te:
ba

Stewart Parker

Born in East Belfast at 86 Larkfield Road, Sydenham on October 20th 1941, (James) Stewart Parker was the son of George Herbert Parker, a tailor's cutter, and Isobella Lynas who had been a book-binder prior to her marriage. Parker was educated at Ashfield Boys' School, Sullivan Upper School and then read for a degree in English Literature at Queen's University where he became involved in the Dramatic Society and friendly with Seamus Deane and Seamus Heaney, graduating in 1963. Sadly, his undergraduate career was severely disrupted by the cancer that he contracted and it would be some years later, in the 1970s, before Parker would work through the psychological effects of this ordeal in his unpublished autobiographical novel *Hopdance*. In 1966 he completed an M.A. thesis in poetic drama on the plays of W.B. Yeats, T.S. Eliot and E.E. Cummings. Parker quickly became known as a poet and one of the Belfast Group under Philip Hobsbaum which included Heaney, Joan Newmann and later Michael Longley. His poems were collected and published as *Paddy Dies* in 2004. In 1964 Parker married Kathleen Ireland and he moved to the US to teach writing at Hamilton College, New York. In 1967, Parker took up a teaching position at Cornell University—where he met the Beat poets Allen Ginsberg and Gregory Corso—returning to Belfast in 1969 as, in Parker's own words, he 'had to come to terms with the place'. Parker started writing his 'High Pop' column for the *Irish Times* in 1970. He also began writing plays for BBC radio: *The Iceberg* (1975) and *I'm A Dreamer, Montreal* (1977) which was televised by Thames in 1979. Other radio plays include *The Kamikaze Ground Staff Reunion Dinner* (1979) and *The Traveller* (1985).

Spokesong, described by Parker as a 'play about the reality' of the Troubles, had premiered to great acclaim at the Dublin Theatre Festival in 1975 and, following a run at the West End in 1977, it opened at the Long Wharf Theatre, New Haven, Connecticut in 1978 and then at the Circle in the Square Theatre on Broadway in 1979.

Parker also served as Resident Playwright at the Kings Head Theatre, Islington and it was here that the Irish-Caribbean musical *Kingdom Come*—a collaboration with the composer Shaun Davey— was first performed in 1978. The stage play *Catchpenny Twist*, first performed at the Peacock Theatre Dublin in 1977, was also adapted for BBC television. A comedy, *Pratt's Fall*, was produced by Glasgow's Tron Theatre in 1983.

In 1982, Parker and his wife separated and he moved to London beginning a new relationship with the playwright Lesley Bruce. During this time Parker wrote extensively for television. His work for the small screen includes *Iris in the Traffic, Ruby in the Rain* (1981), *Joyce in June* (1982), *Blue Money* (1984) and *Radio Pictures* (1985). His series *Lost Belongings* was screened in six hour-long episodes running from April 1987, directed by Tony Bicât. The pinnacle of Parker's achievement as a dramatist is the trilogy published as *Three Plays for Ireland* (1989) comprised of *Northern Star* (Lyric Theatre, Belfast, 1984), *Heavenly Bodies* (Birmingham Reperatory Theatre, 1986) and *Pentecost* (Field Day Theatre Company, 1987). After writing this last play Parker was diagnosed with cancer of the stomach and died in London on 2 November 1988, aged only forty-seven. In his appreciation of Parker published in the *Irish Times* after the playwright's death in 1988, Douglas Kennedy paid tribute to the exceptional qualities of the man:

> Call him one of the foremost Irish playwrights of the last few decades and you'd be paying his remarkable body of work the high praise and respect it deserves. But for anyone who worked with him professionally—or, better yet, could call him a friend—the mercurial wit and depth of compassion which so characterised his plays simply mirrored the mercurial wit and depth of compassion which were so intrinsically Stewart.

The Stewart Parker Trust was founded in 1989 to support the work of emerging playwrights.

Gerald Dawe is from Belfast. He has published seven collections of poetry, including *The Lundys Letter, Sunday School, Lake Geneva* and, most recently, *Points West*. Among his prose works he has published *My Mother-City*, a study of Belfast cultural traditions which includes a profile of Stewart Parker. He is a fellow of Trinity College, Dublin.

Born in Dublin, Maria Johnston studied English Literature and Music at Trinity College, Dublin, where she recently received her Doctorate in English. She reviews poetry for various magazines and is currently preparing her study of Sylvia Plath's poetry as well as editing a collection of essays on European poetry and politics for publication.

HIGH POP

HIGH POP

STEWART PARKER

The Irish Times Column
1970-1976

edited and introduced by
Gerald Dawe
& Maria Johnston

LAGAN PRESS
BELFAST
2008

Publisher's Note
The aim of this collection is present Stewart Parker's journalistic writings on pop music and culture as they appeared in pages of the *Irish Times*. As part of this collection's attempt to recapture 'High Pop' as a *newspaper* column, the publishers have decided—despite occasional repetitions and their sometimes functional nature—to keep the original column headlines and to represent text breaks, no matter how arbitrary, as they appeared in the paper. Similarly, it has been decided to keep all album catalogue numberings as originally listed in the reviews.

Published by
Lagan Press
1A Bryson Street
Belfast BT5 4ES
e-mail: lagan-press@e-books.org.uk
web: lagan-press.org.uk

ISBN: 978 1 904652 59 5

Author: Parker, Stewart
Title: High Pop
The Irish Times Column 1970-1976
2008

Set in Meridien

Printed by Imprint Digital, Exeter
imprintdigital.net

'I am dancing as I type'
—Stewart Parker

CONTENTS

1976

Introduction

I

Some time in the early 1990s, the publisher of Lagan Press, Patrick Ramsey suggested that Belfast playwright, Stewart Parker's 'High Pop' column in the *Irish Times* would make a really interesting book. The idea stayed with me but without progressing any, until a visit to London in 2003 where I met with Stewart Parker's partner, Lesley Bruce. Lesley gave me a box file containing newspaper cuttings, including many of the 'tear sheets', of 'High Pop', which Stewart Parker had kept. As I went through them, one by one, the freshness, energy and wisdom of what he had written, thirty years before, in the early 70s, was clear.

To get a younger contemporary read of the material, I discussed the idea with Maria Johnston, and so began the process of gathering together Stewart Parker's entire 'High Pop' column, which had appeared in the *Irish Times* from April 20th 1970 to the final column, on 2 September 1976. This material is now published here in full for the first time*.

---

*Stewart Parker's significant non-dramatic literary writing, including his John Malone Memorial Lecture, 'Dramatis Personae', along with several poignant and canny reflections on Belfast, his upbringing there, and the unfolding saga of the northern Troubles, as well as various other valuable reflections on Irish theatre and culture, will be published separately by Litteraria Pragensia.

II

Sadly, Stewart Parker died tragically young—at 47—in London in 1988. During the early 60s at Queen's University in Belfast, he had been part of a group of young writers which included Seamus Heaney and Bernard MacLaverty, and by the late 70s, Parker had established himself at the forefront of a (by now) internationally recognised group of writers, including Heaney and MacLaverty, as well as many of his other friends, such as Michael Longley, Derek Mahon and Terence Brown, whose essay, 'Let's Go to Graceland' is an essential guide to the background of Stewart Parker and his drama (*The Cities of Belfast*, 2003).

Parker seems to have had a real talent for making and keeping friends. In discussing this work with those who knew him well, the affection and genuine sadness at his early death, is unmistakable, reminiscent of the reaction to the tragic accident which cost J.G. Farrell's life at a similiarly young age (44) in 1979. This fondness also spanned generations, as Robert Johnstone remarks in his wonderfully astute review of Parker's *Three Plays for Ireland*:

> I met Stewart Parker around 1970. I'd just left school. He was 29 or 30, he'd been to America, one or two of his plays had been on local radio, and Festival Publications had published *Maw* [a poetry pamphlet] ... His flat seemed slightly hippy, in the fashion of the time, and I thought him an exotic figure, with his soft caps and big cigars. He was reviewing records for the *Irish Times*, and was delighted with all the free albums. He was friendly, polite and probably indulgent to what must have been a callow youth.
> —*Honest Ulsterman*, Spring/Summer 1989

Concluding his review, Johnstone notes that Parker 'seemed to belong to a later generation, whose style was more optimistic and playful'. As this collection shows, Parker's mind was lit up with the best that popular music could bring. Like Philip Larkin of an older generation, Parker was well versed in the music-recording world, in Parker's case, from the forties, fifties, through the explosion of the sixties, and into the (much maligned) seventies.

Parker writes with panache, curiosity and a real sense of history. The reader never feels that he or she is in the company of an obsessive snob because Parker wants to share his enthusiasms, not preen himself on how much he knows. His lightness of touch matches his self-confidence; at precisely the right moment he will say what he thinks. 'High Pop' is full of such high points: discriminating (in the best sense of the word) and alert to all who have contributed to the making of the music he is discussing, he rarely leaves out a name in a band, or in the production team. His taste is impeccable too. For a younger generation of readers in search of an iPOD playlist of the best in post-fifties music, there is no better place to start than right here. Parker's 'High Pop' is a kind of mini-history, a fascinating overview of popular music before business took over the music.

You can't help but feel you know the man who is talking through these pages, for stylistically 'High Pop' reads like a conversation, a really intelligent conversation, with one who loves music, rather than with a puppet that loves himself. Parker doesn't giggle or insinuate or patronise the subjects of his column, even when he isn't too impressed with their musicianship, lyrics or production values. He speaks his mind, for sure, but he does so with the kind of respect and belief in artistic values and cultural standards that has, let's be honest, largely disappeared from media coverage of 'popular art'.

Parker had his favourites, clearly, and the Band ('peerless' is his word) are right up there in lights, along with many vocalists and singer-songwriters who he obviously rated very highly—Maria Muldaur, the McGarrigle sisters, Carole King, Sandy Denny, Janis Joplin, Sonja Kristina (Curved Air) and Joni Mitchell. Here's Parker on Mitchell's *Blue*: 'a gust of rain in a dry season...an instant commercial success, but equally sure to be a lasting artistic one'. Like so much else in 'High Pop', he got that and other judgments absolutely right: James Taylor, 'solid gold in a field of corn', Loudon Wainright III, 'one of that handful of genuine originals which sustains your belief in the future', while Steely Dan ('My favourite rock group'), the Strawbs, David Clayton-Thomas (Blood, Sweat & Tears), the Grateful Dead, Captain Beefheart, Jimi Hendrix, DJ John Peel, all come in for special mention.

His changing views of Dylan form a subplot (and topic for discussion all on its own), as does his robust attitude to John Lennon, which varies between reverence and utter rejection. Nor is Parker ever afraid to speak his mind and risk sounding unfashionable or even blasphemous. Thus, David Bowie and Marc Bolan are 'lurid narcissists' and, in terms of the sixties, make up 'the Jacobean fag-ends of the movement' while Led Zeppelin is deemed 'uninteresting', to be more precise, 'a humourless bore.' John Lennon and Yoko also come in for criticism where it is due, as Parker astutely puts it: 'the degree of Yoko's influence and collaboration is in inverse proportion to the quality of Lennon's songs.' Parker does not pull any punches. He is an exacting listener who tires of anything flat, old, re-hashed, under-average and embraces with all his being the original, the novel, the experimental, the deserving. His praise is effusive when called for, his censure bitingly hitting the mark when warranted, making for a body of writing that speaks with authority and genuine interest, is passionate in its opinions and discerning in its judgements—ultimately an exuberant and endlessly engaging read. Rock music, part of 'that vast barbaric confederation known as pop music', is unpicked and the real thing revealed alongside the inauthentic and phony.

He sets high standards. For Parker is one of life's natural detectors of bullshit which may well have had something to do with his roots in east Belfast. The urban, wry and impassioned love of R&B and blues finds strong advocacy throughout 'High Pop'. There's room too for praise for the Incredible String Band, while disapproval for English 'folksiness'—worth, by the way, looking up Joe Boyd's contrasting view in *White Bicycles* (2005). And when he is on home ground, Parker applied the highest criteria by way of honoring the best—Van Morrison, Rory Gallagher, the then 17 year-old Gary Moore, and Skid Row come in for deserved praise. 'High Pop' ventures opinions, insights, asides and (only rarely) rant, as in Parker's irritation at John Lennon's radical chic. Parker also reclaims for a new generation, the great northern lyricist, Jimmy Kennedy, corroborating Derek Mahon's homage in the original version of his poem 'The Sea in Winter' (1979) and in his collection *Harbour Lights* (2005). He also draws attention to fine writing on music such as Charles Gillett, *The Sound of the City*, that 'marvellous bill of goods'.

Parker recognised immediately the particular talents of groups such as Steely Dan, Pink Floyd, Mike Oldfield, the Rolling Stones, without whom today's rock music would be impossible. The roll-call is one of names that have achieved cult status and whose powerful legacy endures right to this day in the best music of the current times. There would be no Radiohead without the innovations of Pink Floyd, no Nick Cave without Leonard Cohen, no American Music Club without Steely Dan, no Tom Waits without Captain Beefheart, and no Metallica without Queen, no Tori Amos without Joni Mitchell and, taking this point to its obvious conclusion, no Rufus and Martha Wainwright without Loudon Wainwright III and Kate McGarrigle! We're still listening to such iconic talents as Captain Beefheart, Joni Mitchell, Jimi Hendrix, the Grateful Dead, Neil Young, the Who and the Rolling Stones. Some names that we should still be listening to have been undeservedly forgotten. Parker reminds us of the talents of such groups as Focus, Manassas, the Incredible String Band and the Mahavishnu Orchestra. Dory Previn too is one of his particular favourites, and is another singer whose talents have endured and are celebrated to this day, such as the tribute by the Scottish group Camera Obscura on their 2006 album *Let's Get Out of This Country*.

The breadth of reference is astounding, ranging from Hank Williams to Karlheinz Stockhausen. Indeed reading Parker's description of the group Henry Cow one is struck by how accurate a description it is of Parker himself if one substitutes 'critic' for 'musician':

> Imagine a young musician who has a taste not only for Stockhausen and Charlie Parker, but also for Cathy Berberian, Kurt Weill, Bob Dylan, Messiaen, the Beatles and Mississippi John Hurt.

Imagine indeed! Parker has not only a rapacious taste and insatiable curiosity for all music but he brings to his writings a dynamic intelligence and insight. There are, throughout this boundless musical road-trip, many incredibly memorable phrases that resonate and seem to leap from the page: Maria Muldaur's voice in performance is described as 'cracking in and out of falsetto like a bull-whip.' Frequently, Parker's observations are so keen it makes one want to laugh out loud, such as his comment on Leonard Cohen's failings:

> Much can be said on both sides about Leonard Cohen's songwriting. But I would have thought that all were agreed on the congenital deficiencies of his singing—the man is endowed, like most of us, with a voice fit for exercising only in the bath.

On the music itself, Parker's descriptions are full of vivid colour, displaying an attentive ear that takes everything in along with a technical knowledge that never grows heavy-handed but instead brings the music to life:

> 'Drop' opens with a kind of enchanted passage incorporating water noises and a music box augmented by the tumbling ethereal use of tape loops. This is a prelude to a duologue between the gnatbuzz of Ratledge's organ and the scholastic agility of Hooper's bass. It's an absorbing number.

'Absorbing' is it exactly. This is a book for everyone who listens to music today, an engaging overview and survey of The Seventies' music, a decade that is recognised as one of the most important in musical history. Parker's words are as fresh today as they were when he first published them in the pages of the *Irish Times*. His voice carries over the decades since this column first appeared, and the joy of reading him is undiminished. 'High Pop' also reveals most about the undying enthusiasms of the man. This collection of his 'High Pop' column reinstates him as a timeless voice, a truly necessary presence, whose rare insight and restless intelligence opens up a century's music, displaying an effortless writing style, humility, humour and sparkling wit. Radiating with lively opinion, incisive argument, formidable knowledge and most of all, a rare and delighting passion for music, no wonder he could write, 'I'm dancing as I type'. We all are.

Gerald Dawe/Maria Johnston
Dublin 2008

1970

THIS IS the first appearance of a new critical column by the Belfast writer, Stewart Parker. Every second Monday, he will review worthwhile records of contemporary popular music.

HIGH POP

The Incredible String Band/*Changing Horses*

MIKE HERON AND Robin Williamson are global villagers. They started out in Scotland as folksingers and nature lovers. Their subsequent musical and spiritual development has incorporated every influence that records, radio, airplanes and success has offered them. They can play all the instruments they buy, some with brilliance and all with competence. Williamson has a voice as true as a choirboy's, but with a formidable range and technique. They have delved fairly deeply into the Eastern religions. All of this and more resulted a few years back in an album called *The Hangman's Beautiful Daughter* which is one of the few unquestionable works of art to have emerged from that vast barbaric confederation known as pop music.

'They're incredible!' said some publicist early on: or at least I hope it wasn't they themselves who coined the name Incredible String Band. To compose and perform under the banner of such hyperbole must be a strain, even for two authentic mystics. Certainly their last album *Wee Tam and the Big Huge* was an extension rather than a development of their work. Now they have a new one out, called *Changing Horses* (Elektra EKS 74057).

The title may be wishful thinking, for there is no noticeable change in content, a few of the songs being familiar from their Irish visit of last year. What is immediately noticeable about the album is its unevenness. It contains their worst piece yet, and one of their best.

The worst unfortunately, takes up a third of the entire album's fifty minutes. It's a Williamson poem called 'Creation', an impenetrable mishmash of apocalyptical images and references to various mythologies. Most of it is recited in a beauteous voice over a chanted background, in what might or might not be a parody of the kiddy prophet Donovan; either way, it's gross self-indulgence.

Towards the end it switches into a pastiche of 1920s megaphone-singing, finishing at last in a lame series of instrumental codas.

The best piece is Mike Heron's 'White Bird'. The lyrics of this are reproduced on the sleeve interspersed with little circular watercolours by Heron, which are images of the song's various phases. To sit with this on your knee listening to the song is a much more rewarding 'multimedia' experience than being blitzed by amplifiers and films and strobe lights. Word, voice, instrument and picture work together in a highly introspective way. The song is a meditation on the co-existence of pain and beauty in the one physical nature (in fact, the hangman's beautiful daughter). At its most agitated it verges on a rock sound, with electric bass and organ, but the heart of the piece is a quiet solo guitar passage, intensely poignant.

***

The other songs are typical examples of the group's work. Two girl friends who have appeared intermittently in previous performances seem now to be members of the band: in 'Sleepers Awake', all four voices join in an unaccompanied hymn which would grace the worship of any denomination. In the amusing 'Big Ted' they do a boogie-woogie chorus on behalf of Ted the pig, who is dead but might be reincarnated as a cow. As usual, a bizarre range of instruments is played in the course of the album, from the kazoo and washboard to the vibraphone, Chinese banjo and saarang, but never merely to show off.

Heron and Williamson share the dangers of all artists working in a popular milieu. To the entrepreneurs they are merely another saleable product, to be beatified while the public wants them, and thrown in the bin when they're no longer selling. The artistic establishment, on the other hand, is either disdainful or patronising. Thus deprived of a healthy critical atmosphere, their work is vulnerable to diseases: in particular to commercialism, pretentiousness and repetitiveness.

The problem is not new, but it has been growing throughout this century, and it is very acute at this moment in the development of pop music, when 'underground' is an actual sales category, like 'Country & Western'.

The Incredible String Band betrays symptoms. Let's hope that innate artistic integrity will restore them fully to health in their next album.

Monday, 20 April 1970

BEATLE ALONE

Paul McCartney/*McCartney*

PAUL McCARTNEY'S GIFT is for melody and lyricism, John Lennon's for surrealism and satire: they don't have Irish blood for nothing. It was the combination of these qualities that produced the Beatles' finest songs and their two larger masterpieces, the *Sergeant Pepper* album and Side 2 of *Abbey Road*. In these they used the recording studio as an instrument and treated the long-playing record itself as a musical genre instead of as a carrier-bag for assorted stage songs. Just how their collaboration was more than the sum of its parts is illustrated in little by the finale of *Sergeant Pepper*, 'A Day in the Life', where a weary and abrasive Lennon lyric is given an extra dimension by the insertion of a fast, nervy McCartney passage in the middle.

***

FROM BEAUMONT and Fletcher through Somerville and Ross to Rawicz and Landauer, it has become axiomatic that collaborators are not so hot when they go it alone. The solo album, *McCartney* (Apple PCS7102), just released, is further evidence. There is melody and lyricism here in plenty, sufficient in fact to make a laughing-stock of all his competitors—except for one: the Beatles. The same principle applies to John Lennon's offerings with the Plastic Ono Band. But where Lennon has gone didactic, McCartney has gone megalomaniac. For not only does he sing his own composition on this album but he produced it too, and played all the instruments, and his wife Linda took all the sleeve photographs of him (and her and his dog and the kids), and she tra-la's a bit too and the first song is called 'Lovely Linda'.

The result is that at times during the album, and most strongly in the five dull instrumental tracks, one reacts as to the neighbours' home movie. But then again there are four songs which are not the work of the boy next door, unless you happen to live beside a man who can write standards as the rest of us write postcards.

The most immediately appealing of them is called 'Junk'. It is the quintessence of that wistful nostalgia which was formerly such a moving foil to Lennon's resigned stoicism (as on the 'Golden Slumbers-Carry That Weight' section of *Abbey Road*). It might serve as an epitaph to the collaboration—

Bye Bye says the sign in the shop window.
Why, why? says the junk in the yard

The tune has that satanic knack for lodging itself in your mind after one hearing, so that you keep catching yourself trying to hum it. To promote this process, there's a 'singalong' track on Side 2.

'Every Night' and 'Maybe I'm Amazed' are love songs with a fresh realism, married love songs, the latter being especially well put together. 'Teddy Boy' is about a rejected mother's boy; again, even while finding it interesting, the treacherous ear laments the passing of 'Eleanor Rigby' and 'She's Leaving Home'.

***

The Beatles formed in 1960 and now they seem to have split in 1970. It's as if they instinctively felt that their corporate identity belonged solely to the decade in which they revolutionised popular music, and to which they virtually contributed a style of life. But maybe the split is only temporary; or maybe, against all the odds, Lennon and McCartney will each develop in unprecedented ways to surpass their former combined brilliance. Maybe the eleven or so Beatles LPs will stop sounding like the Complete Works. There is at any rate another one, *Let It Be*, still awaiting release.

Meanwhile, we must be content with the merely relative excellence of 'McCartney'.

Monday, 4 May 1970

ROOTS

Various/*The Rural Blues*
Various/*The Blue Are Alive and Well*

THREE YEARS AGO, in a cafe in upstate New York, I overheard an American girl say, 'What I really love is British blues!' It sounded ludicrous at the time. But in the abstract, at least, it was no more so than a 16th-century Italian expressing *amore* for English sonnets.

The history of culture is a saga of the migration of art forms. For three hundred years European culture flowed into America. Then the flow reversed itself: many's a school debating society has weighed the evidence as to whether this is A Good Thing or A Bad Thing. It is, of course, all kinds of everything.

Take the blues. They are the downhearted heart of all modern popular music, and it's a Black American heart. The work of men like Lightnin' Hopkins, John Lee Hooker and hundreds of less celebrated singers makes nonsense of labels like folk, jazz, and rock, for it contains the essence of all three. Traditional rural blues are so elemental that you almost sympathise with the purist who will listen to nothing else. The intense quietude of voice and guitar or piano, bending repeated phrases into a wholly personal statement, established a style for the times. For a sampler, there is among current releases a box set called *The Rural Blues* (XTRA 1035) (and in the Decca catalogue is the indispensable Paul Oliver documentary album *Conversation with the Blues*—LK4664).

***

In the big cities the blues, like everything else, lost a little poetry and gained an aggressive cutting edge: the solo guitar or piano grew into a backing group. This was the sound that migrated and excited the ears of ravers like Mick Jagger. In that it has resulted in the best work of groups like the Rolling Stones, this was A Good Thing; in that the bulk of 'British blues' are debased adolescent travesties of the American originals, (as satirized in John Lennon's song 'Yer Blues') it was a deplorable thing. But then again it was the songs and not the singers that moved across the water—as another current release puts it, *The Blues Are Alive and Well* (XTRA 1105).

As with the blues, so with music in general, indeed culture in general. American forms and styles, when assimilated into a personal idiom, translated into the vernacular, can be both valid and exciting:

when their worst aspects are merely imitated (as, for example, in most of our new architecture) the result is squalid and depressing. The problem for pop music is that a lot of people still relegate it in toto to the latter category.

To define and defend one's enjoyment of good pop, this line of argument needs extending. For the 'vernacular' elements of groups like the Who or Traffic are not easy to separate out. It's meaningless to say, 'But they're so English.' Self-conscious attempts at Englishness—like some of the work of a group called Fairport Convention, which tries to fuse English folk music and rock—are as fruitless as sham Americanese. I hope no Irish group is contemplating experiments in ceilidhe-rock.

***

Instead I think the music has to be considered as an international medium, in the same sense that neoclassical architecture was international in the eighteenth century. The roots of the music are all in America—most of them in Black America—but the electric guitar, after all, is no more 'American' than television. The best groups are those that accommodate this international medium to their own idiosyncratic sense of reality. And to hear the very best of them do just that in the recording studio you must get the new Beatles album *Let it Be* (PXSI), finally released last week. Also, there are some superb Irish and Scottish ballads in Kentucky ...

Monday, 18 May 1970

CROSS-BREEDS

Brinsley Schwarz/*Brinsley Schwarz*
The Flock/*The Flock*

THAT FASHIONS AND trends are the food and drink of pop music goes without saying; what is remarkable is the rich multiplicity of them that currently exist. The plagiarists of ten or fifteen years ago could only hammer away at the primitive rock & roll style of the Presley-Haley-Buddy Holly era, and the result was excruciating—

dozens of featureless plastic performers who appeared en masse in rock & roll 'films' and TV shows only to sink without a trace.

Then came the sixties and the extraordinary flood-tide of popular music which burst the old banks and spread out in all directions. The flood is still in full spate and sweeping with it musicians of all persuasions. A new group today, seeking to exploit the fashionable trends for commercial gain has a bewildering array to choose from. There is no excuse for sounding dreary, though most of them still contrive to do so.

Brinsley Schwarz (UAS 29111) is the debut album of a group of the same name. It has been highly promoted, and is obviously a calculated commercial venture. The musicians are experienced and competent and the compositions shrewdly designed to suit the market. The result is easy on the ears and certainly worth 39s. 6d., though probably it has no more artistic value than, say, an attractive art nouveau wallpaper.

The dominant sound is the blending of three voices in high and close harmony, using falsetto. This fashion is the hallmark of the much feted musicians Crosby, Stills and Nash, who pooled their talents to perfect it. The best track on this album, 'Shining Brightly' (also released as a single) is so like them that it would succeed as a forgery. But then the following track, 'Rock and Roll Women', switches to another fashion, the wry quiet song over an unamplified guitar which Paul Simon has made popular. The imitation in this case is a flop, because there's not just a sound to imitate, but also a lyric, and you can't forge poetry.

So it goes through the whole album, echoes of other groups, custom-tailored fashions, all presented in a smoothly professional manner. The group has enough talent to achieve something less highly polished and more their own, but they may lack the hunger.

***

THE FLOCK don't. The bandwagon they are on is the big 7-or-8-piece jazz one from Chicago, which was first set rolling by a group called Blood Sweat and Tears, but the Flock have a just claim to their place on it. They have the real gut need to make their own music, and on their first album (CBS 63733) they do so magnificently, with one major flaw.

Their line-up is a trifle unorthodox: two tenor saxes, a trumpet, amplified violin, guitar, bass, and drums. Five of them also sing. The star is Jerry Goodman, the violinist.

The violin was never really assimilated into jazz, despite Stuff Smith, Stephane Grapelly *et al*; how much less has it been a part of rock! But Goodman is an example of a generation of brilliant young musicians, conservatory-trained, who find no personal fulfillments in either the classical repertoire or contemporary jazz. They have grown up with rock and feel a part of it even though their expertise and musical vocabulary belong to expansive realms undreamt of by Jerry Lee Lewis and His Pumping Piano.

Thus the opening track of this LP, 'Introduction', is a curious thing indeed. At one moment a snatch of atonal intellectualising, at the next an outburst of gipsy passion—is this pop music? It's unlikely to evoke pubescent female screams, but that's no definition. A spontaneous crossbreeding is going on between all manners of music, and like it or not, pop music is the incubator. Personally, I like it. There are moments on this album which are genuinely original. There is gorgeous interplay of reeds and brass in 'Store Bought-Store Thought', and an amazing tour de force on violin in 'Truth'. Instrumentally, the Flock are a vivid new thing.

The major flaw is their lead singer, Fred Glickstein, which is where they lose out to Blood, Sweat & Tears, and he is not improved by the words he has to sing. (No credits are given for the lyrics, and the liner notes are just fatuous puff from John Mayall). He sings sharp and his voice is flavourless.

Rock has always been a snug music and very literary: witness the pun in Beatles or Byrds, the love of outlandish titles, Bob Zimmerman calling himself Dylan after the poet. The Flock's damaging departure from rock is not in working with free form and jazz big band elements, for these enrich and extend the tradition. It is in neglecting the singer and his song.

Tuesday, 2 June 1970

VOICE FROM THE INFERNO

Frank Zappa/*Hot Rats*
Captain Beefheart/*Trout Mask Replica*

FRANK ZAPPA is a Californian rock musician in his thirties who runs two record companies, one called Straight and the other Bizarre. That, as our American cousins put it, is just for openers.

Up until recently he was the leader of a group called the Mothers of Invention which recorded on the Bizarre label. The Mothers were great parodists. They produced, for example, a send-up of the Beatles' *Sergeant Pepper* album complete down to the photographs and lyrics on the album cover. Their treatment of '50s rock & roll hits—what the disc jockeys call 'goldy oldies'—was a version of camp, that peculiarly American compound of incredulous nostalgia and indulgent disdain directed towards the giant junkyard of a culture of obsolescence. But the intention of most of their work was violently satirical, as defined by Frank Zappa in a recent interview: 'We're involved in a low-key war against apathy ... A lot of what we do is designed to annoy people to the point where they might, just for a second, question enough of their environment to do something about it'.

The Mothers pursued this aim for some years with a humour that was frequently savage, occasionally unfunny, but always full of raw vigour and inventiveness. It was, above all, a verbal humour: which was why I was amazed to see in the same interview a scornful rejection of lyrics: 'You have to stick the words on the music to sell it. People still demand to hear some sort of verbal communication: people don't seem to be ready yet for straight musical communication.'

***

As a result of this attitude, the Mothers' albums have contained progressively more and more music and fewer and fewer words, till on their final one, *Burnt Weeny Sandwich* there are only two songs left, both of them belonging to the camp goldy oldies category. The rest is an unsatisfactory musical ragbag. There is a snatch of rocking Stravinsky called 'Igor's Boogie', a gently mocking reminiscence of '30s film music called 'Holiday in Berlin' and a 22-minute rock improvisation, recorded live in concert, called 'Little House I Used To Live In'. The latter is evidently the sound of the future as far as Zappa is concerned. It contains a very gutsy violin solo by Sugar Cane Harris which works up to an exciting controlled frenzy of notes, but long tracts of the rest are very dull.

The blunt fact is that rock music is not revolutionary so far as technique is concerned. It has contributed a few new sounds to the musical vocabulary, but far from tampering with the actual alphabet, it has confined itself to the most basic of letters. This is entirely appropriate to a music which, as Zappa says, is 'electric folk art'. But it means that a 22-minute instrumental must inevitably contain about 15 minutes of boredom, And musical boredom does not annoy people to the point where they change their environment. They merely change the record.

***

This is the sad lesson of *Hot Rats* (Bizarre/Reprise RSLP 6356), the new Zappa album risen from the ashes of the Mothers. His mistake, I think, is to compete with jazz on its own terms. On this album there is left but one stunted song, sung splendidly by Captain Beefheart, of whom more in a moment. The rest of this 'movie for your ears' is— and there can scarcely be a more dreadful word in the context— pleasant. The title of the album and its horrific cover and the names of the tracks (like 'Son of Mr Green Genes') are in the traditional shocker idiom; but the music is incongruously pleasant, occasionally engrossing to listen to, but mostly good background for a party. To utter such blasphemy makes me feel like a hot rat myself.

But then I turn to the Straight label, which has issued a double album called *Trout Mask Replica* (STS 1053) by Captain Beefheart and His Magic Band, and I feel securely maladjusted again. Captain Beefheart, whose real name is of course Don Van Vliet—I flinch at listing the names and instruments of his Magic Band—presents us here with twenty eight of his compositions, ranging from 'Frownland' through 'Dachau Blues' and 'Old Fart At Play' to 'Veteran's Day Poppy'.

No party will survive this as background. There is not an ounce of whimsy in it. Captain Beefheart is a bona fide creative madman in a venerable Romantic tradition encompassing, for example, Baudelaire in his dressing gown making gargoyle faces at the bourgeoisie. A more contemporary kinship is made explicit in one of the song titles: 'Dali's Car'. Whether the bourgeoisie will be excoriated is another matter; there is no questioning the validity of the nightmare, or the searing garish originality of the language used to express it. Frank Zappa has fulfilled his programme, not through his excursions into rock composition, but by promoting the demented poetry of Captain Beefheart, a real voice from within the surrealist inferno of Californian society.

Wednesday, 17 June 1970

LP OR SINGLE

The Kinks/*Lola* (single)
Joe Cocker/*The Letter* (single)
The Groundhogs/*Thank Christ for the Bomb*

PEOPLE INVOLVED IN pop music love to theorise about the relationship between LPs and singles. In the early days a performer or group merely accumulated a sufficient number of single hits and then parcelled them up as an LP much as contemporary poets do. But as the music developed and diversified, things grew less simple and attitudes began to conflict.

In general the LP and singles markets have been drifting increasingly apart. Singles are geared to the hit charts. Most of them are ugly and transient fledglings, squalling each other to death for a peck at the worth of the public's wealth; and the bulk of the public in question is in the vulnerable throes of puberty. There is a Top 40 for albums too, but it is a much more sedate affair. More and more, albums are the fruit of months and sometimes years of thought and preparation. They tend to be aimed at an older and more aware audience and are often in fact conscious attempts at art.

Those who oppose this trend point out that it is tearing the flower of the music away from its roots. They foresee the total surrender of the singles market to teenyboppers and a sterile pretentious artiness overtaking LPs. They have a 'good case', but there are grounds for hope.

At the moment, for example the charts contain some surprisingly good singles as well as at least one first-class LP. The Kinks have finally lived up to their name with a single called 'Lola' (PYE 7N 17961) a very sly song about sexual ambiguity. It manages the trick of appealing to all kinds of listeners at once. The lyrics, and Ray Davies' voice (which succeeds in sounding both shy and insinuating) will delight sophisticates, whilst the brash and simple rock sound will be acceptable on what Frank Zappa calls 'the glandular level'.

Then there is Joe Cocker's 'The Letter' (EMI RZ3027) which is a very swingy number, reminiscent of the heyday of big band music. The clever feature of this record is the tension set up between voice and band. The words of each verse are sung over driving piano chords and then topped by the brass and reeds soaring in. It's scarcely original, but very pleasantly achieved.

Each of these songs would be acceptable on an LP, but they function best as singles. They are red-blooded and entertaining, just

41

as they intend to be, and have no more enduring profundity than they intend to have.

***

Correspondingly, the Groundhogs bring bigger ambitions to the larger format of their current album. On the face of it the ambitions seem doomed. First, they are only a trio of guitar bass and drums, which can be very limiting. Second, Tony McPhee, the leader and composer, has chosen nuclear weapons as his subject-matter; the album is called, *Thank Christ for the Bomb* (Liberty LBS 83295).

Tony McPhee treats it rightly not as an isolated obscenity but as the central fact of modern life. Only his title song is directly about it. The others deal with the connected alienations of urban society. The words are occasionally banal and often hard to catch, but they are carried by the sweep of the whole song-cycle. By constantly varying texture and rhythm the three instruments avoid dreariness, and yet the whole album is based on variations of simple musical phrases to create an emotional unity throughout. This unity is its triumph. The songs are not intended to have the individualist strength of good singles. They are meant to be heard together in sequence and they afford a very rewarding half-hour's listening.

Tuesday, 30 June 1970

ANTHOLOGY ALBUM

Various/*Picnic: A Breath of Fresh Air*

TO KEEP UP with all of the pop groups currently making records, you would have to be both fanatic and rotten with money. You can, of course, chose albums judiciously on the basis of tracks from them heard on the radio; you can even be guided by reviews; but to supplement this, you want some cheap anthologies.

Full marks, then, to EMI for issuing *Picnic: A Breath of Fresh Air* (SHSS 1/2). This is a double album, containing selected tracks from eighteen different LPs issued on their Harvest label. At 29s. 11d., it is definitely Bargain of the Month.

The notion of crowding so many different styles under one roof is alarming at first. But on the whole, the songs have been arranged so that they avoid clashing with one another. For example, there is a pleasant track by the Third Ear Band, a group which combines musique concrète, natural sounds and instrumental music with a strong Eastern flavour. This has been sensibly placed at the beginning of a side and followed by a quiet Syd Barrett song. Similarly, the four worst tracks have been lumped together to make up Side 4, though whether this was intentional or not would be hard to say.

***

The various directions of pop are well represented. The familiar heavy rock sound can be heard on 'Into the Fire' by Deep Purple and 'Twisted Track' by the Battered Ornaments, and a gentler song from the same main stream is the Pretty Things' 'The Good Mr Square'. All three of these cuts make enjoyable listening. On the other hand, the tiresomeness of most British blues bands is well demonstrated by Bakerloo's 'This Worried Feeling' as is the phoniness of most British jug bands by a shoddy track called 'Round and Round' featuring Panama Limited.

So far as the folk revival goes, there is an instructive contrast provided on Side 1. Barclay James Harvest have a folksy song of their own called 'Mother Dear' which is thoroughly mawkish and soft-centred, Shirley and Dolly Collins do the traditional song 'Glenlogie'; they have arranged it for keyboard and brass, but in a way that enhances the song instead of travestying it.

Lonely masculine vocal chords are much in demand these days, especially if they throb with a sad candour. They do so to very good effect on this record, in tracks by Kevin Ayers and Roy Harper. The latter's 'Song of the Ages' is a delicate piece, with the voice double-recorded, but not quite synchronised, a trick that is very effective in intensifying the pathos of the lyric. I had never heard Roy Harper before, but will now get his LP on the strength of this sample: that is how an anthology should work, and why it is to the record companies' advantage to issue more of them.

***

In addition, there are several songs here which are nice to have even if they don't galvanise the listener into an orgy of record-buying. Forest and Pete Brown contribute two of them and Pink Floyd a third, with a number called 'Embryo' which is the only one not otherwise available. It is a slow meditative song which sounds surprisingly like the Incredible String Band. An anthology album can merely be a way of unloading rubbish on the public. But this one really is a breath of fresh air.

Wednesday, 15 July 1970

THE EXASPERATING DYLAN

Bob Dylan/*Self Portrait*

WHAT MAKES BOBBY Dylan run? He is a major composer of popular songs; he also has a tuneless whine of a voice which he keeps tampering with so that it changes from record to record. His songs can be incandescent poetry; they can also be banal and pretentious nonsense. He is an adolescent of 28 with the immunity of a great innovator; in short, the most exasperating figure in pop music.

Dylan fans are like that too (so was Dylan Thomas, from whom the name is borrowed). They laugh all discussion out of court. Dylan cannot err. If you find something to criticise, it's because you're missing the entire experience. And yet even they must have endured a crisis of sorts upon hearing him sing 'Blue Moon'.

The 'Blue Moon'? By Lorenz Hart and Richard Rodgers? The very song, along with that other martini-and-tails workhorse, 'Let It Be Me'. All this and more surprises yet are there for the buying on his new double album, *Self Portrait* (Columbia C2X30050). It opens with a female backing group singing two repeated lines to a string accompaniment, as in TV commercials, for 3 minutes 11 seconds. When you are just about ready to hatchet the turntable, Dylan comes on with a tolerable song called 'Alberta'. No sooner have you relaxed than he oozes into a treacly old country-and-western tearjerker called 'I Forgot More Than You'll Ever Know'.

***

No music can be more soft-centred or sugar-coated than country music, the diet of the white Southern lower classes, and Irish showbands. At the moment it is very fashionable in the rock world, but in its most virile and congenial form. Dylan's own previous

44

album, *Nashville Skyline*, contained some country music with red blood, and his backing group, the Band, have a great rousing country-rock album out. But now he seems to have succumbed to the mushy soul of the Nashville sound. Another example of it here is 'Take Me As I Am'.

Worse than this, though, is to hear him sing his fine song of five years ago, 'She Belongs To Me', in the country-and-western style. All its lyric acerbity and sharp-edged imagery is smothered in twang. The song is rendered boneless. The same thing happens to the traditional song 'Copper Kettle'. In these tracks the social gadfly and visionary of earlier days has become a purveyor of Muzak.

***

And yet the old Dylan is still present here. When a track called 'Minstrel Boy' looms up, you grit your teeth in anticipation of Thomas Moore crossed with a steel guitar, but it turns out to be a new Dylan song with typically mind-teasing lyrics. Better still are the two tracks, 'Little Sadie' and 'In Search of Little Sadie'. These are contrasting treatments of the same set of words which tell the story of a rural murder, pursuit and arrest. They're a sudden gust of reality through a miasma of self-parody, audience send-up and general egomania. They remind you of what Dylan is really about, or what he used to be about: treating the folk music of America not just as a museum but as the source material of a personal art.

He started from that position, writing and singing powerful songs in the style of Woody Guthrie, songs from the very bloodstream of American culture. Since then, his quest for an increasingly personal and contemporary immediacy has led him through the various musical styles of modern America. Presumably this *Self Portrait* is a summation of that quest to date. Thus, all the genres are represented. There is the old rock number, 'Take A Message To Mary', a boogie-woogie, a couple of numbers by prominent contemporaries like Paul Simon's 'The Boxer' and Gordie Lightfoot's 'Early Morning Rain' and so on. But what it all adds up to is a portrait of the artist as a very wayward and very confused young man indeed.

Tuesday, 28 July 1970

ROCK CLIMBERS

Traffic/*John Barleycorn Must Die*
Procul Harum/*Home*

IN THE HYPED-UP world of rock, there is perpetually some newly famous group which is threatening to become a diamond much bigger than the Ritz. Three years ago it was called Procul Harum for a summer, and about eighteen months ago its name was Traffic. Neither group shook the world, but they did establish themselves, and a dedicated band of followers. Each of them has a current new album.

Traffic's is called *John Barleycorn Must Die* (UAS 5504) and it has a self-assurance and tightness that was lacking in their previous work. They were initially touted as the first rock group that had successfully assimilated jazz influences, but even they themselves seemed unconvinced by this claim. The voice of Stevie Winwood, the lead singer, was a strong plaintive wail, but it had none of the freewheeling inventiveness of jazz vocalising; nor did the flute and sax-playing of Chris Wood, which simply lacked facility; nor did Jim Capaldi's drumming, which was clean and driving, but firmly rooted in the rock tradition.

The fourth member, the guitarist and singer Dave Mason, has since left the group, and maybe he was the source of its uncertainty. At any rate, the uneasy whimsy of past offerings has been shed since his departure, and in this album the trio gets down to some serious grooving.

The best track is 'Freedom Rider', and it finally vindicates their hankering after jazz. Fresh and unusual harmonic progressions are combined with excellent flute playing by Wood and a controlled Winwood vocal. It is a tune that Charlie Mingus or Art Blakey's Jazz Messengers could be very happy with, and yet it is distinctively a Traffic tune. None of the other cuts are up to this standard, but they all have the same close-knit driving distinctiveness. 'Glad', which is a 6-and-a-half minute instrumental, has far more vivacity than comparable work on the recent Frank Zappa album.

The puzzler is 'John Barleycorn'. This ancient drinking song is surely among the most elemental of all folk-songs, with its comic pagan allegory of death and rebirth, of the drunken fertility of soil and loins:

For little Sir John's grown a long long beard
And so become a man.

As sung by a rollicking chorus in a pub—or by the Watersons—it has magnificence and a fearful mystery in it. As sung by Stevie Winwood, it has neither. He pinions it with the thumping guitar in a portentous minor key that rock musicians always deem essential to a folk song. Why does he sing it at all? Is it his way of repudiating marijuana? Is it the group's farewell to their former undisciplined frivolities? Whatever the clandestine significance, the rendition is lamentable. But the album as a whole is to be highly recommended.

***

Procul Harum's *Home* (A&M SP 4261) is a very lugubrious affair. The group's big hit of 1967, 'A Whiter Shade of Pale', was a melancholy hymn, combining a solemn organ largo with Gary Broker's mournful voice, and this continues to be their dominant style. Their lyricist Keith Reid seems to have a death-fixation. In 'Dead Man's Dream' and 'Whaling Stories', it takes the form of Gothic horror fantasies; in 'Piggy Pig Pig' and 'Still There'll Be More' it turns nastily sadistic. Inexplicably, the last-named song is the only one in which Brooker's voice sounds cheerful.

Even so, it's a very good voice and the group has the kind of cohesiveness that only comes from experience. They excel at building tension into a slow song; their weakness is that they dispel it with a thundering afflatus at the end. This happens with three of the songs here, and two others ('About to Die' and 'Nothing That I Didn't Know') are presented too melodramatically.

The best song on the album is also the simplest and most direct, 'Your Own Choice', with the excellent lines:

The human face is a terrible place
Choose your own examples.

Procul Harum should develop this aspect of its work and leave the histrionics to lesser groups.

Wednesday, 12 August 1970

SOFT MACHINE

Soft Machine/*Third*

THE NAMES OF pop groups sound increasingly, and appropriately, like those of racehorses. 'On behalf of Renaissance, Deep Purple and Canned Heat, I want to thank everybody,' says Bob Hite at the end of the recent *Canned Heat '70 Concert* album, as though referring to the result of the 2.45 at Newmarket.

On the other hand, there is the Soft Machine (horse of a different colour, running for higher stakes, not in the same race: choose your cliché). The soft machine is a term for the human body coined by William Burroughs to serve as the title of one of his novels. The group of the same name is comprised of four educated English lads who made the *Radio Times* the week before last, and this was because they were appearing in a Promenade Concert in the Albert Hall, on the same bill as the avant-garde composers Terry Riley and Tim Souster.

Prospective listeners should not be deterred by this sudden and suspect respectability. The group's work is in fact extraordinarily good. Recondite would be a word for much of it, and over-cerebral for parts of it, but also innovative for all of it, as well as harmonious, uncompromising and committed. Their double album called *Third* (CBS 66246) is in the shops and should be acquired by anybody interested in music as an organism, alive and growing.

There are four numbers on the album, one to each side. Two were composed by Mike Ratledge (organ and piano), one by Hugh Hopper (bass) and one by the drummer Robert Wyatt. The fourth member of the group is Elton Dean (alto-sax and saxello), and four other musicians are used in the course of the record.

Ratledge is the heavy. His organ playing is breathtaking.

He favours a light strident tone which gives clear definition to the fluid rapidity of his solo work. His two compositions put you in mind of the New Thing in jazz, the work of men like Archie Shepp, Pharoah Sanders and Cecil Taylor, who are correspondingly as deeply into 'straight' music and its experiments with scale and tone as Ratledge is. The pure jazz strain is at its strongest in Elton Dean's alto-playing on these sides, especially in 'Slightly All The Time' where he sounds very like Cannonball Adderley, weaving boldly over a tempo that changes several times, running in 9/4 time for a period. The style of Ratledge's own improvisation is more related to rock, to the work of somebody like the Doors' Ray Manzarek, for example, though far exceeding it in style and complexity.

But the group's real use of rock is not so much a question of style as of machinery: the Soft Machine is an electric band, like the Who or any other hard rock group. If you didn't know that Ratledge was playing the organ, you would swear he was playing the Moog synthesizer. Maybe he will be, on the next album. Meanwhile, he plays other machine/instruments, like the amplifier, the fuzz box and the tape recorder. Tape-loops—which rapidly repeat a short sequence of notes or pattern of sound—have been familiar in the pop world since the Beatles' *Revolver*, and have also been much utilised by Proms composer Terry Riley.

Hugh Hopper's 'Facelift' is a more radical departure still. He has taken tapes of two different concert performances, and superimposed them, again employing overdubbing and loops quite extensively. It ought to be a mess but it never becomes even slightly incoherent, though it's more uneven in quality than the two Ratledge sides. Wyatt's 'Moon in June' though, is the weakest side. He sings on it, in a kind of generalised demotic English accent which is pallid and tuneless. The lyrics are like that too.

Monday, 24 August 1970

BACK TO THE BIG BAND

Blood, Sweat & Tears/*Blood, Sweat & Tears 3*
Matthews' Southern Comfort/*Second Spring*

WHEN YOU OPEN out the sleeve of *Blood, Sweat & Tears 3* (CBS 64024) there is a photograph inside of the nine members of the group in which they all look very paunchy. The music is a bit overfed too.

They are at a difficult stage in their development. They took the lead in re-establishing the big band sound as a popular idiom, which was a feat akin to making the railways profitable again. But that's all blood, sweat and tears under the bridge; now they're a supergroup, experiencing the ultimate accolade of a market flooded with imitators. Where to next?

This album rather marks time. The straightforward numbers on it

49

rely heavily on conventional big band scoring, and as BS&T are a smallish big band with no soloists of stature, these tracks sound a bit commonplace. This is true of the very first piece, 'Hi-De-Ho', despite the addition of a choir of 27 voices. On the other hand, the more exploratory numbers are distinctly over-arranged. Quite the worst thing on the record is a 'Symphony for the Devil' conjured out of the Rolling Stones' song, 'Sympathy for the Devil'. Anybody who has seen the Godard film of the same name will readily agree that the melody of this song quickly palls. Dick Halligan has chosen to orchestrate it into three movements (with subheadings like 'Labyrinth' and 'Contemplation') full of portentous chords from piano and brass.

***

WHAT IS VERY good indeed about Blood, Sweat & Tears is their lead singer, who bears the unlikely name of David Clayton-Thomas. Although his tendency to chew on the words can be irritating, he has a voice with genuine verve and swing for buying the whole album. It combines an affectionate nostalgia for the swing era with a fresh contemporary wit. The band sounds at its happiest too here, playing clean riffs over a very infectious shuffling rhythm.

This is followed by a quiet, sad song called 'Fire And Rain' which Clayton-Thomas handles in a controlled and sensitive way well complemented by some delicate brass arranging. He does excellently also on songs by three other jazz-affiliated singers: Laura Nyro's 'He's A Runner', Joe Cocker's 'Somethin' Comin' On', and Stevie Winwood's '40,000 Headmen'. But again the backing on all of these is far too fussy and inflated. Interpolated into the Winwood song, for example, are passages from Prokofiev, Bartók, Thelonious Monk and Fred Lewis. Such catholicity of taste is admirable, but the effect on a simple dream-fantasy rock song is a trifle overwhelming.

If you prefer the idiom of the Tennessee hills to that of Kansas City, then get *Second Spring* by Matthews' Southern Comfort (UNLS 112) ... except that such a distinction is facile, for the music served up by this group is one of those curious fusions of styles that is making rock music a very diversified affair indeed. Overall, their sound is gently understated and highly polished, and it works best with contemporary songs that are lyrical and tuneful such as James Taylor's lovesong 'Something in the Way She Moves'. Also in this bracket is 'Even As', composed and sung by group member Carl Barnwell.

The most interesting number, though, is the last one, Sylvia

Fricker's 'Southern Comfort'. The words to this are rather disconnected and incoherent, but the music is all of a piece, with fine interplay between solo voice, instruments and vocal harmonies, and an impressive structural development.

***

Their limitation is that with more earthy material they sound thoroughly anaemic. From the deadpan way Ian Matthews sings 'Blood Red Roses', a traditional English song, you would never guess it was a savage war chant. Even with a tamer traditional ballad like 'Jinkson Johnson' the suave harmonies and smooth guitar and fiddle work smother all the darker implications of the lyrics.

This group is easy on the ear and can make a cushy living out of a superficial country-rock sound if it chooses to. But it is capable of better things, and I hope there are more risks taken on its next album.

Saturday, 12 September 1970

NOVEL OR ORIGINAL?

Clover/*Clover*
Gospel Oak/*Gospel Oak*

NOVELTY SHOULD NOT be mistaken for originality: that sums up a lot of what is wrong with our chintzy culture. Novelty has become a fetish.

End of generalised dicta, beginning of particular application. *Clover* (Liberty LBS 83340) is a rare kind of record that should be a bestseller and probably won't because there's nothing new in it. There's also nothing new under the sun, but that's a whole other perspective.

What makes the four members of Clover rare is that they are thoroughly involved in making music and not at all in composing masterpieces. Making music is what gets them up in the mornings, and they don't seem to mind whose music, so long as it kicks back. Their motivation is ... (sainthood? immortality? changing the world?) ... fun.

The album starts with Junior Walker's 'Shotgun', done in lusty vocal style and irradiated by a guitar pattern that gives off sparks. All the guitar work is like this. It bursts with energy again at the end of the next song, 'Southbound Train', where it masterminds a devilish switch in tempo.

Other songs include the old gospel number, 'Wade in the Water' (also available as a single), and 'Stealin'', which has been popularised by Arlo Guthrie but is done here in a far superior manner, lush harmonies lazily rolling over a thudding bass.

The bulk of the songs are in fact their own compositions, but far from desperately striking out towards novelty, they bask cheerfully in the crowded waters of familiar idioms. 'No Vacancy' and 'Monopoly' are country songs with an affectionate parody of the corny metaphor ('There's a room in your heart for every man in town/But there ain't no vacancy for me'). 'Going to the Country' is the most infectious and maybe the most typical song on the album. The others are straight rock tunes, also essentially lighthearted—even the heaviest of them, 'Come', ends with a saucy and enjoyable excursion into Latin rhythms complete with horns and shrieks.

The point about Clover is that they communicate their own enjoyment in making music and it is a communal enjoyment. That has to be the foundation of any genuine originality in rock music. The feel of this record, in short, is not unlike the feel of the first Beatles album.

***

GOSPEL OAK (UNI UNLS 113) is the other side of the coin. This also is a debut album from a new group, but as the publicity blurb says, 'it carries the group's self-penned, self-arranged material,' and a fair cargo of anxiety to boot.

The group should not perhaps be blamed for the publicists' attempt at Instant Myth (just add audience). Even so, the album's shortcomings are partly explained when you know that these four young American lads came together while on holiday in London Town, spent the winter developing their music in the suburb of Gospel Oak, were discovered, recorded, and (last chapter) returned home to be acclaimed as stars. Never having played a concert.

Again, it wasn't their fault that they didn't perform—they had work permit problems—but it still shows on the record. You keep thinking they're going to falter. On the very first song, 'Brown Haired Girl', both voice and guitar go sharp. On 'OK Sam' the guitar solo goes very sharp and in fact disintegrates. Most of the songs end with a fade, a telltale sign of uncertainty.

But the major point is that a new group should not feel compelled to produce an entire album of fresh compositions for its first effort. This is a tyranny of fashion that has grown since the breakthrough of *Sergeant Pepper*. Everybody has to be an auteur, and every song has to make it new.

Gospel Oak just haven't got the resources yet. In striving to be different, they come out sounding not only commonplace but, worse still, thoroughly joyless.

Monday, 21 September 1970

THE BAD WITH THE GOOD

Tony Joe White/*Tony Joe*
The Humblebums/*Open Up The Door*

A BOOK HAS one supreme advantage over an LP or tape cassette— you can skip the dull bits without undue fuss. This physical fact alone should cause performers issuing an album to load every groove with ore, but they rarely do. Two current releases, *Tony Joe* (Monument SMO 5043) and *Open Up The Door* (Transatlantic TRA 218) are especially frustrating in this respect.

Tony Joe White was over in the British Isles a while back, and excited a lot of people with his song 'Polk Salad Annie'. Since seeing him perform it on television—his voice and guitar grunting through the sardonic, sly lyrics—I could think of no nicer possession than an LP of his work. Now I own one and I want to tear out four tracks from it, and throw the rest away.

His ambience is the bayous and swamps of the Deep South, and his songs are the kind that might result if Tennessee Williams were to write a musical comedy. Already half-way through the opening number 'Stud Spider' you begin to weary of the various grunts, gasps and warbles with which he decorates his lyrics. The following song, 'High Sheriff of Calhoun Parish', begins promisingly like a Dylan narrative, but before long you grow aware that it too is going to be overlong and overdone, and you prepare to reject him as just another one-song star.

He isn't, though. There's nothing on this album as good as 'Polk

Salad Annie', but the follow-up singles 'Groupy Girl' and 'Save Your Sugar For Me' are here, and they're all right. The former will surely survive as a laconic comment on a sad little corner of social history.

On Side 2 there is a very tolerable 'Stockholm Blues'. The remaining four tunes are by other hands, and probably the best of these is Otis Redding's 'Hard to Handle' which is slightly more disciplined and a far better song than 'My Friend' or 'What Does It Take'. This latter has a disastrous intervention from the Nashville Horns and Strings plus heavenly voices. Otherwise, the Nashville and Memphis session men who provide the gritty rock backing do a very satisfying job, especially bass player Norman Putnam.

Tony Joe White simply sounds immature on the bad segments of this record. He's over-indulging a talent that hasn't fully formed itself yet.

***

Much the same can be said for the two young lads who perform under the derisory name of the Humblebums on *Open Up The Door*. Their surnames are Connolly and Rafferty but their accents sound Scottish. Rafferty's song 'Steamboat Row' perhaps provides the clue:

> My daddy was a miner,
> Said there was nothing finer
> Than an Irishman who worked an honest day.

Connolly's songs are very rough and Rafferty's very smooth which certainly makes for a good balance, but neither of them has a weighty talent. The former's 'My Apartment', which opens the album, is a vivacious piece about a timorous young man fleeing from various attempts on his virtue 'back to my apartment'. But the other Connolly songs sound as though they had been ad-libbed at a party. His vocal technique and guitar-playing can only be called crude, and the folksy repetitions of a song like 'Mary of the Mountains' are stultifyingly dull. 'Mother' shows that he is capable of writing lyrics with some imagination and tension—again, you want to tear it out and throw away the others.

Rafferty is heavily under the influence of Paul McCartney. In particular, his 'Can't Stop Now' and 'All the Best People Do It' are sub-Beatle songs. His tuneful facility is well exemplified in 'Shoeshine Boy' (with which they had a mild hit) but it's more of a curse than a blessing on him at the moment.

Monday, 5 October 1970

DUBLIN SOUNDS

Dr Strangely Strange/*Heavy Petting*
Skid Row/*Skid*

THE COUNTER-CULTURE is in our midst, my fellow Irishmen. Richmond Park may not have been Woodstock and the Ulster Hall will never be the Fillmore North, but there exists for example a group called Dr Strangely Strange, to name but a few. Managed by a potter from Cork, they have just released an album with lyrics like

And I never even said to her
About the time when I thought I loved a nun;
I'm sitting down here in Sandymount
Waiting for another one to come.

There is also 'Mary Malone of Moscow', a song composed of 'aphorisms and adages ripped off Dublin walls while sheltering from a brainstorm', and an aisling on the pollution of Sandymount Strand.

***

Dr STRANGELY STRANGE is surely a name to be reckoned with; furthermore, they've been in existence for three years and issued a previous album. The main reason for their relative obscurity has to be that their style is essentially the same as that of the Incredible String Band. This is bad luck. The String Band sound is distinctive and closely identified with the one group—in a way that, say, a heavy rock sound is not—and musicians who work in this same idiom are probably doomed to be dismissed as mere plagiarists.

Strangely Strange have certainly been heavily influenced by the String Band but they are not imitators. For one thing, their songs on this album have none of the weighty religious imagery which sometimes threatens to turn an ISB song into a survey of Comparative Theology. They work in a much lighter vein. One song here called 'Kilmanoyadd Stomp' sounds like a parody of the String Band and characteristically counsels the listener against trying to interpret the lyrics. It is interesting to note that both groups are produced by Joe Boyd of Witchseason Productions, and that Ivan Pawle of Dr Strangely Strange played the organ on the ISB album *Changing Horses*.

Pawle has a pleasing introspective song here called 'Sign On My Mind', in which he plays a very plangent penny whistle in counterpoint to a nicely built guitar solo by Gary Moore. Another

Pawle song of great charm is 'Jove Was At Home' which is, to quote the sleeve, a hymn to the lovely Mary Macweeney: marred, unfortunately, by an ill-judged burst into the chorus of 'Ding, Dong Merrily On High' at the end. Harmonium player Tim Goulding contributes a whimsical hymn called 'I Will Lift Up Mine Eyes'; but his main achievement is the celebration of the Dublin graffiti master, which attains an apt musical equivalent to the cryptic lunacy of its subject, and is surely the best song on the album.

The third member of the group is Tim Booth and his best effort is the rollicking 'Gave My Love An Apple'. His 'Ashling' is rather dull and there is an uncertainty of tone in it which is arguably a weakness of the group as a whole. They seem to be rather tentative about their humour as yet, like a shy person making a pun, half-hoping that no one will see it. Perhaps to cover this up they have given the album the wildly inappropriate title of *Heavy Petting*. It is available on Philips Vertigo (6360 009).

***

Amongst Sundry Guest musicians who appear with the trio is Dave Mattacks, drummer with the Fairport Convention (one more group produced by Joe Boyd), and Brian Shields, who plays bass guitar. I've already mentioned guitarist Gary Moore also, who along with Shields belongs to another Irish group called Skid Row. Their first album, *Skid* (CBS 63965) is likewise just released and equally recommended. In fact, its frontal assault effectively complements the gentle skirmishing of Dr Strangely Strange.

Gary Moore is seventeen years old and already a guitarist of prodigious skill. It is instructive to compare his work on the two albums. He adjusts his style impeccably to the context and can range from lyrical delicacy to blazing pyrotechnics. He and Skid Row are still wildly undisciplined and imbued with the clichés of progressive rock; his singing and the group's compositions are thoroughly unformed; but the album is practically livid with raw talent and imagination.

Thursday, 22 October 1970

CONVERSATION WITH A READER

The Band/*Stage Fright*
Tina Turner/*The Hunter & Come Together*

HOLD IT! SCREAMED Parker at the reader's jaded eye as it trickled across his column on the weary trek from the editorial to the Business Page.

Man here wants you, said the eye to the reader's abstracted mind.

Can't you see I'm picking my nose? snarled the reader. Who is he anyway?

High Pop, read the eye, must be an article on wine. Shoo, shoo!

There'll be a form of sexual intercourse at the end, called Parker.

I'm all ears, said the eye, and gave the reader the wink.

Thing is, began Parker, my regular readers are taking a well-earned leave. Both of them. All I would have to say to them would be 'The Band' and they would break out all over in smiles. Because this group the Band has a ... a ... sort of quality, and well, shucks, it's just so durn pleasurable ...

The reader's mouth swallowed a whole yawn.

***

ANYWAY, CONTINUED Parker, clearing his throat, you hate rock music, right? All I'm asking you to do is listen to the Band's new album called *Stage Fright* (on EMI Capitol EA-SW 425). It's their third album on their own, but before that they were Bob Dylan's backing group.

That creep, said the reader.

Forget him, said Parker hurriedly, just listen to the Band. Take off your furrowed face, loosen your ears and open up your mind. These five goodtime musicians have been playing together a long time and their music is so co-ordinated that it sounds effortless, it has a drawl entirely its own. It shares a characteristic of recent good American films like *Bonnie and Clyde* and *Easy Rider*: the sense of being imbued with the whole social history of the United States; an elegiac continuity with the sources of American culture. There's a conscious nostalgia in some of the Band's songs, of course, like 'The W.S. Walcott Medicine Show' on this album. And no other rock group but them could bring off a sentimental lullaby like 'All La Glory'. But the root of the pleasure that their music gives is somewhere subtler than nostalgia or sentiment. Take the opening number here, 'Strawberry Wine', it's just, well, intoxicating ...

Is he writing a bloody thesis or what? said the reader.

Quite right. I'm glad you asked that question, claimed Parker. Because Robertson of the Band has the very same attitude. 'People treat us so much more intellectually and so much heavier than what we ever believe for a minute that we are, and we feel kind of foolish, I wish it was mask upon magic, but it's no big thing. There's no point in writing about it, talking about it. Let's just listen to it.'

***

So? Said the reader.

Er, well, there's also two other albums featuring this terrific soul singer Tina Turner.

We're getting warm at last be-god, said the reader.

She's the wife of guitarist Ike Turner who leads the band and arranges her material. They have a vocal group backing group too, the Ikettes.

Never mind her husband and friends, urged the reader, get to you know what.

The two albums are *The Hunter* on EMI's Harvest label (SHSP 4001) and *Come Together* on the Liberty label (LBS 83350). She's got a really grainy voice, the sort of voice that British singers keep trying to achieve, but it's an inimitable Black voice that celebrates all the moods and degrees of carnal desire. You should hear what she does with John Lennon's 'Come Together' and the Stones' 'Honky Tonk Woman' on the Liberty LP. And the heat she generates on the other album, with songs like Memphis Slim's 'The Things I Used To Do' and Booker T. Jones' 'The Hunter'. It's a voice that wasn't made to talk—singing is its native element. And that's it, you see.

What's what?

That's the form of sexual intercourse I promised you.

I see, said the eye.

Wednesday, 4 November 1970

SPACEMAN HENDRIX

THREE TIMES IN recent months, death has electrified the rock music factory like an alarm bell in a stock exchange. It's hard to know how to interpret these deaths. It's harder still to ignore them and immerse yourself in this month's new releases.

Janis Joplin's is the most pathetic but perhaps the most comprehensible. From the moment she entered the limelight with that raddled face and slept-in hair and the odd irresistible voice screeching desperately towards ecstasy, she took her place as female victim alongside Monroe, Judy Garland, Piaf, and Billie Holiday. Moreover, with her tequila and her heroin and her heavy debt to Bessie Smith, she always appeared an anomaly in the rock world, more a figure from the Jazz Age stranded in the wrong generation. Certainly she never really seemed to find a group with which her express train of a voice could be musically reconciled.

Even so, it is a voice that won't be easily forgotten. Already it begins to haunt, like the voices and legends of those other ladies. Why does this tormented figure of the female victim keep recurring in the iconography of Western popular culture? Some vicarious need must be fulfilled by it. Maybe it's the purging of our own self-hatred and hatred of society through a sacrificial scapegoat. There's the smell of revenge in all martyrdoms.

Al Wilson and Jimi Hendrix died within two weeks of one another. Wilson was a member of the American group Canned Heat and in many ways typified a whole movement. He had glasses and pimples, a music degree from Boston University and a passion for old blues records which he collected avidly. His translation of this Black music into the terms of his own experience and high clear voice (as in 'London Blues', for example, on the *Canned Heat '70 Concert* album) has a boyish poignancy. It makes his death seem even more cruel.

The loudest reverberations have been caused by the demise of Hendrix. It's too early to say how important his work was, though emotional obituarists have been ready to call him 'the greatest rock guitarist ever'. But there is the strong sense of a larger death implicit in his end, the death of the psychedelic antirationalist movement in rock culture of which he was a representative.

***

The most revealing article to have appeared in the spate of reminiscences is an interview in the 6th November issue of *Strange*

Days (the rock paper) with a bizarre figure called Chuck Wain, who apparently directed a film involving Hendrix. 'We had immediate contact,' says Wain. 'One of the ways we had contact is that we both, for the past two years, had been in contact with space ships. Jimi had had the same things happening to him. He felt that he came from another planet.'

To have come from another planet would have made life considerably easier for Hendrix. He had all the colossal problems of a black man who attains a strictly white success: in his case a success initially in England. When he first went through his daemonic routine at the Monterey Pop Festival, blitzing the place with feedback, straddling his guitar and setting it alight with lighter fuel, the American critics ridiculed him as an exploiter of the 'superspade' stereotype.

Later, it became clearer that his music had originality and authentic passion. The *Electric Ladyland* LP is a landmark in the orchestration of electric sound. But the vision it grew from—a vision of life as a continual acid trip, eternal sensual gratification, youthfulness and anarchy—was headed into a blind alley which it has now reached.

The drugs, the space ships, the early graves—these are the familiar properties of all Romantic movements in the arts. At this present stage in the development of rock music, they have turned very sour. The freakout has crashed. Somebody needs to make a fresh start in daylight.

Monday, 16 November 1970

DELTA COWBOY

Stefan Grossman/*The Ragtime Cowboy Jew*
The Rolling Stones/*Get Yer Ya-Ya's Out!*

ANYBODY CALLED Stefan Grossman who brings out an album entitled *The Ragtime Cowboy Jew* is already halfway there (it's on Transatlantic TRAE 223).

On the other hand, the title does raise the wrong kind of expectations: Grossman is not a kind of musical Jerry Rubin. There's no more clowning in his music than there is in the work of that other Brooklyn boy, Ramblin' Jack Elliott, who looks like, sounds like, and for a time actually was a cowboy.

Stefan Grossman isn't in the least like a cowboy, but he does play very impeccable blues guitar, with scholarly annotations like 'this is a bottleneck instrumental played in an open D tuning.' He has, in fact, been a dedicated aficionado of traditional Delta blues for some years, producing a couple of books on the subject. There are two touching tracks on this record on which he plays along with the old blues singer, Son House, who was on his last tour of Europe at the time of recording.

In general, though, the blues tracks here sound like revivalist music in any genre—polished, skilled, but rather academic, a meal that's been meticulously reheated. Luckily, Grossman has not been content with such an achievement, and the bulk of this double album is made up of his own new compositions. He is quoted as saying: 'The blues was always someone else's music, but this is my music.'

'This' turns out to be a collection of melancholy reflective songs, with long musical lines which he handles very pleasingly, and long verse lines which are rather mediocre. It is perhaps seeking too much of a performer that he be not only a virtuoso on his instrument, but a first-class composer, singer and lyricist too. However, the discrepancy here between the expressiveness of guitar and the monotony of voice, between the vivid harmonies and the sloppy, sub-Dylan lyrics, is too great for comfort.

The most successful track is the long, ambitious 'Odyssey', in which Grossman does begin to discover something of his own in a fusion of rock, blues and free improvisation on guitar. It is interesting that he makes use of the excellent electric guitarist, Bernie Holland (amongst other notables from the Transatlantic stable), who can be heard to very good effect on the recent Jody Grind album, *Far Canal* (TRA 221).

***

I was always suspicious of the Rolling Stones (you've got to help me, doctor). Jagger's voice was such a sneering perversion of an American accent. Charlie Watts was Stone Age Man. Their music sounded thin and uninventive. Yet to many of my sensitive friends in America, they were almost figures of myth.

I can see why, from their new album, *Get Yer Ya-Ya's Out!* (Decca

SKL 5065). It was recorded live this time last year during a concert at Madison Square Gardens in New York. 'Live' albums are notorious for sounding entirely artificial, with ailing performances bandaged in over-amplified applause, whistles and screams, but this record shows how they're supposed to sound.

It reveals the Stones as disciplined, professional entertainers, who work like navvies at their craft (or sullen art?) Most of the songs have appeared on other albums but not with the fierce energy they possess here. Side 1 explodes into 'Jumpin' Jack Flash' and roars to an end with an eight and a half minute version of 'Midnight Rambler'. When you turn the record over, even 'Sympathy for the Devil', which bored me to stupefaction during Godard's film of the same name, exudes verve and excitement.

The Stones, in short, are a performing band, and this album presents them at work with the faithful simplicity of a good documentary. When Jagger asks the audience if they're having a good time, you don't feel that it's a cheap showbiz trick, even if it is. The cry of acclamation that goes up is something that the band deserves. They've sweated for it.

It is most satisfying that they supplement their own compositions with two Chuck Berry songs, 'Carol' and 'Little Queenie', for Berry, too, was a performing band. *Get Yer Ya-Ya's Out!* is an unexpected treat, the best album the Stones have ever made.

Monday, 30 November 1970

WHAT TO ROCK TO FOR CHRISTMAS

RECORDS ARE AVAILABLE everywhere, they look all glossy, and they wrap up lovely even when you're stocious with Christmas spirit. A record makes an ideal gift, readers. Unless the recipient already owns it, or doesn't already own a gramophone.

As to the former, detective work is required. As to the latter, if you cherish the recipient dearly and can sustain the departure of at least £40, buy him or her one of the excellent record players in that price range which can be rendered stereo by the plugging-in of an extra speaker (you can reserve the speaker for a birthday present). However, avoid the mistake of my friend Roy's da, who bought the family a lavish stereo outfit, and then spent five bob on a bundle of assorted second-hand records to play on it. Buy second-hand if you must, but don't buy assorted: choose the discs with calculating shrewdness, as follows:

Suppose you want to stimulate Uncle Harry and you don't know what he likes except stout and capital punishment. You could always get him Jimmy Shand or Dana but why not be subversive? Rock has developed into a centre of gravity for all kinds of popular and experimental music. With so many styles and sounds being drawn towards this centre of gravity, there's something in rock for everybody. Surprise Uncle Harry with Crosby, Stills, Nash and Young's *Deja Vu* (Atlantic). He'll never get the four names straight, but he might just be tickled by the ethereal blend of vocal harmonies and the tunefulness of the songs.

Tunefulness is very popular in the rock world these days. You might give James Taylor's *Sweet Baby James* (Warner Brothers) to Aunt Edna while you're at it.

But supposing Uncle Harry is the fiendish drummer in Vin Blank And The Winos and refers to CSN and Y by their Christian names? In this case, buy him Neil Young's latest solo album *After the Gold Rush* (Warner Bros./Reprise). He'll want to have it, even though it's not a quarter as good as *Deja Vu*, and makes the prospect of forthcoming solo albums from the other three a bit forbidding. They should make a New Year resolution to do all their future work together, but they won't.

***

ON THE third hand, supposing you are Uncle Harry: what to get for your glazed young nephew Ringo? Definitely not the two dreaded solo albums by his Beatle namesake, which might do your granny, if she's hard of hearing. Find out if he likes Bob Dylan but has sworn never to buy another album after the pitiful fiasco of *Self Portrait*. If this is the case, give him the current Dylan, *New Morning* (CBS 69001). It's not really a new morning, but it's at least a decent return to the equilibrium of yesterday afternoon, after the aberrations of last night (get it?). There's one rather fine song, 'Sign on the Window', and the rest are blandly pleasant.

To speak more generally, if the recipient claims to be a music-lover and doesn't own the Beatles' *Abbey Road* (EMI Apple), now is the time to introduce him to its second side, which is possibly the finest achievement in rock music. He'll thank you for it years from now, even if he doesn't on Boxing Day. And for the best of that other major force in the development of the music, there is available the Rolling Stones' *Get Yer Ya-Ya's Out!* (Decca).

Showband ravers should be given records by Blood, Sweat & Tears or Chicago; lovers of country and western should be undermined by any of the Band's three albums on Capitol: for opera lovers, there is the Who's *Tommy*, and for community relations with folksong bigots, there is *Just a Collection of Antiques and Curios* (A&M) by the Strawbs, which I'll expand upon next time.

But what shall we give to The Rock-Fan-Who-Has-Everything? I have ransacked the new releases for something really choice and rare, and here it is—a double album, recorded live on Spin RGS 3029/3030 ... of readings and sermons by Dr Ian RK Paisley, DD, MP. Merry Christmas.

Tuesday, 15 December 1970

BOTH PUBLIC AND PRIVATE

The Strawbs/*Just a Collection of Antiques and Curios*
The Incredible String Band/*U*

BACK IN 1957 many spotty young lads were playing that commercial mutation of American folk and country music called skiffle. There was me, John Lennon, Paul McCartney, Dave Cousins and Tony Hooper, for example. Where are the washboards and thimbles of yesteryear? They've gone home to mother. The lads are all spotless and breasting thirty now, and the Strawberry Hill Mob has long come the Strawbs.

Dave Cousins and Tony Hooper are the nucleus of the Strawbs, and for some time they have been creating original music far distant from the days of three-chorded guitarists and the tea-chest bass. The personnel around them has changed several times, the most recent change involving the departure of a cellist and bassist and the arrival of a drummer, a new bassist, and a keyboard wizard fresh from the Royal College of Music called Rick Wakeman. Last July the 'new' Strawbs did a concert at London's Queen Elizabeth Hall and recorded it under the title of *Just a Collection of Antiques and Curios* (A&M

AMLS 994). Any residual Christmas cash or record tokens should be invested immediately in this excellent album.

Cousins writes the songs, and they have three rare qualities: the lyrics are robust enough to stand on their own feet, the words and the melodies are nonetheless interdependent, and the result does not sound like an electric pastiche of traditional folksong. Instead, Cousins has evolved a personal style of very vigorous character, geared to the reedy and rather abrasive timbre of his voice.

***

It's a style that can incorporate both public and private themes. The first song is a decent and businesslike tribute to Martin Luther King without a trace of the mawkish in it. Later, he sings a tender, erotic love song called 'Fingertips', and a most unusual number for a pop group called 'Song of a Sad Little Girl' which was motivated by his young daughter's illness:

> She looks so frail beside you
> As she wears her sick disguise

The centrepiece of the album is the four-part 'Antique Suite', which is perhaps a bit more artily self-conscious than the other pieces, but a moving elegy for all that, evoking the story of a man's life from the mementoes, the 'antiques and curios' left behind in his room.

The songs are fully complemented by the group's playing which now has a richer variety of textures and colours, Wakeman's piano and organ work being especially fine. I hope they get another album out soon, and I hope it contains a song which Cousins says he has written about 'the situation in Ireland' called 'The Hangman and The Papist'.

***

The Incredible String Band's latest, a double-album called *U* (Elektra 2665 001), shows up badly in contrast with the Strawbs: not because the ISB are less talented—the opposite is true—but because they squander and indulge their talents in an increasingly exasperating way.

U was a surreal parable in song and dance staged last year by the ISB and a dance group called Stone Monkey. I have no idea what the show was like (though the photographs look like a cross between a pantomime and the Gang Show), but the music is a ha'penny worth of bread to an intolerable deal of sack. The latter portion is made up of a half dozen interminable Mike Heron compositions, which are tediously over-inflated and sung in the manner of one in great discomfort; and sundry itty-bitties like a mock cowboy song by a Janet Shankman sadly inferior to the Beatles' 'Rocky Raccoon', and a Heron song sung by Rose of the ISB in a very quavering voice indeed.

On the other hand, Robin Williamson turns in four breathtaking songs, as intricately resonant as anything he's done. For these alone I will keep and play the album. But I wish that he and Heron would be at least more self-critically selective about what they release.

Tuesday, 29 December 1970

1971

ANATOMY OF SUCCESS

The Kinks/*Kinks Part One:*
Lola Versus Powerman And The Moneygoround

MUST THE SHOWBIZ go on? It's certainly a difficult institution to outwit. Scores of teenybopper groups are this very minute brooding about whether to 'go progressive'—for the strictly unmusical reason that their 'underground' colleagues have been making conspicuous profits of late.

There's a tricky paradox confronting rock music. It wants to be a liberating, spontaneous, subversive force in society, yet it is the supreme consumer good, the very acme of capitalist profiteering. Record companies rarely talk about artists or songs or records: the word for all these is 'product'. Depend upon it that the growing conflict between the artists and the biz will change the face of the music during the 70s.

The number of groups that can live with the paradox is diminishing. What it involves is the ability to write commercial trivia and then cunningly infiltrate it with literacy; a talent for insinuation, double meaning, working with several levels at once. The Beatles were the supreme masters of this art until they eventually grew tired of it. The Kinks can still turn the trick. Last year they had a hit single with 'Lola'.

> I met her in a club down in old Soho
> Where you drink champagne and it tastes just like coca-cola.

On the surface it was cheerful, unexceptional transistor noise. Underneath, it was a sly and clever joke about the confusing changes taking place in sexual identities.

***

Now they have released an LP called (ahem) *Kinks Part One: Lola Versus Powerman And The Moneygoround* (Pve NSPL 18359). Its subject is this very conflict between art and commerce. Powerman is a pop tycoon ('He's got my money and my publishing rights'). The money-go-round is the machinery of the biz:

Robert owes half to Grenville
Who in turn gave half to Larry
Who adored my instrumentals.

The whole album, in fact, is an anatomy of the conflict and it presumably sums up Ray Davies' feelings after years of grinding out records and doing umpteen American tours. Side 1 opens with 'The Contender' who 'wants to be a winner'. He makes his way to 'Denmark Street':

You go to a publisher and play him your song
He says 'I hate your music and your hair is too long
But I'll sign you up because I'd hate to be wrong

Later, he moves to the 'Top of the Pops', and then ends up caught on the money-go-round. In between, he has been made to 'Get Back In The Line' by the union man and has paid his visit to the dubious Lola.

All of these songs are vivacious and entertaining. They have the sparkle of light revue rather than the scorch of satire: even so, running through them is a genuine desire for change. On Side 2, this is extended to take in urban society as a whole. 'This Time Tomorrow' deals with the unreality of life aboard airliners, and 'A Long Way From Home' with the alienating effects of success.

The most enjoyable single track on the album is 'Ape Man', a witty mock-calypso on the old pop song theme of escape to pastoral simplicity. Ray Davies' innocent-sounding voice is used to best effect here. Elsewhere it sounds as though the recordings were made in his bathroom, and maximum use of your treble control is called for. Also, the two Dave Davies' songs on the record don't quite fit in. Those are my only carps.

Otherwise, his album is something of a landmark in its self-absorption with the music and the industry. Such introspection often signals the point at which a form of expression ceases to appeal to a mass following and becomes a minority art-form. Such was the case with jazz and films. Will this happen to rock? I think so. Will the Kinks go progressive? I hope not.

Monday, 11 January 1971

70

INSTRUMENTAL ROCK

Emerson, Lake & Palmer/*Emerson, Lake & Palmer*

A MAJOR DEVELOPMENT in the pop field is throwing up groups who could easily be confused with estate agents: after Crosby, Stills, Nash and Young, we have Emerson, Lake & Palmer. The great ice pack of established groups is breaking up and the individual floes are drifting into new configurations. The old ideal of faceless group homogeneity is fading. These new 'supergroups' are loose confederations, often uneasy ones, of large individual talents.

Out of three old groups (the Nice, King Crimson and Atomic Rooster) came three gifted performers (Keith Emerson, Greg Lake and Carl Palmer). They have now been playing together for just ten months, and their first album has been released and is already high in the charts. A cynic might be forgiven for accusing them of opportunism. But after hearing the album he would surely re-phrase that to read 'a flair for showmanship', for they make powerfully exciting music.

***

'... THE FIRST SIDE is Emerson, Lake & Palmer as a group—three ideas which have grown from three separate backgrounds to produce a sound. The second side is the work of three individuals having complete expression.' (Keith Emerson interviewed in *Sounds*). This is a clever formula and it works. It allows Emerson, who plays organ, piano and Moog synthesizer to dominate without swamping the other two.

Emerson's fusion of styles is extraordinary. On the organ he plays in odd intervals strongly reminiscent of medieval dance music (as are the clumping rhythms). It's a nobly barbaric sound, particularly when reinforced by the thunder of the Moog, and the first number is indeed called 'The Barbarian'. When he switches to piano in the middle of this piece, the style becomes romantic, almost florid. Finally, the route back to a restatement of the opening passage takes us through some very nifty jazz improvisation on organ.

It's like that all through. Occasionally the profusion of styles defeats him, as in 'Knife-Edge', where he slips into a Bach pastiche, and in the middle section of 'Take a Pebble', where his piano solo is too long and too like the cocktail flourishes of Dave Brubeck's work. But most of the time these disparate elements are held together by the glue of the rock sound itself. Emerson's virtuosity is at the service of a rock daemon and his music is daemonically charged. 'The Three Fates', his solo piece, which begins on the Royal Festival Hall organ, ends appropriately with an explosion.

***

Greg Lake is possibly the nimblest bass player in the business. He gives the bass a full voice in the ensemble where formerly it has been condemned to palpitate with low thuds in the background. Oddly enough his Side 2 contribution is a straight rock song, 'Lucky Man', the most conventional thing on the album; it's in Carl Palmer's 'Tank' that he shines, playing in counterpoint to the electric piano while they together trade phrases with the drums.

'Tank' is an excellent composition. Drum solos seem to me out of place in rock music and I would have been happy enough without Palmer's solo, even though it is his own song. But he matches the high order of playing achieved by the other two, and his solo is well built into the exhilarating climax, with a weird high wail whooping out of the Moog.

Emerson, Lake & Palmer may well become the first group to establish rock convincingly as a wholly instrumental music.

Monday, 25 January 1971

PAP ... GOES THE MEDIA

THE BRITISH POSTAL dispute has deprived me of review albums this week. As a result, I have been lending more ears than usual to the services of the broadcasting media. Much maligned as they are, they are about to be maligned even more. Begging my colleagues' pardon for poaching.

What's galling is that people of discernment and taste all agree that there's too much pop music on radio. Pap music is what they mean. Just as Charles Manson has been consistently described as a 'hippie' in the middle-aged press so all music that isn't explicitly classical or folk or jazz is lumped together as 'pop'; not just by listeners who have no taste for it, but by many of the producers whose job is to present it. On the *Like Now* or *Top of the Pops* kind of television rave-up, you can almost hear them muttering in the control booth: 'Can't tell one of these damned longhairs from another, personally, but they make good television.'

On the other hand, these shows are not really about the music at all but about the 'scene' and that's fair enough. Radio shows, like RTE's *Discs-A-Gogan* or the whole range of BBC air pollutants led in noxiousness by Noel Edmonds fail in quite a different way. They assume that a mid-Atlantic accent pouring out a stream of glib banalities is the equivalent of the work done by American disc jockeys. Instead, it's the equivalent of Walter Matthau acting in Synge. The best American DJs are in fact breathtaking showmen with a real affinity for the music.

***

THE FIRST DJ on this side of the Atlantic who seemed actually to listen to the music and care about it was the BBC's John Peel. His *Top Gear* on Saturday afternoons remains unique in that the music is clearly selected according to personal taste, with no gestures towards the cursed hit parade at all. At the same time, Peel's toneless Liverpudlian mumble is such an extreme reaction to the customary DJ rant that he can turn people away from the progressive tendencies he promotes.

A very different but equally individual path was taken by Kenny Everett, who elevated his task as a DJ into a surrealistic one-man radio revue. His sacking by the BBC for speaking rudely about a Cabinet Minister's wife is one symptom of their befuddled attitude to pop.

On the one hand, there's an avuncular anxiety to offer the kids lots of good clean Tony Blackburn fun, on the other a vague inkling that some of this music is almost serious. Radio Seriousness belongs to the Third Programme and television Seriousness to Sunday morning. Thus we had talks about the music on *Study On Three* last year, and there is the current *Anatomy of Pop* series on BBC1, which you can see if you're a non-churchgoer who doesn't lie in too late.

All the same, the 'Beeb' does try, and has notched up at least two credits. One was for the articulate Tony Palmer TV documentaries on the Cream and on Jack Bruce, and the other for the *In Concert* series on Monday nights—for those who can receive BBC2. This has presented artists like Joni Mitchell, Crosby and Nash, and James Taylor in an entirely straightforward manner. A new series begins soon and will include Leon Russell and Laura Nyro.

There should be much more work of this calibre throughout the broadcasting media and in place of pap. Why? Because quality is healthier than trash; because people who buy records make their choice from what gets broadcast; because the best rock music is the most dynamic of our lively arts; and because the minority audience for that music is certainly no smaller than the audience for symphonic or chamber music.

Monday, 8 February 1971

BELFAST ROCKER

Them/*The World of Them*
Van Morrison/*His Band and The Street Choir*

HOLLYWOOD AND WATTS are two faces of Los Angeles, somehow connected, the ego and the id maybe. Belfast is another such city. Its ghetto face is well known, but it has always had a dream factory too, from the colossal melodramas of the Titanic and the City Hall to current moody superstars like George Best and Van Morrison.

Van Morrison is Ireland's only international rock celebrity. He started out seven or eight years ago as the vocalist in a scruffy rhythm-and-blues group called Them. His own compositions like 'Gloria' and 'Mystic Eyes' entered the English hit parade and achieved a degree of fame for Them, so much so that Decca has recently thought it worth their while to reissue 12 of the group's songs on an album called *The World of Them* (Decca SPA 86).

After the short and hysterical life of Them had ended, Van Morrison both went solo and went—of course—to Los Angeles, where he set about producing himself on a series of solo albums. The last one, *Moondance* (Warner Bros. WS 1835) was quite a commercial success, and he has established himself in America as a major figure in popular music. A new album, recently released, is called *His Band and The Street Choir* (Warner Bros. WS 1884).

Morrison's style has developed into that curious cosmopolitan hybrid called white soul. His writing and singing are essentially derived from the blues and gospel elements of black soul music, from performers like Ray Charles and Otis Redding, but he has assimilated these influences into himself and come up with something distinctively his own. There is a tincture of swing in it, as well as a large measure of Belfast grit.

At first hearing, the melodies all sound rather commonplace and the songs too samey. But the album improves with longer acquaintance. The arranging and production are fastidious and all of a piece. Morrison has built his band up carefully from musicians he has worked with in the past, and they eschew individual flashiness for a tightly controlled ensemble sound, making effectively sparing use of brass and sax phrases. John Plantania, the lead guitarist, plays with self-effacing skill, and does some particularly neat work on the mandolin in 'Virgo Clowns'.

As to the Street Choir, its function seems to be more social than musical, more a part of the sleeve photographs than of the record itself. Morrison has got married—apparently to a girl called Janet Planet, who has designed the sleeve and written a sincere but unfortunately fulsome liner note. What it seems to reflect is the increasing need of rock musicians to create some kind of musical commune in which to work, to surround themselves with souls who are simpatico.

His gift, in short, is for taking shallow, commercial material and giving it enough edge and individuality to make it interesting as well as pleasant. Whether he can repeat this trick on the next album without attempting a new musical departure is questionable. There is a real danger of his work becoming standardised. But in the meantime, on *His Band And The Street Choir*, he has achieved a polished and entertaining crop of songs.

22 February 1971

DISTURBING LENNON

John Lennon/*Plastic Ono Band*

IT'S VERY LIKELY that in the course of the next month, songs by Paul McCartney, George Harrison and John Lennon will all be in the charts simultaneously. Meanwhile, august lawyers gnash their brains publicly over the bitter personality and business conflicts of a group which has been musically defunct for over a year. The Beatles, in short, continue to be as dominant during their afterlife as they were on earth.

But there is, of course, a difference. During the seven or eight years of their unique legendary fame, they didn't merely dominate popular music, they grabbed it by the scruff and rushed it through an astonishing sequence of revolutionary changes. However, this position in the vanguard of rock music, directing its advance, cannot be ascribed to any of the solo efforts of McCartney, Harrison or Ringo since the split-up. Ringo, of course, has at last abandoned himself to the old-fashioned fantasy implicit in the stage-name Starr. McCartney's first solo album was on the level of a home movie. And George Harrison's recent triple LP seems to be predictable and grossly overinflated, though I haven't heard it all through.

Which leaves us with John Lennon and bated breath: will he be the one to break new ground? His album is out (Apple PCS 7124); and the answer is yes.

Lennon was always favoured by the intellectual and literary fans because he was the ironist and punster of the group. He could write and draw with mordant wit and there were clearly emotional depths to his character, which gave to songs like 'Strawberry Fields Forever' and 'A Day in the Life' their profound power to disturb: they expressed not so much stoicism as a numbed hopelessness, a despairing sense of futility which has been deadened by drugs.

***

In this new album, the irony and puns and anodynes have been thrown aside, and the emotions which they filtered or repressed are expressed directly. The result is sometimes harrowing, as in the first and last songs, which are about the desertion by Lennon's father and the death of his young mother when he was still a child. His mother was the subject of an earlier song, 'Julia' a delicate tender lyric of great beauty. What is expressed here in 'Mother' is very different—it is the deprived child's scream of outraged loss. It lays bare a crude emotion which exists to some degree in every human being ever born to woman.

Crudeness or rawness—as opposed to refinement and garnishing—is what this album is largely about. That in itself places it in direct opposition to the general drift of today's progressive rock music, where freakish virtuosity (which helped to kill jazz) is the current fad, and twenty minutes' embellishing of a Scarlatti theme on a synthesizer is thought to be an exciting breakthrough.

By contrast, Lennon has orchestrated his unrefined emotions with unrefined musical sounds. The melodies, never his strong point, are basic rock. The Plastic Ono Band consists of Ringo thudding relentlessly on drums, Klaus Voormann doing the same on bass, and Lennon thumping out two or three repeated chords on the piano. Some of the tracks (notably 'Well Well Well') sound as though the tape was fed through a washing-machine after recording.

Three of the songs—'Hold On', 'Love', 'Look At Me'—reflect Lennon's more tender and wistful side, but the main theme is an angry, contemptuous rejection of past delusions. 'A working-class hero is something to be' he sings in one piece. In another, the climactic song of the album, he lists in a kind of anti-creed the things in which he doesn't believe, from Buddah and Kennedy to Zimmerman (Bob Dylan) and Beatles:

> The dream is over.
> What can I say?

The album is bleak and in places grating. But in another way it's as invigorating as a long draught of fresh cold water. It raises rock to a new level of maturity. Dozens of LPs will soon appear, filled with grim realism. But by then Lennon will most likely be somewhere else.

Monday, 15 March 1971

WEXFORD VISITORS

Curved Air/*Air Conditioning*

OF THE POP groups which were scheduled to appear at the Wexford Tapestry Theatre's excellent festival over this past weekend, the one that interests me most is Curved Air. It's notable that whereas the other eight or nine groups have their origins in the folk music revival, the musicians in Curved Air were 'classically' trained. However, as an example of the confusion currently surrounding such terminology, they recently did a session on a BBC radio series called ... *Folk On 1*. Free love amongst the musical genres has lumbered us with a set of labels as ineffectual as chaperones.

Except, that is, when the love affair between two genres turns out to be a forced marriage, and the parties refuse to co-habit. For my money, that is what happens when you put electric instruments behind a traditional song, as groups like Fairport Convention and Southern Comfort often do. Fairport Convention, by the way, having catered to their fans in the South, at Wexford, will be doing the same for the North, at Belfast's Ulster Hall, on March 24th.

They are skilful and mellifluous entertainers who have written some very pleasant songs. But when they start into 'Sir Patrick Spens' or 'Tam Lin' I reach for my Ewan MacColl. The impulse is not purist but merely commonsensical: if the McPeake family started singing 'Woodstock', I would not be slower in reaching for Joni Mitchell.

This is not to reject the massive impetus that the folk revival has given to contemporary music. Obviously a movement that threw up original artists like Bob Dylan, Robin Williamson and Mike Heron, James Taylor and indeed Joni Mitchell, is the tap root to a hefty share of greenery. It's simply to say that style and content should always bring out the best in one another, no matter what the music.

Curved Air may seem to violate this principle themselves in the piece by which they are best known, 'Vivaldi', in which Darryl Way attacks a bit of Vivaldi with his electric violin, the whole thing turning into an electronic blitz of sound. If it were serious it would be as bad as Stevie Winwood singing 'John Barleycorn Must Die' (or Dylan singing 'Blue Moon'—but, in fact, it's a joke. On their album, *Air Conditioning* (Warner Bros. WSX 3012) they reprise it as 'Vivaldi With Cannons', featuring comic noises from a sympathiser. A somewhat paltry joke, to be sure, but better than straight faces.

The name Curved Air is lifted from the title of a composition by avant-garde composer Terry Riley. They are still too selfconscious about their classical background, but they have the makings of a very good group, a kind of English Jefferson Airplane. Unlike most English girl singers, Sonja Kristina doesn't try to sound black. She puts a lot of cold bite into songs like 'Stretch' and 'Hide And Seek', but my favourite is the poignant 'Situations', and I hope she develops this softer, more expressive side of her voice.

Darryl Way and Francis Monkman—who plays guitar, piano and a whole lot else—have fertile musical imaginations. But their music needs to get funkier and less conceptual. On the album they sound detached from their bass player and drummer, and the songs are sometimes rather mechanical, too obviously 'scored'. However, the promising thing is that they are the first to admit to these faults. They have put a large amount of stage experience under their belts, and at the end of this month they will add to it a seven-week tour of the United States. After they get back, a new album will be completed. It should be well worth a listen.

Monday, 22 March 1971

AMBIVALENT 'DEAD'

The Grateful Dead/*American Beauty*
Family/*Old Songs, New Songs*

THE GRATEFUL DEAD are an almost legendary American rock group and Family is an English group with a big European following. Warners-Reprise have sent me the Dead's recent album *American Beauty* (WS 1893) and Family's *Old Songs, New Songs* (RMP 9007), and I've been playing them as a pair. It makes for an instructive contrast, as well as a pleasant morning.

The Dead were one of the original San Francisco underground groups. Their music has been marinating for years in its environment and by now it is entirely distinctive and very tasty. The communality so desperately pursued in Haight-Ashbury is embodied in the close group harmony of their voices, and in the graceful flow of their playing.

Like the Band, they draw nourishment from the idyllic rural past which lingers in the minds of so many Americans as a dream of lost innocence. But whereas the Band's affinities are with Thoreau, the Grateful Dead are a West Coast group: for all its sweet funk, their music is imbued with restlessness and ambivalence. Songs like 'Friend of the Devil' and 'Truckin" are filled with images of moving on, looking for a home, travelling through the cities.

The ambivalence mostly resides in the tone the lyrics adopt towards drugs, which, like America itself, are at once Utopian and murderous. 'Attics of My Life' is transcendent, 'Candyman' is about the agony of waiting for the pusher to visit town.

It is in this kind of music that the social history of the United States is being recorded, far more than in the newspapers or in the products of the university presses. For this reason, there is no point in judging it by purely 'musical' criteria and especially by the only criterion that most people seem willing to accept, novelty. There are no musical novelties on this album, no weird time signatures nor Mongolian knuckle cymbals. The melodies are all drawn from the blues and country stockpot, the guitar playing of Jerry Garcia is polished, effortless and dead in the centre of the rock tradition. The whole record is sure of itself as an authentic vehicle for American beauty.

***

Family has no such certainties to depend upon. Like so many European 'progressive' groups, it has no affinities with anything except the rest of the international rock culture. Its music is rootless, fretful and mostly loud—with Roger Chapman's voice (a kind of belly-bleat) in full storm, it's apocalyptic.

Old Songs, New Songs is actually 11 old songs re-mixed and re-dubbed and sold for the knock-down price of 149p (29s. 10d.). As an introduction to Family—which it was for me—it's good value. Given the limitations of their chosen style, they're a talented bunch of musicians whose very oddity can produce moments of quirky pleasure.

They have a vibes player (Poli Palmer) and a violinist (John Weider on recent tracks, Ric Grech on earlier ones). With these, and the occasional interjections from flute, saxes and harmonica, not to mention John Whitney's double-necked electric guitar, they avoid the monotony of sound so endemic to progressive groups. As to Chapman's voice, whilst it successfully mauls the lyrics, it could never be called dull.

Monday, 5 April 1971

TOLERABLE TO DULL

Gary Wright/*Extraction*
Don Everly/*Don Everly*
Quintessence/*Dive Deep*
Shawn Phillips/*Second Contribution*
Burt Bacharach/*Portrait in Music*

MOST THINGS IN life are just all right. Reviewers hate to acknowledge that: they want a world which is either 'unsurpassed, breathtaking' or 'disastrous, indefensible'. It's hard to write about stuff that ranges from the tolerable to the dull—that is, nine-tenths of all new records, books, films, experiences. But here goes.

Gary Wright isn't bad. His album *Extraction* (AMLS 2004) is ... well, painless. On 'Get Hold of Yourself' he sounds like Jimi Hendrix, and on 'I Know A Place' he sounds like early Lennon-McCartney. Otherwise, he sounds as competent as he did when he was a leader of the now defunct group Spooky Tooth. The jacket design is striking. It was done by well-known bassist Klaus Voormann who also plays on the album, along with half-a-dozen other good musicians. They sound fine. I probably wouldn't sell this album.

Don Everly is nice. He's half of the Everly Brothers, who are pure trivia, but if they orchestrated your puberty and adolescence as they did mine, you'll feel soft towards them. The album *Don Everly* (AMLS 2007) is conscientiously fashionable: it's solo, it's got all the session musicians listed, it has the words printed on the sleeve (so you can ponder the verbal complexities of 'Tumblin' Tumbleweed'), a bit of studio noise, and poetic self-penned compositions about conservation and suchlike. For a chilling moment I thought that the 'Eyes of Asia' were going to be Vietnamese, but it turns out that they're the eyes of an old-fashioned girl. This album I would sell.

***

Quintessence are worthy. There are six of them and they are the musical representatives of the growing band of people attracted to the religions of the East. Their third album, *Dive Deep* (ILPS 9143), took five months to make. I was expecting a lot of artful fiddling on sitars and gimbris, and there is a little of this, but mostly they are a light rock band with strong jazz affinities.

Every so often there is a vogue for the ambience of the mystic East in jazz circles. There was one in the fifties. I remember. Tracks on this record like 'Dive Deep' and 'The Seer' sound like nothing more than a throwback to that. As music, it doesn't dive more than skin deep. I can't knock it, but I can't keep awake for it either.

Shawn Phillips is a pain. On *Second Contribution* (AMLS 2006) he just drones on interminably, all the songs running into one another. The 'tunes' are just one hackneyed musical phrase repeated and repeated, and the lyrics are a portentous bore. Disastrous and indefensible, maybe? Unfortunately, he has an excellent voice and the arrangements make pleasant listening. It's grimace music rather than retch music. It's like being buttonholed by a mirthless believer in organic food. This album I would give away.

***

But the apotheosis of just-all-rightness is Burt Bacharach. A&M have recently released his *Portrait in Music* (AMLS 2010), on which he arranges, conducts and produces fourteen of his best-known compositions. On one regrettable track, he even sings.

Bacharach would be our Irving Berlin, our Cole Porter, if that kind of musical milieu still thrived (he's even studied under Milhaud). Everybody would whistle 'The Look Of Love' and 'Raindrops Keep Fallin' On My Head' if they weren't already murmuring out of the Muzak. His music is of the '70s: as adroit, efficient and hygienic as air conditioning.

I'm not sure what to do with my copy of this record: there's a big Freudian scratch on it.

Monday, 19 April 1971

SAMPLERS

Various/*Together*
Janis Joplin/*Pearl*

SAMPLER ALBUMS ARE all the rage. CBS are the latest in the field, with a transparent blue one called *Together* (SPR52), a ragbag of sixteen tracks plundered from sixteen of their recent LPs. Given that regular albums cost over £2 and last around 35 minutes—and that this sampler costs 95p and runs for nearly 53 minutes—what is there to criticise? Granted, you will not like all sixteen bands (unless your taste is so catholic as to have given up the ghost) but you're unlikely to hate them all either.

Actually, Side 1 is very listenable. It starts off with the irresistible Johnny Winter's 'Rock and Roll, Hoochie Koo', trucking along, a most infectious noise, the quintessence of old rock & roll combined with the vocal embellishments of the blues. Another good number is Janis Joplin's 'Move Over', her own composition, and surely the best track on her posthumous LP *Pearl*. It moves at just the right speed for her, and allows her to do all the interjections and shouts she could do so well.

Latin rock strikes me as marginalia, but there's a track here from the Santana LP *Abraxas* which works surprisingly well, sounding closer to the Indians of the Amazon than to Edmundo Ros. Last piece on this side is the Soft Machine's 'Teeth' from their fourth album, and it's a splendid stream of nervous energy from Mike Ratledge's organ, set off by very precise phrases from a horn ensemble.

***

Few excursions into modern jazz work as well as this. The Soft Machine have a particular style and sound which has been shaped by their personal concerns. Most other bands are just mulling over tired licks from the group jazz of the forties and fifties: two examples here are from the American groups Ballin' Jack and Dreams. Still, an unusually high level of enjoyment on this side.

Side 2 is more pallid. There is a disappointing 'live-in-concert' piece from Poco, an identikit phony folksong from Tom Rush, the trite old descending scale routine in the Byrds' 'Lover of the Bayou', and a song called 'Fool' by Trees. The girl singer in this group, Celia Humphris, sounds like an elocution teacher. But then all these folk-based English groups have a kind of earnest teacherliness about them.

The best offerings here are Laura Nyro's 'Beads of Sweat' and a pretty little song by Mick Softley called 'Waterfall'. The rest is noise.

***

Which brings me back to *Pearl* (CBS 64188), of which I have at last procured a copy. Most posthumous albums are disastrous, just a bunch of discarded tapes issued in lavishly hypocritical 'memorial' packaging. This one is the opposite. The material is probably the best Janis Joplin ever recorded, and the packaging is just what it would have been had she lived.

Janis's voice was like Euclid's straight line—having length but no depth: all nose and throat, no chest; sounding at its worst like Donald Duck taking off Little Richard. She had no real control over the pacing and dynamics of a song, and in a slow tempo her voice went to pieces. Her forte was the hard driving rock number like 'Move Over'.

Her band on this album, Full Tilt Boogie, is the perfect foil to her strengths and weaknesses. It builds tension where she can't, it propels her along in the rocking numbers and props her up in the clinches. The effect of the album is to dispel a lot of the depressing pathos surrounding her ugly death. It's not the work of a performer in the last stages of disintegration, but of one bringing out the best that was in her.

There is a delightful little unaccompanied song of her own, a parody gospel song, which is entirely unexpected:

Oh Lord won't you buy me a Mercedes-Benz,
My friends all drive Porsches, 1 must make amends.

Monday, 10 May 1971

QUALITY QUARTET

David Crosby/*If I Could Only Remember My Name*
Stephen Stills/*Stephen Stills*

JOHN, PAUL, GEORGE and Ringo were the Fab Four of the sixties: Crosby, Stills, Nash and Young are the Quality Quartet of the seventies—it's our new sophistication. While fidgeting in anticipation of the forthcoming CSNY album *Fourway Street* I have been regaling myself with the solo offerings of David Crosby and Stephen Stills.

Some terms other than 'solo' will have to be devised to describe this new breed of rock album. For in each case the artist has composed and recorded his songs, not alone, but rather with a lavish bit of help from his friends. Stills has Jimi Hendrix playing lead guitar on one track and Eric Clapton on the following one. Crosby calls on 16 or 17 luminaries, including most of the Grateful Dead and Jefferson Airplane—no wonder he called the album *If I Could Only Remember My Name* (it's on Atlantic 2410 005).

Crosby's album seems to demonstrate how much the Quality Quartet are imbued with his ideas, for it sounds for much of the time like another CSNY record. This is most true of an attractive wry song called 'Laughing', about naiveté and gullibility, which has all the poise and relaxed articulateness of the group at its best. It's the kind of song you can listen to all night, smoking reflectively.

'Traction in the Rain' is another excellent song, with a lyric full of original and diverting imagery. Again, it's a piece of mellifluous introspection, and that's what Crosby is most successful at. His political song here, 'What Are Their Names', has a note of self-conscious concern in it as of a man signing his friend's petition, though it sounds great with the tonnage of musical talent he has performing in it.

Elsewhere, this record is easy on the ear, very soothing, maybe a bit too soft-centred on the lusher tracks like 'Music Is Love' and 'Orleans'. There's also an interminable narrative song called 'Cowboy Movie' which I can't entirely follow.

***

Stephen Stills (Atlantic 2401 004) is a winner. Crosby's polished sound is Californian, but Stills was born in Dallas, grew up in New Orleans, and sings like a man who has sustained the odd bruise. Like all Southern performers, he draws instinctively on Gospel and blues, and a number of tracks here feature a funky chorus of voices of the calibre of Rita Coolidge, John Sebastian, Crosby and Nash. Stills's deployment of his chorus and of his various guest instrumentalists is masterly. The album has a truly personal stamp.

This probably springs in the first instance, from the obsessive nature of his songwriting. Nearly all his compositions are about relationships, either his own private ones or the larger ones between men in society. The feelings expressed, whether of bleak pain or light-hearted affirmation, are always clearly genuine.

Side 1 opens with 'Love The One You're With', a most infectious driving rock song loaded with humour; and Side 2 opens with a song of the same ilk called 'Sit Yourself Down'. These pieces exemplify Stills's talent as a popular entertainer, able to make just the right combination of noises that will cause a man to get up and dance. The songs that follow—'Do for the Others' and 'To A Flame'—show his more sombre side. They manage to avoid both self-pity and melodrama, with slightly acerbic lyrics and a restrained performance.

The other songs are extensions of and variations on these opening statements. My favourite is the final one, 'We Are Not Helpless', a fine summary of Stills's outlook on life and of his musical talents, and a natural climax to the album.

Monday, 17 May 1971

SOFT AND PRETTY

The Strawbs/*From the Witchwood*

GIVE ME CHARACTER over prettiness every time—Lynn rather than Vanessa Redgrave, Bunuel rather than Fellini. Dave Cousins' voice may have warts on it, but it's the sound of a real man singing, not a teenage choirboy. Unlike most other groups trying to develop a new music out of the folk idiom, his group—the Strawbs—don't sound pasteurised. Or at least, they didn't before. I'm not entirely happy about their new album, *From the Witchwood* (AMLH 64304).

Their last one, the *Antiques and Curios* one, unveiled the 'new' Strawbs, with a keyboard player, a bassist and a drummer added to the original nucleus of Dave Cousins and Tony Hooper. It was an excellent record, with Cousins' very literate compositions and his nasal rasp being well complemented by the varied sounds and textures of the group. There seems since then to have been a slight revolt in the ranks in favour of more mellifluousness.

***

Two of the tracks on *From the Witchwood* are by Richard Hudson the drummer, and one is by John Ford, the bass player. They all three sound very sub-Beatles. Ford sings like George Harrison and his 'Thirty Days' is straight from the *Rubber Soul* period, sitar and all. Hudson's 'Flight' and 'Canon Dale' are more like Revolver numbers, with filtered voices and multiple tracking and falsetto harmonies. They're pretty to listen to (especially 'Canon Dale') but, as I say, lacking in character.

Which would be fine if it were just Cousins giving the backup lads a democratic chance to step up to the mike. But unfortunately he seems to have been prevailed upon to sing sweet himself. Quite the worst track on the album is his 'Shepherd's Song'. Not content with a tinkling piano and velvet harmonies and Spanish flourishes on guitar and snare drum, he hauls in strings. Nothing else has this degree of schmaltz, but the first number, 'A Glimpse of Heaven', fields a choir and organ and comes very close to having a singalong chorus.

It's not that Cousins can't sing soft: he shouldn't sing pretty. 'In Amongst the Roses' is a very soft song and it's a triumph. All it does is evoke the image of a little girl gathering flowers in the garden of a ruined house. He and Hooper sing alternate verses to a straightforward guitar accompaniment. Lovely.

'Witchwood' itself contains some of the old Cousins nerviness, and so does 'Sheep', though again I don't think the voice-tracking works too well. 'The Hangman and the Papist' is a bit of hokum avowedly inspired by the Belfast riots, but set in the vague past (the hangman finds out that the Papist is his kid brother, you see).

***

Altogether, a lot of hard work and thought has gone into the making of this album, but much of it has served to muffle the group's individuality. I hope they don't end up as just another amalgam of Southern Comfort, Fairport Convention, etc.

Fairport, incidentally, are to make yet another live appearance in Ireland next Sunday afternoon at the Sligo Sounds '71 Festival. On the bill with them is Bridget St. John, one of the best of the university-bred solo performers. She writes and sings wistful, gentle little songs, which can get samey over a long stretch but are very pleasurable in small doses. Saturday afternoon's session was to have been headed by Dr Strangely Strange, but they've finally split up and their place has been taken by Tir na nOg, a very inventive twosome worth watching.

Monday, May 31st 1971

FRISCO SOUNDS TALK

Ralph J. Gleason/The Jefferson Airplane and the San Franciso Sound
James Taylor/Mud Slide Slim and the Blue Horizon

MARTY: ONE THING about the music of the day, one reason it holds, 'cause it's like, it is now, and that's important.

RJG: I went to the Carousel and I was exhausted physically, just beat to where my mind was numb and I was in there about an hour and those bands played so groovy that I stayed there until two in the morning. I felt good.

Marty: Good bands.

RJG: It was like, good medicine. It felt groovy. That's what I look for.

Marty: That's what the musicians look for. That's their main thing is just to play the music and it makes you feel good.

Heady stuff, right? It's from a book about 'Adult Rock', the latest addition to the rock bibliography, which incidentally will soon be massive enough to support its first Ph.D. The book is called *The Jefferson Airplane and the San Francisco Sound* (Pan, 40p.). RJG is the author, Ralph J. Gleason, and Marty is Airplane member Marty Balin. RJG has been going all runny inside about jazz for a fair few years, and is now a large part of the rock magazine *Rolling Stone*.

Making a book out of taped interviews is an operation strewn with traps, and RJG seems to have tripped every one of them—in the extract quoted alone. Some rock musicians are brilliant, colourful talkers, like Frank Zappa and David Crosby. But ... both of these musicians are based in Los Angeles, which commands about the same esteem from cultured San Franciscans like RJG and Marty as your elegant Dublin concert-goer feels for Belfast.

San Francisco may indeed be Culture City, USA, but the five members of its leading rock group have herein recorded lengthy interviews of stultifying banality. These are preceded by an 82-page 'history' of the San Francisco rock scene, which seems a little excessive considering that it only got started in 1965. Still, this part is readable. And the book ends with a very rewarding interview with Jerry Garcia of the Grateful Dead, who talks with an agreeable quiet enthusiasm about the ingredients of his music, how it got started and so on. The book is worth having for this alone.

***

I have no idea how James Taylor would do in an interview, but he's pretty damned eloquent when he sings his songs, or anybody else's for that matter. Already some of the love songs from his first two albums, like 'Fire and Rain' and 'Something in the Way She Moves' have become standards. Now his third album is out, *Mud Slide Slim and the Blue Horizon* (Warner Bros. WS 2561).

Taylor's phenomenal success belongs to the post-Dylan era, but he's actually a very traditional artist. Every age has had a lyric poet who sang: 'My head is full of Spring-time and my heart is full of you.' Taylor's diction even has an old-world quaintness about it, full of usages like 'Do I detect a frown' and 'Forgive me if I say', presumably deriving from his North Carolina origins.

The remarkable thing is that he can make all this new and his own. Underneath the simple lyrics and resonant yet oddly deadpan voice there lies profound melancholy and a whole pattern of irony. It comes out fairly explicitly at times in lines like:

I know you know what I've got to say is an old cliché
Anyway—so they say

But mostly it works as a pervasive atmosphere, as insidiously haunting as the distant owl-hoot of a night train. In the beautiful 'Railroad Song', this very sound is imitated on the violin.

Taylor uses a number of other musicians on the album: mainly the ones with whom he has been touring, like Carole King and Danny Kootch, as well as sister Kate and Joni Mitchell for backing voices. He has been criticised for this by those who prefer him entirely solo, but as he says in a song: 'I've done been this lonesome picker a little too long.' The arrangements are all tasteful and tactful, and they enhance his performance with only a few exceptions (like the overlong title song).

This man is solid gold in a field of corn, and, as RJG might say, I would buy a record of him gargling.

Monday, June 14th 1971

POOR BIG SUR

Various/*Celebration*
Various/*El Pea*

I HAVE IN my hand an LP entitled *Celebration* (AMLS 2020), which is the recorded efforts of six different performers at the 1970 little Big Sur Folk Festival. Nothing demanding about listening to such a disc—simple as inhaling air, right? No. Because I have in my head all the other records I've heard, and all the concerts and rock films and the accumulated lore of the sub-culture. All of which gets called into play in the course of listening, till you have a texture of associations at thick as *Finnegans Wake*.

Thus, Joan Baez's recording of 'The Night They Drove Old Dixie Down' is framed in your memory by the Band's original creation and performance of it, and when she follows it up with 'Let It Be', your mind's ear is hearing Paul McCartney, with all the connotations of the Beatles' split which the song contains. Then you have young Linda Ronstadt imitating old Teresa Brewer singing 'Lovesick Blues', followed by black Merry Clayton (whom you know as a Rolling

Stones session singer) turning both Bob Dylan's 'Times They Are A-Changin" and Paul Simon's 'Bridge Over Troubled Waters' into slow, over decorated gospel songs. It's all a bit wearing.

The oddest bunch of overtones on the album though come through from Kris Kristofferson. After doing graduate work at either Oxford or Cambridge, he lost his heart to country and western music and started singing with an assumed Southern drawl. But if his style is pure Johnny Cash, his content is pure radical chic, in favour of hair and music and against the fuzz and defeatism. Considering that C&W has always been redneck music, the effect is most extraordinary, rather as if Timothy Leary were preaching in the style of Billy Graham.

There are also two numbers from the Beach Boys and one from Country Joe McDonald. The whole thing is a benefit for Joan Baez's institute for the study of nonviolence.

It's a worthy cause and it deserves a better record. This one seems to have been assembled without too much care. The performances, especially Joan's own, are fairly perfunctory, and the chain of associations serves mostly to diminish them.

***

I have in my other hand another LP called *El Pea* (IDLPI). The whizz kid at Island Records who thought of this pun should be knighted forthwith: and it's wittily carried through in the sleeve design with a beautiful photograph of a pea enormously enlarged against a white background. The album is an Island sampler, with the usual good value of these anthology discs, 21 groups for £1.99. But what distinguishes this sampler from those of most other labels is that a number of the tracks are from releases instead of thefts from LPs on current release.

Most interesting to me was a song entitled 'Thru The Night' by somebody called Alan Bown. This is jazz-rock without being too flashy about it. There's a sense of urgency in the phrasing. The singer sounds like a restrained Captain Beefheart and the orchestration of his voice against a descending riff on the horns is very arresting.

Something else that's new and exciting is a Sandy Denny number, 'Late November'. She really does have a rare voice, with the quality in it that actors call presence. Other folkies doing a turn here include Sandy's old group Fairport Convention, the Incredible String Band, Amazing Blondel (these Hollywood superlatives are ceasing to amuse), and Tir na nOg. The latter do a song which is very lyrical and sweet-sounding, but entirely destroyed by its chorus, which goes:

Our love
Will not mildewed grow—no.

If your taste is for the heavies, there are contributions from ELP and Mountain. If it's solo performers you want, you can have Mike Heron, Cat Stevens or Nick Drake. There's even a bit of soul from Jimmy Cliff. Something for everybody, in fact, and all up to the standards of Island fastidiousness.

Monday, June 28th 1971

FEW STARS OR POETS

Carole King/*Tapestry*
Roy Harper/*Stormcock*

FOR MOST OF the sixties, the pop music world was dominated by groups. Now, solo performers have returned to fashion, but with a considerable difference: it's a lengthy leap from Bobby Vee and Neil Sedaka to Elton John and Laura Nyro. Very long, in fact, but not impossible to jump, and Carole King has proved it.

Remember nine years ago a bright girlish voice singing 'It Might As Well Rain Until September'? That was the voice of Carole King, songwriting partner of Gerry Goffin, with whom she had created a string of hit songs such as 'Up on the Roof' and 'Chains' (on the Beatles' first album) and 'Will You Love Me Tomorrow?' This last song, of 1960-61 vintage, now appears on a new album called *Carole King: Tapestry* (Amls 2025), along with some others of 1971 vintage. Carole King has re-arrived.

There's a refreshing unportentousness about her work, probably reinforced by my listening to it in tandem with Roy Harper's *Stormcock* (SHVL 789). Harper is an English singer-songwriter, heavily under the influence of Dylan. He seems to have a genuine sense of concern and of purpose, but none whatsoever of economy or of dynamics. There are only four songs on his album, and not one of them ought to be longer than three minutes.

He's fond of the old Dylan trick of singing a long undulating lyric over a simple repeated chord sequence. This isn't too bad in the first song, 'Hors d'Oeuvres', which is about the sad ironies of a courtroom

91

scene. But even it ends up on a strumming-and-humming, pointlessly long fade. And the other three songs are so windily self-indulgent that I still can't remember which is which, after half-a-dozen plays.

***

Singers used to want to be stars; now they want to be poets. A failed star can turn out to be just an accomplished entertainer, but a failed poet is likely to be a pretentious bore. The percentage of real stars and poets being about equally miniscule, there is a large number of pretentious bores amongst the current host of singer/songwriters. Roy Harper, I regret to say, is one of them.

Maybe because she served her apprenticeship in the star system, Carole King is addicted to professionalism. This doesn't mean that her songs are vapidly commercial. They express personal pains and pleasures in simple, direct language and fluent melodies, sung and played on the piano with a graceful vigour. At the same time, they recognize themselves as pop songs, working with a familiar and limited vocabulary to reach a large audience.

My favourite song from the album is 'You've Got a Friend', because it is the quintessence of the above-named qualities. I must confess to preferring James Taylor's recording of it, he being star and poet too. But it's a song that belongs to everybody—a standard, in fact.

Of all the strands in her tapestry, gospel singing is one of the most recurrent, and 'A Natural Woman ' has already been a hit for Aretha Franklin. In a similar vein are 'Home Again' and 'Way Over Yonder', with the inevitable Merry Clayton doing the backing vocal. Even more attractively exuberant is 'Beautiful', and as a foil to these there is the plaintive and very pretty 'So Far Away'. The only song I dislike on the album is 'Tapestry' itself. It's the only one that tries to be a poem.

Monday, 12 July 1971

MOUNTAIN SLEIGHRIDE

Mountain/*Nantucket Sleighride*
Seatrain/*Seatrain*

FELIX PAPPALARDI USED to produce the Cream. He also has a deftly inventive touch on the bass guitar. That should satisfy any man, but as a member of the group Mountain, Pappalardi also sings, and his voice is just pleasantly nondescript.

Leslie West's voice is as nondescript as a locomotive. Mountain may very well have taken its name from his physique, and he has the voice to go along with it, unfortunately, I can barely comprehend a word he sings. On the other hand he plays the guitar very coherently indeed.

All of which goes to make the album *Nantucket Sleighride* (ILPS 9148) vocally uninteresting but instrumentally rich. Drummer Corky Laing and keyboards player Steve Knight make up the other half of Mountain, which could fairly he described as a heavy group, right down to the exhortation on the album cover to 'play this record at high volume for maximum sonority'. But even at its heaviest, the musical texture never gets muddy. There is a fine group rapport, enhanced by Pappalardi's experienced and skilled production.

These qualities are most evident in the song 'Tired Angels'. There's quite a deal of subtle variety in this track, with West's guitar overlaying a pleasing pattern on bass and organ. Another high point is the one-minute instrumental 'Taunta' in which the four of them prove that they can also play with restraint, and Pappalardi is especially lyrical on bass.

Both of these pieces belong to the album's first side which also contains the title song. A Nantucket Sleighride was the experience enjoyed by sailors in the old whaling days when their boat was being towed by a harpooned whale: this is what the song appears to be about, but I can only catch the occasional word. However, the instrumental work continues to be ingenious, with a kind of rock hornpipe appearing at one point. The first side, then, has a quota of good listening.

The second side is entirely given over to the heavy repeated riff of hard rock, and it's something of a bore. All four songs go on too long, and they sound too alike. Side 1 has barely enough variety but Side 2 has none at all.

***

Mountain strikes me on the whole, as a group with a lot of professionalism and expertise but not a great deal to say. Seatrain is another such group. Several of its members are veterans on the folk and rock music scenes, all of them perform with flair, and their album (EAST 659) has been produced by the legendary George Martin; it's full of cleverness and style, and yet it fails to leave a clear imprint.

Part of the reason is that they are too blatantly jumping on the Band's wagon (I feel ill, too)—there are two songs on Biblical themes and a general air of pastoral idyll.

Vocals are mainly shared between Lloyd Baskin and Peter Rowan, and Baskin is by far the better singer of the two. His performances of 'Broken Morning' and 'Out Where the Hills' (both composed by bass player Andy Kulberg) make these the best songs on the album. He has the appropriate melodious throatiness for this kind of material.

Rowan on the other hand both writes and sings rather insipidly, especially on 'Oh My Love' which is a sub-Buddy Holly number. The most enjoyable feature of the album is a traditional tune called 'O.B.S.' on which he fiddles up a storm. Otherwise, there is a vague but ubiquitous feeling of some vital missing dimension. Seatrain needs a sense of destiny. They need to go their own way and leave the Band behind, for the Band is peerless.

Monday, 26 July 1971

INTROSPECTION IS IN

Joni Mitchell/*Blue*

BLUEBERRIES and waffles don't change their flavour, but the American Zeitgeist does: this summer I sense a mood of stasis, passivity, turning inward. Yesterday's radical oracles about the war and the credibility gap are today's commonplace facts. External reality is a con game. Attention has turned back on the self.

Naturally, this is reflected in the music, in the whole bunch of lonesome pickers currently in public favour. None of them is writing protest songs. The best are scarred dancers from the pop music fandango, all except Joni Mitchell who is a carry-over from the folk boom, except that the term 'carry-over' is insulting to an artist who is developing as profoundly as she. Her album *Blue* (Reprise MS 2038) expresses the mood of the times without doing obeisance to it.

'Blue' is a word that appears in almost all the songs, the dark colour of the album sleeve, and, in the title song, the name given to a beloved. Occasional references are made to the world outside private rooms—

> they won't give peace a chance
> that was just a dream some of us had—

but these are only brief glances away from the pursuit of happiness within the self; mainly sought in a love relationship, but also through the songs themselves.

Joni, in short, is an old-style monogamous romantic, and she recognises it. In a rather wordy song called 'The Last Time I Saw Richard', she recalls a friend who warned her that all romantics end up 'cynical and drunk and boring someone in some dark cafe'. At the end of the song she sees herself in this situation. But meanwhile Richard has got married to a figure skater,

> and he bought her a dishwasher
> and a coffee percolator.

A sense of mischief is one of Joni Mitchell's most individual qualities. It produced 'Big Yellow Taxi', one of the most delightful songs on her last album, *Ladies of the Canyon*.

On the other hand, a modicum of irony was badly needed in the poorer songs from that collection, like 'Willie'. She had an inclination to take herself too seriously, to over-dramatise—the usual romantic failings. These new songs have more subjective depth and sound more genuine.

'All I Want' is the opening number, and it starts off in a very familiar vein:

> I am on a lonely road and I am travelling.

Shades of James Taylor—who is playing guitar on this and two other songs—and of Carole King. However, there is a distinctly un-Taylorish urgency and vibrancy in the rest of the piece, a very feminine outpouring of the ingredients of a good relationship. Following it is 'My Old Man', a fine example of Joni's gift for the original and expressive melody.

***

More conventional is the next song, 'Little Green', which shelters

95

too much behind rather cluttered and confusing lyrics. However, the first side ends with two excellent and very contrasting numbers. 'Carey' is a rousing account of a liaison on the Island of Crete. 'Blue' is an intense and deeply personal love lament, a song of rare authentic feeling.

In the same vein—though necessarily less compressed—is 'A Case of You' on Side 2. This girl can write such literate lyrics! 'California' and 'This Flight Tonight' express the emotions involved in travelling. They have conversational ease, and yet they are full of clear, vivid imagery. 'River' is the weakest song on the record because of its maudlin tone and the mistake of opening and closing it with 'Jingle Bells' in a minor key. Yet even it is worth listening to.

This album is a gust of rain in a dry season. It is sure to be an instant commercial success, but equally sure to be a lasting artistic one.

Monday, 9 August 1971

'JOHNNY WINTER AND'

Johnny Winter/*Johnny Winter And*
Leon Russell/*Leon Russell and the Shelter People*

FRANK FURTER IS currently recording his eighteenth album and I've just listened to an acetate of Side 1, which was finished at lunchtime. Even prior to proper mixing and dubbing, this work is unequivocally a major step sideways in the history of Western music ... it would be nice to be able to write like a real rock journalist, but I can't even stay abreast of the new releases. I keep 'discovering' records that aficionados have long since sent to their aunty's jumble sale.

I've just discovered *Johnny Winter And* (CBS 64117). Not only is this Mr Winter's album-before-the-last-one, it turns out, but the man himself is no longer recording: he's in a mental hospital in Texas, having crashed badly on hard drugs.

On the other hand, why should reviews be obsessed with novelty? Quality usually takes time to seep through anyway—the flashy stuff makes an immediate impact. Johnny Winter has class and deserves to be lingeringly appreciated. I hope that he can soon get himself and then his band together again.

Meanwhile, Side 2 of *Johnny Winter And* doesn't have a poor track on it. It contains two of the three Winter compositions on the record, all of them powerful, raunchy numbers. 'Prodigal Son' is a full-blooded exhortation to hedonism along with an awareness of its price. 'Nothing Left' is about the anguish of waking up needing a fix, a bleak premonition of his recent breakdown. Frantic runs on the guitar express the emotion even more poignantly than his fine voice.

Pain and frustration are the emotional mainsprings of Winter's music (he started out as a blues singer) but the music itself is fastidiously played and recorded. In 'On the Limb', for example, Winter and Rick Derringer sing together and trade lines with a controlled rapport that brings out all of the song's meaning. In 'Funky Music', the last song on this side, they improvise on their guitars in driving counterpoint. Nothing is ever flat, sharp, blurred, fumbled or out of tempo.

Side 1, though, has some mediocre songs on it. Stevie Winwood's 'No Time to Live' presents the lad's most self-pityingly adolescent profile, and 'Ain't That A Kindness' is a dull modern cowboy song in which the group's projection of virile masculinity begins to seem strained. What's great here is 'Rock and Roll, Hoochie Koo', a song to make the very boulders dance. Try it.

***

Leon Russell is another performer with whom I've finally and very belatedly caught up. Having done so, I fail to understand all the fuss that has been made of him. His album is *Leon Russell and the Shelter People* (AMLS 65003) and it's just about all right. As crown prince of that band of former session musicians invariably called 'legendary' who have thrust themselves into the limelight, he is a remarkably uninventive pianist. As for his singing, he somehow contrives to gulp words with his nose, as well as squeaking at the end of every line.

There are really only two songs on the album which involve me, 'Home Sweet Oklahoma' and 'Alcatraz'. The former is a wistful bit of autobiography which sounds genuinely felt. The latter is more typically about a fashionable cause, the Indian seizure of Alcatraz (elsewhere we get ecology, alienation, mysticism)—but the lyrics are surprisingly literate and the music has guts.

Russell singing Dylan is bad news. He rasps through 'A Hard Rain's A-Gonna Fall' in jog-trot time, quenching all the fires of its apocalyptic imagery. 'It Takes a Lot to Laugh, It Takes a Train to Cry' is done as a most unresonant bottleneck blues. But oddly enough, he does a better job on 'Beware of Darkness' than its composer, George Harrison—the awkward, angular shapes of Harrison's music find an apt correlative in Russell's voice.

On the whole, he's probably a very good session musician.

Monday, 23 August 1971

FUSING JAZZ AND ROCK

Heaven/*Brass Rock I*
Supertramp/*Indelibly Stamped*

FIRST OF ALL, there's *Heaven/Brass Rock I* (CBS 66293), a double LP by a group about whom I know absolutely nothing. I don't even know what the album sleeve looks like: CBS have issued the record in a plain sleeve because (they claim) the heavy demand has not given them a chance yet to print on the proper one. So clearly everybody knows about the band except me, which is a downright disgrace for a pundit. A more honourable man would turn in his stylus.

Actually, I can see from the label that Heaven are produced by Rikki Farr, who also produced the Isle of Wight festival, so I infer that they are English. If so, they're one of the best English jazz/rock outfits I've heard. Since the commercial success of groups like Blood Sweat & Tears, Chicago, the Flock and Dreams, a lot of erstwhile jazz cats have been growing droopy moustaches and opting to join what they can't beat.

A great quantity of electricity has been consumed in this process, but not too much has been generated. The accepted procedure for 'fusing' jazz and rock is to overlay standardised rock blare with a few tired raggedy licks on grass and reeds. Heaven, as their name modestly implies, rise well above such trivialities. Their sound is always of a piece and full of inventiveness.

Particularly impressive are their guitarist and flute player, both individually and together. 'Morning Coffee', for example, is a meditative tune too close to Herb Alpert for comfort, but rendered worthwhile by the flute's quicksilver magic. 'Got to Get Away' features an excitingly decorated wall of sound from the guitar.

Other things are less felicitous. This band writes lyrics and sings

98

them like a seal walks. Their lead voice has a bogus Captain Beefheart quality which jollies along the opening number with shouts of 'right on!' and such like. Oddly enough, they sing rather well as a chorus; for example, at the end of 'Song for Chaos', where the ensemble of voices grows very pleasantly out of an instrumental crescendo. However, this same number begins with an awful slow passage on trumpet, piano and jarringly sharp bass.

There are also boring repetitions, a fulsome pop song called 'Dawning' complete with sea noises, and a number of other no-no's but in spite of it all, this is an album to play and a band to watch. They're bristling with good ideas, and they have sufficient expertise and imagination to get them across.

***

I didn't know anything about Supertramp either till I got their album *Indelibly Stamped* (A&M 64306), but the album in this case tells me all. What are they? Well, they're one more group of clean-limbed young men with fine heads of hair and strong tuneful voices and the ability to perform on musical instruments who could equally well be throwing pots or taking the grainy photographs on their album sleeve.

Groups like this are contemporary Aesthetes. The songs they write and record have no justification outside of themselves. The liner notes written by the members of Supertramp illustrate this: each song is related either to other such songs ('"Your Poppa Don't Mind", harks back to the Bill Black Combo of some years ago with shades of Chuck Berry') or else to the manner of its composition ('"Rosie Had Everything Planned" ... written in the middle of the night when we had to do something to stay awake'). Nothing is written to express, communicate, persuade or inform.

Art created for Art's sake can give a certain pleasure if the art in question is well turned out. Unfortunately, Supertramp lack the advantage of extraordinary talent. The melodies are hackneyed and the flautist plays atrociously off-key. It's too bad.

Monday, September 6th 1971

PAPERBACK CULTURE

Gary Herman/*The Who*
David Morse/*Motown*

'ROCKBOOKS' IS A series of short paperbacks about pop music, edited by Phil Hardy and published by Studio Vista. The two I have read are *The Who* by Gary Herman and *Motown* by David Morse. There are others on the Drifters and on Buddy Holly, and presumably further titles are in preparation. So the rock bibliography continues to burgeon: the print culture, in its doddering and obsolete fashion, continues to pant after the new musical express.

It's long since become clear, from the sheer volume of wordage, that a crowd of people have something serious to say about the music (or the phenomenon) and an even bigger crowd are eager to hear it. Yet no-one has so far evolved a suitable style.

'It is the hardest thing imaginable to find a descriptive and analytic language that does justice to any newly emergent form of musical expression' (Meirion Bowen in the BBC book *Anatomy of Pop*). The technical vocabulary of serious music criticism will certainly not serve. In discussing whether soul music is tailored to the requirements of the transistor radio or not, David Morse comments: 'There is an emphasis on synchronic rather than diachronic complexity.' It's just not the appropriate tone of voice.

***

Tone is the crux. Mr Morse knows a bit about music, but he's tone deaf in other respects. He berates white audiences for failing to appreciate and nurture black soul music, and the Motown groups in particular. Yet he never mentions the main objection that can be urged against Motown: its old-fashioned sham emotionalism, its excess of absurd and outdated histrionics. He rejects the contention that some of this music is Uncle Tom material without ever considering the Al Jolson precedents, though he admits that the biggest audience for Motown is the white middle-aged nightclub one.

This insensitivity to tone permits him to discuss, for example, the Four Tops' 'Reach Out I'll Be There' and '7 Rooms of Gloom' (with their almost camp melodrama) as if they were complex realistic portrayals of human suffering. He includes tables and charts of musical and emotional structure, and even invokes Wagner, albeit apologetically. All of which is steadily belied by the photographs sprinkled through the text, in which the performers cluster in strained, stagey postures, as far from expressing their own feelings as James Taylor is from being Johnny Ray.

David Morse likes Motown music and can't put apt words to his responses. What's more, he's far from thick. The best bits in the book come when he turns away from Motown and attacks other critics or the media. There's one excellent section in which he categorises the various approaches to pop music—into ethnic, sociological, political, mass-cultural, Messianist, and rock-elitist—and then disposes of each of them in turn. His jibes at the rock heads are particularly telling: 'The rock ethic assumes that the music to which it is devoted is somehow free from the commercial pressures which operate elsewhere in popular music.'

***

That's only one of the points which is not sufficiently explored by Gary Herman, whose own book fits neatly into category 2 (sociological). In his first chapter he involves you in some dreadful jargon, in which the words 'totemic', 'locus' and 'symbiotic' recur like ragnails. Later, he gives a good account of how the Who developed out of the Mod phenomenon, though he talks about the mods as though they were an isolated teenage eruption instead of merely one in a continuing series.

Monday, 20 September 1971

SAVE US FROM ART

Bernie Taupin/ *Taupin*
Leonard Cohen/ *Songs of Love And Hate*

THERE'S SOMETHING ALMOST likeable about a play or book or record that is entirely disastrous. You don't have to weigh the one hand against the other, the frustrating bad moments against the baffling good ones, as you have to with Leonard Cohen, say. Instead, you can abandon yourself to winces, chortles, puking noises, and yawns, which is what I have been doing listening to *Taupin* (DJLPS415).

I suggest that we junk the word 'art' and all the prescriptions for creativity that are implied by it: whatever is meant by it in theory, it works out in practice as a lot of people self-consciously striving for a fake portentous significance in their work and being indulged in this process. From the Dadaists to our own day, there have been many attempts to smash this Romantic icon of Art, but it continues to be reverenced. The pop industry has been kneeling before it for years now, ever since some literary critic decided that the Beatles were good enough to be Art, and Art became profitable.

Now they're all trying to be Art, and Bernie Taupin has released this album of himself reading his poetry. Bernie is the lad who writes lyrics for Elton John, and Bernie and Elton between them have produced some enjoyable popular songs like 'Your Song' and 'Indian Sunset'. But Bernie is no more a poet than Oscar Hammerstein III.

Attempts at amelioration of this circumstance include the use of heavy voice echo and of background music, played by seven musicians altogether, including Caleb Quave and Shawn Phillips (I trust devoutly that he isn't thinking about recording his poetry.) But nothing can mask the fact that the actual words, lines, rhythms, ideas and sentiments of the poems are execrable. Bernie reads them all in a mournful, apologetic murmur, and try as you will, it's very hard to keep your mind on what he's saying.

You can follow the words in the enclosed booklet, of course, but it's distractingly filled with discrepancies, mistakes and missspellings. As to the music, whilst propping up the words as best it can, it often has the unfortunate efffect of making the voice sound as though it's supposed to be singing especially since most of the poems are written in hackneyed song rhythms.

The ten of them on Side 1 make up a sequence called 'Child'. There are no two adjacent words in it which strike fire off one another. Instead they shuffle dully by, sinking at their worst to the greeting card level:

> All you ever learnt from them,
> until you grew much older,
> did not compare with when they said
> this is your brand new brother.

On Side 2 there are five further pieces, and then a set of three called 'Verses After Dark'. These have a frisson of Gothic horror which makes them marginally interesting; but that's the most that can be said.

***

Getting back to complexities, Leonard Cohen's, third album *Songs of Love and Hate* (CBS69004) has been out for some months now and my feelings about it are still as mixed as its title. The man is clearly gifted, but perversely. He seems obsessed by private images which can cause a song to drone on interminably in a manner that seems arbitrary. For example, the first song on this record, 'Avalanche', is a long sequence of figurative statements put in the mouth of a hunchbacked figure. What is he—devil, earth-god, the soul of man? The clues are entirely obscure.

On the other hand (we're weighing those hands again), 'Dress Rehearsal Rag' is a powerful song filled with the authentic self-loathing and despair of drug addiction:

> Why don't you join the Rosicrucians,
> They will give you back your hope.
> You will find your love in diagrams
> On a plain brown envelope.

Monday, 4 October 1971

IN BETWEEN CAT STEVENS

Cat Stevens/ *Teaser and the Firecat*
Traffic/ *Welcome to the Canteen*

HERE'S AN OPENER for the aficionados: 'Knife Edge' by ELP is drawn from Janacek's 'Sinfonietta', and Cat Stevens' 'Morning Has Broken' uses the melody of the hymn 'Child in the Manger', which was also the tune of my old school song. Eclecticism can go no further.

Cat Stevens is a performer who has suffered from the public's love of categories. He started out some time ago as another clean young singer of disposable top ten songs. Then illness removed him from the business for two years, during which time introspective solo performers became the whole rage. Since his return to the scene, Cat Stevens' work has been falling between the James Taylor and Cliff Richard stools—confessional lament on the one hand, pop commercialism on the other.

This may not be good for trade, but it is far from unattractive to listen to. The worst thing I can say about his new album *Teaser and the Firecat* (ILPS9154) is that there's one song on it ('Changes IV') which I can imagine Tom Jones singing. Husky funk is definitely not the Stevens hallmark. He's a dexterous lightweight with a facility for catchy tunes but also a sophisticated rhythmic sense.

His best songs are rhetorical units built on the repetitions of a simple musical sentence. 'If I Laugh' and 'How Can I Tell You' are excellent examples here. The former has a wry and articulate lyric, the finest on the record, and it is perfectly complemented by the halting, tentative tune. It's a song which has integrity and yet could also be a success in the charts. The lyrics of 'How Can I Tell You' are so threadbare, you can scarcely read them on the sleeve, but they're entirely transformed by the music.

Some of the other songs, like 'Tuesday's Dead' and 'Moon Shadow' are rather nondescript, but they're performed and produced fastidiously. 'Rubylove' is a number in Greek style which sports a bouzouki player—Stevens had a Greek father and Swedish mother—and the middle verse is sung in Greek, with great panache. The bouzouki's nice, too.

***

I want to avoid saying that Traffic has stalled, but the only other phrase that comes to mind is 'has lost its direction' which is worse. *John Barleycorn* was a good album, but since then the group has been vacillating over personnel changes and life in general. A live but far from lively album has just been released. It's called *Welcome to the Canteen* (ILPS9166).

The fault lies partly with the engineers. The overall sound has the approximate qualities of a morgue, and the balance is lamentable, with Winwood's voice hollowly advancing to and receding from the mike. Nevertheless, no engineer could have concealed the fact that we have here a tired rendition of old Traffic songs which are already securely preserved on earlier albums. Side 2 is unforgivable: it consists of a 10-and-a-half-minute 'Dear Mr Fantasy' and an 8-and-a-half-minute 'Gimme Some Lovin'', neither of them even approaching inspiration at any point.

Nor can this he blamed on the three freelance artists—Ric Grech, Jim Gordon and Reebop Kwaku Baah—who have augmented the old Traffic foursome to make up Traffic Etc. Grech plays a buoyant bass, Gordon's drumming shows all the finesse of his amazingly wide experience, and Kwaku Baah plays congas and bongos with tasteful unobtrusiveness. It's possible, of course, that their presence has unsettled Stevie Winwood, but he must have had a hand in inviting them.

At any rate, he sings 'Medicated Goo' and '40,000 Headmen' wretchedly, helped not at all on the latter by some maundering, tuneless flute playing from Jim Capaldi. Dave Mason is marginally better doing his 'Sad And Deep As You' and 'Shouldn't Have Took More Than You Gave', but he has never seemed to me an artist who gives off sparks, despite the praise lavished on his double LP. All in all, it's a rather mournful occasion.

Monday, 18 October 1971

JOHN LENNON'S SECOND SOLO LP

John Lennon/*Imagine*
Loudon Wainwright III/ *Album II*

'CRUDENESS OR RAWNESS—as opposed to refinement and garnishing—is what this album is largely about.' Thus spake Parker in reviewing the first John Lennon solo LP. The second one, *Imagine* (Apple), has now been released, and it contains a considerable amount of garnishing and refinement. On some tracks there are as many as six assorted guitars, a strong section, p. b. and d., saxes, and other multifarious instruments. The producer Phil Spector's taste for a vast hollow shimmering sound with a load of ironmongery round the edges is in evidence. The naked voice has been expensively apparelled.

On the whole this strikes me as an error in judgment, and the album lacks the relentless intensity of the first one. But every record can't be a milestone, which is just as well, and there is always pleasure to be had from Lennon's work. In spite of all his pioneering, he has never lost his gift for writing tuneful, lightweight pop songs, and there are a couple here—'Imagine', 'Jealous Guy', 'Oh My Love', any one of which could be released as a hit single.

Nor is there a shortage of attack. The most successful track is 'Crippled Inside'; realistic words about posing and pretending set to an innocuously jaunty hillbilly tune. In this instance the heavy weight of sound pays off, with three acoustic guitars, two electric ones, and George Harrison's dobro laying down the old fat skiffle noise. However, similar irony does not inform 'Gimme Some Truth' and 'How Do You Sleep', and the effect of these seems to me muffled by the heavy orchestral and group sound (most of which was overdubbed).

There is in addition an element of pettiness in the latter song, which is an outburst against Paul McCartney. Lennon has not succeeded here, as he did throughout the first album, in raising his personal obsessions to a level where they make sense in terms of everybody's experience. But then the first album was a coherent entity. This one sets out to be just a collection of miscellaneous songs, some excellent, a few commonplace, all of them worth a hearing.

***

The naked voice is really getting a hearing these days. For a long time, John Peel has been advocating the work of an obscure New York singer called Loudon Wainwright III, scion of a distinguished family. At last I have a copy of his current album (*Loudon Wainwright III: Album II* on Atlantic) just as he appears to be entering the limelight.

His voice is extraordinarily arresting: high pitched and frail, but charged with a kind of steely urgency which compels you to listen. The burden of his song is identical with that of the young Elizabethan conspirator who wrote from his death cell, 'My prime of youth is but a frost of cares.' Wainwright's cares are the soiled emotional ideals of the young in places like New York City.

He has been unfairly accused of imitating Dylan. Apart from the cryptic imagery of 'Me and My Friend the Cat' and the nonsense verses of 'Glenville Reel', there is nothing on this album that even obliquely resembles Dylan's work. Where Dylan is public and rhetorical, his very wilfulness stemming from his sense of an audience, Wainwright is private, almost painfully intimate, singing to one lone person or to himself.

He's one of that handful of genuine originals which sustains your belief in a future. The only other artist he calls to my mind is, weirdly enough, Tom Lehrer. If you can imagine Lehrer twenty years younger and demented, that suggests the quality of humour in Wainwright's songs. In the pay-off to 'Nice Jewish Girls' he even sings like Lehrer. And how about lines like these from 'Suicide Song':

When you tire of worldly toil
Shuffle off this mortal coil
Turn your body back to soil,
It's OK ...

Monday, 1 November 1971

ROCK, RICH AND RARE

Curved Air/*Second Album*
Elton John/*Madman Across the Water*

CURVED AIR ARE one of the few progressive rock groups actually progressing. Their first album displayed brains, direction and a highly personal style of hard-edged glitter, as well as a certain bloodlessness and a tendency to show off. In their second album (Warner Bros. K46092) these tendencies have been remedied, whilst the intelligence and glitter have been enhanced.

Francis Monkman comes into his own on this record. Apart from his extraordinary contributions on guitar, keyboards and VCS3 synthesizer, he has composed the three songs which make up Side 2, and they indeed carry it away. They have an odd quality of waking dream, at once sinister, innocuous, crystal clear and filled with mystery. There are constant shifts of rhythm, from the gipsy-style violin tune of 'Everdance' to the breezy waltz time of 'Bright Summer's Day', to the subtler shifts within the 12-and-a-half-minute 'Piece of Mind'.

A proper analysis of this last song alone would take up the whole column. It moves from an insistent statement by organ, guitar and trumpets which provides a setting for the opening vocals, through lots of free-style shifting jazz rhythms, to the vocals again, and then a string interlude. During a long piano improvisation, some lines from the Fire Sermon section of 'The Waste Land' are recited, and then there is an electronic passage on the synthesizer with Latin rhythms.

Instead of building this up into an ELP-type concluding blitz, Monkman ends his piece with a series of slow, dreamy flutterings on the synthesizer. Like everything else in the song, this is as unexpected as it is appropriate. Aesthetically and emotionally, 'Piece of Mind' is a joy to listen to.

This is not to belittle Side 1, which comprises the compositions of Darryl Way. His violin marks Sonja Kristina's icy voice with the same dexterity of a top footballer, and his songs partake of the same qualities as Monkman's, even if they don't quite match them. What is important is the way the five members of the group have worked together to create a musical texture which is rich, thick, and rare indeed.

***

Elton John fans should be pleased with his new album, *Madman Across the Water* (DJLPH420). Since becoming all the rage, he has concentrated increasingly on making corn while the sun shines, but this album is something of an improvement on that. Maybe he's growing anxious to demonstrate that he's more than a nine-day wonder as Day nine draws nearer.

A lot of the songs written by him and Bernie Taupin are what literary critics would call versions of pastoral. 'Indian Sunset' is the noble lament of the last of the Mohicans (or one of the last). 'Rotten Peaches' that of a doomed prisoner on the run, 'Levon' the tale of a Jewish pauper in New York who makes good but then has an unhappy son. There's an element of hokum in all this but also considerable expertise. Bernie has the knack of writing phrases that can be sung, and Elton has the slickness to find appropriate musical clichés for them.

Some of his clichés are wearing, though, notably the big crescendo and the habit of singing each song through twice. 'Indian Sunset' is a Hollywood production number with no fewer than three great crashing string crescendoes. 'Tiny Dancer' is a pretty little song to Bernie's wife, Maxine, with an artful 'hook' which could carry it into the charts; but sung through twice, it comes out at six minutes twelve seconds, which is exactly twice the length it ought to be.

The use of strings throughout is very derivative from the Beatles' *Pepper/Magical Mystery Tour* period, but the rest of the musicianship is quite tasty. 'On Holiday Inn', a sub-James Taylor number, Davey Johnstone's mandolin is a delight to the ear, and so is Jack Emblow's accordion on 'Razor Face'. This last song and the title track are the most impressive things on the album and may, perhaps, survive its demise.

***

Finally, a word to Ken Gray with regard to his review in last Wednesday's paper of Charlie Gillett's book, *The Sound of the City*; Johnny Ray and Frankie Laine were not rock singers; sexuality is explicit in the Child Ballads, Wagner, flamenco, Orff, in fact music from every imaginable age and level of society: and finally, may I have his review copy when he's finished reading it?

Monday, and Tuesday, 15 & 16 November 1971

VOICES FROM THE DEAD

The Grateful Dead/*Grateful Dead*
Noir/*We Had To Let You Have It*

THE TIME HAS arrived once more to be grateful for the Grateful Dead. They belong in that tiny handful of groups whose work is definitive, so that to explain things to the man who asks what exactly rock music is, you need only play him one of their albums. If he then asks what's so great about that stuff, you can easily tell him, especially if the record in question is the newly released double album (Warner Bros. K66009).

The raw material here, first of all, is simple in the extreme. It includes those classics from the days of rock-n'-roll innocence, Chuck Berry's 'Johnny B. Goode' and Buddy Holly's 'Not Fade Away' two of the more gritty country and western songs, Merle Haggard's 'Mama Tried' and Kris Kristofferson's 'Me and Bobby McGee'; and the old traditional workhorse 'Goin' Down the Road Feelin' Bad'.

Instead of guying these songs or affecting a fake good-ole-rock-n'-roll style for them, the Dead simply perform them with consummate skill and sophistication. They have travelled the whole progressive route, from psychedelic in-group songs through electronic extravaganzas to return finally to the roots. On the way they have perfected a counterpoint between both their instruments and their voices which lends a distinctive patina to everything they touch. Listen particularly to the constant subtle dialogue between the three guitars. Jerry Garcia on lead, Bob Weir on rhythm, Phil Lesh on bass. As in all good polyphony, the voices are sustaining solo and choric roles simultaneously.

Such a style is capable of great elaboration, which makes the Dead one of the few groups who are justified in playing long numbers. One whole side of this two-record set is given over to an 18-minute excursion called 'The Other One', and it is the most beautiful piece on the album. Like all the others, it was recorded live at various venues. But all the extraneous cheering and announcements have been edited out and a sensible amount of overdubbing has been done in the studio. As a result, the live atmosphere has been retained without the irrelevancies and sloppiness that usually go with it.

***

An album called *We Had To Let You Have It*, which is interesting on several counts, has been released by Dawn Records. It's the recording debut of a four-man Afro-rock group called Noir. According to the makeshift sleeve, they vanished before work on the album was fully finished: the company, unable to discover the group's whereabouts, decided to release the eight tracks as they stood—they had to let us have it. At first this sounds like a stunt to glamourise some mediocre tapes, but in fact the music quickly dispels scepticism.

The thriving pop music of urban black Africa has become quite a vogue of the pinko-grey scene recently: but those heavily ethnic polyrhythms often sound more self-consciously calculated than genuine. Noir, refreshingly, decline to trade in flashy Africanisms. They are an eclectic rock group, and they have what every rock group needs first and foremost, an excellent lead guitarist. His name is Gordon Hunter and he plays with particular eloquence in a song called 'The System'.

They favour an incantatory call-and-response style of singing which derives from gospel and worksongs, whilst drummer Barry Ford has a penchant for an airy bop-influenced type of drumming. All of this adds up to a sound which has considerable variety and expressiveness. It allows them to make rapid vocal and instrumental switches, building up a rich series of crescendoes.

The words are the only unremittingly black element in their music, and they tend to be rather stiff and gauche, especially in 'In Memory of Lady X' which has a sincere but awful spoken lyric. There's also a lack of finish in the recordings-literally. But there's sufficient promise to create a strong wish that Noir may materialise again soon and continue their unfinished work.

Tuesday, 30 November 1971

WOODSTOCK COUNTRY

Van Morrison/*Tupelo Honey*
Charlie Gillett/*The Sound of the City*

VAN MORRISON HAS followed up *His Band and The Street Choir* with another dispatch from Woodstock country called *Tupelo Honey* (Warner Bros. K46114). There he is on the sleeve leading Janet, her long brown hair streaming, on a white horse through the idyllic glades of upper New York state. It's a far remove from sunny Belfast where he started out.

In tune with the new mood of pastoral contentment, there's a developing softness and quiescence in his work. The nicest song on this album, in fact, is a piece of pure domestic sentimentality called 'Old Old Woodstock'. I'm not so happy about the values implied in the line 'my woman's waiting by the kitchen door', but the quiet country-style piano playing of Mark Jordan is most pleasant.

Less sweet but more compelling is 'You're My Woman', which expresses the emotions attendant on the birth of his child. In a refinement of the cumulative repetitions of soul music, he employs more sophisticated rhythmic and harmonic changes than in any of his previous work to build a satisfying series of crescendoes. It's true that he loses the plain-man sincerity of the song by pushing his voice too far at the end, but, nevertheless, this track is evidence of Morrison's rich potential as a songwriter and arranger.

***

Unfortunately, he's no great shakes as a singer and none of the other tracks partake of the integrity of 'You're My Woman'. The title track and 'Like A Canonball' are just commonplace pop songs, whilst 'When That Evening Sun Goes Down' is a composite of three or four standards. As usual, the arrangements are often distinctive—'Wild Night' makes tasty use of steel guitar and horns—but not sufficiently so to outweigh the uncontrollable voice with its irritating hectoring note and the essential thinness of the material.

Van Morrison is revered in the States, and that may be the biggest obstacle to his development. He doesn't strike me as the kind of performer likely to benefit from adulation. At the same time, to be treated as a collaborator by a group as good as the Band can't be altogether bad for you. I had hoped to review the Band's new LP *Cahoots* in tandem with *Tupelo Honey*, for Morrison and Robbie

Robertson sing together on one of its tracks, which they jointly composed. But the album is on Capitol, an EMI label; and EMI (Ireland) seem to dislike publicity: for they've failed to acknowledge my last five requests for review albums.

***

A while ago, in reviewing books about the Who and Motown, I suggested that nobody had yet discovered an effective style in which to write about rock music. Words duly eaten: Charles Gillett's *The Sound of the City* is indeed the marvellous bill of goods that the American critics have said it is. Indeed it's more than they said, for Gillett has overhauled and updated and annotated the American edition amply justifying the delay in the book's appearance over here.

It quickly transpires that 'the best way of writing about rock is identical with the best way writing about bee-keeping or book-binding—commonsensically and unpatronisingly'. Tone is the crux. Gillett's tone throughout is factual, enthusiastic, judicious, neither apologising for the music nor being brusquely condescending to the uninitiated.

For its information alone, particularly on the postwar rhythm and blues scene out of which rock and roll developed, the book must be considered a standard text—the first one on the subject. But the great pleasure of reading it lies in its implied overall theme and its individual critical assessments. The theme is that both R&B and early rock were vital and sane forms of human expression: that the major record companies were caught unawares by their popularity, and proceeded to standardise them into a lifeless commercial product; and that the history of the music since has been a series of rearguard actions. As to the critical judgments, many of them are controversial, and they are likely to be quoted in this space fairly regularly in the future.

Tuesday, 14 December 1971

THE YEAR OF THE LONERS

ROCK MUSIC IS another year older, and in some ways it's appropriately sadder and wiser: for the most striking feature of the music during 1971 was its domination by scarred loners, writing and singing their own introspective observations.

In retrospect, this development was inevitable from the moment that Bob Dylan turned away from folkie protest songs to write the stridently subjective stuff that made him a major rock innovator. But who would ever have predicted then that the typical performer of 1971 would be a 35-year-old divorcee singing uncensored confessional laments? Who, in 1966, would have taken bets on Leonard Cohen, Carole King, Kris Kristofferson, Leon Russell, Dory Previn, or even John Lennon in his own bitter write?

Lennon must, I think, be awarded overall first prize for music in this category during the year (the first 1972 album I look forward to hearing is his *Live Jam*), with James Taylor a close runner-up. For the Most Improved Artist award I would suggest Joni Mitchell, and Loudon Wainwright must surely win the palm as Most Promising Newcomer. Between them, these performers produced in the course of the year a half-dozen albums of literate and mature music which finally opened up popular songwriting to all the concerns and subtleties of lyrical verse. For me they quench the thirst that published verse has for a long time now so dismally failed to satisfy.

Meanwhile, the group scene has continued to languish. A few veteran groups like the Grateful Dead and the Band have gone on refining their style and have contributed brilliant and apparently effortless albums during the year; but others have run out of steam, like Traffic or Crosby Stills Nash and Young, or have become walled into their past successes like the Who and the Rolling Stones. There has been endless disbanding and re-shuffling, but if an important genuinely new group appeared in 1971, I didn't hear it.

***

I have no desire to nominate a Record of the Year, but I know for sure which album I most regret not having reviewed: Captain Beefheart's *Lick My Decals Off, Baby* (Straight Records STS1063). The Captain—alias Don Van Vliet—is entirely peerless, and it is hard to find language that will define or assess him. He is an original, a demented surrealist, a free spirit, an expressionist with language and his Magic Band, which he makes to produce a kind of bubbling atonal rock.

The general effect is of a curiously ordered manic delirium. Of this album the songs seem more sculptured than on *Trout Mask Replica*, but not at the expense of looniness and certainly not of humour: one of them is called 'I Wanna Find A Woman That'll Hold My Big Toe Till I Have To Go'—it's filled with the kind of childlike mock-wicked innuendo which got the title track banned on American radio stations—and another's name is 'The Clouds are Full of Wine (not Whiskey or Rye)'.

This last sounds like the sort of philosophical folk song that might come out of a mental asylum. Similarly, 'Woe-Is-Uh-Me-Bop' is, perhaps, a standard rock & roll song as conceived by a man trapped underground.

There are a couple of engrossing instrumentals, notably 'Peon', in which guitar and bass work out, in a probing and unusually gentle way, the odd jerky polyphony characteristic of Beefheart compositions. But the best track is 'Smithsonian Institute Blues (or The Big Dig)'. This hilarious song makes explicit (as does 'Petrified Forest') Van Vliet's conviction that technological society is the new age of the dinosaurs. His vision of apocalypse is an entirely authentic one.

Wednesday, 29 December 1971

1972

A NEW ROLE FOR DYLAN?

Bob Dylan/*More Greatest Hits*

TEN YEARS AGO, the idea of an album called *More Bob Dylan Greatest Hits* would have seemed risibly satirical, not least to young Bobby Zimmerman himself, an intense white-faced waif toting his guitar round the leftist coffee bars of Greenwich Village. The songs on his first two albums were oracular political anthems and hardbitten love songs, derivative from Woody Guthrie and Lightnin' Hopkins, and far removed from the detested commercial inanities of the hit parade. Some of them reappeared on his *Greatest Hits* album last year and more of them are on *More Greatest Hits* (CBS) including 'A Hard Rain's A-Gonna Fall' and 'Don't Think Twice, It's All Right'. It still seems risibly satirical.

Charlie Gillett says a good thing about Dylan: 'The first rock & roll singers had as nearly as possible been themselves when they sang and played. Dylan and Jagger were after similar musical and emotional effects but played roles to get them.' (*The Sound Of The City*, Sphere Books)

***

DYLAN'S role-playing was such as to make his career seem in retrospect more like a series of one-act plays than a string of LPs. From the plain-speaking country boy of *Freewheelin' Bob Dylan* (1963)—artfully portrayed in the film *Don't Look Back* by a scene where a short-haired Bobby in overalls sings to a bunch of sharecroppers—he moved on to the sneering, aggressive rock singer of *Bringing It All Back Home* and *Highway 61 Revisited* (1965-66). This phase is represented on *More Greatest Hits* by songs like 'Positively Fourth Street' and 'Maggie's Farm', and the wry,

117

exhausted 'My Back Pages' which sums up the whole process of repudiating a past self:

> Ah but I was so much older then,
> I'm younger than that now.

After this came the gnomic narratives of *John Wesley Harding*, followed by the throaty country & western crooning of *Nashville Skyline* and then the dreadful mawkish low camp of *Self Portrait*. Songs from all of these albums except, understandably, the last, appear on *More Greatest Hits*, and there are also two from his most recent album, the so-so *New Morning*.

The curious thing is that they're all jumbled together: thoroughly enough jumbled, what's more, to make the jumbling seem premeditated. I suspect in this the playing of yet another Dylan role, namely that of the commonsense mature man who is indifferent to roles and images. The impression is strengthened by the fact that the album opens with a new recording of a song called 'Watching The River Flow', done in raucously relaxed style with Leon Russell fooling on the piano and a guitarist who sounds not unlike George Harrison; and it ends with four other Dylan songs not previously recorded by him (though familiar in the repertoire of the Band and others) performed in an equally unbuttoned style.

***

These five new tracks ought to have formed the nucleus of a new album. They're the best work Dylan has done for two years. 'When I Paint My Masterpiece', one of the wittiest songs he has ever written, is set in Rome and Brussels, recalling the hysterical days of his concert tours. Having visited the Colosseum, the singer hurries on back to his hotel room for a date with Botticelli's Venus:

> Yup, she promised that she'd be right there with me
> When I paint my masterpiece.

Dylan bawls the song more lustily than Robbie Robertson does on the new Band LP, though on this track and on 'Watching The River Flow' (both produced by Leon Russell presumably in the same session) he sounds as if he has a heavy cold.

The last three songs were recorded as recently as last October, with Happy Traum backing on guitar, banjo and vocals. Together they do a cosy version of 'I Shall Be Released', and an odd arresting piece with an Appalachian flavour called 'Ain't Going Nowhere'. Finally,

'Down In The Flood' is a pleasing emotional pastiche of Mississippi rural blues.

Dylan sounds in form again on these tracks. I hope they represent straws blowing in the wind, and that the commercial cliché of a 'More Greatest Hits' album is just another provocative Dylan game.

Tuesday, 11 January 1972

WONDERGIRL AGAIN

Carole King/*Carole King Music*
Santana/*The Third Album*

CAROLE KING IS Wondergirl. Her *Tapestry* album sold over four million discs and two million tapes last year; and this after ten or twelve years in the business as a successful songwriter. She is applauded by public and pundit alike—by the latter for her unaffectedly mature-woman style and by the former for her unabashedly polished commercialism. Both are in evidence in her follow up to *Tapestry*, which is a guaranteed smasheroo money maker. It's called *Carole King Music* (on A&M) and it travels on down that winning groove.

As before, she throws in a song for old time's sake from the partnership with her former husband Gerry Goffin, the 1964 number 'Some Kind of Wonderful'. It's in a vein of popsy sentimentality which hasn't worn too well. Some of the slower tracks among the eleven new songs—particularly 'Too Much Rain', 'Going Away From Me' and 'Surely'—display a certain strain in attempting to avoid this fate.

What she does superlatively, as ever, is the melodious medium-tempo number that feels-as-good-as-a-tonic. 'Song of Long Ago', with some artful James Taylor lalas in the backing, is such a thing. So is 'Back to California', a number not unlike Paul McCartney's 'Get Back', with Ralph Schuckett very agile on the electric piano. Best of all for my money is 'Carry Your Load' because its unusually intricate tune is perfectly integrated with the lyrics and the several sections of the song are nicely built together.

(All of the tracks are produced with the velvet touch of Lou Adler.

He has avoided a mere repetition of *Tapestry* by fattening out the sound very slightly with wood-winds, brass and percussion but it's done so discreetly you would scarcely notice it—except for Curtis Amy's husky tenor sax solos on 'Sweet Seasons', 'Brother, Brother', and 'Music', all of them solid solos in solid songs. Carole King is no artist, but she's a very pleasing and fully-fledged tradeswoman.

***

My own favourite section of the Woodstock film was that featuring the Latin-rock group Santana. There was an extraordinary exhilaration about the way the flowing camera work and deft editing counterpointed the music, with its weaving Latin rhythms overlaid by heavy electric rock riffs. The group's involvement with its music was apparent too, and so was the high quality of leader Carlos Santana's guitar work.

Santana: The Third Album is a current release on CBS (69015). The music on it doesn't seem quite so magical without the ravishing images to embellish it, but it's still pretty meaty. Although the band comprises seven thundering instrumentalists, interest is sustained by a wide variation of tempo and mood.

On Side 1 this is skillfully achieved by running the tracks together without a distinct break. The rousing opening number 'Batuka' gives way to a slower chanted piece called 'No One To Depend On'. This builds up a head of steam which in turn disperses into a bridge passage in free style. Then there is a soft and evocative song called 'Taboo' which intensifies into 'Toussaint L'Overture', a highly Spanish blockbuster which ends the side.

Side 2 lacks this unity and the group's weaknesses tend to make themselves more apparent. Principally they are the lack of a strong vocalist and the tendency to overdo melodramatic effects like the fire-alarm guitar break. Otherwise this record is a fine stimulant for sluggish wintry blood.

Monday, 24 January 1972

THE MARMALADE

The Marmalade/*Songs*
Therapy/*Almanac*

'ARE YOU STILL following images and trendy conventions—or are you willing to give the Marmalade LP a listen?' This is the stirring question posed to us by the Decca advertising division. It's a question that only arises, of course, because of the effort involved for the hip audience in taking seriously a group calling itself the Marmalade; particularly when the group already has an established reputation for purveying candy pop to the pre-teens.

However, old teenyboppers never die, they just go progressive, and John Peel amongst others has been assiduous of late in promoting the Marmalade as a fully-fledged and accomplished group for the mature audience. So I've been giving the said LP a judicious listen (it's called *Songs* and is on Decca SKL5111).

Let me say at once these boys are smooth. They move around the ring, no sloppy footwork, nice clean punching, they got speed in every department. They're by CSN&Y out of Paul McCartney— melodically versatile, polished harmony singing—and they give us a balance of medium-heavy rockers complete with tempo changes and funky lyrics ... and high-class candy pop ('Sarah', 'Lovely Nights', 'She Wrote Me A Letter').

But the album also has one song called 'Mama' which is extraordinarily touching. It's been haunting me for a week. It catches perfectly the tender vulnerability of a youth turning into a man, with wry, simple lyrics by Dean Ford which are threaded through with little ruminative guitar breaks by Hugh Nicholson. The Marmalade are OK.

***

Dave Shannon and Sam Bracken are Belfast folksingers. Last year they teamed up with an English girl called Fiona Simpson and adopted the collective name Therapy. The group's first job was to record a tape for BBC producer Tony McCauley which I heard and liked, and I'm glad to see that CBS have now released their first album. It's called *Almanac*.

What they do best is material with a period flavour, verging on the quaint. 'Most Peculiar Feeling' is a piece of close-harmony ragtime with a delightfully gentle infectiousness. The sentiments in the lyrics of 'Millionaire' are pure Edwardian music-hall whilst the music is pastiche baroque. And in 'Conversation', a very child-like early fifties kind of pop tune is again built into a baroque structure.

There's no element of parody in these songs such as has become a cliché among other groups—the pokerfaced megaphone-style singing with comic tubas and percussion or florid piano cadenzas. Instead the style sounds natural because it suits Dave Shannon's formalised songwriting, and Fiona Simpson's prim and proper voice.

Unfortunately they try in most of the other songs to be either more grandiose or more easy-going than this and end up sounding wooden. 'Requiem and Renaissance' is flatulent in every respect and 'Sir Ebenezer' is a highly uncomfortable attempt at humour.

The fault may lie partly in the fact that the songs are written to a formula: one song for each of the 12 signs of the zodiac. This is too ambitious and artificial a procedure for an apprentice songwriter.

In addition, the arrangements and production are far too lavish, what with a string quartet, brass trio, oboes, flute, bassoon, bass and drums being plastered over every join. I preferred the simple and straightforward BBC tape.

Monday, 7 February 1972

THE NEW THING?

Osibisa/ *Woyaya*
Midnight Sun/ *Walking Circles*

THERE'S NATIONALISM AND there's international urbanism. While the first continues to motivate real politics, the second has long since dominated real culture. So far as vital forms of expression go, from sport to the higher mathematics, the global village is a fact of life.

Which serves to explain the existence of Osibisa, a London band whose members come from Ghana, Nigeria, Trinidad, Antigua and Grenada, and Midnight Sun, a jazz-rock group based in Copenhagen. Each of them has just had an LP released by the Anglo-American MCA record company. It's a small spaceship, earth.

Osibisa's album is called *Woyaya* and it is their follow-up to a very successful debut album of last year. They have had the misfortune perhaps to be acclaimed as the New Thing by the communications arm of an industry badly in need of a new thing. Their name means 'cross-rhythms' and they have been extolled for the originality of their synthesis of African and Afro-Cuban percussion and in general for their 'wild excitement' etc.

As to the polyrhythms, they're most enjoyable and infectious but far too simplified and refined to be called original. And if you come to the record anticipating an overwhelming powerhouse of sound, as promised by the publicity, you'd do better to look out your old Stan Kenton records. In spite of all the hype, Osibisa are in fact a very superior showband.

***

Probably their biggest virtue is instrumental versatility. Most of them can handle an assortment of percussion as well as their solo instruments, and not just as another example of modish showing-off. They have a fine sense of interplay—particularly evident in 'Move On' and 'Rabiatu"—and at least two excellent jazz musicians, Loughty Amao (saxes) and Robert Bailey (keyboards). All of this affords a rich variety of textures and tones.

What they lack is a good singer, and—really—something to say. 'Be happy!' they exhort us in the opening number, which is rather narcissistically entitled 'Beautiful Seven'. It makes a change from Up Against the Wall, but I can't entirely believe in it. The happiness expressed in some of this music is no deeper or truer than in television theme music.

I can't help wondering if Osibisa aren't being seduced into a new hip version of the old white fantasy about the feckless, foot-shuffling darkies. I'd like to hear what black audiences think of them.

***

Midnight Sun are an easier group to deal with—if you can swallow a Danish lad singing English lyrics with impeccable Ray Charles' phrasing and pronunciation (one of the lyrics is a poem by Edward Lear, to boot). Pianist Niels Bronsted and bassist Bo Stief have for years been providing the backing to distinguished American jazzmen visiting Copenhagen. Bronsted has recorded with Albert Ayler, amongst others, and is a highly fluent and sophisticated musician, if a bit lacking in warmth.

Like many other young jazzmen in a similar position, Bronsted, Stief and a colleague on sax have joined forces with a rock guitarist

123

and drummer. The resulting smorgasbord is entirely tasteful. It's intelligent and literate music, but it lacks some vital nerve. It has a kind of earnest deliberateness which keeps it firmly grounded.

Monday, 21 February 1972

MINUS GARFUNKEL

Paul Simon/*Paul Simon*
New Riders of the Purple Sage/*New Riders of the Purple Sage*

LIKE MOST OTHER established teams, Simon & Garfunkel have split. Everything put together falls apart, sings Paul Simon on his first solo album; and meanwhile Art Garfunkel can be seen acting (excellently) the permanent schoolboy dupe searching in vain for *Carnal Knowledge*. It's all very melancholy. Most of the stuff they produced together was highly accomplished light music of phenomenal commercial value which never quite made it artistically—an overdose of whimsy here, a dash of triviality there. But a large number of people will count the album *Bookends* as a permanent contribution to their lives and a larger number still will continue to enjoy the music as it was employed in *The Graduate*.

Simon was the one who wrote all the words and music and played the guitar. But it seems clear from the solo record (CBS 69007) that Garfunkel contributed more to the team than a harmony line. Simon on his own sounds like a man without a catalyst. The lyrics are still polished and fluent, the music full of bright ideas—'Mother And Child Reunion' was recorded in Jamaica with a reggae group, 'Hobo's Blues' was laid down in France with Stephane Grappelly, and 'Duncan' features a repeated Mexican motif on charango and flutes. Stefan Grossman plays bottleneck on one track and Fred Lipsius (of BS&T) plays his horn on another.

Somehow it all lacks a sense of its own necessity. That's the only way I can account for the album's failure to involve me after eight or nine plays. 'Everything Put Together Falls Apart' is arresting in the same understated intimate way that 'Overs' was; 'Me and Julio Down By The Schoolyard' is an enjoyable bit of lively New York hokum: the other songs are less yeasty but each is meticulously

124

worked out. Yet I don't anticipate playing the album again much. This may be entirely wrong. *Rolling Stone* has greeted it with awed reverence. I still hope that Paul Simon will do something apocalyptic. He still could.

***

Far from splitting up, the Grateful Dead now have a team of seconds in their entourage, a kind of satellite group which goes on stage first at concerts and warms the audience up for the appearance of the maestros themselves. The group's name is New Riders of the Purple Sage, after Zane Grey, and they have put out an easy-going country rock album of great charm (CBS 64657).

Their view of things is right in line with the Dead's—drawing on the themes and conventions of country music to express their own concerns, laying emphasis on polished musicianship and restrained, controlled harmonies. But they're much more lighthearted than the parent group and seem to play strictly for fun.

'Whatcha Gonna Do on the Planet Today?' is a pleasant song and a typical line. 'Dirty Business' is an excellent pastiche of a miner's-strike song with suspenseful guitar effects by Jerry Garcia: 'Glendale Train' is a rather less successful pastiche of a train-robbery ballad. For a strictly contemporary ballad there is 'Henry', the story of a lad driving down to Acapulco to pick up a supply of that celebrated Gold.

A couple of other songs are a shade too popsy—'Portland Woman' in particular will not go down well with feminist fans—and the album as a whole is definitely for light relief. But light relief of this quality is hard to come by.

Monday, 6 March 1972

THE NORTH IN SONG?

WHOLESALERS IN BELFAST have been refusing to stock Paul McCartney's single 'Give Ireland Back to the Irish' (Apple) and it is, of course, banned from the airwaves in Northern Ireland: consequently, I have yet to hear it. But my breath is something less than bated, given the low quality of McCartney's recent work, the blithe simple-mindedness of the song's title, and the abysmal showing of rock music in general as a vehicle for political expression. I have heard McGuinness Flint's anti-internment song 'Let the People Go' (Island) which is also banned by the BBC, and it strikes me as musically trite, politically platitudinous and rather badly performed.

The censoring of these records hardly seems worth arguing about from the vantage point of Belfast. Things in the North have reached a degree of nightmarishness which makes such liberal niceties as a debate on censorship almost a luxury.

***

A more fundamental issue at stake is the capacity of our available art forms to cope with contemporary political realities. For a long time the question has been heard wherever two or three Arts Club dilettantes were gathered together: why has nothing really momentous been written about the troubles? Why has no O'Casey or Yeats appeared? At the level of the lively arts, I recall somebody relishing the thought in 1969 that 'some good ballads should come out of it'.

The ballads that have 'come out of it' so far are depraved, vindictive adaptations of other songs, the literature that has come out of it is stiffly self-conscious and horribly uncertain of itself. Nothing has come out of it except death, agony and a murderous hatred which our forms of expression have shown themselves unable to assuage or define.

To assuage pain and define the overwhelming—those are crucial functions of art, from its lowliest to its most highly developed manifestations. Rock music has been pre-eminent amongst the lively arts in the past decade as a form of lyric expression, assuaging and defining the content of personality and personal relationships. However, it has not developed in narrative or dramatic directions: in other words, it can't handle large-scale public or political emotions or ideas. The typical rock incursion into politics has been shallow and sloganeering, out of either naiveté or cynicism: like 'Chicago' or 'Ohio' by Crosby Stills Nash and Young, or Steppenwolf's 'Monster' or John Lennon's 'Power To The People' or Bob Dylan's 'George Jackson'.

Dylan's early 'protest' songs are something else. They have endured, I think, because they weren't standardised responses to a particular event, but powerfully figurative and prophetic expressions of a whole zeitgeist. When he sang 'A Hard Rain's A-Gonna Fall' at the concert for Bangladesh refugee relief last year, the song sounded

126

more timely than ever. But these songs, and a few others like Country Joe's revue-style 'I-Feel-Like-I'm-Fixin'-To-Die Rag' are isolated successes which have never been repeated.

***

Popular music has not always been at such a loss. I've been reading through a collection of broadside ballads from the sixteenth to the early twentieth centuries called *The Common Muse*, edited by V. De Sola Pinto and A.E. Rodway. This is full of songs about war, repression and similar abuses of power which are full of verve, wit and human observation. Perhaps the last great body of such songs were those of the Great War.

There is no such body of songs from the Cold War or the Vietnam War or the decline and fall of Northern Ireland. Joan Littlewood will be unlikely to mount a stage show about the latter some years hence entitled *Give Ireland Back to the Irish*.

The experiences of the people of Northern Ireland in the past three years—the reality they are living through now—is not quite like anything that has gone before it. The available means of expression are inadequate to encompass it. We will either have to devise new forms or be rendered permanently dumb.

Wednesday, 22 March 1972

DECENT MEDIOCRITY

Jo Jo Gunne/*Jo Jo Gunne*
Wooden Horse/*Wooden Horse*

I FORGET WHO first coined the phrase 'decent mediocrity' but I wish it had been me. The thinking behind it is that for every actual genius on the left wing of culture there are hordes of opportunists, and conmen, and for every sincere upholder of traditional values on the right wing there are scores of philistine snobs, but that somewhere in the middle there is often work being done which is unoriginal yet competent and enthusiastic: decently mediocre, in fact. One invaluable function of this work is to consolidate a position until a new advance becomes possible.

No insult is intended to the two groups under review this week in describing their work as decent mediocrity. On the contrary, it's an affirmation of the pleasure they afford. The first, Jo Jo Gunne, is an American quartet with an album of the same name on the Asylum label. Everything about the album takes me back four or five years to when Buffalo Springfield and the Blues Project and the Byrds were answering the English challenge of the mid-sixties with an American group sound of hugely attractive vigour and fluency.

Since that time the group ethos has largely dissipated itself in superstardom and synthesizers, but Jo Jo Gunne reaffirm it and consolidate it. They stick to their piano, guitar, bass and drums, with no featured solos and no lead singer; everything is tout ensemble. They play extrovert rock music which is evocative of driving towards good times in a big Buick or Chevrolet along an endless hot American superhighway, most especially in the opening number 'Run Run Run':

> Welcome to the party,
> We're all just papers in the wind.

Inevitably this style teeters on the edge of vacuity at times, and indeed topples over in the case of 'I Make Love'. But there is enough subtlety in the music, with expressive melodies full of unexpected modulations and time changes, to reward much listening. Having played it half-a-dozen times, for example, I'm only now beginning to appreciate 'Barstow Blue Eyes', a cheerful love song to a waitress with an undertone of ragtime.

***

Wooden Horse are a new English group with an album out on the York label. Soft accoustic rock is probably the best way to describe their style, with close harmony singing and three guitars strumming underneath just as on the prototype Crosby Stills and Nash album, except that a soprano's voice is on top instead of male falsetto.

The girl is Susan Traynor and her soprano is very sweet and blends perfectly with the melodious tenors of the two lads who sing. For sonority, this album would be hard to fault. Unfortunately the very stoned passivity of the sound causes it to slide into the background of your head as a lulling muzak.

Somebody was clearly worried about this, for attempts are made (by unnamed instrumentalists) to vary the sound and stiffen it up here and there. The biggest attempt is in the track 'Broken Bottles' which is given a full blues treatment on piano, electric guitar and mouth organ. It's a disaster. Like all English groups with any folk orientation at all, Wooden Horse sound like earnest schoolteachers when they try to emote.

But some of their other songs are well worth attending to, particularly 'Feel' and 'Letter'. They've achieved a remarkable degree of flawlessness within the limitations of their chosen style.

Monday, 3 April 1972

EAST COAST SINGER

Judee Sill/*Judee Sill*
David Blue/*Stories*

WHEN I LISTENED at first to Judee Sill, whose debut album is out on the Asylum label, I pigeonholed her as another East Coast, middle-class college girl following in the wake of Joan Baez, Julie Felix, *et al*. It turns out that she's the twice-divorced daughter of an Oakland bar owner who turned to prostitution and forgery to support a bad heroin habit, after having been sent to state reform school for armed robbery.

So why doesn't she sound like Billie Holiday, or at least like Janis Joplin? Presumably, because her experiences haven't affected her in the obvious way. In other words, a curse on pigeonholes.

She sings in a pleasantly relaxed and informal style. Her melodies are fluent and often arresting, most notably so in 'Jesus Was A Cross-Maker', the lyrics of which pour out in an intense stream with the stresses all falling where you don't expect them. This song, sure to be pounced on by other lady singers, was produced by Graham Nash and it features a gospel piano accompaniment and background vocals with just a small touch of strings on a secondary refrain. The piano is exactly right for song and singer.

Unfortunately, the other tracks, which are credited to no fewer than three producers and two orchestrators, lavish upon her multitracked voice every string, reed, brass and percussion caress they can muster. It's not quite as bad as the notorious first album from James Taylor: but it should have learnt the lesson of that record.

Judee Sill's lyrics are as yet too permeated by a fashionable religiose symbolism to express adequately the life and times she's been going through. There's a pathos in the Christian and occult and drug-inspired images of escape which isn't coming through powerfully enough yet. She shouldn't sound just so much like a college girl. For all that, there's an authentic daemon in her songs.

***

The same label has put out an album by a man who used to be Bob Dylan's bodyguard, a member of the tightly-knit Dylan Greenwich Village coterie of the early sixties. His name is David Cohen but he sings under the name of David Blue, which was suggested by another member of the clique as a mirror for Cohen's gruff, nasty and suspicious character.

If this doesn't put you off, let me add that the man has even less of a singing voice than Leonard Cohen and even greater egoism. One of his songs assures a girl who has left him that she'll never find another man of the same calibre anywhere in the world. Another is a limp and interminable complaint about how hard he finds it to make new friends; abandoning his singing career would be a good start.

But the album, which is called *Stories*, is by no means devoid of entertainment value. For David Blue bids fair to be the William McGonagall of contemporary song. One of his pieces, called 'Fire In The Morning', opens with a showy instrumental build-up to the remarkable lines:

> It's an old familiar feeling has its grip on me,
> It's not one of my better days and I'm feelin' weak.

No sooner have you recovered from this than your incredulous ears are hearing:

> I don't have much to offer I know,
> All I really have is my soul.

Regrettably he isn't gifted enough to sustain this level of outrage. The rest of the album is a lugubrious self-indulgent waste of the talents of a number of fine musicians, Russ Kunkei, Ry Cooder, Ralph Schuckett and Rita Coolidge amongst them.

Tuesday, 18 April 1972

NEW OR EARLY BEEFHEART

Captain Beefheart/*The Spotlight Kid*
Ike & Tina Turner/*Nuff Said*

'JO JO GUNNE were born from the breakup of Spirit (writes Michael O'Keeffe of Sandymount) which you never mentioned in your article and in which I think you should have.' I stand justly scourged. Not only was I ignorant of the fact that two of the Jo Jo's were ex-Spirit, but I like their album a lot more now than I did when I reviewed it. The same goes for Paul Simon's solo LP ... and there's coals of fire being heaped there, too. Julian Campbell has written to point out that Paul Simon's first solo LP was actually the *Songbook* album of 1965: 'To me it is his best. It is the LP by which I tend to rate him. It is a pity that he moved away to more highly composed songs on the Simon & Garfunkel LPs.' Shrewd insight.

O the shame.

I'm afraid to hazard a word this week, even though the merchandise under scrutiny bears some names that are highly familiar in this column. Doubts assail me. Take this new Captain Beefheart release, *The Spotlight Kid* (Reprise). It carries the date 1971, but the Magic Band plays on it almost like a regular heavy band, with riffs and solos and a steady beat. Tunes, even. Could it be that this is a bundle of early Beefheart tapes, packaged and released to coincide with his recent tour of England? Or is it a back-to-the-roots effort?

Definitely the latter I would say, but who knows what the mail may bring? At any rate, *The Spotlight Kid* is intriguing listening, like everything that comes out of Beefheart's surreal circus of a mind. It gives the lie right away to the sceptics who have claimed all along that neither Beefheart nor his exotic troupe could really play their instruments. There is some superb blues harmonica playing from the Captain, and the general level of musicianship throughout is excellent.

***

The number that best exemplifies the group's musical imagination is 'Click Clack'. The lyrics begin 'Two trains/Two railroad tracks,' and the accompaniment mimes this, with the guitar playing one train riff and the piano, harmonica and drums playing a different one in counterpoint. In the course of the song they go through several modulations, merging and separating; at the end the guitar riff gradually slows down to a halt while the other one continues unabated. Very satisfying.

Not only is there a train song but there's a blues, and a thing called 'There Ain't No Santa Claus on the Evenin' Stage' which is almost a protest song, and another thing called 'Blabber n' Smoke' which has detectable traces of country and western (just). However, all such categorisation is highly relative in this context. The blues, for example, is called 'Grow Fins' and its refrain runs:

> I'm gonna take up with a mermaid
> 'N leave you land-lubbin' women alone.

This album would probably serve as a good introduction to Captain Beefheart for the unconverted. It's close enough to 'normality' not to frighten too many away. But I'll cherish it one degree less than *Trout Mask Replica* or *Lick My Decals Off, Baby*. Curiously, it tends to maunder a little, with most of the songs going on too long, whereas in those albums supposedly full of free-spirited anarchy there is a paradoxical economy.

***

From a very different area of the pop spectrum comes the latest Ike and Tina Turner album, *Nuff Said* (United Artists). Missing from this are the Ikettes, alas, in their place there is a much slicker band sound, with a lot of cleverly interjected brass phrases, and fast bass lines. The songs are all newish compositions by Ike Turner and two collaborators, and Tina belts them out with the mixture of desperation and aggressive sexuality unabated.

Yet there are times when she sounds as though she's struggling against the smoothness of the band and the production. 'Sweet Flustrations', for example, is a fine song which is spoiled by the voice being pushed beyond the threshold of pain. To my mind her singing demands a very simple, elemental kind of R&B backing, which it gets in earlier albums like *The Hunter* and *Come Together*. All the same, there's a lot of funky music in *Nuff Said*. I think I'll go and play it again.

Monday, 1 May 1972

THE MAN HIMSELF

Gilbert O'Sullivan/*Himself*

THE BLATANT IMAGE-building of the old-fashioned street urchin gear was irritating enough, but what really caused the teeth to gnash was the name Gilbert O'Sullivan. These irrelevancies, plus the lack of a television, have been enough to hold in check my natural-born curiosity about any Irish artist. Today, however, I finally procured his album *Himself* (on the MAM label) and I think maybe the man is a victim of his publicists and managers.

He's certainly the victim of his musical arranger. Song after song is decked out in tasteless muzak clichés: 'Bye-Bye', for example, combines a string line at which even Bert Kaemfert would blench with a few dabs of Tijuana brass. 'Matrimony', which has a Latin-American beat, is permeated with maddening cute little flicks and curlicues.

***

Given all this to contend with, himself puts up a worthy showing. He has a pleasant enough voice with a timbre like Paul McCartney's and something of his phrasing. Possibly from the same influence comes a taste for razzmatazz and music-hall pastiche, complete with do-dee-loo dahs and jokey narratives. 'Permissive Twit' is an excellent essay in this vein, with lyrics that have just enough social bite to be truly funny. The same is true of the words in 'Matrimony', crucified though they are by the orchestration.

Yet, there is something else here, a mournful introspective sense of fantasy, which is genuinely intriguing. Sometimes the songs are pure whimsy (like 'January Git') and at least one is an incomprehensible muddle ('Independent Air'), but four or five of the others have an uncanniness which sets you to thinking. 'Nothing Rhymed', which ends Side 1, is the first indication that there is more to the man than a cheerful false naiveté. It captures a particular kind of pained puzzlement which is a common state of mind in many skulls of our time.

***

'Susan Van Heusen' starts out like a slightly sinister narrative song, but it slides unexpectedly into a first-person lament, and the second verse repeats this pattern; it's a tactic which transforms an interesting

133

song into a fascinating one. 'Thunder and Lightning' is a strong rocker, and 'Houdini Said' has some very arresting moments. My all-round favourite, though, is the last number, 'Doing The Best I Can', which has a straightforward group accompaniment, a robust melody and the best quatrain on the album.

> Take off that silly grin
> Put back that double gin
> You'll need it in the morning
> If I leave you without warning.

The man has a talent worth attending to but I wish he'd change his name, clothes and arranger.

Tuesday, 16 May 1972

CATCHY 22

Stephen Stills/*Manassas*

IT'S HARD TO write coherently in a state of inebriation, and I'm plain stocious at the moment on Stephen Stills' new album *Manassas* (Atlantic). Every song on it is the best one, and there are twenty-two of them.

Stills was in on the birth of super-stardom, and that whole aspect of his career is unattractive. He and Neil Young looked like shaping up as the Liz and Dick of rock music for a while. Nevertheless, when Stills plays and sings his songs, he can have an ego like a dirigible as far as I'm concerned; for, when intoxicating music pours out of the speakers, personality cults fly up the chimney.

Stills seems to have a genius for playing in good bands. He came to the fore in the Buffalo Springfield, one of the ever-diminishing roster of sixties groups whose records are still exciting to hear. Then he super-starred a little before collaborating with David Crosby and Graham Nash in what amounted to a rediscovery of close-harmony singing; their trio album was a joy, better in retrospect than the subsequent (though still very tasty) albums with Young.

CSN&Y would seem to be defunct now. Last year Stills showed his flair again by touring with the cream of session musicians in a big sixteen-piece extravaganza, which resulted in a power cooker of an album, featuring some of the best back-up singing in the history of grooves.

***

Since then he has gathered round him yet another band, Manassas, convened originally just to make this album but then continuing as a proper performing group, so pleased were they with the results in the studio. It's a six-piece with no string section attached, and no horns or sitars or saxellos either—just a sufficient range of guitars, keyboards and percussion to allow for playing in all the multifarious styles of modern rock, which is what they do in the course of the album, with effortless versatility.

Each of the four sides has a title. Side 1 is a suite of songs called 'The Raven', constructed as an unbroken stream of shifting rhythms and textures, as pioneered by the Beatles. The first two songs, which are in straight rock style, slide into a thing called 'Cuban Bluegrass' assisted by the congas and timbales of Joe Lala, and this in turn changes down into blues gear for 'Jet Set (Sigh)'.

The vocals are increasingly traded between Stills and Chris Hillman and there is a corresponding growth of instrumental interludes, so that a genuine sense of build-up and climax is achieved. The 'climax' is typical Stills: a melancholy, very beautiful exequy of thwarted love called 'Both Of Us (Bound To Lose)'.

***

Side 2 is the country music side. With a line-up that includes Hillman (ex-Byrds and Flying Burrito Brothers) and Al Perkins on steel guitar (also a former Burrito) it's hardly surprising that the band can play a magic set of country rock. Stills makes entirely sure of it by using Byron Berline on fiddle. Six songs as fresh and pretty as new gingham dresses.

The other two sides are looser units than these two, but the quality's the same. Side 3, 'Consider', lays the emphasis on philosophical musing, with an excursion into progressiveness on 'Move Around', an odd and arresting song using a Moog.

The last side is just called 'Rock And Roll Is Here To Stay', which is a more ambiguous title than it seems, given the final track, 'Blues Man'. It's dedicated to Jimi Hendrix, Al Wilson and Duane Allman:

Three good men

I knew well
Never see again.

Stills sings it alone with his own guitar, very movingly. I hope it's at least fifty more recording years before his name joins theirs.

Wednesday, May 31st 1972

THE SOFT MACHINE

Soft Machine/*Soft Machine 5*
Matching Mole/*Matching Mole*

WITH THE DEPARTURE of drummer Robert Wyatt, the last vestiges of rock style have departed from the work of the Soft Machine. Rock has bequeathed to them an electronic fluency, a conception of the recording studio as a musical instrument in itself; but the actual music that they make has its source in the cool intellectual jazz of the fifties, of Miles Davis, Ornette Coleman, Chet Baker, Coltrane. In a way, they have done for the white European side of that style what Davis has done for the black African one: refined and abstracted it

Soft Machine 5 (CBS) is their first album without Wyatt. The drummer on Side 1, Phil Howard, sounds distinctly uncomfortable, but John Marshall on Side 2 drums like a man who feels part of the group, and I hope that he is from now on. As usual the song titles, like the numerical titles of the albums themselves, are clipped and impersonal: and the demarcations between tracks are far from identifiable.

This is all in line with the music, which attains on this album to an almost Oriental degree of impersonality. Its essential pattern is identical with that in the songs of Cole Porter or Rodgers and Hart— a prelusive meandering verse followed by the solid pulse of the melody. But the preludes to these pieces are highly ceremonial affairs with instruments making grave and elaborate gestures to one another, whilst the main bodies of the works are generally in arcane time signatures with the most austere of harmonic structures.

The first two tracks, 'All White' and 'Drop', were composed by Mike Ratledge who has always been, to my mind, the group's

136

creative fountainhead. 'All White' opens with Elton Dean's saxello, 'shadowed' by itself on tape, ruminating in tandem with a sustained rumble from Hugh Hopper's bass. Very adroitly they slide into a medium tempo, and the rest of the piece is Dean soloing on saxello, most vigorously, ending with a single note on alto sax. This last touch indicates the growing humour of Dean's work; he even slips in a quotation at one point. 'Drop' opens with a kind of enchanted passage incorporating water noises and a music box augmented by the tumbling ethereal use of tape loops. This is a prelude to a duologue between the gnatbuzz of Ratledge's organ and the scholastic agility of Hooper's bass. It's an absorbing number.

'MC', which closes Side 1, is a Hopper composition consisting entirely of prelude. After a burst of sparklers, the drums lay down a thick swishing carpet upon which the electric piano, alto and bass perform intricate gyrations. Side 2 is most notable for an extraordinary solo on bowed double bass by guest Roy Babbington. Playing a lot of octaves and slurs, he creates the general effect of an enthusiastic but delicate elephant ballet.

Like a lot of art these days, the music of the Soft Machine aims at perfecting itself inside a harshly limited range. The result is diverting and sometimes magical, but it can only be enjoyed a little at a time. The most gratifying development in this album is the new muscularity in Elton Dean's sax playing, though it is rather counterbalanced by the too meagre ration of Ratledge's nervy keyboard work.

As to Robert Wyatt, I for one am grateful not to have to listen to his singing on the Softs' albums any longer. It appears that his urge to sing more was one of his reasons for leaving the group and forming an outfit of his own called Matching Mole, whose inaugural album of the same name has just been released (also on CBS). Wyatt sounds like a Cockney street urchin with a hangover. It's not a pleasant noise. And his lyrics are dismal. The first song on this album, a lachrymose plea to the lovely Caroline Coon, plunges to a new low in this respect.

Instrumentally, the record has inventive patches, but overall it's a very bitty affair with far too much electronic footering around.

Tuesday, 13 June 1972

DON MCLEAN IS NO SEEGER

Don McLean/*American Pie*
Argent/*All Together Now*

I RECALL A critic hailing Louis Malle's *Zazie dans le Metro* as the first film to be created wholly out of the cinema tradition itself, the first to use pastiche, quotation, reference in a way that only those intimate with the tradition could understand. He claimed that this was a sign of maturity in an art form; but it could equally well be a sign of uncertainty

Don McLean's 'American Pie' is a similar phenomenon. To 'get' it, you have to have certain furniture in your mind's attic, items like the Big Bopper, a white sports coat and a pink carnation, the pumping piano of Jerry Lee Lewis, going to the hop, earth angel etc. Given that, the song's appeal is a mixture of sentimental nostalgia, cult, snobbism, and intriguing guesswork. Personally, I love it. Actually it also achieves a kind of elegiac humour which might just keep it afloat in years hence, though I'm doubtful.

At any rate, 'American Pie' is clearly a one-off deal and not a typical McLean song. The album of the same name has yielded another chart-topping single called 'Vincent' which is an appallingly mushy song about van Gogh. And United Artists, eager to sustain the momentum of success, have re-released the first McLean album, *Tapestry*, with plaudits on it from such as Pete Seeger and Lee Hays of the Weavers.

It transpires that songs of protest and lyricism in the Seeger vein is McLean's really characteristic metier. He has a melodious tenor voice, freshfaced charm, a heap of moral indignation about poverty, pollutions, loneliness, commercialism, racism, and he is musically and verbally quite articulate. The trouble is that you can tot all of that up and it still doesn't come out as Pete Seeger.

Seeger's lyrics are frequently banal. Woody Guthrie was no great shakes on the guitar. Dylan basically can't sing. But they all three have something, a daemon, a vision that irradiates their best work so that the shortcomings become almost impressive. McLean doesn't have it, so that his lack of shortcomings becomes an irritation and a bore.

Only one song, 'Magdalen Lane', stays with me and it is the closest to 'American Pie' on the album. It pits a light, inane tune against sardonic lyrics about the degenerating heart of Hollywood and Disneyland. But even it is just all right.

***

Argent is a rather odd group which had essentially a coterie following until the recent success of their song, 'Hold Your Head Up'. The arresting thing about this song is its combination of an hypnotic crude beat and chanted refrain with some very adroit organ soloing and unusual arranging. These idiosyncrasies are in large part the personal style of leader Rod Argent, who once was famous as a Zombie.

'Hold Your Head Up' is the first and finest track of the group's latest album, *All Together Now* (Epic). The kind of spookiness which it engenders is most effective, but elsewhere the group topples into melodrama. 'I Am the Dance of Ages' for example, not content with its pretentious title and lyrics, employs cheap thunder and wind effects full of sounds and fury signifying the usual.

Russ Ballard, the guitarist, appears to be enamoured of this kind of thing. His two songs, 'Tragedy' and 'He's A Dynamo', are badly over-inflated. I can't warm to Robert Henrit's drumming either: he favours an extreme, rock & roll style which rarely moves outside a stiff, inflexible clumping.

But Rod Argent himself is a valuable performer and the album allows him to demonstrate his versatility. On 'Keep On Rolling' he plays some beautiful Jelly Roll Morton-style piano, whilst at the other end of the record and of the musical spectrum he brings off a four-part organ extravaganza called 'Pure Love' which is the equal of anything by Keith Emerson.

Wednesday, 5 July 1972

BLACK INSPIRATION

The Persuasions/*Street Corner Symphony*
Peter Frampton/*Wind of Change*

FOR A LONG time now, Black pop music in America has meant Motown: an essentially old-fashioned dream machine of sequins, lavish nightclubs and melodramatic emotionalism. Only a very few Black groups have been able to earn success doing work of more integrity and honesty.

It took Ike and Tina Turner years of sweat and grind to push their aggressively sensual brand of rhythm and blues to the fore. As for Sly Stone, his attempts to create a style of Black rock, whilst intermittently brilliant, have more frequently been wayward and erratic.

In this context, the first album to be released by the Persuasions in this country, *Street Corner Symphony* (Island), is very invigorating. In a way, it's a revivalist record, and what it seeks to revive is 'acapella', the close harmony vocal style compounded of gospel singing and work chants which used to be all the rage in the black neighbourhoods of Philadelphia and New York (just as barbershop singing was the rage in the white streets). The sound of five resonant male voices blending together in a chord, unadorned by any further instrumentation, is a most pleasurable one, particularly if you've grown accustomed to distinctly unresonant solo voices being smothered in great dollops of schmaltz. But the Persuasions, judging by their choice of material, are eager to update acapella rather than just revive it. In addition to a roster of well-known Soul music hits there are such items as Bob Dylan's 'The Man In Me' and Carole King's 'You've Got A Friend'.

***

Here, I feel, they fall down. The style of the songs sits very uneasily with the style of performance. However, this is not the case with the Soul tracks, like the medley of three Temptations hits, 'Don't Look Back', 'Runaway Child Running Wild' and 'Cloud Nine'. Songs like these acquire a vigorous new lease of life. They've been refreshed at their roots.

The Beatles drew a lot of their early inspiration from Black vocal groups like the Miracles and the Shirelles. In turn, I am reminded of the early Lennon-McCartney work by Peter Frampton, late of Humble Pie. Prior to forming a new group, he has put out a solo album called *Wind of Change* (A&M).

***

Frampton's whole aura is that of the likeable, well-adjusted boy next door. But even though his voice has no particular distinctiveness and the melodies on this album are fairly predictable, there is a musicianly fastidiousness about his work which makes it well worth listening to. What he's best at is relaxed, slowish songs which are sweet without being saccharine. 'Fig Tree Bay', the opener, is a very pleasant lazy easy holiday song. 'Wind of Change', following it, employs sweeping dulcimer chords, again in a style that is soft but never mawkish. Side I ends with a very slow soothing ballad called 'Oh For Another Day'.

The livelier numbers don't come off so well. There's a rather hygienic performance of the Stones' 'Jumping Jack Flash' (the only non-Frampton composition on the record) and a diffuse rave-up at the end called 'Alright', with a kind of superallstars group featuring Ringo Starr, Billy Preston and Klaus Voormann. Even so, this is an album to which it is hard, if not positively churlish, to take exception.

Monday, 10 July 1972

PLAY IT AGAIN, DORY

Dory Previn/*Reflections in a Mud Puddle*

DORY PREVIN STARTED her recording career with big disadvantages and they probably account for the fact that few people seem to have heard her first album: I haven't, for one. First, she had the misfortune to be known chiefly as the divorced spouse of Andre Previn. Second, there has been a glut on the market in recent years of morbidly unhappy singer/composers, particularly female ones. Could anybody hope to hold a candle to Joni? Did we really want a female Leonard Cohen?

Actually, this last is a miserable analogy, put out by lazy-minded pundits. Cohen's thing is singing obscure visionary allegories in a wearied, seamy drawl. Dory Previn takes an opposite tack, at least on her second LP *Reflections in a Mud Puddle* (UA). She sings unambiguous statements in a strong, clear voice. The only thing these two have in common is a pervasively neurotic state of mind, and most of the world has it in common with them.

All the same that title only compounds misgivings, and so does the rest of the material on the sleeve. There's a fearsome photograph, of the lady herself, repeated on a poster inside with her eyes lost in murky hollows behind great saucer spectacles. And there's a listing of musicians which runs to around forty-six names, including a string section of eighteen. Shades of Judee Sill.

But if you can get past all this to the actual grooves, your preconceptions will be dispelled. Instead of the lavish over-arranging and over-production which smothered the Sill album, there is a cunning deployment of the army of musicians, so that they become almost invisible. There is also some very slick production by Nikolas Venet.

Dory Previn's voice is girlish and laconic, with a strong tinge of the pre-war supper dance crooner. On a couple of songs she deliberately guys this style in a delightful way. 'Play It Again, Sam' is a wicked piece of breathy doh-dee-doh nostalgia for World War II. On Side 2, 'The Final Flight of the Hindenburg' is not only sung in '30s vocal style and supported by a perfect arrangement of droopy saxes and violin, but the beginning of the track has been processed to sound like a tinny recording of the period. In another context this would be irritating gimmickry, but in this case it's entirely at the service of the song, which attempts to relate a vivid memory to the recent death of the father who was a part of it.

***

Something else this performer does well is to turn trivial contemporary references into strong imagery—as in 'The New Enzyme Detergent Demise Of Ali MacGraw', which is about an invisible death of the heart, ending with the lines:

> and so it goes, and nobody knows
> I am non
> bio-degradable.

Again, this is cleverly served by the arrangement, with that choice piece of current jargon sustained in sweet harmony by a couple of backing voices and a discreetly anonymous, airport-music style accompaniment throughout, drums and guitar chomping amiably behind vacuous doodles on honky tonk piano, trumpet and strings.

I'm not so sure about her message songs, like 'Doppelganger', 'The Talkative Woman and the Two Star General' and 'The Altruist and the Needy Case'. The first two of these are well enough written, but they have a touch of that uncomfortable archness which often accompanies serious moral purpose. These are all on Side 1; the second side is a suite of songs about her father's death; entitled 'Taps, Tremors and Time Steps'.

This is an arresting and often moving suite, but points up two other Previn shortcomings. Her melodies are rather ordinary and repetitive (no challenge to Joni there), and like all these singers she could fairly be described as self-regarding. Given all that, this is an unexpectedly fresh and tasteful and sensitive talent at work.

Monday, 24 July 1972

JOHN LENNON'S OTHER IRELAND

John Lennon/*Sometime in New York City*

HOW DOES THIS verse strike you as a helpful contribution to our present situation?

> If we could make chains with the morning dew
> The world would be like Galway Bay.
> Let's walk over rainbows like leprechauns,
> The world would be one big Blarney stone.

How does it further strike you when sung out of tune by Yoko Ono to a melody roughly similar to that of 'The Boys from the County Armagh'? You don't believe me? It's all there on the new John Lennon album.

The song is called 'The Luck of the Irish' and it's about this land full of beauty and wonder which was raped by the British brigands and about the pain and death and the glory and the poets of auld Eireland. That's all direct quotation. According to another line in the lyrics, Lennon learned these insights in Liverpool, but it seems more likely that they were gleaned from some boozy New Yorker wearing a green bowler in the Saint Paddy's Day parade.

I'd like to think that the politics of the album's other Irish offering, 'Sunday Bloody Sunday', emanated from the same source. In this, the Protestants of the North are addressed as 'anglo pigs and scotties' and the sentiment is expressed that 'it's those mothers' turn to burn.' Since Lennon pronounces that last word 'boin', it does indeed seem that he's quoting from a source in the Bronx. Still, that hardly reduces the ugliness of the song's crude sectarianism, nor its arrogance coming from an uninvolved pop star.

The entire record is like that. It's called *Some Time in New York City* and its material covers the whole radical chic spectrum. The sleeve is laid out like a newspaper, with the song titles for headlines and the lyrics underneath in columns, and lots of relevant photographs. The banality of the lyrics is uniform. A song addressed to Angela Davis includes the lines: 'They gave you coffee/They gave you tea/They gave you everything but e-qual-i-ty'. 'We're All Water' (a less than felicitous title) asserts that 'There may not be much difference/Between Manson and the Pope/If we press their smiles.' There are other songs called 'Attica State', 'Woman is the Nigger of the World', 'Sisters O Sisters', and 'John Sinclair'.

The melodies have the same odour of manufactured concern as the sloganeering lyrics. They can be instantly learnt, like a vapid catch phrase, and likewise instantly discarded. Somehow Lennon sings his half of it all with a cheerful competence. The band he has put together, a hardbitten bunch of Americans with the name Elephant's Memory, plays a brash but co-ordinated fifties-style rock backing which can slide itself under anything the boss says.

Yoko has composed roughly half of the material and sings on roughly half of it. That's one part of the problem. I can't judge her calibre in filming people's bums, but as a songwriter, political activist and singer, she is tuneless, witless, graceless and extremely strident.

The other part of the problem is the interesting one: Lennon's folly. Literary Romanticism is littered with examples of the political folly of its most distinguished graduates from Coleridge to Ezra Pound. They were all extremists of the heart. So is Lennon. The very depth of feeling that gave us 'Strawberry Fields Forever' and 'Julia' and the entire Plastic Ono Band album has betrayed him into the trite and foolish propaganda of 'Power To The People' and 'All You Need Is Love' and now this colossal debacle, which is undoubtedly the worst record by a major performer, since Dylan's *Self Portrait*.

***

To sugar the pill, a live LP has been thrown in for free. On one side is a jam session done with assorted superstars in London in 1969, and on the other a jam with the Mothers Of Invention at the Fillmore East last year. You won't want to listen to either of them twice.

Lennon's first solo LP was a major and enduring work. His second, *Imagine*, was much lighter and more uneven, but still full of vitality and invention. I devoutly hope that this present excursion with the wife is a temporary aberration which he will come to view in retrospect with a rueful grimace.

Monday, 7 August 1972

BELFAST'S BOY

Van Morrison/*Saint Dominic's Preview*

BELFAST SHOULD NAME a street after Van Morrison. Of all the hard men from the industrial provinces of these islands who made their names during the 1960s by imitating black R&B singers, he alone has gone on to fulfil his promise—and I'm including Eric Burdon and Joe Cocker. He has done it through perseverance, determination, steady toil: so a city that has always prided itself on its Puritan work-ethic could scarcely find a worthier offspring to honour. His voice has never appealed to me as an attractive nor even a particularly expressive instrument. It has a harshly restricted tonal range, the timing is often clumsy, and it tends to go sharp on sustained notes. But the singing is only a small part of Morrison's music. He is an artist who has gradually achieved control over all the components of his material—he writes the songs, orchestrates and produces them. The result is an entirely distinctive sound which is always unmistakably his own.

This control has been growing perceptibly in the course of his prolific output of LPs in recent years, from *Moondance* to *His Band And The Street Choir* to *Tupelo Honey*, and now to *Saint Dominic's Preview*, his new release (on Warner Bros.). The title song on this album strikes me as his most considerable work to date. It's about sitting in San Francisco, watching a band march by, thinking how far he has come from Belfast and the rest of his past, realising that he has achieved what is thought of as success, and yet wondering why he still feels unfulfilled and in transit. He is able to elaborate on all this by means of a much more expansive structure than his songs can usually tolerate. It's rooted essentially in gospel music, but sustained by that peculiar amalgam of urban styles which Morrison has made his own.

There are only six other songs on the record, but four of them are easy-going numbers which swing along very pleasantly. The opening track, 'Jackie Wilson Said (I'm In Heaven When You Smile)' is the best of them, with an integration of voice and instruments which is the tightest that Van Morrison has ever achieved. Borne along on the polished upbeat drumming of Rick Schlosser, the saxes of Jack Schroer and Boots Houston and the guitar of Doug Messenger build up an elegantly funky sound which is irresistible. It's true that the lyrics are trivial—I pray that this will be the last time that a rock song exhorts me to 'let it all hang out' or to get it all together or any other of those mindless apothegms—but the genialty of the overall enterprise triumphs even so.

'Gypsy' is built more or less on the chords of 'House of the Rising Sun', but it features an attractive melding of various rhythms, from modified gypsy fandango to slow blues. 'I Will Be There' is something of a curio, a regular old nightclub piece which you could easily imagine being sung by Buddy Greco, or Al Martino. Messenger does those sophisticated transposed guitar chords, Tom Salisbury tinkles out some pretty cocktail-lounge runs on piano and the sax section moans the right kind of riffs. There is, thankfully, no element of parody involved. The tongue merely favours one cheek rather than the other a little. The shortest song, 'Redwood Tree', is a simple but tuneful ditty.

That leaves the album's two failures, one partial and the other extensive. Unfortunately these tracks last, respectively, for ten and eleven minutes, constituting over half of the entire playing time. Both of them are slow, interminably repetitive, and virtually based on two chords. The notion, presumably, is to build atmosphere and drama. It works to a degree on 'Almost Independence Day', but it founders abjectly in 'Listen To The Lion', where Morrison's voice keeps crooning along low and then unleashing an outburst of melodrama and then resolving into embarrassing bubbling and groaning noises which are prolonged grotesquely.

'Almost Independence Day' has an arresting opening, with nice improvisation on 12-string guitar leading into a hypnotic combination of hissing cymbals and a steady growl on a synthesizer. Some fine effects are achieved, with Morrison using his voice like a train siren, and the sound of fireworks imitated on stopped guitar strings. But again, the thing is grossly over extended.

One final point worth making in Van Morrison's favour. He has the gumption to give employment to such gifted and neglected jazz veterans as Connie Kay and Leroy Vinnegar.

Monday, 21 August 1972

ROCK REGENERATION

ROCK MUSIC HAS given rise to a minor new film genre which was germinated in *Monterey Pop*, and the Bob Dylan movie, *Don't Look Back*, emerged fully fledged in *Woodstock*, and turned tough and sombre in *Gimme Shelter* (about the Rolling Stones' disastrous Altamont concert) and *Fillmore*. All of these document an event, and all of them are part sociology and part propaganda, but their chief concern is to devise a cinematic style for the music itself.

Fillmore is currently on general release in America and so, as it happens, am I. It's a film of some significance. Even though the event which it documents took place over a year ago—the closing down of Bill Graham's Fillmore concert halls in New York and San Francisco—the malaise which that event enshrined has not improved and the state of the music is about the same. For the rock devotee it makes compulsive viewing, compounding as it does exhilaration at the music with shrugged shoulders at the showbiz industry.

Bill Graham is made the star of *Fillmore* in the same cunning way that Dylan was made the star of *Don't Look Back* by showing just enough warts to make him seem intriguingly human but not enough to make him out a punk. The propaganda slant is roughly that Graham created an ambience in which groups, audiences and producers could co-exist in loving trust, that this ambience worked like a charm for a couple of years towards the end of the 60s and that it was then destroyed by the mounting greed and prima donna behaviour of the bigger groups. Sequences of Graham on the telephone trying to set up a set of farewell shows, arguing his way through interminable disputes on fees, light shows, order of performance, billing and so on are alternated with extracts from the actual concerts themselves.

The truth is, of course, that success has spoiled Rock Culture, as it does all entertainment phenomena, through a general hardening of the arteries. As everything got more complicated, from the music itself to the band equipment, recording techniques, promotion and the rest, the original raw vitality of a popular art was spent.

***

But it is equally true that this process is cyclical and that all the lively arts have an endless capacity for self-renewal. The plaintive assertion of the 50s that 'rock & roll is here to stay' turned out to be true in the

147

rocking 60s. This is where the exhilaration of *Fillmore* comes into play. For underneath all the smarting egotistic business hassles, the music pulsates away, alive and well and holding itself in readiness for regeneration. Although there are no startling new groups which open up unimagined horizons, there are veterans like the Grateful Dead and Quicksilver Messenger Service sustaining their excellent standards and there are more minor and derivative groups playing with all-round competence and vigour.

The first of these to appear is a Bay Area big band called Cold Blood which is most notable for a vibrant female vocalist with a resplendent cascade of red hair. She's no Janis Joplin and the band is no Chicago, but together they set up a live current with the audience which transmits itself onto the celluloid. Later, a guitarist called Elvin Bishop fronting a group of the same name plays a remarkable flamboyant solo which drew applause from the audience in the cinema.

More famous is the quartet called Hot Tuna whose set is another musical highlight of the film. A kind of sub-group within Jefferson Airplane, it features Jorma Kaukonen on guitar and vocals; Jack Casady on bass, and the old black fiddler Papa John Creach. The whole combination is an anomaly even in the context of current eclecticism, but it comes off as a tightly integrated, hard driving blues rock, only slightly let down by Jorma's chestbound singing.

One justification of these films, adequate in itself, is that it gives those of us who can't attend the concerts and can't afford limitless record purchases the chance to see and hear groups of this calibre. Cinematically, *Fillmore* counts as nothing more than a budget version of *Woodstock*. But the stereo sound reproduction is crisp and well-balanced, and that's the proper priority.

Monday, 4 September 1972

THE DYLAN LEGEND

Anthony Scaduto/*Bob Dylan*
Frank Zappa/*Waka/Jawaka*

THE LIFE OF Bob Dylan speaks to our own time in the way that Scott Fitzgerald's did to the 1920s or Byron's to the 1810s: the times may be a changin', but the more they do so, the more they seem to stay the same.

For nearly two hundred years now, urban society has provoked from many of its artists a raving egomania, alternately seeking to assert and annihilate itself in excessive sex or drink or drugs, in mysticism or superstition or personal vendettas, in the whole gamut of recognisably outrageous behaviour.

This by now very venerable Romantic tradition has been well sustained in the past two decades—by the original Dylan, by Behan, Mailer, the Beats, Charlie Parker and the rest—but Bob Dylan has a special claim as the man who reached the most immense audience. His influence wove itself into the fabric of the whole culture, from its body language to its politics. For a lot of young people in America and Europe, he was virtually the definitive human being.

To do a successful biography of such a figure demands a regular anthology of talents. Anthony Scaduto, whose book *Bob Dylan* has been published here by Abacus at 60p, lacks some of them but displays the crucial one of a taste for accuracy. The book is an admirable piece of reportage. It's written without eloquence or much elegance, but the fascination of the story it tells overcomes all stylistic deficiencies.

The cliché description of this kind of story is that it 'reveals the man behind the mask.' Scaduto indeed shows us a real man and he demolishes both the sensationalist stories which have circulated about Dylan and the adolescent fantasies which Dylan himself spread around (for example, that he was an orphan, and had an uncle who was a famous Las Vegas gambler).

But in a deeper sense the story of Dylan's career has genuine mythic aspects, just like Citizen Kane's or Jay Gatsby's. In 1956 he was Robert Allen Zimmerman, the skinny son of a Jewish shopkeeper in the small town of Hibbing, Minnesota, doing his Little Richard imitations at high school like a million other middle-class youngsters. By 1961 he had made a pilgrimage to the sickbed of the legendary Woody Guthrie, who announced: 'Pete Seeger's a singer of folk songs, not a folk singer ... But Bobby Dylan's a folk singer.'

Within a year he had an album out and was nationally known. A few years after that and he was the world's best known protest singer along with Joan Baez, with whom he was caught up in a love affair. By 1966 he was a rock & roll king full of vitriolic neuroses and making wild, hallucinatory songs out of his manic, drug-ridden life. After that there was the near-fatal motorbike crash, the secret marriage, the withdrawal into hermit-like seclusion followed by dramatic re-appearances—the whole thing adds up to an authentic and absorbing legend of our life and times.

Or at least of the 1960s. There is a strong feeling from the book, and particularly from Scaduto's gauche and too uncritical analyses of the songs, that Dylan's legend is forever anchored in the last decade. His fraught assertion to the author may prove to be its sad epitaph.

'I still have a lot of talent left ... I can still do it. None of it has left me. All of those people who are down on me, they'll catch up. They'll understand someday. They've got a surprise coming.'

Frank Zappa on the other hand, just keeps on keeping on. He has a rich new album out which is a sequel to *Hot Rats* and a foretaste of the music to be played by his new 20-piece band of the same name. The album, on the Bizarre/Reprise label is called *Waka/Jawaka* and represents a new step forward in his weird Hollywood synthesis of musical styles.

Monday, 18 September 1972

ANGLO-INDIAN SOUND

Mahavishnu Orchestra/*The Inner Mounting Flame*
Chicago/*Chicago V*

JOHN McLAUGHLIN'S MAHAVISHNU Orchestra recently visited England and was accorded a measure of critical acclaim which has stimulated new interest in the group's album *The Inner Mounting Flame* (CBS). Now while it's true that new geniuses are acclaimed every day of the week in the hyper world of popular music, hyperbole is difficult to avoid in describing this record. The most noncommital comment I can think to make on it is that it's electric in every sense of the word.

McLaughlin is an English-born guitarist who grew up playing rock and blues, and then got involved in jazz and Indian music. There's nothing in the least original in that progression, except its end result: a gift for creating haunting, unique melodies, and a dazzlingly original guitar style which is full of passionate intensity.

The religious impulse behind this efflorescence is made explicit in the name of the band, of the album and of the individual tracks. But the music is as devoid of religiosity as McLaughlin's guitar playing is of mere flashiness. His most characteristic technique is to worry a simple phrase or even a single note until he has extracted the last ounce of feeling from it. The numbers are filled with these burning repetitions, pushed higher and higher in a constant emotional ascension. The music is frequently relentless and always muscular, except for one single lapse into maudlin floridity—a free-style piece called 'A Lotus on Irish Streams', which title is perhaps meant as a giveaway.

The Mahavishnu Orchestra is by no means a one-man band. Jerry Goodman, the electric violinist who made a giant reputation for himself when he started out in the Flock, plays with so much simpatico for McLaughlin's music that it's often hard to differentiate their contributions. Drummer Billy Cobham also plays with a quite uncanny degree of group co-ordination. Rick Laird on bass and Jan Hammer on piano are the remaining performers, and although Hammer's work is the least imaginative in the group, it does contribute to the remarkably integrated ensemble sound.

This sound ranges from the quiet lyrical tension of 'You Know You Know', through the cool laid-back opening of 'Dawn' to the wild blitz of 'Awakening'.

It can sustain three melodic motifs and three time signatures simultaneously. It is a mysterious, endlessly intriguing and exhilarating new thing.

***

Of the various groups which re-introduced the big band sound into popular music a few years back, Chicago has proved the stayer. This band always had prodigious musical talent and energy, but it was hard to swallow their rhetoric about revolution, their rather banal excursions into classical music and their insistence on putting out only double and triple and quadruple albums.

Little remains of these affectations in their crackling new release, *Chicago V* (CBS), a single LP of nine exuberant songs. It's true that the first one is entitled 'A Hit By Varèse', but this turns out to be a driving and amusing rocker, with a rising brass slur every so often which is particularly gratifying.

The next two numbers, 'All Is Well' and 'Now That You've Gone' present two contrasting reactions to the end of a love affair, and feature the tight and yet airy harmony singing of the band's three vocalists (guitarist Terry Kath, bassist Peter Cetera and pianist Robert Lamm). Side 1 ends with a song which takes the form of a dialogue between an interrogator concerned about the state of society and a passive uncommitted student. It's written as a simple rock song, but builds in complexity and excitement to the climax of the band singing a capella the line, 'We can make it happen.' By concentrating on drama rather than overt politicking, this song gets the listener thoroughly involved.

Side 2 sustains this admixture of extrovert vigorous tunes made subtle by sophisticated big band licks and constantly varied and economical arrangements. The lyrics are never exactly deathless, but they don't matter a great deal. There's some hope for the western world when a group as musically literate as this can command widespread popularity.

Monday, 2 October 1972

BETWEEN FOLK AND ROCK

Sandy Denny/*Sandy*
Cat Stevens/*Catch Bull at Four*

THE ENGLISH (AND Irish) folk-rock cult has always irritated and bored me on account of my separate but equal passions for real traditional music on the one hand and electric rock on the other. Nevertheless, Sandy Denny has a very haunting voice. And as a sole performer she's moving away from the earnest suburban romanticism of her days with Fotheringay and Fairport Convention into Joni Mitchell terrain.

Her new album, *Sandy* (Island) consists of eight of her own compositions plus Bob Dylan's 'Tomorrow Is A Long Time' and Richard Farina's 'Quiet Joys of Brotherhood'. The Dylan song is the first surprise. She treats it as a relaxed country number, the antithesis of Dylan's hoarse intensity, but also gilds it with some of the pure vocal ornamentation of British traditional singing. With the languorous Nashville tones of Sneaky Pete Kleinow's pedal steel guitar acting as a foil, the result has an unexpected fresh charm.

But the album's main interest obviously resides in her own songs, and four of them have considerable appeal. The opener, 'It'll Take A Long Time', demonstrates the strength inherent in the cool restraint of her vocal style and insinuates itself into your head very speedily, though the lyrics are largely impenetrable. 'The Lady', on the other hand, has fairly simplistic lyrics about singing a song at dawn; but its free-ranging melody is absorbing. It would have gained in expressiveness if accompanied only on piano (like Joni Mitchell's 'Blue'), but even with an inflated string arrangement culminating in a kind of Vaughan Williams finale, it works.

'Bushes and Briars' is an odd, medium-paced number set in a country churchyard, which again benefits from Kleinow's pedal steel work. The last track on the album, 'The Music Weaver', is the nearest thing to a personal statement that she offers us, and it's an attractively melancholy piece, sung with feeling.

Greater personal warmth and involvement is something from which all of these songs would benefit, particularly with regard to their words. Even so, they make pleasurable listening. Less successful are 'For Nobody to Hear', which uses brass and a sax and double-tracked voice in an unhappy attempt to be funky, and 'Listen, Listen', which is just insubstantial. There are also two imitation folksongs, 'Sweet Rosemary' and 'It Suits Me Well', which actually grate. The latter, for which she adopts a fake folkie accent, is especially phoney, but her old fans will probably like it best.

***

Cat Stevens is a more celebrated English singer/songwriter but he can't rock very well either. His new album, with the characteristically gnomic title *Catch Bull at Four* (Island), attempts a generally more aggressive sound than before. Whilst he and his four side-men play extremely well, his voice sounds forced and ragged when he tries to drive it. This is the case in 'Sitting', 'Anglesea' and 'Freezing Steel', none of which is much fun to listen to.

What he does extremely well is the lyrical melancholic song full of quirky musical and verbal inventions. Such a one is 'Sweet Scarlet'. As before, he draws on his Greek ancestry to give us a song in Greek style complete with bouzouki ... except that in this case the words are a poem in Latin called 'O Caritas'. Nice.

The most involving track is a thing called '18th Avenue', a song about a nightmare experienced in Kansas City. The power in the song itself carries over into an extraordinarily articulate instrumental passage, using strings, electric piano and rhythm section. The whole effect is unique. If Stevens is worried about seeming to be only a pretty face, this is the kind of song he should concentrate on. But he shouldn't try to be a shouter.

Monday, 16 October 1972

153

AN EXCELLENT THING IN WOMAN

Chi Coltrane/*Chi Coltrane*

JUDGING BY THE pretty white face on the sleeve of her first album, Chi Coltrane is no relation to her late illustrious jazz namesake. Beyond that I can supply no information about her whatever, except that she sings her own songs to her own piano accompaniment like Carole King and Laura Nyro, and she has as compelling a voice as has appeared on the pop scene this year.

Its rich, husky timbre is a prize of nature which gives her a considerable start on the competition. When soft, gentle and low it is just as King Lear remarks—an excellent thing in woman. It can range from a breathy innocence as in the prelude to 'Goodbye John', through the smoky resonance of 'Turn Me Around', to an almost unnerving intensity of grief in 'It's Really Come To This'.

The latter track, an end-of-the affair song, is the most marvellous example of her artistry on the record. She manages to load her voice with so much emotion that it constantly sounds on the verge of breaking down: yet this actually serves as camouflage for a breath control which keeps every note true and allows her a falsetto at the end which may yet be responsible for somebody's cardiac arrest.

However, quite apart from these plangencies, the girl has lungs like a coalbrick man's, and she belts out half-a-dozen rockers which leave no room for doubt on this score. One of these, 'You Were My Friend', deserves to be a hit single. It alternates short, free-style verses with the blockbuster chorus line of the title, which she sings as a combination of accusation and reproach. It's a consummate pop song, lusty, direct and pulsating with a giant heartbeat.

The other rockers are pleasant but fairly commonplace, with the exception of one ugly number called 'I Will Not Dance'. This is a badly judged sneer at America's rulers on behalf of the younger generation. The monotony of the melody and the fatuity of the lyrics are compounded by the unnatural stridency with which she distorts her voice.

It also has to be said that the writing in general is not greatly distinguished. Except for 'It's Really Come To This', 'You Were My Friend' and 'The Tree' (another climactic falsetto here), none of these songs would stand out from the ruck if performed by another singer. But Chi Coltrane's own voice has the Midas touch.

Somebody at CBS clearly agrees with me. No expense has been spared on the musicians for the session, with such as Jim Gordon on drums, Larry Knechtel and Lee Sklar on bass, Jim Horn handling the horns and Paul Buckmaster the strings and woodwinds. Quality, in this case, has certainly paid off. The album is a snappy, professional job, a pleasure to listen to, and the welcome advent of a genuine new talent.

***

Showing at the New Metropole is the film of the famous concert which George Harrison convened for Bangladesh refugee relief. For devotees of the music, this film is obligatory, quite apart from its purely musical qualities. It offers participation in the one major enterprise to date where the huge juggernaut of pop was successfully harnessed for a humanitarian purpose.

Not that the enterprise didn't leave a trail of commercial backbiting and treachery: what's amazing is that the idea ever got off the ground at all, and that so much money actually reached and continues to reach, the refugee relief fund. This is a tribute to the determination and organising ability of George Harrison, and the film shows as much. However many reservations you may have about his music—and I have plenty—it is impossible not to applaud the way he runs the show, firmly and tirelessly and almost self-effacingly considering that he's never off the stage.

As to the music, the sound reproduction is deplorably muddy. But who could resist the spectacle of Clapton and Harrison trading solos, or the tight-voiced Dylan making his first public appearance in years?

Monday, 13 November 1972

ENGLISH PROGRESSIVE

Yes/*Close to the Edge*
Home/*Home*

THE PROGRESSIVE MOVEMENT in rock music no longer enjoys the vogue it once did, but Yes is one group which keeps the banner aloft: their album *Close to the Edge* (Atlantic) is doing good business in the charts on both sides of the Atlantic without having compromised any principles.

Yes's music shares with that of other English progressive bands

155

such as Pink Floyd a kind of enchanted quality which lends it an odd charm. But it also shares a habit of repetition and overstatement. In *Close to the Edge* the constantly repeated lines and phrases are clearly intended to have a cumulative power, but they do tend to dun the ear a bit.

All of the established resources, from synthesizer to tape loop, are used on the album. With the heavy musical talents of guitarist Steve Howe and keyboards man Rick Wakeman, they are woven into a dense texture which constantly delights the ear with the sumptuous intricacy of its patterns.

Side I is the song cycle 'Close to the Edge' and Side 2 comprises another cycle called 'And You and I' and a long piece called 'Siberian Khatru'. This last title is typically and almost comically pretentious (along with 'Total Mass Retain' and 'The Solid Time of Change') and the lyrics are, as usual, entirely incomprehensible. Yet this is offset by the cheery Lancashire fecklessness and tunefulness of Jon Anderson's singing. And quite apart from their prose meaning, the words as pure sound are uncannily effective.

Not the least attractive noise on the album is Chris Squire's bass, lurching in with odd rhythms, and yet providing a solid underpinning for the others. Bill Bruford (since replaced by Alan White) also contributes very precise and controlled drumming. All in all, it's an album that diverts the ear, even if also bemusing it occasionally.

***

Of the new groups that have surfaced in the last year, Home has attracted a lion's share of attention and acclaim. I find their current album (on CBS) rather dispiriting.

Everything else is there in abundance, musical expertise, inventive writing, taut ensemble playing, even sensitive production. At first it sounds as if it's going to work, with a fine opening track called 'Dreamer' in which Laurie Wisefield and Mick Stubbs trade some fast, tight guitar arabesques. This is followed by a show song called 'Knave' which has a sad, restrained melody, most effective.

With the next piece, a lachrymose number about the poor little rich daughter of Hollywood stars, qualms commence. The excitement, far from building up, is dissipating. 'Rise Up' follows, and it's a frisky enough aubadè, but scarcely affects the pulse. The first side thereupon ends with 'Dear Lord' and to tell the truth, it sounds dreary.

The second side has three songs, and except for an interesting instrumental excursion in the last of them, featuring bowed bass and sweeping cymbals, it's boring.

The problem can be localised in the singing. Leader Mick Stubbs's high, light voice has the earnest piety of a pop ballad singer without the concomitant lung power. His tone and expression never vary.

On a broader level, though, the lack of vitality in Home's accomplished work is symptomatic of an ennui pervading the music as a whole. The huge musical feast of the mid-60s is long over and we're still seeking nourishment from its leftovers; Nixon and Heath have the destiny of the West firmly in hand; and the Woodstock nation has no real Home to go to.

Monday, 11 December 1972

ELECTRONIC CARNIVALS

Nik Cohn/*AwopBopaLooBop AlopBamBoom*
P.F. Sloan/*Raised On Records*
Alice Cooper/*Love It to Death*

MY FAVOURITE BOOK on pop is still *AwopBopaLooBop AlopBamBoom* by Nik Cohn (Paladin). He's one of the few pundits to date who's found a successful style for dealing with the subject: one that's as brittle, pungent, comic and brash as the best of the music itself.

He is particularly entertaining when dealing with the big operators within the industry, men like Lou Adler who was the first producer to realise the commercial potential of protest songs, and who 'set a songwriter called P.F. Sloan to churning out searing indictments of society at the rate of roughly one a week (together they were responsible for 'Eve of Destruction', a round-ticket diatribe against everything)'.

Lou Adler has scarcely missed a trick since then. His most recent coup was the transformation of Carole King from a 1960s songwriter into a 1970s recording star. P.F. Sloan is perhaps hoping for a similar metamorphosis (although he no longer works for Adler) and has released an album called *Raised On Records* (CBS).

157

***

Those of us who can remember 'Eve Of Destruction' vividly enough to blench, need have no fears. P.F. Sloan has sensibly decided that old songwriters neither die nor fade away, they simply swim with the tide. Which in this case has carried him far away from protest to a point somewhere between Paul Simon and Cat Stevens, all three of course being substantially propelled by a Bob Dylan undertow. In other words, he's done a suite of glum songs out of the depths of his damaged ego.

But they're tuneful. And he's obtained the services of a fine bunch of musicians who lay down a very well-rounded and articulate sound throughout, men like Jim Horn, Larry Knechtel and Hal Blaine. Sloan himself is no slouch on the guitar and he can sing melodiously even if the lachrymosity gets a bit wearisome at times. In short, a resourceful man.

The pattern is fairly constant throughout the album: chugging guitar chords first, then voice in with bass and drums, a solid refrain with backing vocals, and a subsequent instrumental buildup to a heavy conclusion. It's done with skill, especially in the title song, a full-blown country paean to gramophone culture, with pedal steel and dobro and a whole lot of wind. Another pleasing number is 'The Night the Trains Broke Down' which features a group called the Neighbourhood Band whose rich sound overcomes the rather lame lyrics.

Lyrics are P.F.'s weak suit. One of these songs begins, 'I once knew a girl/Her name it was Springtime', and another contains the couplet, 'She had a schizophrenic mother/whose mind was in the gutter' which, apart from everything else, is just unsingable. He also sometimes strays from imitation into plagiarism. 'Turn On The Light' is too close to Paul Simon for comfort and 'Sins of a Family' too much of a Dylan pastiche, complete with harmonica and high-voiced harangue.

But in spite of it all, this is an oddly pleasant record, good music to pity yourself by.

***

I would give a lot to read Nik Cohn on Alice Cooper. This is the American band composed of male transvestites whose current stage act, as unleashed in Glasgow recently, includes a live cobra, mock whipping and knife fighting, and the lynching of the eponymous Alice himself as a finale.

Retired colonels will no doubt be dutifully apoplectic, but after all the Jacobean stage accommodated far greater depravities and still contrived a Webster and a Ford. The question is, what kind of music does Alice Cooper play?

The answer is, meretricious music of a colossal melodramatic vacuity. This judgment is based on their album, *Love It to Death*. Shorn of their grand guignol, the lads or girls are pathetic entertainers. And they strike me as symptomatic of nothing more ominous than boredom, the secret black death of the age of the electronic carnival.

Thursday, 28 December 1972

1973

THE RETREAT OF THE HERD

James Taylor/*One Man Dog*
Carole King/*Rhymes and Reasons*

JAMES TAYLOR AND Carole King are two performers just about due to be abandoned. Sensing a retreat by the herd which stampeded so massively in the Taylor-King direction over the past two years, the pundits have been less than rapturous about their respective new album releases. Taylor's *One Man Dog* (Warner Bros K46185) and King's *Rhymes and Reasons* (Ode 77016) This has rather less to do with the intrinsic quality—which is high in both cases—than with the lack of any startling new departures. Taylor still sings out of a resonant melancholia, only now it's described as morbid and boring. King still sings literate and tuneful pop songs, only now it's felt that they all sound the same.

All of this is most unfair, of course, but it reflects a condition of the literary or artistic scenes as much as of the pop music one. Doing a thing in a brilliant way will win you fame: to hold on to that fame, however, you have to keep doing it in other brilliant ways. The Beatles were the greatest exponents of this so far as the musical content of pop goes.

But James Taylor and Carole King just keep doing the same fine thing in the same accomplished way. Which is not to say that their work shows no development. *Rhymes and Reasons* is a funkier and more personal album than her last one, *Carole King Music*, which was in turn a much more sophisticated package than the enormously successful *Tapestry*. And Taylor's *One Man Dog*, his first album for a year and a half, also features new and sophisticated musical settings, particularly in the use of brass and woodwind.

***

James Taylor is the more gifted, the more potentially important and the more vulnerable of the two, and for those very reasons this album is undoubtedly his weakest since the first over-produced one on Apple. He has been labouring, as an introverted and intimate confessional artist, under the appalling burden of mass adulation,

> and they think you've come
> with your soul in your hand
> to set their children free,

he sings in one of these new songs. The inevitable effect of this pressure has been to drive him deeper into himself and constrict his inspiration.

One Man Dog, then, contains only six full-size James Taylor songs. The remainder of the record is made up of one song by the guitarist of his backing group, Danny Kortchmar: one by the wizard guitarist John McLaughlin, the folk song 'One Morning in May', two lame instrumental fillers, and seven song fragments segued together into a kind of improvised suite. Skilfully and sensitively as all of this is presented, there is an inescapable bittiness about the album.

My own opinion, however, is that this man's scraps are more nutritious than most men's feasts. Further, all six of the complete Taylor songs are winners. In particular, nobody should be without the lovely 'New Tune' or the flowing, mournful melody of 'Nobody But You'.

Carole King seems to have no difficulty in being prolific: her only problem, in fact, is the aforesaid aura of déja vu. Three or four songs on this disc are indeed pervaded by it rather too heavily. But half-a-dozen of the others have a cutting edge and a directness not heard before in her work. 'Feeling Sad Tonight' and 'Ferguson Road' are especially fine. Of course, they're not 'You've Got a Friend'. But that's the kind of song that can't be written twice.

Monday, 8 January 1973

ECLECTIC AMALGAMATION

Santana/*Caravanserai*
Colin Blunstone/*Ennismore*

THE ECLECTICISM OF contemporary music can still be rather startling. An amalgamation between the Latin-American percussion band and the electric rock group is unremarkable now, having been successfully developed through three fine LPs by the American group, Santana; but the camels in the desert on the cover of their fourth album, *Caravanserai* (CBS 65299), are a trifle puzzling.

What it means, of course, is the Mystic East. The inside of the sleeve bears a quotation from an Eastern sage, and Side 1 of the album consists of six numbers, beginning with 'Eternal Caravan of Reincarnation', and concluding with 'All The Love of the Universe'. You may want to award grave consideration to these profundities, but in truth they're like a hat which a man might don to act out an idea of the moment.

The music itself on Side 1 is more free-form and impressionistic than in their previous work. The first track opens with the dawn sound of a cricket or a bird, followed by a prelusive saxophone solo, full of hoarse octaves. This launches the full band into some 25 minutes of thickly-textured music, shimmering and shifting at first, more thunderous later on. The only rude shock comes when Carlos Santana suddenly sings a few lines in the fourth track 'Just In Time To See The Sun'. This is one band that would be wise to forget about vocals altogether.

Side 2 is more in their old vein—heavy on the congas and bongos and timbales. The numbers are a bit long-winded, but there's a marvellous climax to the last one, 'Every Step of the Way'. All told, it's a vigorous and creative album, held together by the weaving organ of Gregg Rolie, and with particularly fine work from Tom Rutley on double bass.

***

Colin Blunstone was lead singer with the Zombies back in the days when a group would adopt a name like the Zombies. After they split up he returned to private life for a few years, but latterly he has reappeared as a solo performer. I missed his debut album when it came out a year ago, but his current one, *Ennismore* (EPC 65278), is a smooth and polished job.

In a way it's a Zombie reunion, for production is by Chris White and Rod Argent, the musicians include all the members of the Argent band, and two of the songs are compositions of theirs. But the sound is considerably mellower and more sophisticated than it was in the heady days of the mid-60s. It lacks pith somewhat, but is pleasurably mellifluous for all that.

The opener has already attained some success as a single, Russ Ballard's 'I Don't Believe In Miracles'. It's followed by a quartet of songs which are adroitly varied in style to avoid the potential monotony in Blunstone's breathy, rather uninflected voice. 'Exclusively For Me' is built on very attractive chord progressions and an imaginative string quartet arrangement by Chris Gunning, who has handled the string arrangements throughout most sensitively. 'Every Sound I Heard' has a strong, distinctive melody, and is promptly followed by a folksy, Dylanesque piece called 'How Wrong Can One Man Be', mostly done with just voice and guitar.

On the second side, 'Pay Me Later' has amusing and rather cynical lyrics, whilst the Argent/White song, 'Andorra', is a number about travelling in Spain, complete with castanets and flamenco guitar runs. So it goes, changes of pace and mood from one track to the next. One of the nicest moments on the record is at the end of 'I've Always Had You', where the soft and gentle voice is replaced by a virile alto sax solo, the two joining for the final line.

Monday, 22 January 1973

ANTITHESIS OF A STAR

Boz Scaggs/*My Time*
Paul Oliver/*The Story of The Blues*
Don Short/*Engelbert Humperdinck: The Authorised Biography*

BOZ SCAGGS IS not well known on this side of the Atlantic, even with a name like Boz Scaggs. He has been having a modest success recently with a single called 'Dinah Flo' but otherwise has been known only to connoisseurs of the San Francisco scene and particularly to fans of the old Steve Miller band, in which Scaggs first made his name. At any rate, he has been performing and recording for the past several years and has just released an enjoyable album called *My Time* (CBS).

My own first encounter with the man's work was in the film *Fillmore*, where the diffidence of his stage manner was intriguingly at odds with the assured competence of his guitar playing and singing. He is the antithesis of the rock star: deferential, conservatively dressed, looking like a young minister or an ex-Apprentice of the Year.

The same individualism is subtly apparent in his music. On the face of it, he's yet another white middle-class adapter of black rhythm & blues: on 'Dinah Flo' he sounds just like Van Morrison and on the album's title track he sounds like Steve Stills. However, the more you listen to him, the less he sounds like anything but himself. His voice is as tentative as his manner, issuing in a series of short phrases but with a strong and mellow vibrato. He's very good at pitting this against sustained backing voices.

A good example is 'Old Time Lovin'', my favourite track on the album. This is a gently sardonic departure from 'That Old Time Religion', with gospel organ and growling saxes and Boz's languid throaty vocals being chased from word to word by a trio of ardent backing voices. It's relaxed, smiling music. Rocking-chair rock.

The album was the product of two sessions, one at Muscle Shoals studios in Alabama using session men and the other at CBS San Francisco mostly with the members of his current band. The six Muscle Shoals tracks have been produced (by Boz himself) with a kind of mentholated echo which almost turns the accompaniment into Muzak, despite very alert and tight playing. The four San Francisco tracks have a much more satisfying immediacy. As well as 'Old Time Lovin' they include two rockers, 'Full-Lock Power Slide' and 'We're Gonna Roll', and a strange and very attractive piece called 'Freedom for the Stallion.'

***

SOME YEARS AGO Decca issued a marvellous album of documentary field recordings of the blues. It was called *Conversation With The Blues* and it was put together with a rare mixture of intelligence, sensitivity and feeling by a blues scholar and collector called Paul Oliver. Now, from Penguin, comes another such treasure, a book by Paul Oliver called *The Story of the Blues*.

This is a large scrapbook-size publication, covering the story of blues from West African instruments and dances to Tamla Motown. It's loaded with riveting graphics: the loading plan of a slave ship, police mug shots of Leadbelly, grainy photographs of tarpaper shacks, chain gangs, and bluesmen and women famous and obscure. What I've read of the text contrives to be as entertaining as it's informative.

As a present, it's a gift. It costs 75p. Don't give it to anybody who has no interest in either music or history or sociology or poetry or human nature. Give them instead *Engelbert Humperdinck: The Authorised Biography* by Don Short (NEL, 40p).

Wednesday, 7 February 1973

DOWN AMONG THE THESES

Richard Middleton/*Pop Music and The Blues:
A Study of the Relationship and Its Significance*
Charlie Gillett/*Rockfile*
Ian Whitcomb/*After the Ball*
Horslips/*Happy to Meet*

IDLE JESTS APPEARING in this column have an unnerving way of materialising as serious truths. A few years ago I concluded a piece on the stylistic inter-marriages going on everywhere in music with a quip about 'ceilidh-rock', what an outlandish possibility, etc. Now we have such groups as Horslips, with a line-up including bodhran, organ, whistle and electric mandolin.

About the same time, doing a round-up of the handful of books on popular music then being issued, I passed jolly remarks to the effect that people would be taking PhDs in the subject before long. Actually they were already doing it even then. Now they're publishing the results.

Richard Middleton's *Pop Music and the Blues: A Study of the Relationship and Its Significance* (Gollancz, £4.00) may not literally have started life as a thesis but it certainly reads like one. Mr Middleton is a lecturer in Music in the BBC's Open University and his stultifying academic style gives me my first serious qualms about that laudable institution. A typical sentence: 'For the moment we must note that (the) rupture of the psycho-social premises of the racial situation means that, as far as Negro psychology and culture at least are concerned, the seemingly inexorable "progression" of Negro history is here broken; the mainspring of the everlasting dialectical pendulum-swing is shattered.' Would you let that marry your sister?

It's only fair to say that this is taken from the introductory chapter 'Background to the Blues', and blues writers have always been professorial. But there is no amelioration in the later chapters on Pop. For example, the vocal harmonies of Merseybeat (remember the Swinging Blue Jeans and Freddie & The Dreamers?) provoke analysis of this order: 'Now such a phenomenon strikingly represents in microcosmic form the "centralised individualism" so typical of the social structures of the Post-Renaissance West.'

I confess that I have discarded this book unfinished.

***

Charlie Gillett has far more gumption and style, even though his *The Sound of the City* started life as an MA thesis. He has edited a curious paperback called *The Rock File* (Pictorial Presentation Ltd., 40p), a ragbag of essays, 'playlists', diagrams, photographs, and a log of British hits, 1955-69. This is a delightful oddity of a book, with an entertaining essay on reggae and Curtis Mayfield called 'Johnny Cool and the Isle of Sirens' and another one by Gillett on how to be a rock & roll writer, though personally I think there are too many of us as it is. For addicts only then, but definitely a minor hit.

Since it has already been reviewed in the book columns, I'll just mention Ian Whitcomb's *After the Ball* (Penguin, £3.00) in passing: to say that it's jammed with lore both absorbing and useful, takes a strongly subjective line which is the proper approach to the subject, and is compulsively readable. The over-indulgences, in italics and exclamation marks and narcissism, are pardonable by-products of a very welcome enthusiasm.

The books are crowding out the music. There's just space enough to mention the first Horslips album: *Happy to Meet* (Oats M003). Regular customers already know my distaste for Fairport Convention-style folk rock, and Horslips are doing approximately the same things, with a bias towards Irish folk sources. Nevertheless, there is ample musicianship, a good sound (recorded on the Rolling Stones mobile unit), and it's nice to see a fully polished rock album which is entirely a native product.

Tuesday, 20 February 1973

AMBIVALENCE OF SUCCESS

Joni Mitchell/*For the Roses*

JONI MITCHELL'S 1971 album *Blue* was her masterpiece without a doubt. She has never turned out a bad record, but *Blue* was the one that moved her into the pantheon alongside the chanteuses of other days and scenes like Juliette Greco or Lotte Lenya, the one that suddenly made the personal folk/rock song a definitive genre of our time.

Nobody could have expected its successor, *For the Roses*, (Asylum SYLA 8753) to have the same impact, nor does it; but the same articulate and original sensibility has given birth to it and it meets the standards we've come to expect from this artist. Its twelve tracks range from a simple and lively hit single to a couple of songs that are as subtle, eerie and puzzling as anything she's done.

The hit single is, of course, 'You Turn Me On, I'm A Radio', and it cooks along nicely with Graham Nash playing Dylanesque harmonica and with backing voices and handclapping evoking the right AM Top 40 radio sound. Like all the sophisticated hits since 'Yellow Submarine' and 'Tambourine Man', it's a song of two layers, one straight and the other ironic: as a top tenner it's on the inside looking in.

At the other end of the spectrum is 'Cold Blue Steel and Sweet Fire', apparently a song about heroin addiction. It begins with a swishing carpet of acoustic guitars, bolstered by some excellent electric work from James Burton. When the voice enters it's oddly impassive, crooning and bending notes in a dulled unaccented way quite unlike any previous Mitchell recording. This is counterpointed in turn by a wistful alto sax solo. The entire effect is haunting, hard to dislodge from your head. This song and the equally enigmatic 'Barangrill' which follows it are the most original and successful on the album.

***

'Barangrill' is about waitresses and garage attendants and a mysterious place called Barangrill (bar and grill?). What makes it extraordinary is its melody and arrangement. Various reeds, woodwind, guitars and strings are used deftly and sensitively in a series of repeated phrases which add up to a very distinctive tune and sound. Rarely does a singer/songwriter employ this much orchestration without appearing grossly over-dressed, but the sound here is all of a piece and very tasteful, largely thanks to Tommy Scott who is credited with the beautiful flute and reed sounds. His work throughout the album is a perfect complement to Joni's voice.

Of the other tracks, some are in a too-familiar vein, though all are performed with feeling. The opener, 'Banquet', is a fairly predictable social statement—just a bit too pat—and 'Lesson In Survival' is another of those lover's complaints that slides into a gauche jargon ('Maybe it's paranoia/Maybe it's sensitivity ... Oh baby I can't seem to make it/With you socially'). In a similar style, 'Woman of Heart and Mind' indulges the strain of female masochism that runs through several of her weaker songs. Finally, this artist seems a mite old to be chafing at her mama and papa in the way she does in 'Let the Wind Carry Me'.

These tracks are the album's passengers, but there are more than enough hardworking songs to carry them. 'Electricity' is a highly ingenious and catchy number, full of craft. 'Blonde In The Bleachers' shifts adroitly through several keys in a way that no other pop singer could even attempt, and comments succinctly on pop stardom. So does 'For the Roses' itself: it's the most honest and eloquent statement we've had yet about the ambivalence of pop success.

Tuesday, 6 March 1973

A TOUGH LADY

Carly Simon/*No Secrets*
Poco/*A Good Feelin' To Know*

AMERICA POSSESSES ALL kinds of wealth, but none is more impressive to me than its current generation of female singer/songwriters. Mss. Carole King, Laura Nyro, Janis Ian, Joni Mitchell, Dory Previn, Chi Coltrane ... a host of gifted, bra-less ladies making their own articulate way in an increasingly co-educational society.

Carly Simon belongs to this group and she's not a girl who's prepared to mince, especially with regard to words.

> Daddy, I'm no virgin
> and I've already waited too long

she hollers, in one of the songs on her new album *No Secrets* (Elektra

K42127). In another song, the current hit single 'You're So Vain', she excoriates the amorality and egoism of a former wealthy lover, only to finish him off with the retrain, 'You're so vain, you probably think this song is about you.'

This piece is surely unrivalled as a high-class demolition job but it's a very fine pop-song to boot. The Simon gift for sophisticated bitchiness is matched only by her ability to engage the royalty of pop music as her sidemen. The vocal harmonies here are provided by an un-credited M. Jagger, crown prince of sneering, and their voices blend to perfection. The instrumental work is not exactly slack either, with Klaus Voormann on bass, Jim Gordon on drums and Jimmy Ryan on guitar. It's a driving, wicked number, the best on the album.

All of the other songs have the same hard professional glint, with many layers of sound blended together and given a final polish through a judicious use of strings or woodwind or a choir. My only quarrel with it all is that Carly Simon's voice has sometimes too hard a cutting edge and almost no range of tone colours.

Consequently, the non-attacking songs sound rather lifeless. As if to make up for 'You're So Vain', the following track is a tribute to an apparent paragon of male virtue entitled 'His Friends Are More Than Fond Of Robin': it fails to convince. Similarly, the sentimental hindsight of 'It Was So Easy' comes out platitudinous and the final track, 'When You Close Your Eyes' is a highly-ornamented piece of sweet nothing.

Not all the aggressive tracks work either. There's a horribly stiff and strident version of James Taylor's 'Night Owl' with distinguished guests like 'Paul and Linda', Bonnie Bramlett and Nicky Hopkins contriving to produce an over-cooked mess. But there are also cunning, memorable songs of experience like 'We Have No Secrets' and 'Embrace Me, You Child'. On her own patch of ground, or blasted heath, this woman's hard to beat.

**

Neil Young and Stephen Stills have prospered exceedingly since their sensational group Buffalo Springfield disbanded: the other members of that group who formed a new band called Poco seemed to have done less well when they issued their first album two and a half years ago. It was just another average slice of country rock.

However, Poco has persevered and has quietly built itself up into a band with considerable expertise and expressiveness. Their current album *A Good Feelin' To Know* (Epic EPC 65126) has the mature weight of Stills' *Manassas* album, though it's more restricted to country-style music.

They're extremely good at slow, heavy deliberation as in the two tracks 'Early Times' and 'Restrain' and at ecstatic falsetto harmony singing. Listen particularly to the gospel-influenced 'Sweet Lovin'', a touching Richie Furay tribute to his newborn child, and to 'I Can See Everything' by bassist Timothy Schmit.

Tuesday, 20 March 1973

FRUITS OF VERSATILITY

Edgar Winter/*They Only Come Out At Night*
Argent/*In Deep*

EDGAR WINTER IS one of those adept American musicians who can turn in an excellent performance in almost any style, while lacking unique talents of their own. One of the songs from his latest album says, very appositely:

> I got the blues in my soul but
> my boogie-woogie feet
> Are taking me to rock n'roll.

The fruit of versatility is pastiche and Winter demonstrates this to perfection on the album. It's called *They Only Come Out At Night* (on EPC65074) and it sports on its cover a somewhat hideous photo of the albino wizard himself, in lipstick, spangles and a diamond necklace. This spoof on the current Bowie-Alice Cooper decadence trip is rather coarser than the music that it packages.

What that music does is to transport you through half-a-dozen established modes of rock music, demonstrating the spirit and technique and (sometimes) the nonsense inherent in each of them. The opener 'Hanging Around', is an easy living automobile song, very Californian and infectious. This is followed by 'When It Comes', a rough-voiced punk rocker, with a nice attacking alto sax solo. 'Alta Mira' slides into happy Latin-rock, with close harmony on the choruses, a catchy bouncy guitar riff and an outburst of Latino cries and expletives and whistles at the end.

173

The last track on Side 1, 'Undercover Man', is all mean, macho grunting; a Stones parody done to a tee. As a total contrast to this, Side 2 opens with a sweetly melancholy mid-tempo piece called 'Round and Round', built on McCartneyish changes. This is one of the most successful songs on a very successful album.

'Autumn' is a rather less effective excursion into soft rock, 'Real Good Time' is a fake 'live' performance splendidly done, and the tour ends with a riproaring instrumental entitled 'Frankenstein', which has a bloodcurdling, snarling guitar solo and all manner of other effects.

No individual musical credits are listed: so, all I can say is that Winter and his henchmen run a highly charged and well-oiled rock machine.

***

Argent are an odd little band, combining considerable musical literacy and wit with a weakness for vacuous, boring melodrama. Their new album, *In Deep* (EPC 65475) has a more favourable distribution of these elements than the previous one, *Hold Your Head Up*, but I suspect that I'll feel equally disinclined to play it often. They're four good natured hard working lads who lack some vital spark of judgment.

The first number here, for example, is called 'God Gave Rock and Roll to You'. On the Winter album this assurance would have been unmistakably jokey but here it's delivered with soulful earnestness and at great length—several times greater than necessary, in fact. So that, although the tune is very pleasant and Rod Argent's keyboard work strongly distinctive, the overall effect is rather joyless.

On the second and third tracks—'Only Money', Parts I and II—they move into the zone of vacuous melodrama. Over a leaden, two-note bass phrase, Russ Ballard sings lyrics about going out for a drink and it's always dearer than you think. A rock song about inflation, yet Ballard is a fair guitarist, but he has an agitated bleating kind of voice that only magnifies the banality of his lyrics.

Side 1 ends with 'Losing Hold', which comes on like the heart tugging Act 2 curtain number from the musical comedy version of a novel by say Dostoevsky. It incorporates delayed echo, tam tam, gong orchestra, bass drum and heavenly voice into a wall of sound. Too much.

But Side 2 has a pair of delightful tracks. 'Be Glad' opens with an attractive shuffle rhythm and chunky sound, and slides into a kind of

Frank Zappa collage of incongruous, oddball bits and pieces, including a familiar-sounding mazurka, chimes, a march, and a passage in drawing-room ballad falsetto. 'Christmas For The Free' is the most pleasing and tasteful, pop treatment of the Yuletide theme that I've heard—a warm and gentle tune with sensitive piano work and a sympathetic guitar solo from guest Derek Griffiths.

Tuesday, 3 April 1973

ANOTHER SIDE OF LOUDON

Loudon Wainwright III/*Album III*
Paul Simon/*The Songs of Paul Simon*

LOUDON WAINWRIGHT III has issued his *Album III* (on CBS 65238) which might be described as Another Side of Loudon Wainwright Bringing It All Back Home. In other words, he has moved away from his established style of intimate confessional songs—some of them eerie and some threatening, but almost all highly effective—to a more public, more flip and rugged kind of singing, with the lone guitar backing replaced by an electric rock band.

The band is a solid little country group called White Cloud and they serve him well, but the line of development he's pursuing isn't successful. He's not a rock singer, and his mordant wit on its own isn't enough to see him through. On the opening number, 'Dead Skunk', the band trucks along very pleasantly and Wainwright sings with relish about the guts of a dead skunk splattered across the road: it works the first time through, but it gets progressively less engaging with each hearing. However, this may prove to be his first hit single on the basis of its rollicking tune.

'Red Guitar' starts out intriguingly enough but ends disappointingly in a cliché of irony ('God works in wondrous ways'). 'East Indian Princess' is an unnecessarily vindictive number about an Indian girl who has anglicised herself, and it's not helped by being built on the chord changes of 'Sweet Little Sixteen'. 'Muse Blues' is a passable blues parody, in which he sounds at one point like Van Morrison, but it repeats itself too much. 'B Side' is another song, about bees this time, where the humour wears thin after a few plays.

The album's own B side, however, does have a couple of excellent tracks. The only non-Wainwright composition, Leiber & Stoller's 'Smokey Joe's Café', is handled in a chunkily infectious way. And 'New Paint', a song about trying to conform to the processes of the conventional boy-girl relationship, is a welcome throwback to his thwarted, mixed-up, James Dean glumness.

***

Michael Joseph have published *The Songs of Paul Simon* in a lavish softback format costing £2.95. It comprises some sixty songs from 'Hey Schoolgirl' to the last piece on his solo album, 'Congratulations', with music and guitar tablature, and the lyrics also printed separately. There are in addition photographs sprinkled generously throughout the text, including some very amusing ones of the Simon & Garfunkel teenybopper days. And an introduction by Simon himself.

This latter is far more interesting than the customary foreword. In it he describes the genesis of most of his songs: 'Once I pick a key and start to play, I sing any words that come into my head without trying to make any sense out of them. I tend to sing easy words with a concentration on 'oos' and 'ah' sounds, which are musically pleasing to me. I also like words beginning with 'g's' and 'l's' and words that have 't's' and 'k's' in them. Sometimes during this stream of consciousness singing, a phrase will develop that has a naturalness and a meaning, in which case I keep it and start to build a song around it'.

Most serious pop songs are probably written in this manner, or something very akin to it. It explains the frequently cryptic and puzzling lyrics that abound in today's music, and is a caution against trying to do an I.A. Richards on them. Later in the introduction Simon mentions that the title of 'Mother and Child Reunion' was pinched from a menu in a Chinese restaurant: it was the name of a boiled egg and fried chicken dish ...

Having all the songs in one's lap only confirms my feeling that Simon has never quite made it as a songwriter, except for six or seven of the songs on *Bookends*. Shorn of the very excellent performances and production that this body of work has received, and reduced to cold print, it looks sadly anaemic. But it's been treated very handsomely by the publishers.

Tuesday, 17 April 1973

MUSIC TO HEAR

Mahavishnu Orchestra/*Birds of Fire*
Seatrain/*Watch*

ANOTHER ALBUM BY the Mahavishnu Orchestra has appeared and it will surely confirm their position as the most prodigiously accomplished most advanced and dynamic force in contemporary rock music. You can't do the funky chicken to them. They make the worst possible background music for small talk. What they offer to a society more inundated with 'music' than any other in history is something shocking: music for listening to!

The album is called *Birds of Fire* (on CBS 65321) and it's a straight continuation of the last one, *Inner Mounting Flame*. The metaphor of fiery ascension in these titles is apt for the content of their work. They like to soar and then glide and then soar again, each relaxation of tension allowing an accumulation of intensity, till by the end a terrific power has developed. Billy Cobham's snare drum and cymbals provide the ballast for these flights, but each of the other instruments is astonishingly mobile, switching from rhythm to ensemble to solo playing with lightning rapidity.

Thus Rick Laird's bass, for example, is able to open 'One Word' with a long eloquent improvisation, the other instruments adding little decorative touches: this eventually relaxes into a riff over which John McLaughlin's guitar and Jerry Goodman's violin trade fast coiling phrases. These build to a raucous crescendo which again relaxes, this time into a Cobham drum solo. And the new energy generated by that allows the growth of the awesome conclusion.

All of which goes to demonstrate the impossibility of describing such music. So I'll content myself with a few random observations. McLaughlin, having worked many times with jazz trumpet master Miles Davis, includes here a Davis number, 'Miles Beyond'. It's most remarkable for a Goodman passage in pizzicato. Another innovation is keyboards man Jan Hammer's use of a Moog in the slow number 'Sanctuary'. He handles it with sensitive restraint. McLaughlin himself throws in a fuzzbox solo in a piece called (characteristically) 'Celestial Terrestrial Commuters'.

Many people are scared off this kind of music because it's alleged to be 'difficult'. But the Mahavishnu, whilst challenging you with their virtuosity, the audacity of their inventions, the sheer emotional barrage of their music are never far from familiar rhythmic structures and harmonic progressions. They do in fact slide into them when it serves a purpose to do so, as here on 'Open Country Joy' and 'Resolution' (the titles indicate the purpose in each case). Their very originality is to rehabilitate and to make new the old familiar forms of our popular music tradition.

***

A much less Olympian but nonetheless enjoyable group is Seatrain. Having started out on the Band wagon (I know, but it's the Spring) they have resolved into a group of good-time honky-tonk sophisticates. Their latest album *Watch* (WB K46222, due for release this month) even begins with a party-noise background, and at several points in it they sound just like a jug band. 'Bloodshot Eyes', for instance, has a real Jim Kweskin lyric ('Don't you roll those bloodshot eyes at me') and features a tuba, a kazoo and the ubiquitous barroom piano.

The best tracks are a rousing version of Dylan's 'Watching the River Flow' and Al Kooper's 'Flute Thing'. This latter number is a throwback to that pioneering group of 1964-67, the Blues Project. It's a shimmering, spritely piece, done at least as well here as on the original Blues Project album. The flutes of Andy Kulberg and Jill Shires are as limpid and airy as can be, and they do a marvellous free passage in the middle of the track mainly in the lower register, like the murmurations of a highly pleasurable wind.

Tuesday, 1 May 1973

SURVIVORS OF THE 60s

Faces/*Ooh La La*
Leonard Cohen/*Live Songs*

REMEMBER HOW, IN the 60s, we were always being bombarded with 'new faces'? Face was a key word. Having face was having style, being utterly of the moment—with it—on display, acting David Hemmings photographing Jean Shrimpton posing on the set of Julie Christie's new film. The Mods called their pop idols 'faces', and one of their groups responded by naming themselves the Small Faces.

It all referred to the primacy of appearance, image, the media being the messages, just as in the Elizabethan comedy of humours. Today's lurid narcissists, like David Bowie and Marc Bolan, are the Jacobean fag-ends of the movement, a degeneration into sexual melodrama, vapid and joyless.

But some heroes of the sixties have matured into serene survivors, and amongst them are Rod ('The Mod') Stewart and his Faces. Maybe elegance is not quite the word for a man with the hairstyle of the Greater Crested Grebe and the Voice That Smoked A Thousand Cigarettes. Even so, in the gloss of the music, in its seemingly effortless panache, there is a considerable degree of deliberate fastidiousness, finesse ... style in fact.

A lot of this originated with Chuck Berry, and the Faces have done the most stylish new version of a classic Berry song. Their own writing is often like latter-day Berry, as in the single 'Cindy Incidentally', with that distinctive chugging tempo and lyrics like a short play ('Cindy get your coat on, leave the rent with the gent in the penthouse.')

***

This is included on their latest album, *Ooh La La* (Warner Bros. K56011), the delights of which begin on the sleeve: it sports the face of a gentleman in evening dress whose mouth and eyes move if you squeeze the top of the album down. When you tire of this, you can turn to the more substantial pleasure of the first track, a raucous jeu d'esprit called 'Silicone Grown', about a lady who's got more front than the 'Haig Museum'.

Far from treating the other Faces as a backup band, Rod Stewart sits out on three of the album's ten tracks, and on 'Flags and Banners' he just plays rhythm guitar, leaving the vocals to bass player Ronnie Lane. This is an admirable strategy: Lane has a lighter voice, closer to folksong technique than to Stewart's abrasive urban style, and it is much more suitable for this odd, engaging song. Lane also plays highly attractive bass lines, and the two songs here which he wrote himself—'Glad and Sorry' and 'Just Another Honky'—have very infectious laid-back melodies which are clearly developed out of his own bass phrasing.

The Faces are one of those bands who devote themselves to a tightly-meshed and yet fluid ensemble sound, and it sustains them through even such a fundamentally dull instrumental as 'Fly in the Ointment', which opens Side 2 of this album. They can play quite tenderly, as in 'If I'm On The Late Side', and they can play stomping, driving, hardcore stuff, which they do on 'Borstal Boys'. This opens with the noise of a hooter which is incorporated into the music, and it proceeds as a real old delinquent rocker.

But the best song on the record is the title track, Lane's and Ronnie Wood's 'Ooh La La'. It's about the singer's grandad warning him of female wiles, of the onstage glitter and the backstage reality of the can-can dancers. Although they're in Ray Davies and Paul McCartney territory here, there is neither parody nor manufactured nostalgia in the song. The past is simply a natural part of everybody's vocabulary, and they treat it with the same polished cheerfulness as everything else. This is a beguiling song on a very beguiling album.

***

Much can be said on both sides about Leonard Cohen's songwriting. But I would have thought that all were agreed on the congenital deficiencies of his singing—the man is endowed, like most of us, with a voice fit for exercising only in the bath.

Studio production can do, and in this case has done, an extraordinary cosmetic job. But who on earth decided to put out an album of his live performances? It's called *Live Songs* (on CBS 65224) and apart from one new deadpan song called 'Queen Victoria', recorded in 'a room in Tennessee', it's entirely atrocious.

Tuesday, 15 May 1973

MAGNIFICENT SEVEN

Manassas/*Down the Road*
Led Zeppelin/*House of the Holy*

MY FAVOURITE ALBUM of last year was the double one on the Atlantic label which marked the debut of the Stephen Stills group, Manassas. I negotiated a daring journey across war-torn Belfast specially to see them on a friend's colour television. I very nearly flew to London just to catch their concert at the Rainbow until reminded of the air fare. Their album has been on my turntable at least once a week since it came out, and its shine remains untarnished. In short, I'm a fan.

What I like about this particular magnificent seven is that they stick to a conventional line-up of guitars, keyboards and percussion, and play music which is eclectic without being faceless, simple but never inane: in fact, it has its own distinctive and unmistakable sound. Of all the good groups involved in a middle-tempo mellow kind of rock, emphasising the pedal-steel drawl of country music and close-harmony singing—like the Byrds, Burritos, Poco and most recently the Eagles—I find Manassas to be supreme.

Picture my delight, then, in laying hands on their second album, *Down the Road* (Atlantic K40440), which has just come out. It's much skimpier than the first—just two sides, totalling under 30 minutes of music—and it's altogether a more lightweight production, with no song suites or extended pieces, But it's still the choicest morsel for many a day.

It kicks off with the familiar solid beat laid dawn by Dallas Taylor's drums and Joe Lala's percussion, in a Stills number called 'Isn't It About Time'. This is in the same vein of social commentary as the previous opener, 'The Song of Love', and it employs the words of the title in a strong, vivid chorus. Next comes a Chris Hillman song, 'Lies'. Hillman's voice is an excellent complement to that of Stills, earnest and slightly mournful, and well suited to the rather bitter lyrics about betrayal in this piece.

***

Still's taste for Latin-American music, well served by Joe Lala's congas and timbales, is fully indulged on this record. The third song, 'Pensamiento', is sung and spoken in Spanish in a high, impassioned voice, and with the most birdlike of flute solos by guest Sydney George.

Side 2 has another such song called 'Guaguanco De Vero'. Its chorus is sung by the whole group in a smooth, seamless close harmony: at one point they stop all the accompaniment except percussion and continue to sing it half-a-dozen more times, and this is a highlight of the album.

'So Many Times' is a slow and melting country waltz, full of plucked mandolin and soft harmony, rather like 'Jesus Gave Love Away For Free' on the first album. 'Business on the Street' picks the tempo up again, with the backing voices shadowing that of the lead singer much in the style that Lennon's voice used to be echoed by those of McCartney, Starr and Harrison. The opener on Side 2 is a succinct little piece called 'Do You Remember the Americans?' with a succession of instruments dominating the accompaniment, the banjo yielding to the pedal steel guitar which is followed by acoustic guitar and then mandolin. Very different is 'Down the Road', a drug blues for which Stills adopts a gravelly voice, funky low guitar phrases and the backup singing of Pat Arnold.

Naturally, the album has flaws. 'City Junkies' is a choppy affair, with rather monotonous piano and uncharacteristically rough harmony singing. On the last number, 'Rollin' My Stone', there's a backdrop of echoing guitar and organ noise which makes for a very muddy sound, though this may be partly the fault of my machine. I can foresee, though, that the sound throughout will be a great deal muddier by the time I've got tired of playing this album.

***

Led Zeppelin are an enormously popular group, and their current album *Houses of the Holy* (Atlantic K50014) has been wildly successful, just like their previous ones. I had intended to speculate on why I find them most uninteresting. But the answer's simple: all the genuine rock artists have had some dimension of humour in their work. *Houses Of The Holy* contains a single attempt at a joke, at the end of Side 1, and it dies the death. Led Zeppelin are a humourless bore.

Tuesday, 29 May 1973

LOOKING BACK

Paul Simon/*There Goes Rhymin' Simon*
Alan Price/*O Lucky Man Soundtrack*

THE ONE DEFINITE trend of this decade so far is nostalgia for other decades. The nineties, twenties, thirties, forties and fifties have all been plundered for fashions and sounds and television serials. Mary Quant is now reported to be preparing a museum exhibition of the sixties (with herself perhaps as a major exhibit).

The new Paul Simon album (CBS 69035) has a streak of nostalgia for earlier forms of popular music—it's the excuse for the title, *There Goes Rhymin' Simon*—but he has placed it in the service of his own contemporary ideas, and the result is a highly individual, tightly packed album, much better than his first solo effort.

The first lines of the first song ('When I think back/On all the crap I learned in high school') dispel any forebodings about sentimentality which might have been aroused by the grubby photo of teenybopper Simon on the sleeve. Apart from 'Take Me to the Mardi Gras', all of the lyrics are nervy, sceptical, New York-ish, often dramatising a situation wittily or mournfully—Simon at his most characteristic and best. Two of the songs contain writing as true as anything he's done. 'Tenderness' is a quiet, telling reproach to a woman:

Much of what you say is true...
But there's no tenderness
Beneath your honesty.

In a different vein altogether is an agitated monologue by a tenant in a large apartment building, called 'One Man's Ceiling Is Another Man's Floor'.

The nostalgia lies in the deployment of musical sounds. In 'Tenderness' and 'Loves Me Like A Rock', Simon has used the vocal backing of a venerable black close-harmony group called the Dixie Hummingbirds. In 'Mardi Gras' he uses the Onward Brass Band from New Orleans and the beautiful falsetto gospel voice of the Reverend Claude Jeter. In 'Something So Right' he has brought in Quincy Jones to do a movies-style string arrangement.

***

All of this sounds fey and fussy but it has the same rationale as Simon's peregrinations around the recording studios of the western world (most of these tracks were done at Muscle Shoals Studios in Alabama). He collects different sounds, and different kinds of sound in order to create a very personal patchwork. My only regret about this album is his rip-off from the Bach cantata 'O sacred head, sore wounded' for use as the pretentious and wrongly entitled 'American Tune'.

Without having actually seen the Lindsay Anderson film *O Lucky Man*, it's difficult to know precisely how the Alan Price music and songs function in it. But on the strength of the album of the original soundtrack (WB K46227) it seems likely that Price has evolved a new genre: the film song which is condemned neither to be aural wallpaper behind the credits (or some vivid action passage), nor to be rudely forced as a nightclub or stage performance into the action.

As a matter of fact, it has to be confessed that I've read two magazine features about the film, seen Alan Price interviewed on TV, and caught a few clips of the film itself. So I happen to know that the songs, performed by Price and a group of musicians in a studio, are simply slotted into the film between certain episodes—a sort of objective cabaret/chorus.

***

This allows them to be good songs in their own right, and they are. With the sole exception of his marvellous treatment of the Randy Newman song 'Simon Smith and the Amazing Dancing Bear', Price's work has been rather aimless since the original Animals broke up. But in these songs he comes into his own. They have a wry, worldly realism which at no point sounds affected and is often very funny, as in the Price version of nostalgia, about the corner of the hometown street where he used to stand with his mates:

And sing the old songs,
We called them dole songs.

The musicianship throughout has a fastidious simplicity. In fact, the only feature of the album which marks it as a soundtrack is that there are a mere seven songs in all (the title song is reprised). Even though the instrumental tracks are played with finesse and imagination, the album does feel unduly abbreviated. But maybe not after seeing the film.

Tuesday, 12 June 1973

LATTER-DAY COWBOYS

The Eagles/*Desperado*
Arlo Guthrie/*Last of the Brooklyn Cowboys*

IN A RECENT despatch, I expressed a preference for the Stephen Stills group Manassas over all those other bands working in the same approximate idiom: namely, a mellow rock sound emphasising the pedal steel drawl of country music and close-harmony singing. 'Country rock' is too restricting a term for it, and 'soft rock' makes it sound no more virile than a stick of that well-known Edinburgh confection, whereas it's a dynamic and exciting kind of music.

Anyway, Stills has been (if you'll pardon the expression) instrumental in developing this style, through his work with Buffalo Springfield, Crosby Stills Nash & Young, and now Manassas. These bands, along with the Byrds, have exerted an enormous influence and one of the most recent groups to show it has been the Eagles, a five-man outfit from California which is extremely popular in the States, though less well-known here.

To judge from the Eagles' LP *Desperado* (Asylum SYL 9011) they are one of those country-influenced groups who believe strongly in simplicity. Apart from a mouth-organ phrase at the start, and an intrusion of strings on one track, they never move outside guitars, bass and drums, with occasional banjo and mandolin licks. All of their attention is directed towards playing these classic instruments with polished togetherness, and they do so very agreeably. The electric guitar playing is particularly smooth. I think Bernie Leadon is the guitarist but no credits are listed.

As to lyrics, the album is a suite of cowboy songs full of conventional cowboy sentiments. The lads appear on the sleeve duded up as cowhands in yet another sepia-tinted mock up of the Old West. A large number of rock performers like to think of themselves as latter-day cowboys, and the identification is constantly hinted at here: 'a life on the road/Is the life of an outlaw man.'

This is a potentially interesting theme, but little is made of it. We're told about Doolin Dalton riding into town for a showdown, about the saloon getting out of control, about the loveless life of the desperado all within a sequence of highly predictable chord progressions. There is a wallow in glorious maudlin called 'Tequilla Sunrise' which stands up to several plays, and another such called 'Saturday Night' which is even more lachrymose and somehow incorporates a quotation from Yeats. The only two numbers which really demand attention are 'Certain Kind of Fool' and 'Bitter Creek": the words of these are sung as though they were meant, and there's attention paid to dynamics and texture. 'Bitter Creek' creates a particularly good interplay between solo and backup voices.

Stills has demonstrated that this kind of pop song can be an effective mode of self-expression and can also be musically rich. The Eagles have got the expertise and their album is easy on the ear, but they don't appear to have a lot to say, nor do they draw sufficiently on their musical resources.

***

The cowboy fantasy is indulged on Arlo Guthrie's new album as well. It's called *Last of the Brooklyn Cowboys* (on Reprise K44236) but it has in truth only the one cowpoke ditty, with the refrain:

> It ain't right and it ain't wrong
> To hear a cowboy sing an
> old-time song,

which is unquestionably true.

The rest of the album is an odd and disarming ragbag. It begins with Sligo fiddler Kevin Burke playing the reel 'Farrell O'Gara', proceeds with Arlo singing a heavily orchestrated 'Gipsy Davey' (attributed to his father Woody, when even I know how old it is), and continues on its crooked way with popular songs of the '20s, '30s and '40s, including the old yodelling hill-billy number, 'Lovesick Blues'.

Side 2 opens with Dylan's 'The Gates of Eden' sung in Guthrie's relaxed and rather deliberate way. Then there are a couple of his own cherubic compositions, one of his father's, and Kevin Burke doing another reel along with Ry Cooder on bottle-neck guitar and Arlo on banjo.

I forgot to mention the piano rag which Arlo plays on Side 1, rather efficiently, in conjunction with bassoon, clarinet, oboe and flute. Monotonous this kid is not.

Wednesday, 27 June 1973

EMOTIONAL CRISIS

Jo Jo Gunne/*Bite Down Hard*
Judee Sill/*Heart Food*

MAYBE THE REAL energy crisis in Western society is going to be an emotional one. Just now (through eyes that are admittedly under-slept) the world of cities looks debilitated and done. Such human energy as remains appears to be wholly malignant: energy to murder, spy, blackmail, betray, exploit. Gratuitous and prolonged violence is ruling the box offices—vicarious energy for impotent audiences, presumably. Creative energy is extremely scarce, and supplies may well run out long before oil does.

This is all in connection with two new record albums on a label piquantly called Asylum. They're entitled *Bite Down Hard* (SYL 9005) and *Heart Food* (SYL 9006). The former is the work of a group called Jo Jo Gunne, whose name comes from a song by Chuck Berry: whose music in turn expressed and released the kind of elementary creative energy of which this society is drained. That, in fact, was the original, miraculous appeal of rock and roll. It had the pulse of life itself; it was unrefined, joyful, crude energy.

Jo Jo Gunne, who grew out of another group called Spirit, have tried to sustain this quality in their music. They did so very effectively on their debut album (SYLA 8752) of last year, playing unadorned, driving ensemble stuff, which retained the primal matter but managed as well to be musically interesting and verbally vivid. *Bite Down Hard* disappoints in comparison. The energy now sounds a bit manufactured and spurious.

The most noticeable signs of this are the introduction of a synthesizer on '60 Minutes to Go' and the over-indulgence in spacey echo and electronic distortion on tracks like 'Rhoda' and 'Special Situations'. There's also a slight degree of campiness present, for example in the title 'Rock Around the Symbol', which opens with a cymbal marking the offbeat. And I think it's time for sanctions to be introduced against all poems about writing poems, novels about novel-writing, and rock songs about rock singing, like '60 Minutes to Go'. Narcissism is the last word in boredom.

The best tracks here are the most unaffected: 'Ready Freddy', 'Take Me Down Easy' and 'Wait A Lifetime', which is a slowish number using piano arpeggios for the verses and a good bluesy mouth organ in the choruses. This last number is welcome relief from the relentless monotony of tempo in the other songs, which again contrasts disappointingly with their first album. Maybe the problem is the replacement of Mark Andes on bass by Jimmie Randall. But it seems more likely that they've mined their particular vein to exhaustion.

***

Heart Food is also a second album, from singer-song-writer Judee Sill, but in her case it marks an advance. Her first LP suffered from the over-lavish attentions of three producers and two orchestrators. This one she herself co-produced with Henry Lewy, and the gain in sensitivity and symmetry is remarkable. Also, the songs on her first album were concoctions of occult, psychedelic and Biblical imagery which appeared merely to be reflecting fashionable trends in a diffuse and rather obscurantist manner. These new songs, on the other hand, are explicitly religious and employ the familiar language of Christian mysticism.

Inevitably a suspicion of Jesus Freakishness is aroused, especially as the credits extend special thanks to God. But there's nothing crass or excessive about the songs. They all have a genuinely hymnal quality, with strong, flowing melodies harmonised often intricately in three and four parts. And without borrowing anything from black gospel music they still manage to be songs in the popular tradition, though in a highly disconcerting way.

It's disconcerting enough to be reminded of St John of the Cross and Anglo-Saxon devotional verse by songs with titles like 'When the Bridegroom Comes', 'The Phoenix' and 'The Pearl'. But weirder still are the pioneer and cowboy elements which Judee Sill mixes into her highly subjective mythology, and the pronounced Californian accent in which she delivers it all.

Clearly this is not a sound likely to evoke mass hysteria, but it's extraordinarily successful on its own terms, and certainly quite unique. The only really large mistake comes at the very end, in a rather subtle processional song called 'The Donor', where she sings a series of kyrie eleisons. These are words which already bear too heavy a religious and cultural burden to be appropriate for this context.

Otherwise, Judee Sill is a prime exponent of the principle that the devil is not entitled to all the best tunes.

Tuesday, 10 July 1973

SIXTIES STYLE

Shaun Davey & James Morris/*Davey and Morris*
Buddy Miles/*Chapter VII*

THE YORK RECORD label is a small subsidiary of Decca which seems to specialise in finding and recording good new artists from these islands. They've just put out an album by the duo of Shaun Davey and James Morris (*Davey and Morris* FYK 417) supported by eight excellent English and Irish musicians. Two old Strawbs are involved—Tony Hooper producing and Richard Hudson drumming—and there's an assortment of strings and keyboards (Donal Lunny is credited with one of the year's more eccentric set of instruments, namely banjo, bouzouki and bodhran).

Like most of York's output, the sleeve is very plain, minimum info or promo. Expectations are aroused of something folksy, worthy and cheerless, and confirmation of this seems imminent from the chugging, unimaginative guitar chords which open the first song, 'Town Crier'.

But no sooner is the ear composed for slumber than it begins to notice the rather cunning chord progressions heavily underlined by Morris's thudding bass, and then the pleasantly warm voice. By the time the banjo and harmonica make their entrances, the song has established a strong presence. What we have here, it transpires, is a nice surprise, a light rock album bereft of pretentiousness and full of variety.

The noticeable influences are impeccable. There's a very attractive song called 'Window', surrealistic ruminations through an open window wedded to a sensual, funky guitar strut, a combination that can only be called Lennonesque. There's a touch of the McCartneyesque too, particularly in the opener to Side 2, a mournful and lavish number called 'Who Stole My Land', with the big orchestral sound on the chorus. 'Grape Street' has something of the style and sentiments of one of Bob Dylan's 115 dreams, and there are two songs reminiscent of the Mike Heron/Robin Williamson sound, 'Blue Smoke' and 'Ishkamir'. This last piece has mystic Eastern lyrics so demented that it sounds like parody, but it also has very tasty passages of fiddle and viola playing.

Davey and Morris have assimilated these first-class influences: there's nothing narrowly derivative about the album. Nor is it a denigration of their work to say that it's rooted in the mid-1960s, at least for those of us who were of age during that burgeoning era. 'You Come Now', in particular, sports a group sound and lyrics that already have almost a period flavour.

The only flaws in this album are poor sound balance on some tracks and a Side 2 that's decidedly weaker than Side 1. 'Hey Susie' has vocal and instrumental tracks slightly out of tune with each other, an overall dragging of feet, and extraordinarily weak singing on the chorus, as though the lads were doing their first audition. 'Banjo' also has uncertain vocals. It's as though the Side 2 cuts had been rushed through with limited studio time in hand.

Nevertheless, this is a refreshing set of songs and I look forward to more.

***

Buddy Miles and his band have come out with their *Chapter VII* (On CBS 65406) in a vile sleeve done up to look like a studded, tooled leather book. Having missed out on the previous six chapters, I've no pre-conceptions about the music, except the vague impression that it has never been too well received by the critics; which treacherously predisposes me to favour it.

Miles is a large expanse of drummer who has played with many luminaries in his time—Hendrix, Carlos Santana and Stevie Wonder are all pictured inside the sleeve—and his band is a seven-piece, including brass and sax. On the whole the band sounds musically capable of taking off if given its head. But on virtually all of the tracks it's constricted by monotonous and static arrangements.

Unexceptional, then—but also unexceptionable, nice enough road-band textures and crisp playing to hold the attention. All except for one number of stultifying inanity, which unfortunately happens to be the last and the longest (at 6 minutes, 20 seconds). It's an embarrassing, maundering thing called 'There Was a Time'. It has the effect of a drunken, exhibitionist bore at the fag-end of a party telling you his life story.

Tuesday, 24 July 1973

GREEN ELEGIES

Benny Green/*Drums in My Ears*

BENNY GREEN IS one of those Sunday paper reviewers from whom I took my opinions when I was a teenager. In his case the opinions were about jazz. He accorded the subject a breadth of vocabulary and an elegance of style to which it was far from accustomed. At the same time he was himself a practising musician, whose baritone could be detected amongst the sax section of many's a British group. He knew music, he knew the scene too, he was discerning, he was witty but in earnest, and it pains me now to state the conclusion that he was fundamentally wrong.

Drums in My Ears (Davis-Poynter, £2.50) is a collection of his reviews from the late fifties up to last year, arranged into chapters entitled 'Saxophones', 'Avant Garde', 'The Singer Not The Song' and suchlike. It allows the reader to locate precisely the Green articles of faith. Preeminent amongst these is the belief that jazz is a unique art form: 'While the rest of the arts have been cooking over a slow fire for a few thousand years jazz has been thrust into the pressure cooker of contemporary life, so that it has moved from primitivism to neoclassicism in fifty years'.

The first thing wrong with that is the implication that 'contemporary life' is an era unto itself, and the few thousand years preceding it a quite different era, whereas the truth is that the past fifty years, however extraordinary and momentous, are still only a half-century and there have been other such half-centuries. It follows that to equate the process which led from (say) cave paintings to Rubens with that which led from King Oliver to Stan Getz is comically absurd.

***

Jazz is not a major art form like painting. It is a genre of popular music, like operetta, music-hall and rock. It is organic to the history of popular music in the same way that the short story is organic to the history of literature.

Benny's faith in the autonomous stature of jazz leads him into many frustrations. He adopts a highly elitist position, in which some of his most treasured jazz is seen as 'a music too esoteric for marketing on a mass scale'. When this position is caricatured by the vapid pretentiousness of Dave Brubeck or the dinnerjacket solemnity of the Modern Jazz Quartet he becomes excessively wrathful and expands a disproportionate amount of time in excoriating these unfortunate. Goldwater is Nixon's fiercest critic, by the same token.

But a further frustration is provided by the fact that even some of this music is enjoyable—Paul Desmond's alto for example, and John Lewis's compositions. The case of Lewis leads Green into that ultimate dead-end of his philosophy: '... I found the performance of 'Pierrot' a genuine creative experience. It is indeed magnificent, but it is not jazz.' Instantly there floods back into the memory a thousand sterile arguments about what is or is not jazz. Goodbye to all that.

So far as Benny Green is concerned, jazz is Lester Young and Charlie

Parker, Coleman Hawkins and Zoot Sims, a form of music which takes the melodic inventiveness of composers like Cole Porter or Jerome Kern and improvises from it with considerable harmonic virtuosity and mellifluousness, usually upon some species of saxophone.

***

I share his love of such music: but regret the exclusiveness of his attitudes to it. As the book comes closer to the present day, the tone becomes increasingly elegiac and the attitudes increasingly preposterous, e.g. 'The welcome reappearance of the bossa nova albums confirms the view that while the music industry spent the 1960s being distracted by loud noises from the nursery the real innovations in the composition and treatment of popular songs were taking place elsewhere'.

Apart from acting as a refreshment for Stan Getz, bossa nova was of minimal importance to anyone and died the quick death of a thousand similar fads. It was a narcotic for tired industrialists, and a commercial, dishonest fantasy about life in Brazil. To elevate it above the work of John McLaughlin, Joni Mitchell, Jack Bruce, Keith Emerson, Paul Simon—random examples of excellent rock musicianship and/or composing—is the last infirmity of a noble mind.

Wednesday, 8 August 1973

ALIVE AND WELL

Johnny Winter/*Still Alive and Well*
Natural Acoustic Band/*Branching In*

JOHNNY WINTER BELONGS to that sad band of gifted people whose careers have been blighted by drugs. For a long time he was out of action altogether, undergoing hospital treatment after a collapse. His comeback has been launched with an album confidently entitled *Still Alive and Well* (CBS 65484).

Rick Derringer has remained a loyal collaborator of Winter's and so has bassist Randy Hobbs. Derringer, who wrote the best-ever Winter song, 'Rock And Roll Hoochie Koo', has contributed two compositions to this new record and a smattering of his highly accomplished guitar work, as well as producing the album. I'll swear that he also is the lead singer on the anonymous country number 'Ain't Nothing To Me', and possibly on his own 'Cheap Tequila'.

The album is very like previous Winter efforts—his work has not been impaired since the crack-up, but neither has it noticeably developed. There's the same throat-tearing vocals, the same fluent but constantly abrasive guitar breaks, the same pervasive harshness and attack. It's monochromatic music, brilliantly done within its narrow limits but wearing in large doses. And if a particular song itself happens to be melodically anaemic, the style becomes grindingly monotonous.

This applies to the two Mick Jagger/Keith Richard songs on the record, most especially to 'Silver Train' (due on the new Stones album) which achieves the same continuous sneer and muddiness of sound which the Stones favour, but without their personal schtick. 'Let It Bleed' is slightly better—it's a slightly better song—but still not a success.

While we're on the poorer tracks, I may as well mention the title song, 'Still Alive and Well', which Derringer presumably wrote especially for Winter's return. It may be good therapy, but it has an infantile tune and never gets near lifting off. Winter's own blues 'Too Much Seconal', is pretty scrappy, with Jeremy Steig overdoing the heavy-breathing-and-humming-into-the-flute trick; but it has an attractive mandolin obbligato by Winter.

The other tracks are much stronger. The old Arthur Crudup/Willie Broonzy song, 'Rock Me Baby', is classically transformed from a drawling blues into a bullet-like rock number. 'Cheap Tequila' is a full-blooded lament for an ageing lady on the skids. Winter plays some beautiful slide guitar licks on 'Rock and Roll', and Derringer shows his skill on the pedal steel model in 'Ain't Nothing To Me'.

On the whole, though, I could wish that Johnny Winter had some of the eclecticism of his brother Edgar, whose recent album (*They Only Come Out At Night*) is a far more attractive and entertaining proposition than *Still Alive and Well*.

***

I've finally caught up with the album *Branching In* (RCA Victor SF8314) by the Natural Acoustic Band, an English trio which has enjoyed good notices. Their most notable feature is Krysia Kocjan, a diminutive little girl with an astonishingly big voice, virtually operatic in its range and power.

She plunges you in medias res with the opening track, a passionate vocal outpouring entitled 'Running Into Changes'. Her writing is sometimes equally fine: 'Money', the best song on the album, is a trenchant piece of social commentary, in which Money is personified as a successful London model. I also like her 'Moontime Writer' ('Word machine by your bed/Alone in the city/So much to be said'). Her other two compositions 'Little Leaf' and 'Road to the Sun', are in a more familiar folksy-sweet vein which is pleasant enough but rather wet.

The remaining members of the trio, Tom Hoy and Robin Thyne, are not in the same league as Krysia. In particular their harmony singing is highly uncertain—'Follow Your Love' is excruciating. But they play their various instruments capably enough and they certainly don't sabotage the album, which is several cuts above the usual English folk-rock output.

Tuesday, 21 August 1973

RELIGIOUS REVELATIONS

Carlos Santana & Mahavishnu John McLaughlin/
Love Devotion Surrender

THE ROAD TO Damascus is heavily trodden by the artistes of popular music. Music being an activity of the soul and pop stardom conversely involving such carnal excesses, performers as a group are peculiarly susceptible to salvation. This can be quite hilarious, as with the long succession of evil rock & roll stars in the late 50s who suddenly found Jesus (Tom Matthews has a fine poem about such a figure, in his Ulsterman Publications pamphlet, 'Foolstop':

I wish he had died like Buddy
and Eddie
Oh Teenangels
His latter-day happiness appals
me).

But it can also be a valid and deeply-felt response to a personal reality, as with the beboppers in the 40s and 50s who adopted the Muslim faith and the new identity that went with it.

Considered in isolation, a performer's religious revelations may strike most people as preposterous, just as (say) Yeats's attitudes to the occult were preposterous. But it's the music that counts—if it's authentic, the rest is mere footnotes.

A good example is the John Coltrane album, 'A Love Supreme', one of the great jazz achievements of the past 15 years. The liner notes were written by Coltrane in embarrassing, religiose free verse and led one to anticipate the earnest heartiness of a gospel hall. Instead, there were two continuous sides of astonishingly simple, virile music, executed with such conviction that it holds your breathless attention. It expresses both affirmation and intense searching, universal emotions which will draw a response from anyone, whatever their faith or lack of of it.

***

All these weighty observations arise from the appearance of a new album called *Love Devotion Surrender* (CBS 69037) which brings together two highly celebrated guitarists, Carlos Santana of the group called Santana and John McLaughlin of the Mahavishnu Orchestra. They're pictured on the cover dressed in white, beatifically posed, in the company of their guru, whose full name appears to be Sri Chinmoy Lighthouse.

The title of the album comes from Sri Chinmoy, whose essay on Love, Devotion and Surrender constitutes the liner notes. This essay packs in quite a range of quotations—St Augustine, Shaw, Dante, St Francis and Tagore—but otherwise its platitudes seem to me as unexceptionable and as nearly meaningless as anybody else's.

The music, however, is an intriguing combination of the airy spaciness which Santana achieved on their last album, *Caravanserai*, and the blistering assault which characterises McLaughlin's band. Musicians from both outfits are employed on the album: Mahavishnu's relentless drummer Billy Cobham and pianist Jan Hammer, and Santana's rock-solid bassist Doug Rauch and percussionist James Lewis. Also featured are Khalid Yasin (Larry Young) on piano and Armando Peraza on congas.

And what should the first number be but Coltrane's 'A Love Supreme'. Since this takes its departure from a simple four-note phrase repeated liturgically, everything depends on what you make of it; and what is made of it here is inevitably something less potent than the original, more manufactured, an act of homage rather than a new insight.

But the dialogue between the two guitars, which gets underway here, is thoroughly fascinating. Carlos Santana works a lot with sustained notes, with overtones and feedback, with trills, and passages in the lower registers—he's a mainstream rock guitarist. McLaughlin is the virtuoso, screaming away at breakneck speed. Each shows up the other's limitations: Santana's paucity of original invention, and McLaughlin's lack of nuance or subtle finesse. One elegantly savours a rather restricted vocabulary, whilst the other gabbles away eloquently on a single topic. They're well matched.

The second track is another Coltrane piece, 'Naima'. This is done beautifully on acoustic guitars, but again is more homage than discovery. 'The Life Divine' is a McLaughlin original and they're able to extend themselves more freely on it. Side 2 has just two tracks, a very long and rather over-indulgent piece called 'Let Us Go Into The House of the Lord' and a tenderly lyrical 'Meditation'.

Tuesday, 4 September 1973

A TRIO FROM THE MOORS

Back Door/*Back Door*

THE DEBUT ALBUM *Back Door* (WB K46231) by the group of the same name is a pleasurable surprise, but it carries with it one of the most uproarious blurbs ever to disgrace a record sleeve: ' ... when Colin Hodgkinson and Ron Aspery traded the rat race of London for the provincial seclusion of Redcar and conscripted Tony Hicks from nearby Middlesborough, little did they envisage that they were about to direct a totally different outlook on what we know as contemporary music.' This and much more comes from an article by Roy Carr of the *New Musical Express*, which is reprinted on the sleeve along with several other such puffs from the trade journals.

Still Back Door are a publicist's dream—a progressive musical trio who set up as resident group in the picturesque Lion Inn on the Yorkshire moors, endure a string of rebuffs from the record companies, finally record an album by themselves, selling it through friends and topers, until it trickles through to the London critics, who go into such ecstasies that the plucky trio are signed by the great Warner Brothers: the final Hollywod touch. It sounds too good to be true, and it is. Back Door are not the new Cream nor the new breakthrough in popular music. They're an excellent trio who play fifties-style small-group jazz with later embellishments, in a style which combines wit, whimsy and finesse. It's music to be relished and cherished, but—or maybe therefore—I can't see it making the lads into superstars.

***

Hodgkinson plays fender bass, Aspery plays alto and soprano saxes and flute, and Hicks plays drums. And no sooner had I listened to a few bars of their fluent, thoughtful interaction, and registered titles like 'Vienna Breakdown', 'Plantagenet' and 'Waltz For A Wollum', than I was plunged into memories of such as Jimmy Giuffre and Jim Hall, Chico Hamilton and the MJQ, all those stoic exponents of Cool whose wistful, introspective and sometimes rather bland music orchestrated my adolescence. Back Door are quite squarely in this tradition but they avoid the blandness through the playing of Aspery and Hodgkinson.

Aspery is a brilliant imitator of alto sax styles and he runs through a kaleidoscope of Parker harmonies and Coltrane attack and Giuffre sweetness, never pausing long enough to plagiarise, and ending up with an expressive variety all his own.

But with Colin Hodgkinson, Back Door have their strongest claim to musical innovation. Heretofore the bass guitar has been used largely as an electric substitute for the double bass. Many players have occasionally strummed it or played the odd bit of melody on it, but essentially it has been used largely as an electric bass line underpinning the lead and rhythm guitars. Hodgkinson takes it at its word and plays it as a guitar—with harmonic, melodic and percussive functions all going on at once. The effect is dazzling, though it can probably only operate in this kind of intimate chamber setting. 'Catcote Rag' is a Hodgkinson cool piece and it really is a new experience, a twangy, virile guitar rag in a deep register, without the rather elephantine freakishness that double-bass pieces tend to have: it's more like a baritone sax as compared to an alto sax.

Tony Hicks' drumming has the right degree of intimate finesse, and the three instruments together make up a seamless garment. The numbers they play on the album are all short, a series of intimately worked cameos. They are full of catchy and witty melodies and this, combined with the versatile variety of the playing, prevents the trio format from ever becoming samey or repetitive.

My favourites are 'Plantagenet', a slow piece just for bass and flute, 'Turning Point', on which Hodgkinson does some extraordinary chording under Aspery's quirky soprano, and 'Back Door' itself, a funky strutting number full of squawks and rasps, very infectious.

Tuesday, 18 September 1973

QUAINT COMBO

John Hammond, Mike Bloomfield & Dr John/*Triumvirate*
Glencoe/*The Spirit of Glencoe*

IT SEEMS NOT unlikely that every big record company has an office called 'Supersessions' where a producer sits all day doing cost-benefit analyses of hypothetical albums like *Tiny Tim and Jimmy Osmond: A Meeting of Giants* or *Boy Meets Girl: Janis Ian and Alice Cooper.* Certainly, supersession albums continue to appear and they get odder all the time. This month we have *Triumvirate* (CBS 865659) which brings together John Hammond, Mike Bloomfield and Dr John The Night-Tripper, as quaint a combination as they come.

John Hammond—son of the famous Columbia producer who has signed up many legendary figures, including Bob Dylan—is a young blues singer and guitarist who bases his style on the classic black performers of the rural past. Mike Bloomfield is a veteran of the rock revolution, an electric guitarist who came to prominence with the Paul Butterfield Blues Band and who has freelanced around many groups since then. Dr John is really Mac Rebennack, and a unique kettle of fish gumbo indeed. He's a white, middle-aged singer and pianist who has been a feature of the New Orleans music scene for many years; his style is based on voodoo and creole sources and was for long an underground cult until the opening up of popular music in the last few years created a wider audience for it.

It's not surprising that their attempt at collaboration foundered after the first two weeks, and the project had to be started afresh. What is surprising is the degree of pleasure which the resulting album affords. Presumably the studio was gambling on the fact that all three performers were experienced and highly seasoned entertainers. If so, the gamble has paid off in regard to two elements—Rebennack's arrangements and Hammond's singing. The excellence of these, both separately and together, is what carries the recording. Bloomfield is extraneous to it—insofar as his contribution can be detected at all it seems ill at ease, and out of place.

***

There are five tracts of southern rhythm and blues which cook along irresistibly. The opener 'Cha-Dooky-Doo', has a light, infectious piano riff from Rebennack, and there's a magic moment in the middle where a guitar run is suddenly complemented by a nifty horn line. The horns—trumpet, trombone and sax—are played by long-established sidemen for whom Rebennack has written very deft and subtle charts. Side 2 opens with another of these Delta R&B numbers, a Dr John song called 'Sho 'Bout to Drive Me Wild'. It's a sultry shuffle which Hammond sings impeccably over a richly textured backing which includes a trio of girl singers and a baritone sax.

As well as these, there's a couple of straightforward blues. 'Last Night' and, B.B. King's 'Rock Me Baby' are just OK, but John Lee Hooker's 'Ground Hog Blues' sounds as if it was recorded at 4.30 a.m. with everybody in a coma. The record ends with a piece of candy floss called 'Pretty Thing', the only track which sounds like run-of-the mill pop.

Throughout Hammond sings (and plays harmonica) with the energy of a man who wants every song to be the best, and he communicates the bawdy wit and relaxed sensuality of the material very effectively. His singing, combined with the mosaic of punchy riffs and stresses which characterises Rebennack's arrangements, go to make an album as appealing to the ear as it is to the feet.

***

Glencoe are a Scottish band whose album is called 'The Spirit of Glencoe', but it has more of the spirit of Woodstock, being a set of fairly standard rock numbers with the usual lyrics about love and karma and downers and signs of the zodiac and getting high and playing in a band. The singing has the throaty tunefulness and breathy harmonies which are ubiquitous now and the musicianship is competent throughout, with stylish guitar work by John Turnbull.

Some of the tracks, however, are marred by string arrangements which are lifeless and full of dandruff. And the album as a whole lacks any special quality which would give it lasting value. It's pleasant but forgettable.

Tuesday, 2 October 1973

COUNTRY MATTERS

Kris Kristofferson & Rita Coolidge/*Full Moon*
Mike Oldfield/*Tubular Bells*

THE SUDDEN PASSION for undiluted country and western music which broke out a few years ago amongst some of the rock generation is a very odd phenomenon; and one of the oddest products of it is Kris Kristofferson. How a former Oxford Rhodes scholar with a PhD, ends up in the disguise of a rough, honest cowpoke, a bosom pal of Johnny Cash, wearing his heart of corn on his sleeve, is entirely beyond me. While the attitude of Kristofferson songs like 'The Law is for the Protection of the People' or 'Beat the Devil' are slightly more robust than those of the standard C&W dose of lachrymose selfpity, the style of delivery is the same. He's got the authentic maudlin huskiness to perfection. Which is why I only like 'Me and Bobby McGee', his most successful composition when somebody like Janis Joplin is singing it.

Rita Coolidge from Tennessee is a different case. A session singer who moved out of the chorus into the spotlight, she has a marvellously restrained tensile voice. She excels at the slow burn, at building a meditative number, phrase by sad phrase, up to a peak of controlled emotion. This is, of course, a bequest to rock from gospel music, and Rita did indeed learn her licks in the church choir.

There is no reason in the world why these two should record together—except that they are romantically intertwined. If John and Yoko, why not Kris and Rita? Their album is called *Full Moon* (A&M AMLH 64403) and it has two songs written by them jointly. The first of these, 'It's All Over (All Over Again)', is a very ordinary song in which they sing alternate lines, Rita's cool stylishness showing up the desperate groaning vocals of Kristofferson and his exaggerated phoney Southern accent. The second one, 'I'm Down (But I Keep Falling)', is much better, partly because of a strong lyric, and sensitive guitar playing by one of the many distinguished guest musicians; but mainly because Rita has control of the vocals, with her voice double-tracked.

This is the general pattern of the whole album. 'Hard To Be Friends' is again mainly Rita, with Kristofferson only coming in on harmonies, and it's an absorbing piece with wonderful suspended bass lines by Lee Sklar. 'From The Bottle To The Bottom' is a Kristofferson number, with a typical chorus:

That's the way I've been feeling,
Since the day I started falling
From the bottle to the bottom
stool by stool,
Learning hard to live with
losing you.

'Take Time to Love' is a piece they sing to one another over soupy strings, like two plastic figures in some gruesome Hollywood musical comedy. 'I Heard the Bluebirds Sing' is a hoary and innocent hillbilly number which they render lifelessly. But to be fair, there are moments throughout the album when they sing well together and at least one whole trick which came off. It's 'After The Fact', one of the few songs which moves faster than a crawl, and it stirs up a little gospel-style fire. Still, I'd rather listen to Rita's solo album, *Rita Coolidge* (A&M AMLS 2015).

***

Mike Oldfield's *Tubular Bells* (Virgin Records V2001) really is something completely different. Oldfield is half composer and half prankster, creator of a mosaic of beautiful and hilarious and sometimes tedious sounds, a kind of English Frank Zappa. He plays the piano and glockenspiel and flageolet and all manner of organs and guitars and so on, but his real instrument is the recording studio. Each side of this album is a complete composition, using multi-tracking, tape loops and all the other resources of the modern studio.

In each case he begins by building up a rich polyphony from a number of short repeated themes on the multifarious instruments, like a bank of shimmering sparkling lights. From this he works through a series of shifting textures and moods, including some very funny ones, like guitars imitating bagpipes, or Viv Stanshall introducing each instrument as it plays the theme, with the tubular bells as the climax. It's restful and good-humoured music, if a little whimsical and longwinded to stand up to a lot of playing.

Tuesday, 16 October 1973

DEXTEROUS DUTCH

Focus/*Focus at the Rainbow*

FOCUS IS THE name of a Dutch band whose unique style has won for them a unique kind of popularity: they have achieved more critical and popular success than has any other group from continental Europe. Last May they gave a concert in the Rainbow Theatre in London which was broadcast on the BBC's *Old Grey Whistle Test*. The live recording of that performance is now available on *Focus at the Rainbow* (Polydor 2442 118), and it serves as a perfect introduction to their work for those who haven't encountered their existing three or four LPs, since it features the most outstanding compositions from those albums.

The group's fluent bassist and drummer provide a very solid and responsive underpinning, but the undoubted stars of Focus are Thijs Van Leer and Jan Akkerman. Van Leer plays organ and flute and carries the major composing credits. Akkerman is the ace guitarist. Together they make music which weds the dexterity of modern jazz to the rude passion of rock, and has other qualities all their own. There's the Puckish whimsy of Van Leer's weird falsetto vocals, wordless wailing and yodelling, for example. Above all there's the flowing, deliberative melodies which are irresistibly cinematic.

The flavour of the movies strikes me as the most distinctive feature of Focus's work. At times—like the end of 'Focus II'—they sound like John Barry. What they have done is to take the melodramatic impact of film theme music and transmogrify it into a genuine musical emotion of their own. They achieve an 'epic' quality without any of the vapid orchestral histrionics which the term has come to imply.

***

Possibly I've been over-influenced by having first heard their hit 'Sylvia' when it was played during an intermission at the pictures. Whatever the case, I should like to place it on record that the cinema concerned was the Curzon on the Ormeau Road in Belfast, and to commend whichever enlightened projectionist was responsible. 'Sylvia' is one of the most infectious and euphoric pieces of popular music ever recorded. It appears on this album, albeit in a shortened version.

Focus is entirely unlike any American group, and probably the nearest British equivalent would be a band like Argent. But nobody in Argent could match the musicianship of Jan Akkerman. He uses the electric guitar vocally, incorporating the whole range of tone colours which electric distortion provides. He's at his best in soulful, hoarse statements, like the opening of 'Focus II', but he has many other expressive voicings. For example, on the long second track which has the teasing title 'Answers? Questions! Questions? Answers!' he gets totally inside a dazzling cumulative solo. My only reservations about his playing is that he sometimes can't sustain the flow of ideas all the way through a fast solo—in this particular case, he does falter into aimless doodling in the last few minutes.

Nevertheless. Akkerman is one of the most pleasurable performers to have emerged in recent years, and he has a flawless rapport with Van Leer, whose fluid chording on the organ bolsters the romantic outpouring of the guitarist. Van Leer also acts as a quirky and energetic foil to the often mournfully introspective Akkerman, whilst remaining an outstanding musician in his own right. His flute solo on 'Answers? Questions!' is as pretty and sensitive as they come.

One final important point is that Focus play dance music. 'Hocus Pocus' is on at the moment, and I'm dancing as I type.

Tuesday, 30 October 1973

COLLABORATORS

Man/*Back into the Future*
James William Guercio/*Electra Glide in Blue Soundtrack*

ROCK GROUPS HAVE employed a wide range of startling collaborators, but some kind of prize is due to the British group Man for co-opting an entire Welsh male voice choir. If you should happen to acquire their double album *Back into the Future* (Liberty/UAD 60053/4) and begin, as I did, by playing Side 3, you may feel that some labelling machine has gone crazy. For swelling out of your speakers will come the throbbing male ensemble sound of the Rhondda valley.

There are very few kinds of music which strike me as akin to torture, but this is one of them: so the onset of electric instruments on the second track comes as no small relief. This is a long number

203

performed by the five members of Man, with a lot of atmospheric work on a synthesizer, the atmosphere being heightened by the male voice choir ooh-ing in the background. It all happened at a concert in London's Roundhouse last June and Side 4 consists of one other number from this live recording.

'Jam Up Jelly Tight' is the name of it and very proper too. It has all the spontaneity of a jam session and yet a very tight intricate interplay between the instruments, particularly guitars and organ. There is also an impressive control of dynamics and a superb flute-like passage on the Moog. This is the work of a highly sophisticated group, entirely in charge of their instruments, listening intently to one another, and extending the experiments of the San Francisco acid-rock groups of yore in a wholly individual way.

Their weakest points are lyrics and vocals, and this fourth side is all the more successful for having almost none of either. The first two sides are the studio LP, and whilst the standard of workmanship is high throughout, I find it less exciting and rather more commonplace—although not too many groups could handle the time signatures they so often adopt. 'Just For You' is a very pleasant tune, but the harmony singing is a bit rough. 'Back into the Future' itself is a strained and somewhat pretentious piece about time travel. 'Don't Go Away' is a straightforward commercial pop song.

The best of these tracks—for its title alone—is 'Never Say Nups To Nepalese'. The lyrics here are again held to a minimum, and the instrumentals allowed to work out some fascinating patterns. It also has a nice tinge of eccentricity.

..*

What should a film soundtrack album attempt to do? Evoke the film for you, either in anticipation or retrospect? Or ignore the film and offer you the incidental music as a work of value in its own right? Recently, some soundtrack scores have outclassed their films: Isaac Hayes' score for *Shaft*, for example. And Alan Price's songs for *O Lucky Man* certainly stand on their own as the best set of numbers this artist has done in an age.

The soundtrack of *Electra Glide in Blue* (UA-LAO62-H) takes the former option, and includes bits of the film's dialogue and action in between the tracks. There are big disadvantages to this. By the time the film comes round, I expect to be heartily sick of these little snippets from it. Furthermore, it will be robbed of some of its surprises—such as a cop reciting a solemn stream of invective and then explaining to his men that this is a catalogue of the 'vocal harassment' they can expect at a forthcoming rock concert.

The interest of *Electra Glide in Blue* for rock fans is that its producer and director is James William Guercio, the éminence grise behind the big band Chicago. Guercio has naturally composed the theme music for his film as well, and has used most of the Chicago musicians—along with a whole raft of others—to play it.

However, this is not a rock music film. It's the story of a young man who returns from Vietnam and becomes a motor-cycle cop. It sounds like an outstanding film, but its incidental music doesn't make a satisfying album—there's a bit of '50s rock n'roll, a couple of spoony country numbers, a hard rock freakout by the trio Madura, and a whole lot of mood music from the vast band. Plus all those snippets. Maybe it works better after you've seen the film.

Tuesday, 13 November 1973

BATH WARBLER

Neil Young/*Time Fades Away*
Cheech & Chong/*Los Cochinos*

NEIL YOUNG ALWAYS sings as if he's in his bathroom: a man not so much singing as acting out a fantasy of himself as a singer. He forms the words, breathes and projects as though he were talking, and has as much difficulty hitting and maintaining the right pitch as somebody like Walter Matthau probably has. In fact, on one track of his current LP called 'LA', he sounds very like Walter Matthau.

What makes him different from other people who warble in their baths is that he composes the kind of songs which they will want to sing. His gift for melody exceeds that of his peers and sometime collaborators, Crosby, Stills and Nash, and he writes lyrics which are always of interest and sometimes achieve powerful imagery, as in his song 'Helpless'. He has neither Crosby's mellifluous voice nor Stills' range and depth of emotion, but once a song of his enters your head, you can't get it out again.

The album is called *Time Fades Away* (Reprise 54010) and it contains eight songs recorded live on tour with four or five

205

musicians, at least some of whom were in Young's former band Crazy Horse. Lyrically, the songs are largely autobiographical, with a good deal of reference to the singer's young days in Canada; musically, they often have the flavour of other performers. The title track, for example, is a semi-R&B piece which would fit Mick Jagger and Keith Richards like a glove. 'Don't Be Denied' is a pure Band number, complete with Robbie Robertson narrative and phraseology, but with a rather clearer message.

The two nicest tracks are rather Joni Mitchell (all these Canadians must have something in common)—introspective reflections done by Young alone at the piano. 'The Bridge' is a lovesong built on some beautiful, subtle harmonic changes, with a harmonica introduction and coda also attributed to Young. 'Love In Mind' is yet more plangent and sung very well for once.

The same can't be said for 'Last Dance'. This has the loose, extended structure of a CSN&Y number, and sure enough Crosby and Nash put in a guest appearance on it. All of them manage to sing atrociously. On this track, even the instruments sound out of tune. It ends with Young chanting repeatedly 'No, no, no.' Fair comment.

***

Some time ago the rock culture finally produced its own pair of stand-up comedians, but they've had very little impact on this side of the Atlantic. They're called Tommy Chong and Cheech Marin— otherwise Cheech and Chong—and their act is heavily American, in the best traditions of Mort Sahl, Lenny Bruce et al, but with an emphasis on drug jokes.

Their album, *Los Cochinos* (Ode SP 77019), opens with a funny but not hilarious piece called 'Sergeant Stadanko', about a narcotics cop giving a lecture to a class-room of delinquents at Our Lady of 115th Street High School. This is followed by a dire spoof commercial about VD and a strained psychiatrist's office routine about a boy who keeps putting everything up his nose.

However, the final track on Side 1 is the album's success. It's a nonsensical 12 and a half-minute dialogue between two neanderthal teenagers who have smuggled some of their friends into a drive-in movie in the boot of the car. It's a great pity that the rest of the album doesn't match up to the inspired idiocy of this routine.

Tuesday 27 November 1973

LISTENING LIVE

Dory Previn/*Live at Carnegie Hall*
Humble Pie/*Eat It*

I ONCE SAW the Lionel Hampton band play at a country club in Upstate New York. They had been hired for a local college prom and I managed to spirit myself in along with all the white sports coats and ball-gowns, who had come only to dance and who ignored the band entirely. Never have I seen a more bored and somnolent group of musicians. The drummer actually played with his elbows resting on the kit. Then, out of the blue, the MC announced that the next half-hour was to be relayed live on local radio. The band suddenly sprang into life and played thirty minutes worth of scintillating classic swing music.

The very same thing can happen with recordings. Every artist likes the reassurance that there's somebody out there actually listening: some can't perform at their best without it. For them, live recordings are much preferable to studio ones, despite the loss in quality and the instrusions of applause and announcements.

***

I never would have expected Dory Previn to be such a one, but her double album *Live at Carnegie Hall* (UAD60045/6) is a revelation. She's first and foremost a songwriter, and it always seemed likely from her lavishly arranged and elaborately produced records that her voice and presence weren't that strong. Furthermore, I never could warm to her songs. They were adult and literate, sensitive and honest, but there was some crucial element of humanity missing from them. I anticipated therefore, that her live album would be as big a disaster as Leonard Cohen's.

Instead, she sounds transformed on it. There's a tangible flow of goodwill from the audience and she blossoms in it. Her voice has a new vibrancy and it's beautifully complemented by a five-piece band calling itself Angel's Flight—acoustic and slide guitars, p. b. & d.

The album also gains from being a virtual 'Best of Dory Previn', for it contains the sixteen strongest songs culled from her four studio LPs, plus two new numbers. It opens and closes with the song which first established her as an original and highly gifted song-poet, 'Mythical Kings and Iguanas'. It also has those extraordinarily frank and tender songs of insight into male impotence and female desire, 'Don't Put Him Down' and 'When A Man Wants A Woman'.

These seem to me the highlights, but there's plenty more that's excellent: 'Mary C. Brown and the Hollywood Sign', 'The Lady with the Braid', 'Left Hand Lost' and many others. Taken together, they outweigh the less attractive side of Dory Previn, present here in a line like, 'There is nothing that I haven't endured or encountered in my long downhill trip' from a new song called 'Be Careful, Baby Be Careful'. This kind of ego-flagellation may be suitable raw material for art, but she doesn't succeed in transmuting it.

Still, this is an album for the collection and it establishes her as a contemporary singer and songwriter of considerable weight.

***

The English group Humble Pie have also issued a double album (*Eat It*, AMLS 6004), the fourth side of which is a live recording made at a concert in Glasgow. Again, this side has an edge to it missing from the other three, even though the sound quality is none too good, with the vocals just a sort of high-pitched tearing noise in the background. There's a blistering guitar solo on 'Up Our Sleeve' and a long and lively treatment of the Motown number 'Road Runner'.

However, Humble Pie's leader Steve Marriott strikes me as the least distinctive of the former mods. His voice has none of the dissipated elegance of Rod Stewart, or the honest tunefulness of Roger Daltrey. When Peter Frampton, a fine songwriter and guitarist, was working alongside him, the band had a certain style and vitality. But since Frampton's replacement by the less gifted Dave Clempson, the group has become more or less a Marriott vehicle. All the original numbers here are his.

There's a strong vein of gospel in many of them, and Marriott has emphasised it by hiring a female trio of black gospel singers from the US to sing backing. This is indeed a piquant situation, the young white English imitator being accompanied by the middle-aged black originals. They sing beautifully, but he maunders away incoherently. And the songs themselves sound very third-hand. Definitely for Pie fans only.

Wednesday, 12 December 1973

THE YEAR'S DISCS

THE 'PLAYLIST' IS very much in vogue in the pop music papers these days; a playlist being simply the discs to which a reviewer or critic has been listening—for pleasure rather than duty—during the previous week or month. Drawing up such a list at the close of the year can be a surprising, even guilt-ridden experience.

For example, I find that a couple of the albums which I acclaimed as major achievements when they first came out have not been on my turntable more than two or three times since. One such is this year's Mahavishnu Orchestra album, *Birds of Fire* (CBS 65231). The passion and originality of John McLaughlin's work is undiminished on this record, and I still consider the band to be in the front rank. But on closer acquaintance *Birds of Fire* hasn't stood up as well as the preceding *Inner Mounting Flame*. It's really an appendage to the latter rather than an advance upon it.

On the other hand, nothing that I panned during the year has subsequently won its way into my heart. Nobody else had much to say for the Dr John/Mike Bloomfield/John Paul Hammond collaboration, *Triumvirate* (CBS S65659), but it has continued to afford pleasure in this household since its first spin. Its chunky musical textures and sensuous wit are rich enough to stand a lot of listening.

***

The album which I've played most is Paul Simon's *There Goes Rhymin' Simon* (CBS 69035). Every time I pick it up I wince at the title, but if there's been a better song than 'Tenderness' written during 1973, I haven't heard it—unless it's 'One Man's Ceiling Is Another Man's Floor' from the same side. Apart from the sheer quality of lyric writing in these songs, and their musical expressiveness, which contains a large element of brilliant pastiche, there is running through the album Simon's concern to achieve the exact musical metaphor and style for every song, which makes it a series of discoveries. With this record, he has at long last fulfilled the enormous promise which has made him a very wealthy man in the last ten years.

Another record which rarely gets a chance to cool around here is *Focus at the Rainbow* (Polydor 2442 118). Focus lacks the virtuosity or intensity of a band like the Mahavishnu Orchestra, but they have other important qualities which that band could use—notably humour and an unsyrupy lyricism. They're a modest, unshowy foursome, and the affection they inspire in their audience is very evident on this invigorating album.

Affection also fills the groves in surprising amounts on the Dory Previn *Live at Carnegie Hall* double LP (UA LA 108-H2). It seems that the confessional artist is rewarded with a loving audience for showing her or his pain nakedly in public. Miss Previn's own stage personality comes over very sympathetically, and her often bitter and very candid songs are greatly enhanced by this live setting. This is an album to be played only in certain moods and when the stamina is strong, but it'll continue to satisfy those particular needs for a long time to come.

***

What else did 1973 bring? There were the sly, wry songs which Alan Price wrote and recorded for the film *O Lucky Man* (WB K46227). There was another stylish, strutting album from Rod Stewart and the Faces called *Ooh La La* (WB K6011). These have both won plenty of needle time.

As for new faces, there were two debut albums by different English performers, both rather oddball but original and enduring. One was *Back Door* (WB K46251) by the group of the same name, an English trio of bass guitar, alto/sop. sax and drums. In some ways a curious throwback to fifties West Coast jazz, Back Door are nevertheless remarkable in the rich flow of ideas they can sustain from such a limited instrumentation. The other album was *Tubular Bells* (Virgin V2001), a quaint and delightful fantasy conjured up on a multiplicity of instruments by a 19-year-old prodigy called Mike Oldfield.

Not a bad year, then, if not a historic one. It looks as if rock & roll is here to stay, but whether or not it'll save the world is still an open question.

Tuesday, Wednesday & Thursday, 25, 26 & 27 December 1973

1974

ROCK BOTTOM

Various/*Solid Gold Rock & Roll Vol 1*
Roxy Music/*Stranded*

IN 1974 THE revival of fifties rock & roll must surely come to an end. Simply, there's nothing left to revive. It's been a very piquant trend. People like me have found themselves pondering the purchase (at full 1974 prices) of bright new glossy albums of recordings which they threw out twelve years ago. All those teenage fantasies—electronically altered to simulate stereo. The shelves of the record shops and supermarkets are loaded with them, and they're practically all a take-on.

For one thing, most of the budget 'Great Hits of the Fifties' albums are not the original recordings at all, but imitations of them done cheaply by hack session men. Either that, or they're inferior 'cover' versions made at the time to ride in on the coattails of the hit. People buy these albums because they respond to fifties' song titles rather than group names. Plenty of veteran fans can hum 'Will You Love Me Tomorrow' but few may recall that it was the Shirelles who first recorded it—rather than the Chantels or the Caravelles or the Shangri-Las. Groups in those days flashed by like showers of meteorites.

The safest bet is to buy compilation albums issued by the important record companies from their own archives. For example, I've just succumbed to Vol. I of Mercury's *Solid Gold Rock & Roll* (Import, SR61371). Mercury was one of the first labels to sign up vocal groups in the High-school idiom, and this album contains several deathless classics of the genre. There's the delirious camp banality of the Diamonds' 'Little Darlin'', the gum-chewing innuendo of 'My Boyfriend's Back' by the Angels, and the baby-doll breathiness of 'You Don't Have To Be a Baby To Cry' by the Caravelles.

Such riches would have been enough in themselves to sell me the album, but the Big Bopper's 'Chantilly Lace', which I have been known to do as a party-piece clinched it.

Otherwise, this album is again something of a con. It has two or three other rock & roll numbers, less distinguished but still genuine. However, it opens with the Crew Cuts' 'Sh' Boom' which is pre-rock & roll barbershop music, and its last five tracks are all from the middle and late sixties. 'Mendocino' by Doug Sahm was a 1969 hit, and so was Steam's 'Na Na Hey Hey Kiss Him Goodbye', if I remember rightly. Pleasant songs, certainly, but scarcely solid gold.

The fifties revival formalised that hapless decade into a style. New groups started to appear with hair greased back and leather jackets. It was just another way to be flash, a macho alternative to transvestism, another glam posture. The most enduring of these groups has been Roxy Music, whose third album *Stranded* (Island ILPS9252) is currently available. Listening to it right after 'Little Darlin'' and 'Chantilly Lace' gives you a very vivid idea of how far the music has travelled in the intervening years.

Amongst other things we've had the Beatles, Dylan, and rock, Lou Reed, the moog synthesizer, the Incredible String Band, and the emergence into popular taste of the sexual and spiritual underworlds. Elements of the lot of them are present in Roxy Music music, along with words like 'predilection' and 'Zarathustra' which would have amazed the Big Bopper.

The group's singer and composer, Bryan Ferry, goes in for carefully aesthetic images sung in a broadway, eerie kind of way. Instrumentation includes sax and oboe, and synthesizer, with a lot of electronic 'treatments'. The effect can be threatening, as in the opener, 'Street Life', a lurid paean to bodily commerce; but it can also achieve a kind of overcivilised melancholy which is very absorbing. 'Sunset' and 'Just Like You' both have this quality. In fact, the album's only disaster is 'Psalm', the 8 and a half-minute murder of a disjointed, tuneless gospel song.

Ferry sings at one point, 'Nothing is there/For us to share/But yesterday' which could be a sad comment on the fifties revival. But I gather that he has now left Roxy Music, so it may turn out to be a postscript to the whole extraordinary craze.

Thursday, 10 January 1974

'SUPERSTARS'S' UNSUPER SONGS

THE BELFAST theatre-going public is currently under the spell of *Jesus Christ Superstar*, with the film at the ABC Cinema and the stage production at the Lyric Theatre both doing a roaring trade. Many words, most of them pious have been lavished on the religious content of this show, on its social value, its presentation, production and so on. Not much has been said specifically about the music, which audiences and critics seem to accept unquestioningly as authentic rock music.

Yet the venture started out as nothing but music—first as a pop single, then as a Decca LP set, the success of which led to its being mounted as a lavish stage extravaganza on Broadway. It's not a 'rock opera', then; nor is it even a pop musical. It's 20-odd songs based on some of the climactic events in Christ's career, strung together into a continuous whole and presented with dance and spectacle. In other words, it's modelled on the standard television Top Twenty show.

From the first brooding bars of the overture it's clear that a composer with a musical training is at work. Andrew Lloyd Webber did, in fact, study at the London Royal Academy of Music. His overture conforms to stage musical conventions in being an orchestral fantasia on the show's big numbers. It's given a rock coloration by the use of electric instruments, but basically it's the usual pseudo-symphonic mishmash.

***

The songs themselves run the whole gamut of popular styles. Tim Rice, the lyricist, who was a trainee record producer at EMI, employs a bizarre mixture of styles, with snatches of the Gospels, worn-out jive talk ('this Jesus is cool'), public school locutions, the debased jargon of television, and musical comedy rhymes ('a faded, jaded mandarin'), all jangling together.

Thus, crowded by lepers and beggars, Christ yells: 'Don't push me!' like an irritable commuter. At the Last Supper, the disciples sing, 'Always hoped that I'd be an apostle/knew that I would make it if I tried/Then when we retire we can write the Gospels/So they'll all talk about us when we died', than which nothing could be feebler. Unless it's Christ's cry to God in Gethsemane: 'Show me just a little of your omnipresent brain.'

It would take a lot more than Webber's clever pastiche to redeem such lyrics. For the songs sung by Jesus and Judas, he borrows

215

mostly from Motown, particularly in the driving bass figures and vocal falsetto, which is overdone to the point of caricature. The other important figure is Jesus's groupie, Mary Magdalene, and she gets to sing the sweet ballads—'Everything's Alright' in lilting waltz time, and 'I Don't Know How To Love Him', the throbbing showstopper. They at least have pretty tunes, albeit of a very brittle kind.

Otherwise, there's a little bit of everything—except originality. Caiphas and Annas sing a form of recitative: in the film the former does a bullfrog rasp and the latter a kind of reptilian boy-soprano whisper. Pilate bellows out a spot of Pirate King pantomime melodrama, and Herod is given a spoof 1920s routine ('Show me Jesus you're no fool/ Walk across my swimming pool'). Commercially, it's all very adroit; artistically, it's less than worthless. Far from entertaining me, it set my teeth on edge and kept them that way for two hours.

Pop music can express religious experience—listen to the work of Judee Sill or John McLaughlin. It can also work in extended forms—listen to *Sergeant Pepper* or the Who's *Tommy* or Yes's *Close to the Edge*. These are amongst the authentic achievements which will continue to flourish after the Webber-Rice Plastic Jesus show is dead, buried and beyond resurrection.

Tuesday, 29 January 1974

TRIBAL SOUNDS

Allman Brothers Band/*Brothers and Sisters*
Gallagher and Lyle/*Seeds*

CIVILISED LIFE IS crumbling all round us. There's panic-buying of toilet rolls; and, increasingly, record companies are declining to send out review albums because of the vinyl shortage. It makes you cherish what you've got, especially if you've got something that smiles, something like the Allman Brothers Band's *Brothers and Sisters* (Capricorn 47507) or Gallagher and Lyle's *Seeds* (A&MAMLS 68207).

Benny Gallagher and Graham Lyle, two refugees from famous groups, have developed a kind of Scottish Simon & Garfunkel act.

Their work is highly professional, but the harmony singing is simple and unaffected and the homely sound of Gallagher's accordion figures prominently in the backings. The opening number on *Seeds* is a measure of their genuine charm: they manage to sing the praises of a morning in the country without setting your teeth on edge.

Not all their songs are as lightweight as this, though. 'A Misspent Youth' has a few wry words to say about pool rooms and youth clubs. Better again is 'Remember Then', a sensitive song about meeting an old flame, with the strongest lyrics on the record. 'Sleepyhead' is a delightfully drowsy catchy number.

These are the highlights of the album. The rest is extremely pleasant, but more predictable. There are a couple of rather self-conscious essays in the folk idiom, one about the Highland clearances and another called 'Cape Cod Houses'. The title track, 'Seeds', is a country number with a lot of nice dobro in it, but the lyrics are too contrived. Otherwise, the songs are well-turned commercial efforts, any one of which could do well as a single.

The Allman Brothers Band was named Band of the Year in the *Rolling Stone* Music Awards for 1973; yet the group is scarcely known on this side of the Atlantic. The main reason is that they've been playing around the festivals and on tour in America for years, but they've never had a big hit single—at least not until this current album and the song from it called 'Rambling Man'.

What's great about the Allmans is that they combine all the expertise of 'progressive' rock with the entertainment value of traditional pop styles. 'Rambling Man' is a country number with corny lyrics about having been born on the seat of a Greyhound bus and being a rambler ever since, but out of this the band develops a marvellous repeated figure over which guitarist Richard Betts plays a brilliant solo. Likewise, 'Jelly Jelly', is a four-square, traditional 12-bar blues, but they make it mint new with their tight ensemble playing and control of dynamics.

All seven of the tracks on *Brothers and Sisters* are of the same high standard. The husky vocals of 'Come and Go Blues' build-up towards a flowing instrumental ending. On 'Southbound', the vocals are backed up by a series of fast and beautiful ascending runs. 'Jessica' is a long instrumental with that breezy, deceptively effortless quality of their playing. The last track, 'Pony Boy', draws on the elements of traditional blues to celebrate the band's enjoyment of its own music.

The Allman Brothers are at the centre of a tribe, as are other American groups like the Grateful Dead and the Band. Groups like these have developed an instinct for communal expression which is unparallelled. It shines like a good deed in a world where people hoard toilet rolls.

Tuesday, 5 February 1974

LENNON WITHOUT YOKO

John Lennon/*Mind Games*
Brinsley Schwarz/*Please Don't Ever Change*

IT'S BEEN A year and a half since John Lennon's last disastrous album, *Some Time in New York City*, challenged Bob Dylan's *Self Portrait* for the distinction of being the most appalling lapse in quality ever marketed by a major artist. It seemed then as though the combination of political naivety and collaboration with Yoko had finally annihilated Lennon's intuitive creativity for good. But it hasn't. A partially restored and Yokoless Lennon appears on a welcome new album called *Mind Games* (Apple PCS 7165).

Although not physically contributing to the music, Yoko is still strongly in evidence as theme and subject matter. The sleeve contains a Declaration of Nutopia—a 'conceptual country' which has 'no land, no boundaries, no passports, only people', the declaration being signed by the two of them. The music, however, is mercifully free of such limp whimsicality.

The work which it most insistently recalls is *Imagine*. There's a similar heavy instrumental sound; no string section this time, but a mellotron and much else besides. There's also a similar emphasis on melody. And there's even a song called 'I Know (I Know)' with phrases about 'yesterday' and 'its getting better all the time', which sounds very like an apology to Paul McCartney, a companion piece to 'How Do You Sleep' on *Imagine*.

Finally, the songs cover the same range as on that LP. 'Mind Games' itself is a slow, deliberate celebration of Lennon's predilection for verbal and musical fantasy and magic. 'Tight As' is an earthy medium-rocker. 'Aisumasen (I'm Sorry)' and 'One Day (At A Time)' are both love songs to Yoko, lyrically soppy but musically interesting. The former has a subtle, Gospel-style melody, while the latter has the dreamy, spellbinding quality of numbers like

'Across the Universe', sung in spacey falsetto with marvellous backup singing from a female group.

There are two facile sloganeering numbers, 'Bring On the Lucie' and 'Only People'. But these are more than outweighed by the album's two highlights. First, there's 'Intuition', which has the kind of attractive, breezy tune and nodding rhythm you might find in an ideal stage musical, with literate, self-aware lyrics and a tasty melange of electric instrumental sounds. The other number is the closer, 'Meat City', the album's one dose of Lennon bile, with screaming guitars, whipped-up vocals and distinctly nasty lyrics ('Chickinsuckin mothertruckin City shookdown USA').

On most of the songs, a rather soupy rock & roll echo is employed which blunts rather than sharpens the emotional impact of the voice, particularly when it is also multi-tracked. The overall sound is also sometimes muffled, which is a pity, for the musicianship on this album is easily the most excellent of any Lennon solo record.

Overall, though, partisans of the intellectual Beatle—and I'm one—can only cheer *Mind Games*, once they've finished sighing with relief.

***

The five members of Brinsley Schwarz have long since overcome their infamous super-hyped debut of three or four years ago to become a pleasantly easy-going band. I can easily imagine enjoying their work in the atmosphere of a pub concert.

Transferred to record, it's less compelling; still, *Please Don't Ever Change* (UAS 29489) would make a good party album. It's got a couple of oldies—the vocal group number 'Speedee', with a backing chant that goes 'bah bah ba-deedle-it'; and the Goffin/King song 'Don't Ever Change', which has nice harmony singing. Otherwise, there's a mixed bag of their own country and rock & roll numbers, as well as a preposterous parody of an old-fashioned Latinate pop song called 'Down In Mexico'.

Friday, 22 February 1974

LAST SUMMER

The Band/*Moondog Matinee*
Bob Dylan/*Planet Waves*

IT'S NO GOOD decrying the thrall of nostalgia in which popular culture is gripped at the moment. Nostalgia is what pop music, at least, is all about. If you listen to it at all, you've measured out your life in it a little: last summer's songs define last summer, and all the things that happened to you in it, for the rest of your life.

So it is that Clarence Frogman Henry's 'Ain't Got No Home' plunges me years back into the torrid, carnal murk of a Newcastle, Co Down, amusement arcade. Nobody could ever equal the deliberate, dogged banality of the original; most groups today would want instead to camp it up unbearably, which would be as clever and amusing as scrawling boobs on a photo of Gracie Fields. But the group known as the Band instead treat the song with humorous attention and respect. They blend their own swirling but tightly organised sound into some fifties-style growling saxes and come up with a brand of revivalism which is nutritious.

The album in question is *Moondog Matinee* (Capitol E-SW 11214), named for the historic Alan Freed radio show of 1953. It contains ten songs which the Band used to sing when they were just another teenage group from Toronto called Levon and the Hawks. There are two other New Orleans numbers besides 'Ain't Got A Home'—Allen Toussaint's 'Holy Cow' and the great Fats Domino's 'I'm Ready', which lacks the sensuous happiness of the original, but has exactly the right sax sound, of a frog with laryngitis playing a kazoo.

'Great Pretender'—the Platters' hit—is the only other track which doesn't quite come off, and it's simply because the song demands a backing of vocal harmonies, and sounds strained without it. Otherwise, there are riches galore. Junior Parker's 'Mystery Train' has the Band at its best, with organ, guitars, accordion and drums all working with filigree distinctness and yet achieving that overall chug-along sound which is so irresistible. They make Chuck Berry's 'Promised Land' sound like their own composition. And they end the album by rehabilitating that very beautiful Sam Cooke ballad 'A Change Is Gonna Come'.

***

The Band, of course, first became famous as Bob Dylan's backing group. And they are now with him once more in his re-emergence into the public eye, with a massive American tour and a new album, *Planet Waves* (Island ILPS 9261).

Dylan's last album of new songs, *New Morning*, came out in 1970. The first track on *Planet Waves*, 'On A Night Like This', sounds very much like the work on that previous LP, facile and rather forgettable. In fact, the similarity exists throughout the whole eleven tracks—except for two redeeming features.

One is the good old Band itself, which does sterling work for its boss, building atmosphere behind his voice and shifting the instrumental textures subtly to accommodate the moods in each song. This is particularly extraordinary when you consider that the album was made in three days.

The other thing about *Planet Waves* is that some of the old Dylan magic is unquestionably there. Personally, I can't be bothered any more speculating on what the lyrics mean (especially without a lyric sheet), on what the liner notes mean, on what position Dylan is adopting. I'm irritated by his singing the slow version of 'Forever Young' horribly off-key and by his tuneless harmonica blowing.

Yet there's no escaping his fascination: the edginess of 'Going Going Gone', the obscure stomping relish of 'Tough Mama', and the 1965-style voice hissing out menacing compliments in 'Something There Is About You'; the drama is all there. One line in 'On A Night Like This' goes, 'If I'm not too far off/I think we did this once before.' He's done it all more than once before, but it still can get a hook into you.

Tuesday, 5 March 1974

LIVING DEAD

The Grateful Dead/ *Wake of the Flood*

WAKE OF THE Flood (K49301) is the best Grateful Dead album since the immortal *American Beauty*. Which makes it a highly suitable record with which to launch their own record company, Grateful Dead Records. This venture takes rock band tribalism a large step further on the road to self-sufficiency; for the Dead are not merely recording their own music, they're also handling the pressing and distribution in the US (over here, distribution is in the hands of the WEA Group). If the Dead can make this work—and no group is better equipped for the task—they will have established complete control over their work and unfettered communication between themselves and their highly devoted public, something unprecedented in the 'pop music industry'.

I suspect that a list of credits—and possibly also a lyrics sheet—are accidentally missing from my copy of the LP. At any rate, their absence is the only serious carp that I have. Bob Hunter's lyrics are always full of intriguing images, but they're often difficult to catch from the Dead's singing, which is the weakest component of their whole sound. As to the playing, everybody knows that it's Jerry Garcia on lead and pedal steel guitars, Bob Weir on rhythm and Phil Lesh on bass, Bill Kreutzmann on drums and Keith Godchaux on piano—but who's playing the fiddle on the opening track? And the reedy alto sax on the second one? Or is it a soprano sax?

The use of extra instrumentation throughout is an indication of change. For the past few years they've been heavily committed to simplicity and to roots—concentrating on live performances, on country songs and on old rock & roll numbers. *Wake of the Flood* is in some ways a return to the gnomic intricacies of their underground days. But it has an eclecticism which would have been unthinkable in the days before the underground went legitimate.

***

It opens with 'Mississippi Half-Step Uptown Toodleloo', which is one of those deliberative, mid-tempo numbers, with a hint of boogie rhythm in it, which draws you in irresistibly. 'Let Me Sing Your Blues Away' (not the Claire Hamill song) employs a folksy, homespun tune; but it's rendered strange by some very stoned harmony singing and double-tracking, and by the abrasive sound of that saxophone.

The other two tracks on side I are slow and meditative. 'Row Jimmy' is awash with pleasurable melancholia, the excellent lines,

That's the way it's been in town
Ever since they pulled the jukebox down.

occurring near the end. It has good droopy guitar breaks, and what sounds like a strong female voice singing harmony on the choruses. But again, the unexpected is there, in the shape of a Latinate arrangement, with one of those rasping percussion devices, and percussive phrases on the guitar and piano. 'Stella Blue' is a most delicate and lyrical number, with the same suspended rhythm and floating bass line as 'Attics of My Mind'.

Side 2 opens with 'Here Comes Sunshine', which is startlingly similar to George Harrison's 'Here Comes The Sun' on 'Abbey Road'. It has the same childlike feeling, with a simple tune alternately spelt out by the lead guitar and sung in harmony, and what may be a Moog doodling in the background. The remaining three tracks are collectively entitled 'Weather Report Suite' and are the work of Bob Weir.

'Prelude' is an upbeat, jazz-influenced piece. The playing is tight and energetic, but Weir's lyrics are a bit flowery-powery, and the singing, particularly on the chorus, is distinctly shaky. 'Part One' opens with a rather baroque passage of chording on acoustic guitar, and then slowly builds up, with pedal steel and organ, a richly sensuous sound. 'Part Two (Let It Grow)' is a magnificent Spring anthem, with a most lovely alto sax solo and orchestral punctuation to provide a big ending to a beautiful album.

Tuesday, 19 March 1974

PRINE LYRICS

John Prine/*Sweet Revenge*

JOHN PRINE IS one of those singers whose success became possible the day that Bob Dylan met Johnny Cash in Nashville. In fact, his voice sounds at different times like both these men's, and often uncannily like Dylan's; and he was helped to fame by another graduate of the same school, Kris Kristofferson.

It follows that the strength of his work lies mainly in lyric-writing. His tunes are merely rudimentary vehicles for words, and they invariably remind you of other tunes. On his new album *Sweet Revenge* (Atlantic SD7274), the tune of 'A Good Time', for example, is very close to that of Dylan's 'Tonight I'll Be Staying Here With You', and 'Christmas in Prison' has almost the same tune as a song my grandfather used to sing to me about the theft of certain apples by a party named Johnny.

But the versifyin' is something else entirely; Prine is indeed a considerable folk-poet, with the ability to dramatise commonplace themes in a wholly original way. The first track on *John Prine* (K 40357), his first album, was about marijuana, but it had the delightful title of 'Illegal Smile'. Side 2 of the same record opened with an anti-Vietnam song, but again the sentiments were brought alive by the mordant wit: the number was called 'Your Flag Decal Won't Get You Into Heaven Anymore'. Perhaps the album's finest track—and still Prine's best song—was 'Sam Stone', the story of a Vietnam veteran who dies of a drug over-dose: a ballad which will surely carry into posterity a grim and shameful chapter of American social history.

***

Prine's second album, *Diamonds in the Rough* (SD7240) extended his concern for society's victims like 'Billy The Bum' or 'The Torch Singer' but it had a heavier country bias than its predecessor; with a less sombre kind of humour in songs like 'Everybody' (about an encounter with Jesus) and 'Yes I Guess They Ought To Name A Drink After You'.

Now comes *Sweet Revenge*, which follows a familiar path, towards a heavier rock sound, with more surreal and subjective lyrics, often edged with bitterness and menace—in short, it's his 'Another Side of John Prine' album.

After admittedly short acquaintance, I find it less satisfactory than his previous work. The wit and imagination are still there, but more in brilliant flashes, and though he can do the Dylan rough-diamond folkie voice better even than Dr Zimmerman himself, he can't do the nihilistic sneer which goes with the rock sound, simply because there isn't any vitriol in his system. He just doesn't sound comfortable with backup singers and keyboards and a horn section here and there.

On top of all that, a self-conscious poeticism has seeped into numbers like 'Blue Umbrella', 'A Good Time' and 'Mexican Home'; 'Onomatopoeia' is an unconvincing attack on showbiz exploitation and 'Nine Pound Hammer' is a not very good old song which he sings not very well.

However, 'Christmas in Prison' is an outright success, with some genuine wild poetry in the lyrics. So is 'Please Don't Bury Me' on a lighter level, and 'Grandpa was a Carpenter', a simple and unaffected piece of autobiography. There's plenty in the album to sustain your interest. Prine has by no means lost his way, even if he has poked up a few blind alleys.

Tuesday, 2 April 1974

UNRIVALLED JONI MITCHELL

Joni Mitchell/*Court and Spark*

THERE ARE A few, just a few, artists in popular music whose new album releases are major events awaited with bated breath. One such is Joni Mitchell. She has an unrivalled range of talents: she sings like an angel, composes like a composer and writes lyrics like a poet. She plays deft and expressive piano and guitar. She can arrange quite large-scale instrumental resources in an unmistakably personal style. She even looks good.

All of this is so extraordinary in a scene of eurovision marionettes, wizened children and sex-mutated circus acts, that her work shocks the ear afresh each time. It's something to live with and assimilate gradually. For the initial few hearings, her last album (*For the Roses*) seemed to me very beautiful but not as profound as her preceding masterpiece *Blue*; but having played it constantly for a year and a half, I rate it now on a par with *Blue*. It'll take at least as long to come to as full acquaintance with *Court and Spark* (Asylum SYLA 8756), her new work.

***

The title comes from the opening song, which personifies love as an itinerant street musician looking for a woman to 'court and spark'. The singer, mixed-up and unsure as ever, resists his advances because she can't let go of Los Angeles, the 'city of fallen angels'. Her singing is throatier and more soulful than of late, and the backing is a full group sound, with piano and steel guitar and chimes featured.

This is the pattern for the whole album. Although the lyrics are as personal as ever, her voice is direct rather than intimate, soaring over fat accompaniments which often swell to orchestral proportions. 'Help Me' is a real pop song, with walloping drum and cymbal, backup singing and brass lines, addressed to a man who loves his loving 'but not like you love your freedom.' 'Free Man In Paris' has Jose Feliciano and Larry Carlton on guitars, and Crosby and Nash singing vocal harmonies with her.

The following two tracks are run into each other and are in her familiar vein of disconsolate self-analysis linked up to unhappy social situations; in fact, the second song is called 'Same Situation', the first one being 'People's Parties'. The imagery in both cases is strikingly vivid and well observed, but 'Same Situation' builds up to an awkward and rather soppy climax, with strings arranged by Tom Scott. It's interesting that the next song, 'Car on a Hill', which contains a far more successful use of quite complex instrumental colouring, was arranged by herself.

***

The peak of elaborate orchestration is reached in 'Down To You', with Joni playing a clarinet, and a fleet of phrases from various of the woodwinds bobbing on a sea of guitars, keyboards, brass and strings. This I find a little too ornate, and the lyrics also seem rather written to order, generalised abstractions.

But 'Just Like This Train' is a relaxed and brilliant train song, 'Raised On Robbery' a light-hearted rocker, with Robbie Robertson playing the guitar and 'Troubled Child' a moving treatment of emotional breakdown, with lovely muted trumpet work by Chuck Findley. Finally, there's the delightful surprise of her cool, masterful singing of 'Twisted', the old Lambert-Hendricks-Ross number which I've cherished for years. It's a performance which proves beyond doubt that Joni Mitchell could have made it to the top on vocal ability alone.

Thursday, 18 April 1974

AN EXCITING DISCOVERY

Steely Dan/*Pretzel Logic*
Captain Beefheart/*Unconditionally Guaranteed*

ALTHOUGH *PRETZEL LOGIC* (Broba SPBA 6282) is the third album from the American band, Steely Dan, it's the first one I've heard and the most exciting discovery in an age. Their lyrics are literate and interesting, with none of the usual hackneyed, get-it-together catchphrases that are now the staple of rock songs. Their vocal harmonies are beautifully crisp and true. But best of all, they've achieved the most successful use yet of jazz elements in a rock-group context.

This becomes clear right away in the first track, 'Rikki Don't Lose That Number', where drummer Jim Hodder's deft cymbal work and offbeat rim shots display a breadth of vocabulary beyond the reach of most rock drummers. It continues into 'Night by Night', which has superbly mellow brass and sax lines wholly of a piece with the group's guitars and singing. This is followed by 'Any Major Dude Will Tell You', which demonstrates their ability to do a song which is catchy as well as intelligent.

The last track on Side 1 indicates where their ears are. It's Duke Ellington's 'East Saint Louis Toodle-O', with the 1927 Bubber Miley trumpet solo done on wah-wah guitar. It's is an endearing and entertaining tribute from one kind of popular music to another.

'Parker's Band' on Side 2 pays tribute to the great jazz altoist, but wholly in rock form, with only a slight reference to be-bop phraseology. 'Pretzel Logic' itself is a song about past ideas of stardom, with very tasty horn riffs and guitar work. There are lapses on the album—'Barrytown' has a sub-Dylan tune and vocals—but nothing like enough to prevent it from being a wholesale triumph.

***

Who is bawling out, with a certain anguish, 'Happy love song, make me feel all right,' in that ragged, masculine voice? Could it be, say, P.J. Proby? It could indeed, but it isn't—it's Captain Beefheart, the erstwhile Dada King of rock music; and that middle-of-the-road pop group backing him, boosted by brass and saxes, is his erstwhile atonal Magic Band.

For those fans, like me, who were transfixed by the unique mania of *Trout Mask Replica* (the double album produced by Frank Zappa) and *Lick My Decals Off, Baby*, the new Beefheart LP (*Unconditionally Guaranteed*, on Virgin V2015), is very bewildering-like going into a Salvador Dali exhibition and finding reproductions of watercolours featuring flowers and cats. It has been heralded, certainly, by his recent work and by interviews and pronouncements. We knew he was turning to simpler, more conventional songwriting. But we didn't expect that he'd actually go soppy.

Perhaps the explanation lies in his shared authorship of the songs with his wife, Jan, and one Andy Di Martino who also produced the album and shared the arranging. At any rate, there's but a shadow of the old Beefheart here—in the nutty lyrics and upturned vocals of 'Upon The My-O-My' (released as a single) in the double-entendres of 'Sugar Bowl' and 'Peaches', and in a couple of powerful harmonica breaks.

Otherwise, all is sweetness and sunshine, in wholesome pop songs

227

with titles like 'Magic Be', 'This Is The Day' and 'Lazy Music'. Zoot Horn Rollo proves conclusively that he can play the guitar very well, and there is attractive, gutsy sax and flute work from Del Sommons. But God be with the old days.

Wednesday, 1 May 1974

THE WAY WE WANT OUR WOMEN

Kiki Dee/*Loving and Free*
Carol Grimes/*Warm Blood*

THESE ISLANDS HAVE produced any number of fine rock groups and male singers, but nary a single female artist of stature. Why are there no lady Van Morrisons or Rory Gallaghers or Paul McCartneys? It's a question raised every time a new girl contender comes along to be KO'd in the first round. There are plenty of TV pop stars, the Cillas and Lulus and Clodaghs. There are also a fair number of crystal-voiced folkies, but even the best of them (Sandy Denny, Maddy Prior) are just pretty voices, with a closely-circumscribed repertoire. Beyond that, there are a handful of maverick singer-songwriters— Claire Hamill, Joan Armatrading—who seem to have the ingredients right but aren't quite cooking yet.

It can't be genes, it has to be in the nature of the society: because in America they've got Joni Mitchell, Carly Simon, Dory Previn, Maria Muldaur, Chi Coltrane, Carole King ... an apparently inexhaustible supply of women who can write adult, individualistic songs and perform them with emotional honesty and directness. We don't seem to want our women to be adult individuals. The popular demand is for television Cindy Dolls on the one hand, and on the other, fresh-cheeked virgins with the voices of boy sopranos.

For the women who try in their music to express themselves rather than some male fantasy, the pitfalls are demoralising. For one, they almost invariably come out sounding like mere imitations of the above-mentioned American competition. At the very least, they can't escape invidious comparisons.

***

Kiki Dee is an example. From the opening bars of her Rocket album *Loving and Free* (PIGL5), you know you're in the company of an intelligent and mature performer with a relaxed, mellifluous voice floating over some pretty guitar chording and harmonics. The trouble is, you also know she sounds uncomfortably like Rita Coolidge. With maybe the occasional touch of Carly Simon ...

It isn't just the singing, it's her writing too. She favours the cool, slowly building, gospel-country style which Rita has made her own. All four of her own compositions on the album are in this vein. 'Rest My Head' is particularly nice, with plain, strong lyrics about contemplating a strange city from a hotel room window. The other six numbers, from a variety of composers, have been chosen with discernment to make a strong, well-filled album.

Rocket is Elton John's own label, and there's a strong Elton John presence on the album, mostly to its advantage—in his co-production, in his piano and mellotron playing on half the tracks, and in the collaboration of several fine musicians associated with him, notably Davey Johnstone on guitars and B.J. Cole on pedal steel. But not so much in the two rather trivial John/Taupin compositions, 'Lonnie and Josie' and 'Supercool', a fast rocker which only demonstrates that Kiki Dee's voice is too light for full-blooded wailing. Only a few shades better is the Free number, 'Travellin' in Style'.

The song which really scores for me is 'Amoureuse', credited to Sanson/Osborne. The words are those of a girl lying awake beside the sleeping form of the first man with whom she has made love. Kiki Dee's style is perfectly suited to this, and the backing sensitively mirrors the girl's fears, hopes and longings.

Carol Grimes is an English singer who has worked her way through folk, blues and pseudo-jazz styles. For *Warm Blood* (Virgin CA2001) she has gone to Nashville to record with some of the celebrated session men there, in an attempt to achieve genuine country funk. Alas, she just sounds like the rebel of the fourth form getting it on at the tennis club hop.

Tuesday, 14 May 1974

STEWART PARKER

SATISFYING MARIA MULDAUR

Maria Muldaur/*Maria Muldaur*

SIX OR SEVEN years ago in America there was a record by the Jim Kweskin Jug Band which I played almost until it was worn smooth. It contained a number of whacky, funny songs like 'Never Swat a Fly' and 'Blues in the Bottle'. But the thing that made it special was the singing of Maria Muldaur, particularly on 'Richmond Woman' which had qualities of sensuousness, with an understatement far in excess of the humble demands of Jug Band music.

Such a voice stays with you and makes hungry where most it satisfies. So the announcement some months ago of a Maria Muldaur solo album coming long after the passing of her Jug Band career, was great news. And having finally managed to get hold of a copy, I can testify that *Maria Muldaur* (Reprise M.S. 2148) is a great record.

The distinctiveness of her voice frustrates definition. It seems fragile and steely at the same time, as natural as breathing and yet full of artistry. It resists categorisation: it is neither a blues voice nor a pop nor a cabaret voice, but is instead able to absorb all such styles into itself, as the album's range of material demonstrates.

None of the eleven songs was previously known to me, but they have all already entered my bathroom repertoire. They range back in time to the Dixie-style Jimmie Rodgers song 'Any Old Time' and the bawdier 'Don't You Feel My Leg', both done with a goodtime swing and panache. From more recent New Orleans music come Doctor John's 'Three Dollar Bill', and still in a very simple vein is Dolly Parton's country number 'My Tennessee Mountain Home'.

These last two are rather slight, but the quality of Ms Muldaur's backing musicians as well as her voice irradiates them. She has Dr John himself on piano, Jim Keltner on drums, Richard Greene on violin; some of the finest session names in America are sprinkled throughout this album.

***

ON THE other tracks, they and she are able to stretch. There are two songs from the pen of guitarist David Nichtern, who also plays on the album. 'I Never Did Sing You a Love Song' is an attractive ballad complemented by 'Long Hard Climb', also in a fairly lush pop idiom;

230

'Midnight at the Oasis', by contrast, is a zany and delightful jazz vein of sophisticated humour.

This description applies equally to the Dan Hick's number, 'Walkin' One and Only', a tour de force in the course of which Maria turns into a superb vocal trio. As a Desert Island disc choice, this track would be hard to pass up, but amazingly even it is surpassed by the remaining three songs.

These are the contemporary numbers, the work of two new young female composers. Kate McGarrigle's 'The Work Song' is about the fantasy world of minstrel songs which we all carry in our heads, and the rail world of black slavery which gave rise to it—but done in a wry, personal and honest way.

Wendy Waldman's 'Vaudeville Man' also looks to the past, to the old trouper philosophy of her father. But her 'Mad, Mad, Me' the album's climax, is something else entirely—a dark, profound, disturbing love-song, sung by Maria Muldaur with an intensity and depth that induces awe.

What finally distinguishes this singer is her intelligence. Behind the voice you sense a mind, matured and sharpened by a fullness of experience, expressing itself with grace and integrity.

Tuesday, 4 June 1974

INDEPENDENT VIRGIN

Slapp Happy/*Slapp Happy*

VIRGIN RECORDS HAS been known for some time as a London record retailer, offering cut-price albums by mail to readers of pop music magazines. But since last year it has become even better known as a full-fledged record company with a steadily growing list of album and singles releases.

Every history of rock & roll will tell you that all the innovative discs were made by 'indies'—small independent companies usually run by a dedicated individual (like Sam Phillips and his Sun Records) backing his own taste, and that mass popularity led to the swamping of these by the huge record corporations, which led in turn to anonymous mediocrity. This trend has intensified over the years, as small labels, unable to beat the big companies in the competition for new artists, have joined them in unwieldy amalgamations. All the more reason, then, to applaud the arrival of a new independent label in these islands, particularly when it has already proved a commitment to new artists, a willingness to take risks, and an ability to discover genuine talent.

Each one of these qualities was most successfully demonstrated in Virgin's very first release, Mike Oldfield's *Tubular Bells*, which became a kind of instant classic. None of their subsequent records could have been expected to repeat that coup but they have released one this month which is, initially at least, just as fascinating.

It's from a trio called Slapp Happy, and the album (on V2014) has the same name. The songs on it are sung by a girl called Dagmar, and written by Peter Blegvad, who backs her up at times, and Anthony Moore, who plays keyboards. Complementing them are a number of other musicians, some not named, but all extremely good.

A booklet of the song lyrics accompanies the record and it's worth having, for they are often clever and richly humorous. 'Michelangelo', for instance, has lines like:

> Work and toil, well he ain't no dilettante,
> He conceives in oil and Vatican chianti.

This has a jaunty, childlike tune and the sound is characteristic of many of the cuts: it has no middle. On top there's drums and accordion, a strummed mandolin and occasional bassoon: on the bottom there's bass and a few jug sounds; but nothing in between, no rhythm guitars or equivalent to fill out the sound. The effect is flat and yet dreamlike, and is reinforced by the cold and slightly hollow sound of Dagmar's singing.

'Casablanca Moon' (this group is nothing if not cosmopolitan) is a witty verbal fricassée concocted from Sydney Greenstreet movies and '30s secret agent novels. The first part of 'Mr Rainbow' is a pretty setting of a poem by Rimbaud, but the second part is two florid, garbled verses which would have been better omitted. And, of course, pretentiousness is the chief occupational hazard for a group like this: what's surprising about the album is that it contains so little, with the fresh nuttiness of the music often cancelling out a trend towards poesie in the words.

Furthermore, several of the songs are done in a silkily commercial style rivalling Michel Legrand. At least one, 'A Little Something', seems to be a straightforward (and very good) pop song, but 'The Secret' is a sly pastiche. All in all, there is both variety and originality in the album, and also some blowing of a high quality—Henry Lowther's trumpet on 'Dawn' for instance, and Geoff Leigh's ravishing sax solo on 'Slow Moon's Rose'.

Wednesday, 12 June 1974

RELENTLESSNESS

Henry Cow/*Unrest*
Kevin Coyne/*Blame It on the Night*

IMAGINE A YOUNG musician who has a taste not only for Stockhausen and Charlie Parker, but also for Cathy Berberian, Kurt Weill, Bob Dylan, Messiaen, the Beatles and Mississippi John Hurt. Now imagine four other musicians, equally eclectic, who reflect all these tastes in their playing and composing. What you've got is a group calling itself Henry Cow, for reasons known only to its members.

It's not unusual for a person to have this range of musical tastes, but it is most unusual to have them all indulged on the same album, as they are on Henry Cow's *Unrest* (V2011)—well, maybe not all, but a considerable variety nevertheless. The opening track, for example, starts out quite funkily on bass, piano and drums, with arresting guitar phrases. But soon some quaint woodwind stylings take over, contributed by the one female group member, Lindsay Cooper, who is academy-trained in bassoon, flute and oboe.

The second number opens with an impressionist essay on piano by Tim Hodgkinson, and then moves into a cool, striding modern jazz tempo which accommodates some impressive improvisation-including a bubbling sole from Miss Cooper on that reed most intractable to jazz performance, the bassoon.

These pieces are called, respectively, 'Bittern Storm Over Ülm' and 'Half Asleep; Half Awake', not titles that are likely to bust the charts. But Henry Cow does have a firm following, probably much larger than that of many leading performers in the pure jazz or avant-garde music genres. And they deserve it, for musical ability and for the imagination to forge a unity out of their diverse influences.

Having said all that, I have to confess that their music finally

233

leaves me cold. It lacks wit and sensuousness, which couldn't be said of any of the ladies and gentlemen mentioned above in the opening sentence, except maybe Stockhausen, whose music may have all kinds of qualities for all I know. The second side of this album is especially dry, comprising as it does a considerable amount of free-form doodling, electronic messing about and meandering impressionism.

Ultimately, what the ear misses most is melody, which is in even shorter supply here than on Soft Machine albums. So long as you're going to employ other hopelessly unprogressive elements like harmony and recognised tempi, you might as well throw in a few good tunes here and there. Without them, the music grows increasingly relentless.

***

Relentless is also the word for Kevin Coyne's *Blame It on the Night* (V2012), but in this case there are no compensations whatever. 'Nobody remembers me, nobody knows my name' he sings on one track: unfortunately, I for one remember the gruesomeness of his voice and lyrics all too well, and quite a few people seem to know his name after the critical success of his first album.

Yes, grown men have been known to praise his work, and I can't begin to imagine why. In general, it seems as though he's trying to be the English Loudon Wainwright, all pained voice and naked confessional. In the process he works through a series of awful singing imitations of Roger Chapman, Dave Cousins, Gilbert O'Sullivan, Van Morrison, Bob Dylan and Robin Williamson.

The lyrics are about the River of Sin into which we are repeatedly assured he is falling, about a number of things which are Signs of the Times, about how he Believes in Love, but beseeches us all to Don't Delude Him, and tells some girl that Wanting Her is Not Easy; and about Taking a Train. That's Side 1.

The delights of Side 2 I shall leave you to discover for yourself.

Tuesday, 25 June 1974

234

FROM THE WAITING ROOM

James Taylor/ *Walking Man*
Geoff and Maria Muldaur/ *Sweet Potatoes*

JAMES TAYLOR'S NEW album *Walking Man* (Warner Bros. W2794) seems strongly apposite to this summer of '74 in America, where I happen to have been living for the past month. The country has the calm and apparently resigned and indeed very pleasant atmosphere of a vast waiting-room; verdicts and disclosures flow in, but everybody still keeps waiting for the mythic showdown, the final accounting, or at any rate a finale to the national psychodrama.

Taylor's passive, melancholy style suits this mood well. But there's more: the song 'Let It All Fall Down' addresses the political situation directly:

> I just now got the news
> He seems to tell us lies
> And still we will believe him
> Then together he will lead us
> Into darkness, my friends.

The chorus calls for a dropping of all deception and pretence, but it's undercut by the languor of the singing and the comparative lushness of the arrangement.

Other songs make more indirect commentaries. The protagonist of 'Walking Man' is headed towards a Holy Land which is merely a 'hypothetical destination'. At the other end of the album is Chuck Berry's song of ten years ago about the poor boy from Virginia who makes his way by bus, train and plane to what was then the 'promised land' of California. As for presenting the rock culture as a mode of salvation, Taylor warns us in a droll, effective number that 'mama knows and papa knows/That rock 'n roll is music now'—it's been co-opted, it's safe and respectable.

This David Spinozza production is the most elaborately orchestrated and arranged Taylor album since his debut on Apple. On 'Rock 'n Roll Is Music Now', the elaboration pays off, with tight, exciting jazz/rock lines, some punchy riffs from a seven-piece horn section, and high-class background vocals from Mrs Carly Simon Taylor and the (Paul) McCartneys. Elsewhere, there's sometimes treacle. 'Hello Old Friend' opens like a remember-when song from a romantic film musical, and keeps this up with oboe and French horn

235

obbligattos gilding the voice whilst it is meanwhile swathed in sweeping strings.

Taylor himself seems somewhat uneasy about the lavish orchs, and even apologises for them in 'Me and My Guitar'; 'I hear horns,' he sings, and sure enough the horn section blows a line; 'I hear voices,' he adds and so do we; 'I hear strings,' he concludes, and he's right again. He then goes on to sing that these 'extra things' serve only to confuse him, that it's essentially just him and his guitar and that we're to pay no attention to the man behind the curtain. But that's not easy when there's at least ten men behind the curtain, plus a string section and a horn section.

Nevertheless, Taylor's voice is richer and deeper here than it's ever been before. And if the lyrics are sometimes correspondingly muddier than before he's still capable of a touchingly simple and beautiful lullaby like 'Daddy's Baby'. All in all, this is a seductive album which has subtly captured the tone of its time and place.

***

Maria Muldaur's unlikely and heartening break through into mass popularity continues to happen, with her solo album and the single 'Midnight At The Oasis' both high on the American charts. Hungry for more of her work, I have obtained one of the two albums she made with her former husband Geoff Muldaur—*Sweet Potatoes* (Warner Bros. MS2073).

Unfortunately, Maria sings solo on only two of the ten tracks, and I find her ex-husband's work on the other eight rather coarse-grained and pedestrian. But the two tracks are magic. On the old jazz standard 'Lover Man' she rivals Billie Holiday for wistful magnetism. On 'Sweet Potatoes' she turns in a performance of pure sensuous beauty. She is without a doubt the brightest star in the firmament this year.

Tuesday, 6 August 1974

COUNTRY COOKING

Joy of Cooking/*Cross Country*
Chi Coltrane/*Let It Ride*

ONE OF THE treats of a visit to America—for the rock-music fiend—is the chance it affords to acquire slightly obscure albums which have eluded one in the old world. For years I've been hearing occasional snatches of a San Francisco group called the Joy of Cooking, but their work has been practically unknown in these islands. Then, for a period towards the end of last year, a song called 'I Want To Be The One' got a fair bit of airplay on the BBC and became a minor hit. It was done by Toni Brown and Terry Garthwaite, the two women who led the Joy of Cooking, and it came from an album they made together in Tennessee, mainly with Nashville session musicians, called 'Cross Country' (Capital ST 11137).

At long last I've got my paws on this record, and it's a little treasure. Garthwaite and Brown are light years away from the all-girl rock group ballyhoo, which thankfully seems to be spent. The maturity and simplicity of their work are equally lacking in pretentiousness. Like Garbo in *Ninotchka*, they don't make an issue of their womanhood. But it's present all the same in every word they sing and write.

Cross Country belongs in part to the pilgrimage-to-Nashville genre which was inaugurated by Bob Dylan's 'Nashville Skyline' seven years ago; the dobro players and pedal steel guitarists of the 'home of country music' have been hired by some pretty quaint visitors since then. However, Brown and Garthwaite are not interested in C&W pastiche. The nearest they come to it is on a pseudo-Johnny Cash number called 'I Don't Want to Live Here', but even in it the lyrics are distinctively their own, dealing with a wife who's quitting the fat, slothing TV moron and betting addict who calls himself her husband.

The opening song, 'Done My Cryin' Time', is a tight, vigorous rock number, with Vassar Clements' fiddle sailing excitedly over a chunky band sound. The two voices are well matched, Garthwaite's slinky and of the earth while Brown's is more ethereal, but the two of them close enough in timbre to blend harmonically. This shows up attractively on the slow, countrified numbers, 'Going Isn't Easier' and 'Come To Me Now'.

In between these two tracks there lives the glorious 'I Want To Be The One', a rock song that is now firmly established in my personal permanent Top 50. Punctuated by an irresistible guitar figure, the sly voice sings siren verses to a married man, pointing out that she can make love to him, talk to and befriend him in ways of which his wife is incapable. The harmony voice swoops in to underline particular words. It's a rare mixture—for pop music—of irony, joy and female sensuality.

Side 2 adds to the album's variety. 'Midnight Blues' catches the innocence of the teenage girl duos of early rock & roll, while overlaying it with womanliness. 'I've Made Up My Mind' is a sultry and slightly aggressive love song. 'When All Is Said' is another piece of funk but qualified this time by a mourning country wail of sadness in the chorus.

Terry Garthwaite and Toni Brown are neither poets, musical innovators, revolutionaries, prophets, nor leaders of any movement. In the climate of today's popular music culture, that in itself would serve to make them extraordinary if their music didn't already do so in its own right.

***

FROM A delight to a disappointment. When Chi Coltrane (white, female and no relation to John) came out with her debut album nearly two years ago, I was greatly taken by it, although it received scant attention; so much so that I failed to procure her recent second LP, *Let It Ride* (Columbia KC 32463). Now I have it and it's a sad disaster. Most of the numbers are uncontrolled soul imitations, synthetic freakouts. On the few numbers which approach the vulnerable, fragile lyricism of the earlier record, her voice has been fuzzed over echo and strings.

She still has immense promise. I hope she, or her producer, recognises and learns from the mistakes on this album.

Tuesday, 20 August 1974

WENDY HAS ARRIVED

Wendy Waldman/*Gypsy Symphony*

WENDY WALDMAN ISSUED her debut LP in America last September called *Love Has Got Me*. But what has really brought her work to the attention of discerning fans is Maria Muldaur's solo album on Reprise, which contains two Waldman compositions: the jaunty 'Vaudeville Man' and the haunting, riveting 'Mad, Mad Me', arguably the finest track on that remarkable record. The emotional depth and artistic breadth of these two songs bespeak at the least an important new songwriting talent.

Further evidence is now at hand in the second Wendy Waldman album, *Gypsy Symphony* (Warner Bros. BS 2792), on which she sings 'Mad, Mad Me' and eleven of her other songs playing a little guitar, dulcimer and piano, and receiving a credit for the string and horn arrangements. Oddly enough, on early acquaintance with the twelve 'new' songs, these arrangements and the sound in general are more impressive than the actual writing. There is a marshalling of quite formidable contrapuntal resources which no other singer-songwriter has ever entirely brought off.

The reason may be that Wendy Waldman's father is a well-known composer of film and television theme music and her mother a concert violininst. She has the kind of genes that are clearly at home with horn and string sections, piano, synthesizer guitars, bass, Afro-American percussion and other miscellaneous effusions all going on at once. This album has as rich and complicated a palette of sounds as any in its category, but it never gets blotchy or gaudy. It's always a pleasure to listen to.

***

Her voice is light and without particular individuality, but it has a lot of vigour and throaty expressiveness. On 'Mad, Mad Me', for example where comparison with Muldaur's performance is unavoidable, she uses her girlish timbre to good effect particularly in swooping up to an impossibly high falsetto near the end. Elsewhere, she often sounds like a young Carole King, with a more sophisticated edge. However, to my ear the voice track is sometimes mixed down too low, rendering the words inaudible—especially on 'You Got to Ride'. This is my one gripe about an otherwise superb production job by Charles Plotkin.

The song lyrics tend to be restricted to 'A man and a woman, the joy and the pain', and are not always entirely fresh, but neither are they prominently featured. As to the Waldman style of composition, it runs the gamut. Like most of her peers, she has been exposed to an enormous range of types of music, and she has assimilated all of them into her own styles. 'You Got To Ride' is a rhythm & blues train number, with a virtual big band sound. 'The Good Love' is a gospel song celebrating a love affair in which 'the worst times are better than the good times before.' 'My Name Is Love' is an odd childlike song with rapid lyrics and a beautiful soprano sax obbligato.

***

My favourite number is 'Cold Back On Me', which closes Side 1. It has an insistent light chugging rhythm and a melody which consists of one compelling phrase constantly repeated. The complex arrangement is fascinating, with continuous embellishments and metamorphoses of instrumental colour and texture. But the overall effect is curiously innocent and quite dreamlike: a mixture of hypnotic R&B repetitions and youthful fantasy.

Side 2 has a striding blues called 'Baby Don't You Go' and a folksy song, catchy but insubstantial called 'Northwoods Man'. 'Come On Down' is a familiar R&B invocation with a tinge of Beatles, and 'The Road Song' is just what it says.

It all adds up to a heady brew well worth the sampling. With these talents at her disposal, Wendy Waldman is clearly no momentary sensation, but has arrived to stay.

Wednesday, 4 September 1974

DUTCH TREAT

Focus/*Hamburger Concerto*

A NEW RELEASE by the Dutch group, Focus, is always an occasion for good cheer. Focus is one of those rare bands with a sound all their own, instantly recognisable. When you break it down, none of its individual elements is particularly original: it's the blend that's unique. Musicianship is combined with Puckish whimsy, spacey cinematic melodrama with genuine lyricism, jazz flavours with classical flavours, and the whole thing is presented with a kind of casual insouciance.

Hamburger Concerto (Polydor 2442 124) is the name of their current album. It opens disconcertingly with a cut called 'Delitiae Musicae', which is listed as 'traditional' and sounds 17th-century, with Jan Akkerman playing a flute and Thijs Van Leer a recorder, both very well. With 'Harem Scarem' we leap into the more familiar sound of Akkerman's damped-string fast chording on electric guitar, leading off a full-blooded rock number.

The range of instrumental and electronic sounds on this album is wider than in their previous efforts. On top of his customary keyboards and flute playing, Van Leer throws in at various points both synthesizer and mellotron work, as well as fooling with vibes, an accordion and the organ of St Mary the Virgin, Barnes, London. Bassist Bert Ruiter and drummer Colin Allen handle between them a vast array of percussion instruments. As you would expect, the record sometimes gets a little cluttered, but not seriously. Mostly it's a natural extension of their previous work.

The third track, 'La Cathedrale de Strasbourg', is one of their romantic filmic numbers, with the piano and guitar in a soulful dialogue. Typically, however, it's undercut by the eccentric singing of the title by Van Leer. 'Birth', which closes Side 1, takes off from a delicate harpsichord introduction into stomping drums, organ and guitar. There's a marvellous flute solo with the guitar gurgling along underneath. The textures throughout are dynamic and the structure, built as usual on a simple theme, wholly impeccable.

***

Side 2 contains the Hamburger Concerto itself, in SIX movements—Starter, Rare, Medium I, Medium II, Well Done and One For The Road. I haven't quite figured out yet where each one begins and ends, but the overall effect is irresistible. It owes something to late-period Beatle arrangements—in fact, one of its leit-motifs, a series of descending chords, comes straight from the climax of *Abbey Road*, Side 2. But it's worthy of its influence. It manages to perfection the blend of hilarity and good music implied in its title.

The opening is a kind of comically dignified baroque procession, done with synthesizer, guitar and timpani. Then it moves through the 'Abbey Road' chords into a passage of Van Leer vocals which includes his yodeling and a ludicrous parody of operatic singing. After this, Akkerman, who is not especially prominent on one side takes the centre of the stage. Working with a heavily filtered sound, he displays his virile romantic imagination to perfection in a long guitar interlude which builds up a powerful head of steam.

This winds back down to the opening chords accompanied by handclaps. Then Van Leer sings us what sounds like a Dutch carol as a prelude to a heavily rocking finale; a cinematic barrage of sound, which concludes with the guitar imitating a clock chiming the half hour.

This summer, the McDonald's chain of hamburger joints in America—where you do your eating 'under the golden arches'—was proudly advertising the fact that its patrons had now consumed a grand total of 14 billion hamburgers. Consumption of *Hamburger Concerto* is unlikely to be quite on this scale but it's a taste sensation worth indulging. In fact, it's a whole meal in itself.

Tuesday, 17 September 1974

THE FIFTIES

Robert Greenfield/*Stones Touring Party*

ROCK 'N ROLL is twenty years old now, and its days of innocence are gone. Not that it ever seemed innocent at the time; one of its most exciting original elements was the sexual frankness which it appropriated from black music, albeit somewhat timorously at first.

But frankness about sex has become commonplace now, and we can see that it's not after all the equivalent of honesty or of truth, much less of happiness. And the joyous sensuality of early rock & roll has evolved into a parade of garish fantasies drawn from the collective mania of the sexual demi-monde closer to Hieronymus Bosch than to Eros.

Everything else to do with the music has grown up in the same way. Big concerts today are as often as not armed confrontations between surly audiences and massive security forces, with the cosseted stars performing at a safe remove. Pep pills and joints have been superseded by cocaine and heroin; on the Rolling Stones' 1972 American tour the most popular drug was amyl nitrate, in the form of capsules which could be cracked under people's noses. Their medical function is to ease the agonising pain caused by a heart attack.

***

The source of this information and the occasion of these observations, is Robert Greenfield's book *Stones Touring Party*, published last week by Michael Joseph at £3.00. It's a 337-page account of a major tour describing (in the words of the blurb) ... 'fifty-four nights and days of drugs, drink and random debauchery ... the crazy exhausting enormously exciting brutal punishing life of a rockbiz tour.' Yes indeed, folks. That's what it is. But luckily that's not the way in which it's written.

Greenfield is an old *Rolling Stone* magazine hand, and he writes in the bright nervy style of that particular brand of the New Journalism, which I for one find immensely readable. Combined with the reptilian fascination of the subject matter, it makes for a book as compelling as it is nauseating. It's the most complete account yet of how a large segment of the rock music world now shares the values of Harold Robbins and Ian Fleming and Richard Nixon, i.e. people are objects to be exploited for gain and pleasure, enemies exist to be screwed, and personal material gratification is the supreme aim of life.

Playboy magazine fits in there too. On their visit to Chicago, the Stones Touring Party stayed at the Hugh Hefner mansion, where drugs and bunnies were passed from hand to hand like candy bars. At other points on the tour, there were other diversions: ripping the plumbing out of hotel bathrooms, bringing groupies on to the private jet and filming the sexual junketings with them, and at the very end joining the New York jet set for an exclusive party at which a naked lady burst out of a cake and four black dancers shuffled to the music of Count Basie.

The worst aspect of it all is the way the particulars constantly express disdain for these wretched values. Jagger announces at one point that he would never give an interview to *Playboy* 'on principle' ... having just spent four days as an honoured Playboy in the Hefner inner sanctum. Keith Richards complains of being treated like 'a product'. Jagger even has the amazing temerity to criticise the audiences for not being politically involved; 'I think you just have to make your country a better place to live and bring up kids in and think in, and sitting at home taking smack and listening to records just ain't gonna do it. '

No wonder people feel nostalgic about the fifties.

Tuesday, 8 October 1974

243

OLDFIELD OPUS 2

Mike Oldfield/*Hergest Ridge*

WITHOUT HAVING done any market research whatsoever, I would suggest that the audience for rock music albums falls mainly into the 25-35 age group, and is in search of a little sophistication and intelligence on top of your basic beat. How else to explain the fact that Mike Oldfield's *Hergest Ridge* (Virgin V2013) is currently number one in the *Melody Maker* album chart, and his *Tubular Bells* is number two?

Tubular Bells, you may remember, was a maverick disc of 'symphonic rock' which last year went from obscurity to cult status to public performance on a TV culture programme. A fragment of it has now become that programme's signature tune, and 20-year-old Oldfield has become 1974's most unlikely pop star.

The opinions I expressed in reviewing the work have remained unchanged: namely that it comprises a polyphony of beautiful and hilarious and sometimes tedious sounds, created by a man whose real instrument is the recording studio, and that whilst musically restful and good humoured for much of the time, it's also a bit whimsical and long-winded to stand up to a lot of playing.

***

Hergest Ridge is the follow-up; it has zoomed straight to the number one spot on the strength of its predecessor's reputation, and it strikes me as one of the dreariest records ever made. Gone are the humour and the rich polyphonic textures. The tedium and whimsy have taken over.

It's easy to sympathise with the appalling dilemma of an introverted and retiring musician who suddenly finds himself with a monster hit album (so successful that a version employing a full symphony orchestra is being made) whilst still in his teens. The pressure on the lad during the gestation of opus 2 must have been enormous. But it would be a greater disservice to him to overlook the album's failings than to attempt a definition of them.

The basic processes are the same as before, with Oldfield playing a range of string and keyboard instruments and employing massive overdubbing, tape loops and the like to build up his multilayered sound. Some woodwinds played by other hands also appear here and there, but to little effect, though a stray trumpet passage on Side 1 is some relief from the general blandness of the sound.

The composition is melodically very impoverished and harmonically repetitive. When Oldfield does hit on a new thought, he blatters away at it ad nauseam. The major theme of the whole piece is undistinguished and sounds suspiciously close to a section of *Tubular Bells*.

Insofar as there is variety, it encompasses a kind of directionless browsing through a series of innocuous, uninteresting musical statements, and a fast, thudding repetition of the main theme with various tinkering embellishments. In the middle of Side 1, this latter style works itself into a passage which might serve to accompany an inter-galactic chase sequence in a sci-fi movie. But this is but a brief awakening in an otherwise undisturbed slumber.

Tuesday, 15 October 1974

GEORGE AND IRA

Robert Kimball & Alfred Simon/*The Gershwins*

IF THE '20s were roaring and the '60s swinging, what are the '70s turning out to be, as they near their half-way house? Nostalgic, mainly, for all those earlier decades. The two biggest trends in recent popular music have been the rock & roll revival and the ragtime revival, and the next one bids fair to be a Kern-Berlin-Porter-Gershwin-Rodgers revival.

Indeed this is already under way. Rock luminaries like Harry Nilsson and Bryan Ferry have recorded some of these inter-war oldies, with mainly horrendous results. Paul Simon is reportedly pondering an album of them. Mr Porter has received lavish attention in the pictorial biography *Cole*, and the stage show of the same name which has done good business at London's Mermaid Theatre. The 1926 Gershwin musical *Oh Kay* has also been revived in the West End. And now they—meaning George and Ira—get their book in turn, entitled *The Gershwins* (Jonathan Cape, £9.50) from the team that brought you *Cole*: designer Bea Feitler, assembler and editor Robert Kimball (augmented this time by Alfred Simon).

The Gershwins is big and voluptuous, as befits a book costing £9.50. After a short, straight biography of the two brothers, we're

245

given a 250-page collage of diary entries, letters, recollections, sheet music, lyrics, paintings and sketches by and of both brothers, and of course scores of photographs. In one sense this is the raw material of a biography which we can write in our heads as we peruse it. But in fact it has all been painstakingly and imaginatively arranged into what is literallly a documentary account of the lives and careers of its two subjects.

***

They were the Brooklyn-born sons of Morris Gershovitz from old St Petersburg, and their first joint composition to be performed in a musical comedy made a splendidly fitting declaration—'The Real American Folk Song is a Rag'. The lyricist, Ira, was 21 at the time. The composer, George, was just 19. This song was quickly forgotten about until Ella Fitzgerald recorded it in her *Gershwin Songbook* album in the late '50s, at which point it became immortal.

Ragtime was of seminal importance to George Gershwin. He had a genuine affinity with black music, and when he was still only eighteen, his piano playing caught the attention of the great Harlem rag pianists like James P. Johnson. It's this quality which has made Gershwin compositions the most popular vehicles amongst jazzmen. How many jazz solos have been constructed on the chords of 'I Got Rhythm' or 'Summertime' or 'Embraceable You'?

George Gershwin died suddenly of a brain tumour at the age of 38. Ira is still alive today. Somehow that seems appropriate to their disparate personalities. They were the tortoise and the hare: George was mercurial, scintillating, the handsome boy at the centre of the party, accompanied by a succession of beautiful women. Ira was and is stocky, bespectacled and self-effacing. Most people even today think that Ira Gershwin was George's wife or sister. George tossed off the music with prodigious energy: Ira then took it home with him and proceeded methodically to apply words to it.

His achievement in doing so shouldn't be underestimated. He may not have had the corrosive sophistication of Cole Porter or the verbal virtuosity of Lorenz Hart, but he had an amazing gift for transmuting the way people talk in the street into vividly singable words, sometimes hilarious and sometimes very gentle. What could be more delightful than the abbreviations of "S wonderful' and the pronunciations of 'Let's Call The Whole Thing Off', or more tender than 'Someone to Watch Over Me'?

Songs like these have never died, so they don't need to be 'revived': but if fashion decrees that they are de rigeur for this season, it's all right with me.

Tuesday, 29 October 1974

PERSONAL LIST

Henry Pleasants/*The Great American Popular Singers*

AN ECLECTIC TASTE in music is becoming more and more respectable. One man who has succumbed to it splendidly is Henry Pleasants, music critic of the *International Herald Tribune* and editor of *Stereo Review*. He has formidable credentials as a commentator on classical music and particularly opera, not the least of them being his survey of operatic performing styles from the dawn of opera to the present day, *The Great Singers*. But he has been glad to tell the world of how, at the age of fifty, he started to appreciate popular music as well; and he is now presenting us with chapter and verse in a new book entitled *The Great American Popular Singers* (Gollancz, £3.75), a study of twenty-two performers from Jolson to Streisand.

Books like this often come a cropper, a recent example being Professor Wilfrid Mellers' study of the Beatles, *The Twilight of the Gods*, a dreadful farrago of musical jargon and critical gibberish. At first sight Henry Pleasants' book looks alarmingly similar: it's a big heavy hardback with an introduction, the first paragraph of which invokes the 'terminological and categorical conventions of our time' arising from a 'dichotomous musical society'; and with a glossary at the back of terms like mordent, roulade and tessitura.

Yet you only need to get half-a-dozen pages into the text to realise that you're on to something, entertaining, illuminating, even thrilling. Pleasants is both articulate and candid. Contrasting his present love of Bing Crosby's work with his loathing of it in the 'thirties, when he and his friends were opera snobs, he says: 'It seemed, when heard from our point of view, to be saccharine, lugubrious, cello, maudlin, musically slovenly, lacking in vocal virility and incisiveness, short of range—in brief, just something tasteless for schoolgirls to become excited about.' Which is as lively a description of orthodoxy as has been heard from a latter-day heretic.

247

***

The book has an intriguing thesis—that the American popular singer of today is closer than the contemporary classically-trained singer to the older, original objectives and conventions of European singing. Pleasants directs particular attention to matters like enunciation, vocal embellishments and rhythmic sensitivity. But he always comes back to the central point of the primacy of text in popular singing, the way in which the singer's art is aimed at achieving maximum expressiveness for the words.

His pursuit of this theme through the historical fluctuations in singing styles is masterly, but the bulk of the book is taken up with the twenty-two short essays on particular singers. Naturally, his list is a personal one. He fails to convince me that Johnny Cash or Barbra Streisand deserve their places—to me they represent bogus integrity and bogus histrionics respectively. His wholesale exclusion of 'folk' singers, and his glumness about the younger present-day performers both seem a bit wilful.

However, he is sensitive and wise about Ethel Waters and Billie Holiday, enviably precise about the nature of Ella Fitzgerald's supremacy, fascinating about Peggy Lee's arranging and bandleading expertise, and never less than readable about figures as diverse as Hank Williams, Aretha Franklin, Elvis and Mahalia Jackson.

Wednesday, 13 November 1974

THE GUINNESS SPOT MUSIC SESSIONS

THE GUINNESS SPOT has undoubtedly become the most distinctive institution of the Queen's Festival in Belfast. This year it was moved back to its former home on the campus—the South Dining Hall, an oblong box beside the Whitla, erected about 13 years ago as a temporary structure. Sitting on moulded plastic in this overcrowded, smoke-filled refectory with its awful acoustics and Double Diamond banners, you wonder why you're enjoying yourself. That's the work of a worthwhile institution.

The Spot was filled during the first week mainly by folk groups, culminating on the Saturday with a magical performance by the

Watersons from Yorkshire. The excellence of this group transcends categories, so that everyone from the most rigid purists to those with a folk phopia can enjoy their work. On the other hand, the bulk of the audience was only there for the beer and the clamour of its applause at the end was greatly exceeded by the loudness of its conversations during the singing.

The Watersons sing ritual songs of the elements, of the seasons and of eating and drinking. Without accompaniment, they blend their four voices in superb harmonies, often employing the intervals typical of medieval music, which are so appropriate to the modal airs of their traditional material. Outstanding in this concert were their wassail songs, like 'Three Jolly Gentlemen', 'Here We Come A-Wassailing', and a slow one in free rhythm with the most extraordinary sustained harmonies.

But everything they did was a delight, including their solo numbers. Mike Waterson, who has one of the great story-telling voices of folk singing, did an English Napoleon song, 'The Eighteenth of June'. The new member, Martin Carthy, who has a nasal but very intense singing style, with a glissando like a blues singer, was especially fine in his version of 'Bonnie Boy, Billy Boy'. And the girls gave us their splendid girl-disguised-as-soldier song, 'Rub-A-Dum'.

***

Tuesday night was trad jazz time, shared between two local bards under the trombone of Rodney Foster and the trumpet of George Chambers respectively. Musical raggedness was subsumed in good cheer, and the appearance of a sousaphone towards the end consolidated the benevolence of the proceedings.

On Wednesday and Thursday nights, yet another kind of traditional music was featured-the Blues. The admirable Jim Daly Blues Band warmed the audience up in preparation for the Mighty Flea from Chicago, with his quartet of British Session musicians. The Mighty Flea turned out to be a personable man called Gene Connors, who was a first-rate showman, an acceptable trombonist and singer, and a non-purist whose 'Blues' extended from 'Shake, Rattle and Roll' to 'I got Rhythm'.

Friday night was the climactic Guinness Spot, with a triumphant return visit from the man who played tenor sax alongside Lester Young in the 1939 Count Basie Band, George (Buddy) Tate. Playing with the local Billy White Trio who always rise magnificently to these occasions, he conquered a packed audience which was so noisy that the promoter twice appealed for quiet and finally shut the bar early.

The moment of conquest came early in the second set with a barnstorming 'C-Jam Blues', on which the Buddy Tate flute proved itself almost on a par with the Buddy Tate tenor. Before this he had played some beautiful ballads, notably 'Satin Doll', which had been scarcely audible over the din. After it, he was able to do a 'Body and Soul' which had the audience attentive and enraptured. To finish off, he got them on their feet dancing a stomping number with a rock beat, which he reprised for encore. Great showmanship. Great jazz.

Wednesday, 27 November 1974

THE DANCE BANDS

Albert McCarthy/*The Dance Band Era*

A FEW WEEKS ago I had the pleasure of interviewing for radio the man who played tenor sax alongside Lester Young in the 1939 Count Basie Band—Buddy Tate, in Belfast for the Queen's Festival. For him, the Swing era is a personal experience: for me, a collection of book chapters and old recordings. It was a delight to talk to him and later in the evening to hear him play as well as he has ever played, which means superbly.

With Buddy Tate at the interview was the English jazz writer Albert McCarthy, who has perhaps done more than any other individual in recent years to uphold the cause of Swing music, in terms of editing magazines, writing books and making recordings. But unlike most jazz scholars, he's no snob. His new book is called *The Dance Band Era* (Spring Books, £1.95) and, affirming the fact that we tend to love best the music by which we grew up, it expresses unabashed delight in idols of his youth such as Bert Ambrose, Jack Hylton and Lew Stone.

Purists of the jazz big band school tend to dismiss dance bands as commercial hacks churning out musical clichés for an undiscerning audience. Unfortunately, the distinctions are rarely as simply drawn as this in real life. McCarthy cites the extraordinary career of Paul Whiteman, a favourite butt of the jazz enthusiasts. Whiteman started

250

with the Denver Symphony Orchestra, then formed a dance band which became the toast of high society, until in 1924 he was able to put on a pretentious and patronising concert in the Aeolian Hall, New York, entitled 'An Experiment in Modern Music'. Its climax was George Gershwin's first performance of his 'Rhapsody in Blue'.

However, Whiteman was subsequently to hire and feature one of the great creative figures of jazz, the cornet-player Bix Beiderbecke. Part of the Beiderbecke legend is the belief that he compromised his integrity by playing Whiteman's music, and was thereby driven into the drugs and dissipation which caused his untimely death. But, again, a recent biography has demonstrated that Beiderbecke was delighted to get into Whiteman's band; as was Mildred Bailey a few years later, and Billie Holiday in 1942.

***

THE FACT is that musicians rarely categorise in the rigid manner of critics. Louis Armstrong's favourite listening in the early thirties was the famous wide vibrato of Guy Lombardo's sax section, 'The Sweetest Music This Side of Heaven'. On the other hand, they can be devastating in their reaction to bad craftmanship. McCarthy quotes a former sideman with the Eddie Duchin band who said: 'I'll say this for the man, he was the only musician I've ever known who could play a thirty-two bar solo with thirty-two mistakes and get an ovation for it afterwards.'

The Dance Band Era is presented in this book as stretching from 1910 to 1950, with its peak in the late thirties, when jazz finally broke through into popular taste, and the great bands of Goodman, Basie, Herman, Ellington *et al* combined commercial success with artistic excellence. For the rest, McCarthy gives a very full and meticulous account. Even if most of it will only engage the hard-core enthusiast, the pictures are great and the price is most certainly right.

Wednesday, 11 December 1974

LABOUR OF LOVE

Carla Bley/*Escalator Over The Hill*

A FEW YEARS ago in America, I kept hearing about a mammoth work composed and recorded by jazz pianist Carla Bley, employing a huge and stellar cast of jazz and rock musicians, recorded on a small private label and available only by post. It sounded like the ultimate in underground mystique. But the invaluable Virgin Records have now got hold of the thing and released it in the British Isles: it's called *Escalator Over The Hill* (JTA 411-13), it's comprised of three LPs (six sides), and it's a fascinating and important piece of music.

Its realisation was a dedicated labour of love spanning five years. Miss Bley decided to write an opera in collaboration with her writer friend Paul Haines, who began plying her with verses by post. These triggered off her musical imagination; so that, according to her own account, 'I began to feel as if I was not writing music so much as reading poetry, with the resulting music as the painstaking and complicated by-product of revelation.'

Personally, I am thoroughly grateful for her revelation, since I've experienced none of my own. The words of *Escalator Over The Hill*, sung, spoken and chanted, leave me generally mystified. There are characters, with names like Ginger, Doctor and Sand Shepherd, some of whom have two incarnations. There are localities, mainly in and around 'Cecil Clark's Old Hotel'. There is apparently a running dialogue between eastern and western cultures. And the nature of time seems to be a central theme, since the work is subtitled 'a Chronotransduction'. That's as far as I've got.

***

But it seems likely that this libretto is as unimportant as those of most of the classical operas—which are often incomprehensible in their own way. The music is the major event, and it's as good as a feast. It's broken up into twenty-five segments, ranging from a 13-minute overture played by a big jazz orchestra to a 13-second passage played by a mainly amateur scratch band. It's arranged around several groupings of this varied kind, each of which has a title and plays a dramatic role.

In the 'Orchestra' sections, there is thrilling solo work by tenor saxman Gato Barbieri and trombonist Roswell Rudd. The leader of the 'Desert Band' is another superb jazz soloist, trumpeter Don

Cherry. As for 'Jack's Travelling Band', this achieves one of the most triumphant collaborations in the short history of intelligent rock: guitarist John McLaughlin and bassist Jack Bruce, recorded in 1970-71, when they were both at a peak.

Bruce also shares with Carla Bley herself the main vocal burdens of the work, and again he does brilliantly, with vocal lines that are sometimes tortuous. Other singers (there are many of them) are equally fine, notably Linda Ronstadt, otherwise known as a fairly ordinary pop/rock performer, who sings the role of Ginger. And I am indebted to the work for introducing me to the gorgeously velvety voice of Jeanne Lee.

There is much more-including Andy Warhol's superstar Viva, a calliope passage, and the splendidly comic chorus with a real opera singer taking part—and the musical styles encompass Kurt Weill and musique concrete as well as the best of contemporary jazz and rock. Carla Bley's struggle to get the work recorded and sold, in the face of indifference from the commercial record companies, deserves high praise. The fruits of that struggle deserve a wider audience.

Wednesday, Thursday, Friday 25, 26 & 27 December 1974

NEW REPERTOIRE?

Cleo Laine/ *Cleo Close-Up*
Various/ *Rodgers and Hart in London*

'A BASIC PROBLEM is repertoire', says Henry Pleasants in his book *The Great American Popular Singers*, which I reviewed here some weeks ago. He's referring to the kind of singers he admires, those of considerable vocal endowment and maturer years, who've been left stranded by the wave of pop/rock/soul which has engulfed show business for the last fifteen years. The repertoire problem, for these singers from big bands and musical comedies and nightclubs, is finding suitable new songs instead of repeating the old standards year in and year out.

Cleo Laine—'the greatly and justly admired English jazz singer' as Pleasants describes her in passing—has met this problem by having a go at everything from Shakespeare to Schoenberg. She not only has the warmest, most womanly voice in the business but also one of the most awesomely equipped, with a range approaching four octaves and a jazz sensitivity to rhythmic and melodic embellishment.

The trouble with most contemporary material is that it doesn't call enough of this equipment into play. Thus her most recent album, *Cleo Close-Up* (RCA LPL15026), is a most pleasant, interesting and resourceful record, illustrating the alchemy which she can work on sometimes indifferent material, but only occasionally allowing her to scale the heights of which she's capable.

The two producers—husband John Dankworth and Mike Vernon —have created a rich and modish backdrop for her voice by using a fairly big studio band, with drums, bass and pedal steel guitar to the fore, and backing singers. It's sometimes quite a large sound, but never too much for the gorgeous tone-colours of her voice to master.

Several of the songs are in the contemporary soul idiom, notably Mark James' 'Keep the Faith' and two Stevie Wonder numbers. There are also some pop ballads and Todd Rundgren's rocker 'I Saw the Light' in all of which she does some lovely wordless singing in unison with the orchestra, soaring to the ethereal heights in the middle of the Rundgren piece.

But the two outstanding tracks for me are 'The Sun the Moon and I' and 'Wish You Were Here'. The former is none other than Yum-Yum's song from *The Mikado*, transmuted into something unrecognisable and magical. The latter was written for her by her bass player Daryl Dunswick and is a charming number fashioned out of holiday postcard clichés. She imbues it with an atmosphere of warm-hearted yearning which will melt the snow off your roof.

The market in bargain re-issues keeps growing all the time, and whilst it contains a high proportion of re-processed rubbish, there are also some genuine treasures. One such is *Rodgers and Hart in London* on EMI'S World Records label (SH 183). It contains original cast recordings of shows from *Lido Lady* in 1926 to *Up and Doing* in 1940, featuring artistes like Jack Hulbert, Cicely Courtneidge and Jessie Matthews.

So used have we become to hearing songs like 'My Heart Stood Still' or 'Small Hotel' or 'This Can't Be Love' done by singers like Cleo Laine we forget they ever formed bits of musical comedies. Here they are available again in all their quaintly endearing elocuted purity.

Tuesday, 31 December 1974

1975

WORST WISHES

MY HOPES FOR our popular music in 1975 are mainly negations of things that went on in 1974. To start with a safe bet, I hope that the androgynous glitter-and-glam movement dies a fast and early death. Also, that the fifties revival at last expires. That the Beatles once again fail to get reunited. That Bob Dylan doesn't make another tour and issue another live album. That the twenties revival at last expires. That the Rolling Stones break up. That the Sixties revival at last expires.

All of which is unnecessarily jaundiced, but the fact remains that nothing very new has been happening during the past year. The most exciting new sounds, in my opinion, came from an American group called Steely Dan, whose album *Pretzel Logic* (EMI SPBA 6282) was a major highlight. Every one of its eleven songs is a distinctive and highly accomplished statement, both musically and lyrically; the ones that haunt me most are 'Rikki Don't Lose That Number', 'Charlie Freak', and 'Monkey in Your Soul'.

This group seemed to be taking rock music to a high level of literacy without losing any of its pungency and energy. But alas, the word is that they have split up. Much the same comments apply to the Allman Brothers Band, whose *Brothers and Sisters* album seems to have marked the limit of their potential. A marvellous album it is too—one for all seasons.

So far as solo performers go, the only new artist to whet my appetite (musically), has been Wendy Waldman. Her *Gypsy Symphony* album, whilst unmistakably the work of an apprentice, still bears evidence of impressive song-writing talent, especially in 'Mad Mad Me'. Which inevitably brings up the name of Maria Muldaur, whose solo album with that song on it sold its way all through the year, with the single from it, 'Midnight at the Oasis', projecting her into the hit parade. I look forward to hearing her second album, *Waitress in a Donut Shop*, more than to any other pop music experience.

Joni Mitchell worked her magic again in *Court and Spark* (EMI SYLA 8756), in which she sustained the brilliance of her *For the Roses* and *Blue* without in any way repeating herself. Having proved herself without equal as a contemporary lyricist on those two albums, she turned her attention to arranging and singing on *Court and Spark* and turned in one of the most musically interesting albums of the year. Focus also contributed an album of rich musicianship, the comic, eccentric, sentimental and splendidly named *Hamburger Concerto* (Polydor 2442124).

***

There were plenty of other worthwhile records from established artists in the course of the year, but I want to give an extra plug to Carla Bley's *Escalator Over the Hill* (Virgin JT 4001). This work was actually finished three years ago, but it has only recently become available in this country. It's a set of three LPs, it comprises several scratch groups of musicians, drawn from the top flights of the jazz and rock scenes, as well as many singers and speakers, and it's impossible to describe in a few words.

Suffice to say that it represents a rare commitment to the highest musical values, that musicians like Jack Bruce, John McLaughlin, Don Cherry and Gato Barbieri play at the top of their form, and that makes it a genuine attempt to do something original. And after the Year of Nostalgia, I'm left with nostalgia for nothing at all except originality.

Tuesday, 7 January 1975

MARIA MULDAUR AGAIN

Maria Muldaur/*Waitress in a Donut Shop*

THE APPEARANCE OF Maria Muldaur's *Waitress in a Donut Shop* (Reprise K 54025) will thrill and delight the fans of her first LP, a constantly growing band. This second album follows the pattern of the first very closely. Guitarist David Nichtern, who composed the ineffably looney 'Midnight At The Oasis' and lovely 'I Never Did Sing You a Lovesong', contributes another winner here, a slow, wistful number called 'Oh Papa'. Wendy Waldman ('Mad Mad Me' and 'Vaudeville Man') is represented by the lightweight 'Gringo En Mexico'. Kate McGarrigle's 'Work Song' is paralleled here by sister Anna's 'Cool River', a more commercial, gospel-styled number. Once again there's a New Orleans composition (Allen Toussaint's 'Brickyard Blues') an old bawdy song ('It Ain't the Meat, It's the Motion') and a country number ('Honey Babe Blues').

The production team is the same, Joe Boyd and Lenny Waronker, and most of the excellent musicians are once more in evidence, with guitarists Amos Garrett and Greg Prestopino to the fore. But there's an additional musical bonus. Three of the numbers have been arranged and conducted by swing-era veteran Benny Carter, using a ten-piece band of his peers—the likes of Harry 'Sweets' Edison on trumpet, Bud Shank on alto and Ray Brown on bass. They open the proceedings with a Fats Waller composition, 'Squeeze Me', they sing as well as swing along on 'It Ain't the Meat', and they also feature on the album's best track, 'Sweetheart'.

***

This song is the lament of a waitress in a donut shop whose beloved is a customer with a sweetheart of his own. It's attributed to one Ken Burgan, a new name to me, and it has exactly the kind of jazz flavoured, sophisticated lightness of touch which suits Maria Muldaur's voice to perfection. Another highlight—and again something of a departure—is the Leiber/Stroller song, 'I'm A Woman', the only number on the album familiar to me from another performance—Peggy Lee had a hit with it several eras ago. Maria belts it out with liberated virility, her voice cracking in and out of falsetto like a bull-whip.

The only track which strikes me as unnecessary is the old spiritual 'Travellin' Shoes', which is sung in close harmony a capella with Kate McGarrigle, Garrett and Prestopino. The harmonies are not as close as they might be, and the whole piece is definitely not in harmony with the rest of the record. It's also true that none of these songs can quite match the best of the first album like the breathtaking rendition of Dan Hick's 'Walking One And Only' or the superb 'Work Song'.

***

But that's carping. There are more than enough riches here to satisfy anybody. Every number has been sensitively tailored to get the best possible fit between song, voice and backing. Listen to Paul Butterfield's harmonica on 'If You Haven't Any Hay', old Doc and Merle Watson playing guitars on 'Honey Babe Blues', and Plas Johnson's tenor solo on 'Squeeze Me'. Maria Muldaur deserves backing of that order. As they say in Hollywood, she's tops in my book.

Wednesday, 22 January 1975

WHITE TRASH

Randy Newman/*Good Old Boys*
Van Morrison/*Veedon Fleece*

I'VE BEEN CATCHING up this week on two albums which have been out for a while, Randy Newman's *Good Old Boys* (Reprise K54022) and Van Morrison's *Veedon Fleece* (Warner Bros. K56068). Both of them are by performers who've been around for the best part of a decade now, writing and singing their own very personal kinds of songs. Both of them are as maturely conceived and as well-made as one would expect from artists of this much experience and reputation. But they're also both rather under par, not up to the best of the albums which have preceded them.

Good Old Boys is a 'concept-album', a genre increasingly rare these days. The concept is 'white trash': all of the songs are about the representative experiences and attitudes of lower-class whites in the American Deep South. The opening song, 'Rednecks', is typical:

> We talk real funny down here
> We drink too much and we laugh too loud
> We're too dumb to make it in no northern town
> And we're keepin' the niggers down.

There's an accurate eye for the reality of life in these insulated, deprived communities which is worlds away from the generalised, chic, self-righteousness of a song like Neil Young's 'Southern Man'. Instead of merely wagging a finger at bigotry, Newman attacks its causes: the impoverishment of body and mind in decaying hamlets and cities, the humiliation of failure and presumed inferiority. One of the best songs is 'Kingfish', which expresses the defiant populism of the notorious governor of Louisiana from 1928-1935, Huey P. Long who was himself a good old boy, and revered for it across the South. Newman prefaces 'Kingfish' with a strong rendition of a populist campaign song written by Huey P. Long himself and called 'Every Man A King'.

There are songs of escapist drinking, of maudlin lovesickness, of historical disaster. They cover a range of musical styles, from ragtime influences of 'Rednecks' and 'Birmingham' through the blues structure of 'Guilty' to the reggae beat of 'Naked Man'. The trouble is, they all sound fairly bland and ordinary if you don't attend to the words.

Sometimes the arrangements are too soupy, as on 'Marie', which is vastly overburdened with strings. Often, Newman hasn't come up with arresting enough melodies to match his excellent lyrics. But overall the problem is in the 'concept.' Randy Newman is at his best, in my view, with a small group in a nightclub ambience singing those random ditties of his which manage to be whimsical and sinister at the same time. I don't think the adoption of set roles suits him, however expertly he brings them off.

***

Van Morrison's best work, looking back, was the album *Astral Weeks*, with its long, trailblazing, meditative songs like 'Madame George' and 'Cypress Avenue', uniquely combining nostalgia, drama and a personal mysticism in a kind of white soul style. He has recorded many first-class numbers since then, but none of the attempts to recapture the *Astral Weeks* blend has been entirely successful.

Most of *Veedon Fleece* is thereby summarised. The songs are slow, emotive, atmospheric. As ever, the musical arrangements are fresh and very attractive, with some particularly fine writing for woodwind and strings by Jeff Labes. My favourite number is 'Cul-de-Sac' where Morrison's vocal mannerisms really intensify the effect of the song, as he stutters and growls and then screams his way to the climax. Otherwise, he tends to overstrain both himself and the listener.

Tuesday, 4 February 1975

THE BEST OF JONI

Joni Mitchell/*Miles of Aisles*

IF YOU DON'T possess anything by Joni Mitchell, but feel you might like to, then her new album *Miles of Aisles* (Asylum SYSP 902) is the record to get. It's a double-LP set of sixteen classic Mitchell numbers and two new ones, all of them recorded live in concert. If you're already sufficiently sold on the lady's genius to have acquired her studio albums, you'll still want it. More so, even.

Often these live recordings of 'greatest hits', expensively packaged, are record-company expedients for squeezing extra mileage out of a performer's career, particularly if the career in question is showing signs of stalling. But not with this lady. Her songs are performed and recorded here with such fastidious professionalism that it takes the applause at the end to remind you that it's all been done live. And what has been done live is a set of fresh and creative new readings of familiar songs by a mature artist with a rich oeuvre upon which to draw.

She ranges from the youthful feyness of 'The Circle Game' and 'Both Sides Now' to the nervy sophistication of 'People's Parties' from *Court and Spark*, her latest album. The distance travelled is considerable, but it's a direct route, and she emphasises this by jumbling up the chronology; the album's divisions are instead stylistic, with sides one and four featuring heavy arranging and backing from Tom Scott and his LA Express, whilst sides two and three are mainly just Joni with her guitar or piano.

She opens with 'You Turn Me On, I'm A Radio', her hit from *For the Roses* and 'Big Yellow Taxi', her recurrent hit from *Ladies of the Canyon*, both of them full of exuberant wit. Singing with a jazzy looseness and swing, she regenerates them both, boosted by the marvellously inventive vigour of Scott and his band.

***

Since *For the Roses* Scott's collaboration has been crucial to Joni Mitchell's development, and the work he does for her throughout this first side is a joy to the ear. Switching to atmospheric tension in 'Rainy Night House', he creates a lovely interplay between flute and voice. The side ends with the most amazingly successful reincarnation of all, since the number itself is the most dated imaginable—'Woodstock'.

The rest of the album is not quite at this rarefied level of achievement, and the second disc is in general a notch or two down from the first; but the differences are marginal. After the rich band sound, some of the guitar accompaniments on the middle two sides sound rather thin. 'All I Want' and 'People's Parties' in particular suffer from the lack. On the other hand, 'Woman of Heart and Mind' sounds better than the original, and the hoary 'Both Sides Now' is stiffened by a tincture of group backing.

The only real miscalculation on the album is the glib, upbeat treatment of 'Carey' from the album *Blue* on Side 4. 'The Last Time I Saw Richard' from the same album suffers, too, from a misplaced gag. But the album ends with the affirmation of two new numbers, 'Jericho' and 'Love Or Money', both of them crackling with verbal precision, musical taste and a romantic sensibility of a high order.

Tuesday, 18 February 1975

ENGLISH ROCK

Stackridge/*Extravaganza*
The Strawbs/*Ghosts*

THE STRAWBS AND Stackridge are both English groups pursuing a distinctively English rock style. Stackbridge is by far the younger outfit of the two, but they've made their mark. *Extravaganza* (Rocket Records) however, is my first taste of them. Toothsome. I like it.

Their sources are in the George Formby kind of music hall, filtered to some degree by Lennon and McCartney. Indeed there's a Sergeant Pepperiness about much of the album, festooned as it is with clowns and dancers in period gear. Andy Davis sings his wry army song 'The Volunteer' in a manner not unlike Ringo's, and the vocal harmonies on 'Highbury Incident' inescapably evoke the Fab Four in their prime.

It's surprising and creditable how much vitality they can generate from the idiom. 'Spin Round the Room' and 'Grease Paint Smiles' both make effective use of showbiz imagery. 'Benjamin's Giant Onion' manages to be whimsical without setting your teeth on edge. These three were co-written by Rod Bowkett who plays keyboard in the band.

The song that stands out though, was contributed from outside the band by Phil Welton. It's essentially an attack on the lip service habitually paid by society to Christianity but it's the insidious deftness of the words and music which makes it so remarkable. 'Happy in the Lord' is the title and refrain, trilled repeatedly to a serenely jolly tune, and interspersed with verses which reduce the atrophied precepts of organised religion to absurdity:

> While the players white the summer breeze
> Whiter yet the holy empire
> He won't get the green stuff on his knees
> He just holds the bowler's jumper.

Stackridge are a six-piece band and they achieve quite a big and varied instrumental sound. Three of the tracks on the album are instrumental, all of them accomplished and exhibiting some of the same wit as the songs. Even if they sound a trifle samey—and even though Stackridge, on this showing, is not a group of earth-shattering originality—*Extravaganza* still remains a very entertaining and pleasurable achievement.

***

Dave Cousins is the only old original Strawb left in the group, and he must be growing nodes on his larynx by now. It certainly sounds that way in *Ghosts* (A&M), the new Strawbs album. Gone is the rasping attack of yore, replaced by a mellower, hollower sound, attributed on the sleeve to David Cousins, and swathed in mellotrons and moogs.

Ghosts has its quota of fatuities. There's a subsection of a song entitled 'Impressions of Southall from the Train' which opens with some lines of sociological pseudo-poetry being intoned by voices of Frankensteinian portentousness. Better yet, there's the choir of Charterhouse school going 'aaaaah' in their chapel as Cousins sings 'Darlin' I Love Ya'.

Still, the old campaigner knows a few clever dodges. 'Lemon Pie' is an infectious song with a pleasantly silly refrain. 'Where Do You Go' builds another catchy tune on a chug-a-lug rhythm. Either one or both could be an acceptable entry in the charts.

Friday, 7 March 1975

SOUNDS UNCOMPROMISING

Slapp Happy & Henry Cow/*Desperate Straights*
Tom Newman/*Fine Old Tom*

THE SMALL INDEPENDENT British label Virgin Records, continues to issue the most consistently progressive recorded music in these islands. One notable feature of their output is the way the company's artists work on each other's albums. Collaboration of this kind has contributed to the success of two very interesting recent releases, *Desperate Straights* (V 2024) and *Fine Old Tom* (V 2022).

Two groups—Slapp Happy and Henry Cow—have come together to make *Desperate Straights*, and the territory which it inhabits lies somewhere on the frontiers between European cabaret, contemporary 'serious' or 'straight' academic composition, and progressive pop. The resources for such an excursion are contained within the two groups. Slapp Happy consists of songwriters Peter Blegvad and Anthony Moore, whose high-toned and often arcane lyrics are sung by a German girl called Dagmar in a voice like Lotte Lenya's only icier and more 'schooled.' Henry Cow is a ferociously cerebral jazz/rock group featuring Fred Frith on guitar, which plays at prodigious levels of invention and volume.

Together they have come up with thirteen tracks of varied, uneven, but highly distinctive music. Something of its nature is suggested by the fact that the nearest approach to a piece of straight rock music on the album is a setting of 'He gave his back to the smiters' from Handel's 'Messiah'. Elsewhere, intricate musical textures and tricky time-signatures abound: the arrangements are highly detailed and energetic.

The nearest approach to humour is the opening number 'Some Questions About Hats' (' ... can a hat aspire to higher things?') But this is explicitly rejected in 'A Worm is at Work', which expresses the writer's self-doubt about his attainments and the temptation to escape into easy cynicism. 'Bad Alchemy' is about self-doubt of a sexual kind, a bad dream causing the protagonist to ponder: 'Am I hermaphrodite? Neither one nor quite the other?'

Not all the songs are as accessible as these. 'Europa' has an over-ambitious lyric which tumbles into pretentiousness, and there is a whiff of languorous aestheticism about songs like 'Strayed' and 'Riding Tigers'. Also, the two instrumental tracks are self-indulgent—the title track is a piano waltz by Moore full of Romantic ennui, whilst 'Caucasian Lullaby' is a long free-form piece for clarinets and piano. But a few such excesses are permitted to an album as artistically uncompromising as *Desperate Straights*.

***

Fine Old Tom is a different kind of record, but equally distinctive. It features the work of Tom Newman, whose name is new to me, but who appears to have been working on some of these tracks since 1972. Like Virgin's star performer Mike Oldfield—who plays a lot on this album—Newman is a wizard of overdubbing, and often appears here in choral proliferation.

He takes us through a sequence of popular styles, starting with the hoarse passion of a slow '50s-style rocker called 'Suzie' (which acknowledges its Everly Bros namesake), moving through a Chuck Berry-like raunchy stomper called 'Poor Bill', and four tracks later, getting to John Lennon's 'She Said, She Said'. This has been recorded in the open air, with no backing other than birdsong and some percussion (table and sleigh bells?) The vocals have been overdubbed in very wide harmonic intervals which are often dissonant. The effect is eccentric and yet an appropriate extension of Lennon's original interpretation.

Throughout the album Newman effects an odd marriage between technical expertise and homespun ruggedness. He keeps time by tapping the mike stand or slapping his thighs whilst dazzling feats of musicianship are being accomplished (guitarist David Duhig plays some superb breaks). This kind of idiosyncrasy informs the whole enterprise.

Thursday, 20 March 1975

CREATIVE LADIES

Phoebe Snow/*Phoebe Snow*

ANY PARTY WHO wants to argue that women can be superior to men in artistic creativity should turn their attention to the class of people who sing their own compositions. A most astonishing proliferation of female singer-songwriters has appeared in America in recent years, and there is no end in sight. Phoebe Snow is the latest name, with a debut album from A&M Records which is richer, more mature and more distinctive than many artists achieve after years of experience.

Miss Snow starts out with big natural assets—a kind of bronze contralto voice and a jazz ear for phrasing. Her voice is strong, almost brassy when projected, but with a gorgeous warm vibrato and even a girlishness in the upper registers. It's a marvellous instrument, and that's how she uses it, with instrumental flexibility.

***

Producer Dino Airali (one assumes) has had the astuteness to complement this with some elegant backing—such as jazz tenorist Zoot Sims, one of the legendary Four Brothers in Woody Herman's band, and swing veteran Teddy Wilson. The arrangements are most unusual (a harpist plays on three tracks, beautifully on 'Take Your Children Home'), and double bass is preferred to electric on most tracks, with Chuck Israels' plangent swing providing all that's needed on top of Phoebe Snow's rhythm guitar to make 'San Francisco Bay Blues' an unexpected gem.

This old Jesse Fuller number, plus another standard, 'Let the Good Times Roll', are the only non-Snow compositions on the album. Her own songs are fairly melancholy and downbeat, but the writing is excellent, music and lyrics both. What can you say about a writer who mimics *Macbeth* with 'I strut and fret my hour upon the stage' ('Harpo's Blues'), or builds a refrain round the question 'Do you like or love/Either or both of me?' Best of all is a verse (too long to quote) in 'It Must Be Sunday' which constitutes the ultimate comment on New Year's Eve parties.

Musically, Miss Snow is steeped in the phraseology and rhythmic patterns of mainstream jazz and blues. But she perceives them with the ear of a rock-era child, and the harmonic shifts and melodies which emerge are very personal. She's not confined to one style either, even if the numbers share a similar kind of pace and mood: 'Either or Both' has the flavour of a country song, with David Bromberg playing a dobro.

The album commits very few errors. A couple of numbers have ill-advised string intrusions, but they're mercifully short. The last track, 'No Show Tonight', with Dave Mason on lead guitar, is the nearest thing to a rocker and it sounds slightly uncertain of itself. But *Phoebe Snow* is definitely an album for the permanent collection.

***

Meanwhile, the hunt for a British equivalent continues. Kiki Dee is finally achieving her just deserts as a singer, topping magazine polls and packing concert halls. She has a very good single out on Rocket Records of the Nancy Wilson song 'How Glad I Am', putting the number across with a womanly zest which few British or Irish performers can achieve. But the flip side shows her unfortunate weakness as a writer: it's a limp and self-conscious ballad called 'Peter'.

Thursday, 3 April 1975

TOP 40

Ian Whitcomb/*Tin Pan Alley: A Pictorial History (1919-1935)*

FORSTER, IN *A Passage to India*, satirises a young missionary who contends that in the many mansions of his Father's house there may well be room for monkeys. Jackals even ... '... and the wasps? He became uneasy ... and oranges, cactus, crystals and mud? And the bacteria inside Mr Sorley? ... No, no this is going too far. We must exclude someone from our gathering, or we shall be left with nothing'.

Much the same problem is encountered by the devotee of popular music. He will certainly give houseroom to 'Manhattan' by charming Rodgers and Witty Hart. Their 'Blue Moon', even. And 'Over the Rainbow'? How about 'I'm Always Chasing Rainbows', or 'Tiptoe Through the Tulips' or 'It's a Sin to Tell a Lie'? How about 'Any Place Where I Make Money (Is Home Sweet Home to Me)'?

All of them can be found in Ian Whitcomb's new book, *Tin Pan Alley* (Wildwood House and EMI, £2.95). It's subtitled 'A Pictorial History (1919-1939)' and it does have a scattering of pictures, and a series of short, breezy essays introducing each of the six sections, but it consists in the main of the words and music (and original cover illustrations) of forty songs. They stretch from the end of the First World War with the high-spirited query about returning doughboys, 'How Ya Gonna Keep 'Em Down on the Farm (After They've Seen

Paree)', to the outbreak of the Second World War and the obscure and haunting German cabaret song which was to be cherished by both armies, 'Lili Marlene'.

Whitcomb's *After the Ball*, which appeared two years ago, was a bright and lively full-length account of pop-music 'from ragtime to rock'. This book is also bright and lively, but also a little sloppy and silly. Its historical passages often read like hasty rehashing of material in *After the Ball*, and they show up badly against the meticulousness of other recent books on the subject, like Henry Pleasants' *The Great American Popular Singers*. Also, no rationale is offered for the choice of songs, and it's hard to infer one.

For example, there's nothing in the book from the greatest Alley-man of them all, Irving Berlin, so this selection can hardly be considered the period's Top Forty. Not all of the songs were even hits, though most were. Either they represent Whitcomb's private taste, or they represent what could be obtained in the way of copyright permission. It would be nice to know.

***

But all this detracts very little from the pleasure of the book, particularly if, like me, you are prepared to embrace the lot all the way down to the bacteria inside Mr Sorley. For, as his title indicates, Whitcomb's not dealing here with the virtuosi or prophets of popular song, but with the commercial pros, whose work is almost anonymous—composers like Nacio Herb Brown, Walter Donaldson and Fred Fischer, lyricists like Arthur Freed, Al Dubin, Gus Kahn.

You remain unmoved. Try humming a few bars of 'You Were Meant for Me'. It's in the book; it was written by Brown who also tossed off things like 'Singing in the Rain' and 'You Are My Lucky Star'—all with words by Freed. Or how about 'Love me or Leave me' (Donaldson) 'Dardanella' (Fischer) or 'I Only Have Eyes For You' (words by Dubin). All of them well-turned, attractive songs, all of them alive and well half a century on, and all of them available in *Tin Pan Alley* for just over seven pence a number.

Tuesday, 15 April 1975

A GOOD ACT, BUT ...

George Melly/*It's George*
Swamp Dogg/*Have You Heard This Story*

GEORGE MELLY'S AUDIENCE appeal was fully demonstrated on his Irish stage appearances. He has cornered the home market in the good-time songs of black America between the wars—from the licentious ditties of those oft-mentioned New Orleans brothels, through the breezy urban blues of Joe Turner and Jimmy Rushing to the irresistible sentimental humour of Fats Waller.

George has a good comic act and he's under no illusions about it musically, as is clear from the engaging interview with him in the 5 April *New Musical Express*: '... I'm doing what Emlyn Williams does when he goes on stage and reads bits from Dickens dressed as Dickens. People may then go and pick up a Dickens book and start to read it and find a new world, and a marvellous one, which they wouldn't have otherwise considered.'

This works well enough on stage, where he can evoke the spirit of, say, a Bessie Smith song without actually having to sing it as well as Bessie. But he can't strut his stuff inside a gramophone; the records are cheerful, unpretentious, but definitely amateur-night.

The most recent of his three albums, *It's George* (Warner Bros. K56087), has something old and something new. There's familiar trad stuff like 'Trouble in Mind', 'T'Aint No Sin', Kid Ory's 'All the Whores Go Crazy' and Duke Ellington's 'It Don't Mean A Thing'. There are three songs written by John Chilton, leader of Melly's backing band, The Feetwarmers.

Most welcome to me, though, are the Tin Pan Alley songs—'Hard-Hearted Hannah', 'Lulu's Back In Town', and best of all, Johnny Mercer's 'The Waiter and the Porter and the Upstairs Maid'. Numbers like these don't get aired enough, and sheet music of them can be hard to come by. Full marks to George for giving them a boost.

***

As to the songs of black America today, how about 'My Hang-ups Ain't Hung-up No More', or 'God Ain't Blessing America'—two of the titles from *Have You Heard This Story* (Island ILPS 9299) by Swamp Dogg, the alter ego of composer/singer/hustler Jerry Williams Jun. Swamp Dogg is about the same weight as George Melly, but in every other way dissimilar. Where Melly flaunts a moped to mock the false values of show-biz, Dogg straddles the groaning bonnet of his Rolls Royce Silver Shadow.

The songs also revealed rather different preoccupations. Dogg opens with an LSD number and proceeds with an alarming number of medical references, indicative of acute hypochondria—these are the first lyrics I've ever seen containing the words 'electrocardiogram', 'hyperventilation' and 'phenobarbitol'. He's also adept at ringing startling changes on familiar themes. In 'Did I Come Back Too Soon (Or Did I Stay Away Too Long)', the protagonist loses his wife to another ... another woman, that is. The love song 'I Wouldn't Leave Here to Go to Heaven' contains some theology:

> I'm not putting it down, but heaven's a place I've never been.
> I can't get my hopes up high, for sometime I got to die
> To see
> You ain't no hearsay ...

All of this is delivered in an energetic high-pitched voice, over a splendid backing of hardcore bluesy soul. In fact, the whole album is thoroughly musical, good to dance to and quite unique. Swamp Dogg's bite is as good as his bark.

Tuesday, 29 April 1975

HEARD IT BEFORE?

Bad Company/*Straight Shooter*
Little Feat/*Feats Don't Fail Me Now*

A NEW WAY with an old wheeze—that's originality, in popular music as in most other things, and it's surprisingly rare. Novelty, yes, and proficiency even, these are not lacking in Today's Music. But a lot of it's just the old wheezes performed in the old ways.

Proficiency badges might well be sported by the four members of the English group Bad Company, whose album *Straight Shooter* (Island JLPS 9304) is currently high in the charts. Each of them has a distinguished pedigree. Singer Paul Rodgers and drummer Simon Kirke were once half of Free, whilst the lead guitarist and the bass player are ex-Mott The Hoople and ex-King Crimson respectively.

Given all that—and the success of the album—and the fact that its first track, 'Good Lovin' Gone Bad', was a number one hit single—these boys hardly stand in need of cossetting. So allow me to confess that I intend to trade *Straight Shooter* in for something a bit more durable. It's not exactly bad company, but every move it makes is predictable.

Starting with the very song titles, 'Feel Like Makin' Love', 'Weep No More', 'Wild Fire Woman', 'Call On Me', you can write the lyrics to these in your head before you even switch on the stereo. Having written them you can perform them internally with the standard machismo anguish. Finally you can parcel this up with the customary chording, bass-lines, drum patterns and guitar breaks ... and thus conserve energy by not playing the record at all.

Some of this is intentional. Rodgers has said: 'Simplicity is music for me. Our record was purposely underproduced for that effect. We like to build and cut it off and leave everyone lots of room to put themselves into it.' Fair enough, as a reaction against baroque excess. It probably works beautifully in a live performance, where the audience can envisage itself as part of the group. But a record needs more. Proficiency is a means, not an end in itself.

***

Feats Don't Fail Me Now (Warner Bros. K56O30)—to make an odious comparison—is an album for the collection. It's been out for some time, but didn't do much business until the group (Little Feat) appeared in concert in London's Rainbow Theatre and brought the house down.

The mainspring of Little Feat is one Lowell George, guitarist, co-writer, singer and producer. He used to be a Mother of Invention and there's some of Frank Zappa's zany and spirited eclecticism in the Feat's music. There's also a lot of the Southern white funk which is much in vogue in America these days, and a smidgeon of Los Angeles sophistication.

The group's originality lies in the disposition of these familiar elements. With musical good taste, imagination and dynamism, they provide the ear with a constantly changing kaleidoscope of sound. A six-piece band can too easily fall back on sheer volume for its own sake—particularly one composed of keyboards, two guitars, bass, drums and percussion. This band never comes near doing that.

A quite remarkable feature of the album is the uniform quality of the tracks. Not a bummer amongst them, though I dislike the way the vocals are all mixed down too low for the words to be entirely audible, especially as they sound interesting. The homogeneity of the record makes it hard to choose an outstanding number, but I'd settle for the contagious title track itself, 'Feats Don't Fail Me Now'.

Tuesday, 13 May 1975

ROCK ALBUM

Steely Dan/*Katy Lied*

TWO OF THE most gifted writer-performers on the American rock scene in these curious times are Donald Fagen and Walter Becker. Hip collegiate types from the East, New Yorkers down to every last split-end, they would probably have gone to Southern California a generation ago to write sophisticated, cynical screenplays. This being the seventies, they've gone there instead to write sophisticated, cryptic rock songs, under the group name of Steely Dan.

Last year's Steely Dan album *Pretzel Logic* was considered by many critics, including this one, to be the sharpest number of the season. Their new release, *Katy Lied*, (ABC Records ABCL 5094) has not fared so well. Some pundits are annoyed at Becker and Fagen's abandoning of the 'group' aesthetic, in favour of hiring whatever musicians they want for specific assignments. Annoyance has also been expressed at the perplexing and inconsequential lyrics.

There may be a germ of justice in these strictures, but the fact remains that *Katy Lied* is the most interesting rock album thus far in 1975. In almost any one of its tracks you'll find more musical richness, diversity, and surprise than in entire albums by other groups. All their trademarks are here—the long, strong melodic lines, the biting vocal clarity with beautifully precise harmonies, the changing textures, with rhythmic shifts and instrumental breaks which are a working model of style expressing sensibility.

And of course, the baffling, often weird lyrics. Certainly I prefer lyrics which attempt to make sense. But most rock songwriters are reluctant to have their banality so rudely exposed, and since lyrics were stricken by acidosis nearly a decade ago, they've been able to shelter behind portentous gibberish. Becker and Fagen are rarely

273

portentous, and their obscurity can be entertaining, with a Pinterish undertone of menace.

***

TAKE 'Everyone's Gone to the Movies': an invitation to some kids to come and watch Mr La Page's films in his den. We aren't told what kind of movies these are, and the lines get creepier as they go on: 'Don't tell your mama/Your daddy or mama/They'll never know where you been'. Or 'Daddy Don't Live in That New York City No More'. Again, the apparently innocuous statement of the title gets clouded over by something more unsettling as the song progresses. Daddy's activities, no longer pursued, appear to have been rather squalid: keeping a secret love-nest, drinking his dinner from a paper sack. By the time the childlike catalogue reaches its final item, it seems fair to assume that daddy may have met with a bad end: 'Daddy can't get no fine cigar/But we know you're smoking/Wherever you are ...'

These numbers are admittedly more accessible than most, and 'Movies' is copyrighted 1972. Another song on the album called 'Any World (That I'm Welcome To)' dates from the following year, and its lyrics make a very direct statement: 'Any world that I'm welcome to/Is better that the one I come from'.

Becker and Fagen have found a welcoming world in rock music. The danger is that they'll become immured in their own little private corner of it to the point where they lose touch with the rest of us. 'Your Gold Teeth II' and 'Rose Darling' have lyrics which are not only unintelligible but uninteresting. To that degree the carping is justified. Still *Katy Lied* should tide us over nicely until the next Gary Glitter release.

Friday, 30 May 1975

THE BIG SIX

Alec Wilder/*American Popular Song: The Great Innovators*

AT LAST ALEC Wilder's definitive study, *American Popular Song* (OUP, £3.25), is available in paperback. It was first published three years ago and has been deferred to ever since as a kind of instant classic. Small wonder, since Wilder is only the man who composed the tender 'I'll Be Around', who hobnobbed with the likes of Mildred Bailey and Bunny Berigan and Fats Waller, and who played his way through seventeen thousand songs in the preparation of his manuscript.

All of which would amount to very little, of course, if he were unable to write well. But he writes with just those qualities which he finds missing from the songs in *South Pacific*, to wit, 'fire, impact, purity, naturalness, need, friendliness, and, most of all, wit.' He expresses to perfection my own response to those bland and pompous ditties: 'I almost feel as if I should change into formal garb before I listen to them.'

Formal garb would be highly inappropriate gear for embarking upon the odyssey of 'American Popular Song'. Shirt sleeves are called for, plus a friend who can play the piano, if you lack that happy attainment. Wilder's subtitle is 'The Great Innovators 1900-1950'; his interest lies, not in social history or show business or biography or even very much in lyrics, but in the nuts and bolts of musical composition. Before you're nine pages into his text, noted staves have popped up and specific examples of harmonic and melodic development are being analysed.

Many people—and not only those as unversed in musical theory as I am—are frightened off by such procedures, when applied to popular songs. But there isn't even the faintest whiff of academicism about Wilder's methods. He's like a seasoned and committed professional, leading you backstage by the hand, and marvelling with you at the intricate magic of the machinery. The most rudimentary grasp of musical structures is all that's required. Certainly I sometimes get lost in a welter of enharmonic changes and diminished fifths, but never for long, and always with enough faith in the author to know he's not just waffling.

***

After a brisk and concise opening chapter on 'The Transition Era' (1885-1914), he devotes a chapter each to six of the 'great innovators': Kern, Berlin, Gershwin, Richard Rodgers, Cole Porter and Harold Arlen. In each case he chooses the songs which he considers most innovative and assesses them quite rigorously.

Like all worthwhile literary companions, Wilder has a firm set of personal values for which he wants to argue a case. He believes in a hierarchy of quality, with theatre songs mostly at the top, then film songs, then Tin Pan Alley. He dislikes an abundance of repeated notes, which leads him to denigrate Gershwin ... causing at least one reader's pulse to accelerate sharply.

He also believes that his tradition is the great tradition of American popular song, and that after 1950 came the deluge of amateur mediocrity and rock infantilism. This I regret as a limitation of vision, however understandable. But it's the only bum note in an otherwise massively satisfying symphony, which incidentally finds room for the work of seventeen other composers besides the Big Six, as well as a host of outstanding individual songs.

Friday, 6 June 1975

SCOTT JOPLIN

Peter Gammond/*Scott Joplin and the Ragtime Era*

THE HISTORY OF popular music is littered with more tragic corpses than the entire body of Jacobean drama. Poor Stephen Foster ... poor Scott Joplin ... two seminal figures whose frustrated lives both ended on the skids in New York. Their sufferings had little to do with their creative abilities, but a lot to do with public taste and racism.

Thanks to Joshua Rifkin and *The Sting*, Joplin's classic ragtime style is now finally vindicated. This time last year you couldn't walk into a theatre or a party, or even down the street, without hearing the graceful and spritely melody of 'The Entertainer', a smash hit only seventy-two years after it was published—undoubtedly the greatest 'sleeper' the trade has yet known. Since then the craze has ebbed considerably, but the distinctiveness and importance of ragtime in the pantheon of popular music has been permanently established, and its devotees will continue to defend its interests with the same fierce partisanship as the fans of Dixieland jazz, music-hall and the other genres.

***

They, and some of the rest of us, would like to read a fully-researched biographical study of Joplin. Unfortunately, Peter Gammond's *Scott*

Joplin and the Ragtime Era (Angus and Robertson. £3.00) isn't it. Nor does it claim to be—'to be honest', says Mr Gammond in his opening sentence, 'there is not a great deal of intimate detail known about his daily life or background.' But, as he reassures us later on, '... there is no doubt that some worthy and assiduous American scholar will do his best to remedy the situation by some difficult research into the misty past to produce a definitive Joplin biography.'

This tone of chummy amateurishness is not uncommon in books about pop music and jazz by English writers. Perhaps it's meant to disarm criticism; but it can scarcely justify the fact that, of Mr Gammond's 200-odd pages, exactly twenty-seven are devoted to the life and career of Scott Joplin. These are divided into five 'chapters', and interspersed with background material which constitutes, in short, the bulk of the book.

'A flagrant piece of bookmaking' is a phrase favoured by literary critics, I believe. Pundits, would be better advised to procure from Oak Publications (New York) the standard work which is Gammond's major source, *They All Played Ragtime* by Rudi Blesh and Harriet Janis. Nevertheless, *Scott Joplin and the Ragtime Era* is not without usefulness.

It has admirable appendices—listing relevant books, sheet music and records respectively. The latter list is especially useful as it includes classical compositions modelled on ragtime (by the likes of Debussy, Satie and Stravinsky). There is a very good chapter enumerating and describing all of Joplin's works in the order of their appearance.

***

And even a scissors-and-paste job on his life is worth having, until the real thing comes along. It is, to say the least, a story of great human interest. Born the son of freed slaves in the Reconstruction South, and coached by a local German music teacher, he ran away at fourteen. For years he played the Negro jigs and minstrel songs of the honky-tonks and brothels, nursing a vision of transmuting them into a dignified Black American art music.

His 'Maple Leaf Rag' of 1899 was a popular success which secured for him a regular publishing outlet. With the proceeds he embarked on his life's ambition—to create a black ragtime opera.

His first effort, *A Guest of Honour* (1903), was almost wholly ignored and is now lost. His career ended with the protracted and futile struggle to mount his second opera, *Treemonisha* (1911). He died in a state hospital after a mental and physical breakdown induced, according to the death certificate, by syphilis: a terrible end for a man who strove, against all the odds, for acceptance and respectability.

Thursday, 19 June 1975

A LOOK AT THE POP WEEKLIES

POP MUSIC AND journalism both deal mainly in the ephemeral—so it's not surprising that the tabloid pop music weeklies contain the highest trivia quotient in the whole world of publishing. The bulk of them appear to have been written and produced by a manic computer, which has been programmed by a warring army of publicists, representing every group in the world.

What is surprising is that anything worth reading ever emerges. But there have, in fact, been numerous attempts at quality, and not all of them have foundered; at least a couple of the current papers continue to delight the thinking fan.

The market giant is *Melody Maker*, 'the world's biggest selling music weekly.' It has always followed majority tastes, and its catholicism is well exemplified by the cover of the 14 June issue. Beside a photograph of Steve Harley is a big headline—'Marvin Gaye Coming!'—and underneath is a smaller one adding the tag, ... 'and Johnny Cash.' Thus are the fans of rock, soul and country music respectively, attracted to the product.

Within the fifty-six mammoth pages, they are each accorded their own sections, along with the followers of jazz and folk. But the emphasis is inevitably on the Pop thirty, which dominates the famous charts on page 2. Opposite this there is, for example, an article entitled 'The Price of Teeny Lust'. It turns out to be about the tee-shirts, jigsaw puzzles, key rings and other consumer spin-offs which are sold in their millions to the pubescent girls who follow the Bay City Rollers and the Osmonds.

***

YOU can also read a detailed history of Tammy Wynette's single, 'Stand By Your Man' and the ad section offers access to everything from mail-order cavalry boots to 'Orgy dirt cheap: Wanted, four fun-loving people to share Cornish cottage.'

All good value for 12 pence, but I find it enervating. Although the reviews have surprising bite, the overall effect is that of an impersonal mass of indigestible information.

Until a few years ago, the *New Musical Express* was an unexceptional competitor. Then a mob of young rock writers took over the editorial offices, and suddenly it became a paper with style. The style can raise hackles, based as it is on a kind of hysterical cynicism, but its energy and humour, and self-mockery make it irresistible. Their Bay City Rollers piece in the June 14 issue is headlined, 'Smiles and Milk: New Threat to Nation's Youth.' They also have a review of a Loudon Wainwright concert, headlined 'Thank God I'm a Shambling Buffoon'. The review is favourable.

Although the Lone Groover strip cartoon has been regrettably dropped, the thrills section has now been expanded into a fourpage ragbag of absurdity, scurrility and satire. It leads off this week with photographs of a Don McLean fan having an enormous picture of his idol tattooed on to his back.

***

The pioneer for a lot of this was, of course, San Francisco's *Rolling Stone*. *NME* writers like Peter Erskine and Charles Shaar Murray have retained some of the febrile iconoclasm of the early days of *Rolling Stone*, whilst the house writers of that organ (Joe Eszterhas, Tim Cahill, Jon Landau *et al*): have gone on to become respected New Journalists.

The magazine itself has long since stopped being a rock-music mag, and become the intellectual forum of the rock generation, or something. Of the four major articles in the June 19th issue, one is about rock music: the others deal with Vietnam, Cuba, and a world conference of genetic scientists. The emphasis is heavily American, and so is the price—30p. I still buy it because it still occasionally comes up with something superb, but its self-importance is setting in like rigor mortis.

Some things don't change, of course. In all three of the issues mentioned you can read a description of Mick Jagger's mascara.

Thursday, 26 June 1975

'SIXTIES STYLE

Oscar Brown/*Between Heaven and Hell*
Pilot/*Second Flight*

THE BEST RECORD I've procured in recent months is Oscar Brown Jr.'s album *Between Heaven and Hell*, which was made in 1962. It turned up in my local record shop as a stray import; and I mention it because Brown was an important figure, an artist of rare quality, who appears to have disappeared in the rock deluge which came after him. I'd be glad to hear from any reader who's been in touch with Brown's activities during the past ten years.

Lest you doubt the man's importance, let me quote the opening lines of the opening song on this album:

Permit me to introduce myself, the name is Mr Kicks,
I dwell in the dark dominion, way down by the River Styx.

If that sounds familiar, then you're remembering the Rolling Stones' rip-off, 'Sympathy for the Devil' ('Allow me to introduce myself, I'm a man of wealth and taste'). Brown was writing daring lyrics when it was still audacious to be daring.

For example, he penned the *Paradise Lost* of pop music, a song so witty that it never goes stale, 'Forbidden Fruit'. Nina Simone's reading of it (on her album of the same name) is a classic. He also expressed his Blackness, in songs like 'Excuse Me For Livin'' and 'Elegy (Plain Black Boy)' with an astringent pride which was well in advance of the times.

Passing through Chicago in 1966, I saw Oscar Brown's name outside a nightclub, and didn't go in; just one of life's many regrets. More recently I saw a tribute to him by Clive James, critic and lyricist, as the man who made it all seem possible. As the dust settles on the sixties, his work looks better and better. There are any number of people nowadays writing and singing songs which are witty, pungent, sophisticated and personal. But Brown's 1962 songs can still hold their own in such company. They have a magic preservative not much in evidence these days: style.

***

The classic British 'beat group' sound crystallised in the early Beatles records, and taken up by the likes of the Hollies and Bee Gees, continue as a living tradition: witness the work of a young quartet from Scotland called Pilot. Their album *Second Flight* (EMI EMC3075) is constructed, as all albums used to be, of a dozen three-minute pop songs, any one of which (excepting the instrumental '55° North 3° West') could have been issued as a single.

This is pleasant, bouncy MOR music, with titles like 'Love Is', 'To You Alone', 'Do Me Good' ... plenty of soft vowel sounds making up singable words which don't impinge too severely on the cortex.

Pilot started out as a trio, and it is the three original members who supply most of the beat group trademarks—the breezy ensemble singing, the jangly piano and foursquare drumming and bass patterns. Characteristic bursts of orchestral sound have also been added by producer Alan Parsons.

The songs are all more or less on the same level of amiable extroversion, and all more or less disposable, but a rather more arresting note is sometimes sounded by the new boy, guitarist Ian Bairnson. He doesn't get much chance to cut loose from the group format, but when he does, there is a hint of deeper waters.

Thursday, 3 July 1975

GRAND OLD ALLEYMAN

JIMMY KENNEDY IS a debonair and distinguished-looking gentleman who constitutes Ireland's gift to Tin Pan Alley—and what a gift. Everytime you do the Hokey-Cokey, assert that 'twas in the Isle of Capri that you met her, meltingly inquire whether the listener's mother came from Ireland, or raucously point out that Constantinople is now Istanbul, you're quoting a work of vintage Kennedy.

Furthermore, if you go down in the woods today—to darkest Co. Dublin—you'll find him at the piano in his study, still in pursuit of winners, like 'The Teddy Bear's Picnic', which was his first real monster hit in 1932. The tune of this title had been written by an American in 1907 for Teddy Roosevelt's 1908 election campaign, Roosevelt being fond of an occasional bear-hunt in the Dakotas between whistle stops. The English music publisher Bert Feldman had acquired it and tossed it to his new young staff writer. J. Kennedy, in December 1930, who was asked to apply suitable words for a children's show in Manchester. This achieved, the number lay on the shelf for two years, until Henry Hall came seeking bait wherewith to lure listeners from *Children's Hour* to his own radio show on another channel. The old picnic number was half-jokingly proffered, performed on the air, and the switch board lit up. Hall's record of it ultimately sold three million copies.

But this being showbiz, Kennedy got no royalties on any sales before 1947. (According to him, Feldman found the song's success irksome and not the kind of material he wanted to encourage from his staff writers.) Never mind, he was making very good for a young man who'd reached Denmark Street, W1, via Portstewart, Co. Antrim (his hometown) and TCD (his alma mater) and the Shaftesbury Grammar School, Dorset.

Since he taught French at the latter, his career to that point was quite similar to Samuel Beckett's; thereafter, the similarity rapidly diminished. More taken by Gershwin and Kern than Proust and Gide, he thrashed out a few ditties on the staff-room piano, nipped down to London in the half-term and touted them round the publishers. When one firm finally offered him three guineas each for three of them, he accepted with alacrity. It was 1928, fame beckoned, and he'd sold three songs outright. One of them, 'Hear the Ukeleles', was done the following year by the music-hall legend G.H. Elliott, by which time the three guineas were long spent.

It was not an auspicious time to break into songwriting. In the Crash of '29, record and sheet-music sales evaporated. His freelance earnings during the first year were £90. It was a buyer's market. Woolworth's put out sixpenny records, and he recalls being asked to write eighteen songs for the B-sides of these, at £3 a song. In a weekend. And doing it.

Business picked up, he had a hit with the lyrics to a Continental tune, 'Oh Donna Clara', and became Lyric Editor at Feldman's. Denmark Street was the British Alley, with over a dozen publishers, and the work was brisk and lively, what with supplying words to tunes from abroad, writing second verses to American hits (to allow the extra plug of three choruses), penning accordion waltzes, and whatever else was required.

An Austrian refugee, Will Grosz, supplied the melody to 'The Isle of Capri' and Kennedy got the idea for lyrics from a newspaper article on Gracie Fields' Capri villa. Feldman turned it down on the grounds that the line about the 'plain golden ring on her finger' implied adultery, and Reith's BBC would never broadcast such degeneracy. The tune was passed on to other lyricists for treatment, but none of their efforts was up to the original.

Kennedy refused to change the offending line, so finally a release was granted and the piece offered to another publisher. He agreed to risk publishing it if Kennedy would accept a 50% cut in royalties. He did, the song was broadcast, and requests flooded in for 'the one about the ring on her finger'. Many listeners had never heard of Capri, others thought the phrase ran, 'I Love Capri', but they all devoured the number—an instant standard.

Also with Grosz, he wrote 'Harbour Lights' and 'Red Sails in the Sunset'. The former was suggested by the name of a pub in Hampshire which he passed one night; as to the latter, it was built round a memory of Major Scott's boat sailing off Portstewart, seen in the sunset from the family house on Strand Road. He thinks the boat still exists, at Portrush. The Ulster Folk Museum ought to investigate; if this isn't folklore, what is?

His other major collaborator in the thirties was Michael Carr: together they wrote words and music for three shows, and they produced the world smash 'South of the Border', which had another homely inspiration. Kennedy's sisters went for a trip to California, and they sent him a card from Tijuana saying '... today we are south of the border' ... idea ! By a pleasing coincidence, the number took on a new lease and clocked up its biggest ever sales when re-recorded in the sixties by Herb Alpert's Tijuana Brass.

In January 1940, 'South of the Border' was No. 1 and 'My Prayer' No. 2 on the American charts—and the author of both was in the mud of an Ack Ack Battery. Asked for a number for the troop sing-song, he knocked off '(We're Gonna Hang Out) The Washing On The Siegfried Line'—one of those war songs that seizes the moment, its flavour and smell, and preserves it for ever after.

He finally got to America in 1947, on contract to a publisher there, and stayed till 1960, hobnobbing with the likes of Porter, Berlin, Rodgers, Arlen and the rest of the gang. Berlin he found unpleasantly conceited; his favourite team of the lot is Rodgers and Hammerstein, the kings of schmaltz, and his favourite number 'If I Loved You' from *Carousel*. At the same time he says of Cole Porter: 'he makes me feel that I'm not a lyric writer at all'.

Most of his own work in America was country and western, of all things—but he points out that its roots lie in the Scots-Irish immigrant culture and Moody and Sankey hymns, and for a man from Portstewart this was wee buns. 'God's Little Candles' and 'Down the Trail of Aching Hearts' are two of the lachrymose titles from this period.

During the sixties, he lived in Switzerland in semi-retirement, but in 1971 he came home again, to Mr Haughey's tax relief, and he's still writing. Recently he has contributed his own kind of comment on the strife in his native province, with a song called 'Let There Be Peace'. We're lucky to have him—an Alleyman for all seasons.

Friday, 11 July 1975

ICE-COLD MAMMA

Carly Simon/*Playing Possum*
Adrienne Johnston/*Adrienne Johnston of the Johnstons*

CARLY SIMON'S NEW album, *Playing Possum* (Elektra K52020) is fascinating for many reasons besides the high quality of her writing and singing. For one thing, it might almost as well be described as Richard Perry's new album, so crucial is that distinguished producer's contribution to the total sound. He employs all the facilities of a modern studio to produce a big spacey atmosphere; but such is his reticence and restraint in this instance that there is never any sense of the production intruding or growing rank and lush.

Instead, Ms Simon's voice is subtly reinforced and enhanced by a wide range of instrumental sounds—the players as always being of the first rank—and by such devices as a cunning blend of vocal and electronic sound, so that it's often difficult to tell them apart (for example, in 'Look Me In The Eyes' and 'Waterfall'). In purely aesthetic terms, this is a beautiful recording.

But of course the album has a subject-matter, and that's absorbing too: it's an affirmation of sexuality, as indicated in most of the song titles—'After the Storm', 'More and More', 'Are You Ticklish'. The expectations aroused by these are of a raw and earthy red-hot-momma routine. But the renditions are remarkably chaste and dreamy, the voice ethereal rather than orgasmic. Carly Simon has wisely stuck to her own territory rather than trying to ape Tina Turner or even Maria Muldaur. This is refined, white and affluent eroticism.

A couple of the songs are not directly involved in this theme. The title number is addressed to a man who has worked his way from radical chic through mysticism to married bourgeois contentment.

284

It's too deliberate an attempt to emulate the success of 'You're So Vain'. But Billy Mernit's poignant 'Sons of Summer' is one of the loveliest things on the album.

***

Meanwhile back home. Adrienne Johnston has entered the female singer stakes with an album of her own (on IEMC 6002). Folk buffs will know her from her work with the Johnstons, whose reading of 'The Curragh of Kildare' can still melt my calloused eardrums. She has a bright, clear, unforced voice, which she applies on the album to nine songs written by her husband Chris McCloud and composed by himself (two), herself (three) and Paul Brady (five).

A lot of professional care and expertise has been lavished on this album. The lyrics are literate and of the moment, their mood well exemplified in the chorus of the opening number: 'So many country songs/that aren't quite real,/And he never hears a city song/About the way he feels/And he's weary of nostalgia/And so tired of looking back/He's out searching for tomorrow/On that good old railroad track.'

The arrangements by Don Fraser use orchestral instruments in a vivid and sometimes dramatic way. There's a particularly fine atmosphere created in a song called 'Too Late Now', which has a strong set of lyrics about a relationship which is beginning to falter. The following track, 'Long Ride in the Morning', a retrospective look at the protest song has been cunningly if a trifle ornately arranged by the soloists involved.

The album's weaknesses seem to me, after a couple of hearings, to be melodic and vocal. The tunes are quite adequate, but they have no particular flavour; there's a rather assembly-line kind of impersonality about them. This is reinforced by Adrienne Johnston's voice which doesn't vary much from track to track. She has the same problem as other folk stars who have crossed over into pop music—a vocal spectrum limited to cool primary colours, which can produce a rather remote and schoolmistressy effect when applied to contemporary material.

However, you can judge for yourself on 28 July when Adrienne Johnston and Chris McCloud are featured in an RTE television show.

Thursday, 17 July 1975

BIRTH OF THE BLUES

Samuel Charters/ *The Legacy of the Blues*
Various/ *The Legacy of the Blues*

IT'S ONLY NOW, when the century is three-quarters over, that the Blues are being given full recognition as the quintessence of its popular music. Books, articles and records abound; and these are in themselves a symptom of decline. The arts of primitive and classical blues singing are carried on by old black survivors and their young white imitators, and looked upon with indifference or contempt by the new black generation because of their tone of plaintive stoicism. It's significant that Samuel Charters' new study is entitled *The Legacy of the Blues* (Calder and Boyars, £1.50, paperback).

Charters is slightly afflicted by reverence but not by the other besetting sin of the aficionado, pedantry. His involvement is a deeply personal one, he knows his bluesmen and loves them, and it's hard not to be reverent in the face of the emotional intensity generated by performers as supreme as Lightnin' Hopkins or Memphis Slim. His book is subtitled 'an informal study' and 'a glimpse into the art and lives of twelve great bluesmen.' It ranges from old country blues singers like Big Joe Williams and Bukka White through the Chicago style of men like Sunnyland Slim and Mighty Joe Young to younger men like Snooks Eaglin, who sometimes plays in places like the Playboy Club in New Orleans.

It's a short, conversational book which doesn't get into anything really scholarly or general, but one of its most interesting sections is a short chapter called 'The Language, the Voice', which takes a look at the language of the blues in the context of the history of Black writing in America. A few slaves made it into print in the 18th century—but only by dint of aping the iambic pentameters and poetic diction of white society, like 'Phillis Wheatley' of Boston (and later London) or by doing the same for ballad doggerel like Lucy Terry of Deerfield, Mass. Meanwhile, a black dialect was evolving, its early forms captured in the fragments of the Gullah language of the isolated Georgia Sea Islands which were transcribed in the 1880s. Charters sees the blues as the form in which this dialect finally found its artistic outlet—'Of all the things that are the legacy of the blues, it's probably this that is the most important: that with the blues, the Black American, for the first time, was able to speak with his own voice.'

A sampler album of the same title (on Sonet SNTX-1) has been released simultaneously with the book. It features all the bluesmen dealt with in the book and is available from Sonet Records, 12 Needham Road, London W11. The whole package should appeal very strongly to those who already have an acquaintance with the music. Rank beginners will be better off with the marvellous big Penguin, *The Story of the Blues*, by Paul Oliver, and the two albums which go with it on CBS (M) 66218. Paul Oliver was also responsible for the documentary album, *Conversation with the Blues* on Decca, which I would recommend to anyone.

***

I have received a letter from a reader called (I think) Helen K.R. Wiley which deserves to be quoted in full: Sir, In your article. 'High Pop-Grand Old Alleyman', on Friday 11 July, you refer to the boat which inspired Jimmy Kennedy to write 'Red Sails in the Sunset'. This yacht was not owned by Capt. D.F. Scott but by Albert Clarke, of Kerr Street, Portrush. It was called Kitty of Coleraine and was the only yacht with red sails in the area at that time. I myself was sailing in this craft when Jimmy Kennedy wrote the song. Capt. Scott—not major—owned a white-sailed boat of the Jewel class called the 'Ruby'.

All of which is a song in itself, and an invitation to a protracted and scholarly correspondence.

Thursday, 24 July 1975

PLAYING PAUL

Wings/*Venus And Mars*
Gwendal/*Gwendal*

FOLLOWING UP ON the success of *Band On The Run* last year, Paul McCartney's Wings have released an album called *Venus and Mars* (EMI PC&C 254) which has zoomed to the top of the charts in both Britain and America. Which must be very satisfying to the soul and chequebook of the ex-Beatle, who was written off by the critics for the blandness and complacency of his work. Particularly as it has been achieved without the benefit of extensive public performances, either on the stage or on television. Songwriting, production and promotion have sufficed.

No expense has been spared on the latter two elements. The first striking thing about this album is that it looks and sounds lavish. The packaging includes two poster-sized photographs, and even the inner sleeve has a glossy planetary design all over it. To make the disc itself, McCartney drew on the finest record-making and musical talents of two cities, New Orleans and Los Angeles—basic tracks and brass in one, mixing and strings in the other. No austerity in this enterprise: everything's the best that money can buy, from the fat sound of the opening theme, 'Venus and Mars', to the lovely quicksilver sax playing of Tom Scott on 'Listen To What The Man Said'.

McCartney himself is in excellent voice throughout—deep and vigorous, with none of the over-forcing which has sometimes marred his singing in the past. As to Wings, they're a virile, efficient band with Linda keeping decently back and new American member Joe English laying down a full-blooded drum sound.

But when you get down to the heart of the matter—the songs themselves—the issue becomes clouded. Certainly they're commercially adroit, and 'Listen To What The Man Said' is a single of high quality. They sustain interest, they're varied in tone and tempo, they never get entirely mawkish. The trouble is that the man who wrote 'Yesterday' and 'Blackbird' and 'Mother Nature's Son' has set himself the highest of standards, and when he doesn't reach them, you can't but feel the lack.

Perhaps some of the songs on *Venus And Mars* will survive, but I doubt it. When you mentally compare them (and it's unavoidable) with the McCartney standards, they seem to have been conceived and executed at one remove. 'Venus and Mars' and 'Magneto and Titanium Man' are comic-strip in tone. 'Love in Song' and 'Letting Go' and 'Call Me Back Again' are pleasant, straightforward romantic numbers. 'You Gave Me The Answer' is thirties pastiche. 'Spirits of Ancient Egypt' has a hip, nonsense lyric and a heavy rendition, whilst 'Treat Her Gently-Lonely Old People' is a weepie. The album ends with a jokey rock version of the Tony Hatch theme to the awful TV soap opera *Crossroads*.

The one non-McCartney song is Jimmy McCulloch's anti-drug composition 'Medicine Jar'. It's not a great song, but in an odd way it has a greater impact than the rest because it is at least trying to say something. It's not just a pretty face.

***

Those who like their traditional music laced with jazz or rock—and vice versa—will enjoy the cut-price EMI album *Gwendal*. The group of this name is a French five-piece, and this is their first release here. They draw quite heavily on Irish folk tunes, but there are also Breton titles, and a track called 'Texas Quickstep'.

It's not a branch of contemporary pop to which I personally respond, but I like this group better than most, their music is entirely instrumental, the cuts are crisp and tightly played, and the flute player in particular knows his way around the instrument. Unlike most groups of this kind, they seem to have at least as much grounding in the jazz end as in the ceilidhe.

Thursday, 31 July 1975

DOWN THE TRAIL OF ACHING HEARTS

The Eagles/ *One of These Nights*
Jimmy and Tommy Swarbrigg/ *That's What Friends Are For*

LEAN BACK IN the old rocking chair and pour yourself a strong one, we're heading down the trail of aching hearts with five muchachos called the Eagles. I missed their last excursion, *On the Border*, but their reputation has been building and with country groups disbanding in all directions, they've got the Nashville end of Sunset Boulevard pretty much to themselves now.

Their new album is called *One of These Nights* (Asylum SYLA 8759) and it's a ripe set of eight country-rock songs and an instrumental. The title song opens the proceedings with refreshing gusto. It's sung by drummer Don Henley who has an attractively husky voice full of soulful sincerity, but manages to sound quite leery here: he's in between the dark and the light, the wrong and the right, searching for a woman who's the daughter of the devil as well as being an angel in white, and though she may have her demons and desires he's got a few of his own. Great stuff.

This is followed by the high voice of bassist Randy Meisner complaining about 'Too Many Hands' being laid on her. Percussion beats out an urgent tattoo under some thick acoustic guitar chording. After such brooding melodrama, 'Hollywood Waltz' slides down as easily as the 'Tequila Sunrise' on the *Desperado* album, to which it bears some resemblance. The Hollywood waltz is being danced by another Beverly Hills casualty, on the skids, deserving kind affection since she gave more than she's taken We're all in this together, all maudlin through and through.

Side 1 ends with the instrumental, a Bernie Leadon mini-symphony which starts out arrestingly on the banjo and then loses its way in a welter of strings and special effects. Not Eagles territory this.

A quick flip and the mood is restored. 'Lyin' Eyes' is the choicest number on the album for my money. It deals with a time-honoured situation, young girl married to older man. She's headin' for the cheatin' side of town every night, and there's no way to keep it quiet: 'You can't hide your lyin' eyes/And your smile's a thin disguise.' Glenn Frey sings it well, but could scarcely go wrong with lines like that.

'Take It to the Limit' and 'Visions' are not up to this level, they're just OK. The first is another high-pitched Meisner melodrama, and the latter is a rock number by new member Don Felder, with the vocals mixed away down. 'After the Thrill is Gone' returns us to homily on the range, love without passion is no love at all, etc., sung in lovely plaintive harmonies by Don Henley and Glenn Frey.

The album ends with another disappointing Leadon composition, 'I Wish You Peace', a real Cliff Richard piece of saccharine piety. But never mind. More than enough riches here to see you through a lost weekend, played and recorded with that American brand of ostensibly effortless excellence.

***

Just room for mention of the new album from Jimmy and Tommy Swarbrigg, *That's What Friends Are For* (EMI IEMC 6003). It takes its title from their Eurovision entry, and comprises twelve songs much in the same vein—unpretentious and pleasant if rather bland. More pop music. It was recorded in an Irish studio to a high professional standard of playing and production.

Thursday, 7 August 1975

MUSICAL BIKES

Richard Ballantine/*Richard's Bicycle Book*

IN RECENT WEEKS a single called 'My White Bicycle' by the English group Nazareth (on Mooncrest Records) has scored a modest success. Had the singing been better and clearer, the guitar work more interesting, the production a bit brighter, it could well have been the hit of the summer. For pop singles are largely a branch of fashion, and few things are currently more fashionable than the bicycle.

The trend has been gathering momentum for some time. 'My White Bicycle' was in fact written and first recorded around 1967-8, inspired by a scheme to solve Amsterdam's traffic congestion and pollution distributing free bicycles (painted white) around the city centre. This plan was the work of those erstwhile Dutch yippies, the Provos, whose values and ambitions—to rescue the city and make it a better place for its inhabitants—were the exact opposite of those of our own folk-heroes of the same name.

The white bicycle idea was never fairly tested, but the principles behind it have continued to gain force with the help of the crisis over energy and inflation. Habitual cycling, until recently thought of by the people of sensibility and taste as (at best) eccentric, has suddenly become terribly chic. I've been registering this because I've just written a stage play about bicycles involving a fair bit of research into the subject. Everywhere I look now, in the high-class Sunday papers, on glossy magazine covers, on television, one of the humble machines is in the clutches of some smiling glamorous person.

This new image has been reinforced by the publications, which have been appearing to service the growing market. Pan have published a 'manual of bicycle maintenance and enjoyment' called *Richard's Bicycle Book* by a young American cycle freak called Richard Ballantine.

It's a marvellously comprehensive and well-researched and readable book—possibly the best there is on the subject, certainly for £1.25—and it has an evangelistic opening chapter which ends with the words: 'the salvation of the world is the development of personality and identity for everybody in it. Much work many lifetimes. But a good start for you is Get a bicycle!'

***

The last time people were talking in those terms was during the

1890s, the first and greatest decade of the 'safety bicycles' popularity: and the period which produced the greatest bicycle song and in many people's opinion the greatest music-hall song of all, 'Daisy Bell', popularly known as 'Daisy, Daisy'. This was composed and written in 1892 by a man called Harry Dacre, and popularized around the halls by singer Katie Lawrence. There can scarcely be a person alive who doesn't know its chorus, but not many people are familiar with the three excellent verses which Dacre wrote. I particularly like the saucy imagery in the final one:

> You'll take the lead in each trip we take
> Then if I don't do well
> I will permit you to use the brake
> My beautiful Daisy Bell.

According to Robert A. Smith in *A Social History of the Bicycle* (American Heritage Press, 1972) there was a host of cycle songs in the American Tin Pin Alley of the 'nineties. He cites titles like 'Mamie, My Bicycle Girl', 'I Love You, Bloomers, Bicycle And All' and 'Get Your Lamps Lit'. He even mentions a musical farce produced on Broadway in 1895 called *Bicycle Girl*. If any reader has copies of such material, or its ilk, I'd be very eager to photocopy it.

Maybe the bicycle renaissance of the 1970s will produce its own crop of songs. I hope so. 'My White Bicycle' may not be a masterpiece, but it's better than the more typically named flip side— 'Miss Misery'.

Thursday, 14 August 1975

NEW NAMES

Clifford T. Ward/*Escalator*
John Dawson Read/*A Friend of Mine*

IT'S A RARE week indeed which affords the opportunity to enthuse about two new names. New to me, that is: Clifford T. Ward has had three albums out now, and the current one, *Escalator* (Charisma CAS 1098) has sent the musical press into raptures. Still, he's scarcely a household name.

As for John Dawson Read, he is entirely a newcomer, and all the more welcome for being a mature man with a separate career as a graphic designer. His debut album, *A Friend of Mine* (Chrysalis CHR 1075), is light years removed from the usual record company 'product'. Both his songwriting and his singing are imbued with qualities lke gentleness, relaxation, humility, lyricism.

If he sounds like anybody else, it's the early James Taylor (and on a few tracks, like 'My Time', he sings uncannily like him) but without the constant melancholy and literary symbolism. He has a priceless voice, light and mellow, lifting high notes from the air with apparent effortlessness. The song's subjects range from 'superficial things' to the growing inner vision of a friend who's going blind to 'Good Living'.

His most extraordinary knack is to take a really corny subject—e.g 'Rain'—and make it work as if nobody else had ever thought of it. This particular number has a lovely, flowing melody, and the voice is sensitively complemented with some single-string acoustic guitar work by Alan Hodge. 'All the time in the World' is a simple love song with a ravishing over-all sound—a soaring melody buoyed up on the rich chords of a small brass choir.

What other contemporary songwriter could create an acceptable song about a family picnic 'Sallyalley Sunday'? It's a bit wordy, but there's just enough grit—throwing a bag of tupperware into the jeep, daddy sloping off to the boozer—to keep it from cloying. It also has a very pretty flute obbligato.

In fact all of the instrumental arrangements and overdubbing are an enhancement to Read's voice and guitar—except the string. Maybe I'm over-sensitive to the sound of swelling catgut, but I can't understand why every solo performer's voice has to be swathed in it.

Never mind, this record should be acquired immediately by all persons of taste and discernment.

***

Clifford T. Ward seems almost brashly commercial by comparison, but of course that's nonsensical, as is instantly demonstrated by his use of the phrase 'a slave to rock and mud': referring not to a pop fan but to a coal miner. It's just that he's very versatile and slick, turning his hand to several different styles in turn.

Because of my own musical predilections, two of the tracks on *Escalator* strike me as marvellous. There's the title song, a tightly played jazz number with alto saxist Pete King in full flight, and nifty lyrics about modern technology being ok since he met his girl on an escalator. Then there's 'Cellophane', an outright winner. It's a lighthearted, catchy, jokey, Simon-and-Garfunkely song, entirely irresistible. He's insane and inane over Cellophane, she elevates him like a steel crane, but then in the same machine-like way she drops him back down again.

It's only fair to say, though, that Ward's real forte is the big ballad, and most of the other tracks are in this vein—Atlanta in flames, soft focus and glycerine, a warm swelling in the bosom. It's not my cup of treacle, but he does it very well.

Thursday, 21 August 1975

RENAISSANCE ROCK

Consort of St Sepulchre/*Medieval and Renaissance Music*
Buddy Holly & The Crickets/*The Chirpin' Crickets*

SMALL WONDER THAT the secular music of the period 1200-1600 AD has found an audience amongst rock fans. To begin with, the bulk of it is heavily percussive dance music. Also, the instrumentation accords with contemporary tastes—loud and brassy (e.g., cornetti and sackbuts), reedy and vibrating (e.g., krummhorns and rauchsfeife), but with a vividly contrasting sweetness in the viols, lutes and recorders. Perhaps there's the added fact that the music is solidly grounded in concrete particulars, often indeed in plain arithmetic—its mysteries grow out of a very democratic simplicity.

Like a lot of other people, I first came to it in adolescence through an enjoyment of the oldest Christmas carols. Performances on record then—of which there were few—tended to be decorously church-choir. But groups like Musica Reservata and David Munrow's Early Music Consort have since rediscovered or reinvented the genuinely popular qualities of the music, by playing it on authentic instrument and singing it with folk gusto rather than concert-hall refinement.

***

Dublin is lucky to have such a group in the Consort of St Sepulchre, and the rest of us are lucky now because they've just released an album (on IEMC 6005). Produced by Donal Lunny, himself a figure of note in Irish traditional music, and promoted by EMI (Ireland) along with their latest pop release, it deserves to bust the charts. If you consider something called *Medieval and Renaissance Music* to be beyond you or beneath you just ask the man in the record shop to play you one number from this album.

The first one, for example, an upbeat love song from Scotland belted out by Lucienne O'Kelly in a manner which eclipses the entire recorded output of the Bay City Rollers and all such milksops. If you prefer something bawdier, try 'Hey Trolly Lolly Lo', in which cow-milking takes on a whole new significance,' or 'Calabaza', which is described in the notes as 'a Spanish song of about 1500, full of double meanings and erotic images.'

Initiates will particularly enjoy Vanessa Sweeney's fast rendition of 'Angelus Ad Virginem', beloved of Chaucer's randy clerk in 'The Miller's Tale', and Peter Sweeney's stirring version, over pounding tabours, of 'L'Homme Armé', a medieval popular song which formed the basis of many settings of the Mass, including the magnificent one by Josquin.

The most gorgeous sounds on the album occur when the whole consort of six instrumentalists and four voices performs—as on a French theatrical song by Gosse, and the sad, stately 'Hélas Madame' from the court of Henry VIII. But equally effective in a different way are the utterly simple dance tunes, like the estampie played on sopranino recorder by Jennifer Robinson, and the great Provencal troubadour song 'Kalenda Maya'.

Congratulations and indeed gratitude are due to Barra Boydell, Andrew Robinson and the whole Consort for getting this music together, and to EMI for recording and releasing it. Let's have more.

***

Buddy Holly is one of the concrete particulars of today's rock music. His influence is everywhere; he continues to be imitated by performers who were four or five years old when he died in a plane crash which immediately became a rock & roll myth.

For those tired of imitations, the real thing is again available. The 1958 album, *The Chirpin' Crickets*, has been reissued, complete with the original cover (on MCA Coral CDLM 8035). It contains twelve songs, including 'Oh Boy', 'Not Fade Away', 'Maybe Baby', 'That'll Be The Day' (need I say more).

Thursday, 11 September 1975

STICKING TO THE STYLE

Procol Harum/*Procol's Ninth*
Be-Bop Delux/*Futurama*

WHEN ROCK GROUPS start hiring symphony orchestras, watch out. They're about to change their name to Hubris and record an octuple-album called *Vanity of Vanities.*

Many fine groups have gone down that sunset road, and there-by perished, at least until Ken Russell finds the time to make a film about them. I had rather assumed that Procol Harum were such a one. But bless me, they've just released their ninth album, *Procol's Ninth* (Chrysalis CHR 1080) and there isn't so much as a first violinist on it: just the group with the odd bit of brass embellishment. Furthermore, it's a highly entertaining and lively and very musical album.

The distinctive Procol Harum style was established in their first and biggest hit, 'A Whiter Shade of Pale', which roughly speaking had imitation-T.S. Eliot lyrics sung over an imitation-Bach organ toccata. Those who can still hum it—I'm afraid it was eight years ago, ravers—will know what I mean. With lugubrious singing from Gary Brooker, composer and organist.

Subsequent album work revealed an additional penchant for drama, especially of the doomy kind. All of which culminated in the excellent *A Salty Dog*, a front ranker from the heyday of the concert album, but also the first on which they used orchestration. Since then Procol have sounded dull and vapid to these ears, whatever about gold records

It has to be the producers who have made the difference this time: none other than Jerry Leiber and Mike Stoller, the men who wrote 'Yakety Yak' and 'Searchin'' and all those other Coasters hits of a dozen-odd years ago. Hip isn't in it. There's even one of their own compositions here—'I Keep Forgetting' from 1962—and there's no way of mistaking that it's the classiest song on the album. The mastery of metre, the percussive consonants, the wit ('And this stubborn old fist/At the end of my wrist/ Keeps knocking on your front door.')

But credit to Gary Brooker and his four gifted minions. They play and sing together with grace and symmetry throughout the disc. Brooker's music has a harmonic versatility which allows for all manner of pleasing instrumental patterns, and the boys take full advantage of it. I particularly like the opener, 'Pandora's Box', which is very much mainstream Procol in its stringing together of portentous cultural references and images. The publicity describes it musically as 'Gothic-calypso', which is splendid and apt.

The weaker tracks are towards the end, and their weakness mainly resides in Keith Reid's lyrics. He's never been a strong writer either in form or content; but when he gets into being whimsical about his own writing, as in 'Typewriter Torment' and 'Without A Doubt', he's downright awful. There's also a lacklustre version of 'Eight Days A Week' which is nothing without the Beatle's vocal harmonies.

But *carpe diem*. It's so great to hear a long-established group which can once again make refreshing, shapely, living music.

***

I've been trying for weeks to get in a word about Be-Bop Deluxe. They deserve a mention for the name alone, but in addition they have a very impressive album out on the Harvest label called *Futurama* (SHSP 4045). They're a three-piece, and the motivating genius is one Bill Nelson, who composes, sings and plays all the keyboards and guitars.

His guitar work is of the pyrotechnic variety, but it's not just exhibitionism, it's purposeful and accomplished, sometimes unnervingly so. His conceptions are grandiose and range from the purest hokum and self-indulgence to three consecutive numbers which have drama, humour, melodic strength—'Maid in Heaven', 'Sister Seagull', 'Sound Track': dynamic rock music.

Friday 19 September 1975

MUZAK-MAKING

Poco/*Head Over Heels*
Gentle Giant/*Free Hand*

MOST POP IS as processed and characterless as slot-machine coffee. That's only to be expected in the world we've made. What's genuinely regrettable is when an intelligent group, aiming at a personal statement, just produces more standardised product. Naturally, it tends to happen to groups which have been working together for a long time, though the process isn't inevitable (as witness the fine, new Procol Harum album, reviewed here last week). At any rate, a lot of the new Poco album—*Head Over Heels* (ABC Records ABCL 5137)—is no more distinctive than a muzak tape. Which is sad for a band which traces its lineage back to the Buffalo Springfield.

Enough of turntable philosophy, let's get down to particulars, starting with the good bits. The first track is right in line with 'A Good Feelin' To Know', homespun sentiments expressed in radiant vocal harmonies over a strummed acoustic guitar. 'He's gonna keep on tryin', he's through with lyin' and tired of cryin'. It bursts out of the speakers like a rich peal of birdsong.

On Side 2, 'Flyin' Solo', is composed by the same man, bassist Timothy B. Schmit, and is equally effective in a different way. It's one of those loping numbers which gradually builds in power, solo voice being joined by harmony backing and then efflorescing in a guitar solo. Which fits the lyrics nicely. 'Sitting' On a Fence' isn't bad either, though it sounds very like a Stephen Stills song. It's a driving Latin number with a lot of lively percussion, and a kind of all-purpose warning against sitting on fences.

The rest of the album I find hard to remember without close scrutiny of the lyric sheet. There's 'Lovin' Arms', 'Let Me Turn Back To You' and 'Makin' Love', which are all identikit country-rock songs, largely indistinguishable, except that the last one's faster.

There's 'Down in the Quarter', an 'atmosphere' song about New Orleans with feeble lyrics and a corny string arrangement. There's 'Dallas', a Steely Dan song, the only non-Poco offering on the record—with all its fascinating weirdness buried under a top-heavy, cloying arrangement. And there's two or three others, all too familiar, all too forgettable.

***

Head Over Heels is Poco's tenth album; *Free Hand* (Chrysalis CHR 1093) is the eighth from Gentle Giant. This is something of a cult group, comprising five Englishmen who like to fool around with elements of baroque music and jazz in their intricate rock compositions. I've heard very little of their earlier work, and I'm not tempted to explore it further by co-leader Ray Shulman's comment on this new disc: 'The change isn't that dramatic from our other albums ... we've tried not to be so technical and introduce some genuine emotion as well.'

All I can say is that *Free Hand* sounds like the creation of a gifted, sophisticated, musical computer. The words, first of all, are sung in a cold voice, often in choirlike harmonies, and cannot be understood. But when you check the lyrics sheet, you find that they're almost entirely meaningless verbiage anyway.

The numbers tend to be constructed of various complicated riffs repeated in various difficult time signatures. On the title tune, for instance, keyboards, guitar, bass and drums play a set of quicksilver figures which are intricately interwoven. The result is clever and sometimes quite beautiful, but it constantly moves towards an impersonal formality which leaves this listener stone cold. For all the slick production, ingenious multitracking and musical expertise on their album, it has a pervasive feeling of mechanical anonymity. There's nothing very human in it.

Thursday, 25 September 1975

IN BETWEEN

Melissa Manchester/*Melissa*
Moonrider/*Moonrider*

LADIES AND GENTLEMEN—Melissa Manchester!

You cannot applaud a name like that. How did she arrive at it? Is there a discarded sheet of paper in her waste-basket covered in crossed-out possibilites—Sybilla Sheffield ... Wanda Wigan ... ?

No clue is given on the sleeve of her album *Melissa*, released by Clive Davis's Arista label (with the rather coy index number ARTY 104). But the lady herself stares out fetchingly, with a muted Bette Midler aura of high camp sleaze. And this is pretty much what I expected the music within to sound like—fair to Midlerish.

In actual fact, it's wholesome Carole King whose work is instantly evoked by the first track, 'We've Got Time'. Miss Manchester lays out some melodious, soulful chords on the piano which are crisply extended and reinforced by a tight studio group. Meanwhile she sings 'as long as we keep an open mind, we've got time,' in a light, accurate voice, lacking in character perhaps, but equally devoid of harshness or strain.

The last track on Side 1 is even more under the King influence, as witness the lines: 'Why should I care about being unfair/Nobody's home when you need 'em/Even after you love 'em and feed 'em,' done very wry and sincere. It's called 'This Lady's Not Home', and apart from the obtrusive influence, it's a nice song.

In between this pair come one piece of disco fodder called 'Party Music' and two very interesting numbers. There's 'Just too Many People', which is a driving mid-tempo song sporting an unusual verse melody built on suspended unresolved chords, which gives way to a simple hook guaranteed to slice through traffic or any other noise and implant itself in your helpless mind. Then there's 'Stevie's Wonder', a tribute song. It uses a fast, breathy descending run as the main feature of the tune, which gives way to a fascinating instrumental coda, based on Wonder's style, with guitars and percussion and strings muttering over a bass punching the on-beat.

***

Side 2 opens with an actual Stevie Wonder song, 'Love Havin' You Around'. There's a big group of musicians on this, and it moves along, with Melissa giving full expression to the sensuousness of the lyrics. 'Midnite Blue', a lover's plea to make up after a rift, is again her own composition, not very original but affecting for all that. 'It's Gonna Be Alright' is another disco track, 'I Got Eyes' a light and very pleasant little song and 'I Don't Want To a Hear It Anymore', the last and best piece which the album offers.

It's by Randy Newman, and it concerns a woman who can hear the neighbours through her thin bedroom wall discussing her husband's adultery. Melissa sings the first half with just her own piano backing which is greatly refreshing. She does full justice to a very fine song.

Melissa Manchester is not well-known over here. I hope people will give her album more than a single hearing. It repays closer acquaintance.

***

Moonrider (Anchor ANCL 2010) is the first album from the relatively new group of the same name, an English foursome endeavouring to play American soft and country rock. The lads have a lot of experience—guitarist John Weider is ex-Animals and ex-Family, vocalist and producer Keith West has been playing in groups for over twelve years.

300

Their album is pleasant and easy on the ear, but it ain't the Eagles. It isn't even Poco, whose latest collection I was somewhat severe with last week. There's a kind of foolhardy heroism about an English group attempting this music. Moonrider are probably up to it instrumentally —Weider is first rate, and Bruce Thomas is a very gifted bassist—but vocally (and in their lyric-writing) they're plain weak.

Thursday, 2 October 1975

SOFT ROCK ARISTOS

Souther-Hillman-Furay Band/*Trouble in Paradise*
Pink Floyd/*Wish You Were Here*

THERE'S A VERITABLE aristocracy now of veteran soft-rock musicians in California. They freelance around, teaming up in varying permutations, as complicated to sort out as the affaires of the Bloomsbury group. As often as not these brief alliances call themselves by the lordly, hyphenated surnames of their leading members—and such is the case with the Souther-Hillman-Furay Band, which has just come out with a polished and beautiful album called *Trouble in Paradise* (Asylum SYLA 8760).

With a combined pedigree involving such groups as the Byrds, Poco and Manassas, this band could be forgiven for indulging itself— as most of the others invariably do. But in fact its six members play and sing as if they were trying to win a talent contest. Since they are in fact highly gifted and mature musicians, the result has to be a first-rate album. And so it is, folks.

They begin by demonstrating that the band can rock, just to clear the air. The number is 'Trouble In Paradise' itself, and it's a driving bluesy piece, written and sung by John D. Souther, with an attractive finale on flute and then electric piano, both instruments being handled by Paul Harris. This is followed by Chris Hillman's 'Move Me Real Slow'.

Hillman has always played the second banana to performers like Roger McGuinn and Stephen Stills, but I find his brand of depressive integrity consistently appealing. 'Move Me Real Slow' is a rollicking number, with lyrics full of sensuous overtones, but Hillman gives it an extra edge with the characteristic mournful note in his singing. He sounds like a man feeling sexy, urgent and hopeless all at once.

The remaining member of the starry triumvirate, Richie Furay, makes his bow in the third track, 'For Someone I Love'. He is, of course, a major exponent of the plangent country-rock sound, and this song is as sweet as they come, with the most honeyed of backing harmonies from the others.

The variety exemplified in these three tracks extends over the rest of the album, with a constantly changing swirl of instrumental sound. Souther's 'Mexico' has a Latin beat and Latin acoustic guitar. It's a confession of a man's infidelity while his wife was away. She was on a holiday in Mexico spending her daddy's dough, and he guesses he got so lonely without her he had to let somebody know. 'Love and Satisfy' is another Hillman ditty, greatly enhanced by the dobro playing of Al Perkins.

Side 2 opens with the high, pure voice of Furay doing his 'On the Line', followed by a slow, melodious number of Souther's called 'Prisoner in Disguise'. In all these songs, the vocal harmonies are of the highest order, but they reach their apogee in Hillman's 'Follow Me Through', which is a high point of the album, with a mid-way switch of tempo to an upbeat Latin rhythm, followed by a fine guitar solo, then the voices again, and a fade-out on piano and guitar trading solos.

The album ends with Souther's 'Somebody Must Be Wrong', which sports a strong and pretty tune. It goes out on ecstatic high harmonies behind the final chorus. Which is a fitting end to a very pleasurable record.

***

I had meant to write about the Pink Floyd's new album as well. It's called *Wish You Were Here*. It exemplifies again their habit of stretching out basically sound ideas to the point of vacuity, but it has its moments of excellence—enough of them to save up for next week. This'll do for an appetiser.

Friday, 10 October 1975

FED UP WITH IT

Pink Floyd/ *Wish You Were Here*

THE MUSIC OF the Pink Floyd is very English; like cricket, it moves with a slow and repetitive deliberation, occasionally erupting into movements of unexpected drama. To appreciate it, you have to attune your mind to this premeditated but seemingly casual slow motion.

All this occurred to me while listening to the new Pink Floyd album, *Wish You Were Here* (Harvest SHVL 814). It was only afterwards that I read about the Pink Floyd XI, which plays regular fixtures against such other eminent cricketers as the Roy Harper XI. So there you have a thesis topic for some future music student: the influence of cricket on English progressive rock.

This is the first Floyd album for two years, since the hugely successful *Dark Side of the Moon*. The delay may be partly explained in the theme of this new work, which is one of sardonic disenchantment with the rock music industry and with their own success. The most explicit statement of this comes in 'Have a Cigar', the song of a record company shark, with lines like:

We're just knocked out. We
heard about the sell-out. You
gotta get an album out.
You owe it to the people.
We're so happy we can hardly count.

***

Listening to successful, wellheeled performers moaning wearily about their disillusionment can be a tiresome experience. But the Floyd's situation has an extra piquancy: the visionary who virtually moulded the band in his own image, and led it through the early days of public ridicule and critical abuse was guitarist Syd Barrett. After the public and press had begun to catch up with his music, and to heap rewards upon it, he dropped out and became a recluse, which he remains to this day.

The remaining four members of the group are still in Barrett's thrall, to some extent, and the whole album is like a dialogue between them and him. It opens and closes with a direct exhortation to him, called 'Shine On You Crazy Diamond'—'You reached for the secret too soon, you cried for the moon ... come on you painter, you piper, you prisoner, and shine!' The middle two songs are satirical of the pop-showbiz scene which Barrett rejected, as the titles indicate: 'Welcome to the Machine' and 'Have a Cigar'. Then comes the title song.

This poses the inevitable question: who was right? Is it better to work on within the system or to reject it and retreat into your own mind? Addressing Barrett rhetorically, the lyric asks: 'And did you exchange a walk-on part in the war for a lead role in a cage?' Whether he did or not, they wish he was there.

The nature of this dialogue gives an over-all shape to the album and tightness about its individual parts which is not always common in the Floyd's work. Musically, there are longwinded patches, such as the opening, which resolves after a kind of Vaughan Williams mellotron chord, into an interminable bluesy guitar passage. But there are also many felicities, such as a ravishing Dick Parry sax solo at the end of the first track, hoarsely eloquent.

'Welcome to the Machine' employs mechanistic sound effects which are effective in a comic-strip way, and 'Have a Cigar' fools around with perspectives and fades as well as sporting the strongest Dave Gilmour guitar work on the record.

All in all, it's full of fascination, and a very fine album indeed from a band which many critics had written off.

Friday, 17 October 1975

IN THE MAINSTREAM

Orleans/*Let There Be Music*
Batdorf and Rodney/*Life Is You*

AT FIRST I thought *Let There Be Music* (Asylum SYL 9023) was going to be yet another rock & roll revival album, for it starts with the good old chomping chords of Buddy Holly's 'Not Fade Away'. But these lead us into a bright, vigorous song called 'Fresh Wind', delivered in crisp vocal harmonies by a four piece band of considerable flexibility and verve. The band is called Orleans and is itself a fresh wind, even if blowing in the prevailing directions.

In other words, don't look here for the oddball genius of a Steely Dan or the strong-flavoured individualism of a Little Feat or an

Allmans. Orleans is a mainstream American rock group, content to work within the established conventions like many fine groups before them (Jo Jo Gunne comes to mind). What makes them stand out is their taste, their panache and above all the sheer quality of their performance.

The second track, for example, could scarcely be cast in a more classic pop-song mould 'Dance with me/I want to be your partner/Can't you see/the music is just starting/Night is calling/And I am falling/Dance with me'. They put this time-honoured imagery over with such vivacity that it's one of the most attractive songs on the album: a timely demonstration of simplicity operating as a virtue.

Their success is partly explained by their set-up. Band leader John Hall composes the music for his wife Johanna's lyrics, takes the lead in singing the results, and plays mainly first guitar parts. However, Larry Hoppen supplies a kind of twin lead guitar part as well as handling keyboards. His brother Lance plays bass, and Wells Kelly is the strong and discreet drummer who holds the sound together.

All of them play with such facility that the music of ten sounds wholly natural and effortless. In 'Time Passes On', a couple of strong and simple melodic phrases are developed into a flowing tune of considerable prettiness enhanced by soothing backing harmonies, and flawed only by an awkwardness in the lyrics. In the title song, the band displays its heavy guns with funky and infectious guitar work by Hall. This should do well as a single.

Side 2 keeps up the standard. 'Business as Usual' is all about staying oblivious to the world's plight and wrapping yourself up in your own affairs—it has a particular resonance for those of us who live in the North. 'Cold Spell' is another semi-political song about conservations, done with great urgency over a wah-wah guitar and a thudding bass. The other three cuts are less compelling—'Give One Heart' in particular is a rather sanitised reggae number—but taken for all in all, this is a very pleasant album indeed with which to beguile the cool autumn evenings.

***

Life Is You (Arista Arty 112) is a debut album from a duo called Batdorf and Rodney. Presumably on the grounds that if two lads called Simon and Garfunkel can make it, why not two lads called Batdorf and Rodney?

The problem is that their names are the only original or striking thing about this pair. They sing very smoothly together, but their melodies fail to linger on and their lyrics may be summed up with justice in this example: 'As long as I'm with you/I hear singing/As long as I'm with you/Bells keep ringing'.

What value the album has comes from the high-class studio sound and rich instrumental mix achieved by producer and arranger Tom Sellers. It's a beautiful package but not much of a gift.

Thursday, 23 October 1975

OUTLAWRY

The Outlaws/*Outlaws*
Dr Feelgood/*Malpractice*

LAST WEEK I was enthusing about the apparently effortless excellence of a new American rock band—and this week I find myself doing the same thing yet again. The supply from that teeming republic seems well-high inexhaustible. Last week Orleans, this week the Outlaws.

Their chosen name is the only lame thing about this band, or at any rate about their album *Outlaws* (AL 4042). They were the first band signed by the famous Clive Davis to his new Arista label, and this debut album contains a gravely worded rave from the chief himself. One listen is enough to confirm that the man has not lost his ear for music.

The Outlaws are a 'Southern' band, which is the fashionable thing to be at the moment, but they aren't irritatingly pushy about it. There's a lot of progressive Nashville in their material, but there's also a lot of Los Angeles in the vocals and a solid core of rock & roll. There are five of them, and like Orleans, they go-in for two lead guitars— played with prodigious talent by Billy Jones and Hughie Thomasson. These two also share the singing with rhythm guitarist Henry Paul, whilst all five band members write songs.

These are musically excellent, lyrically just adequate. The titles really contain the lyrics. 'There Goes Another Love Song' is the very comment of your average bar-room romantic—somebody's singing about me again, he continues. 'Song for You' is the first opportunity for Thomasson and Jones to unfurl their dual lead guitar technique,

306

as well as their nifty high vocal harmonies. 'It Follows from Your Heart' is a melancholic philosophic number written and sung in a plangent, quavering voice by Billy Jones. Very Neil Young, 'Cry No More' has the tempo and some of the chords of 'Sweet Little Sixteen', and trucks along very satisfactorily.

Side 2 is more country-flavoured, opening with a terrific burst of fluent, banjo-like guitar work called 'Waterhole' and continuing with Henry Paul's 'Stay With Me', which is almost undiluted Nashville, ending on excitingly high harmony singing. In 'Keep Prayin'' the voices are as interestingly blended as the guitar lines. 'Knoxville Girl' is a rousing number, reminiscent of the Eagles, and it leads into the album's climax, 'Green Grass and High Tides'.

In this track, the Outlaws extend themselves musically for the first time, and the result is amazing. The two guitarists seize the musical structure by the scruff and frog-march it through an increasingly dazzling series of variations, culminating in a blitz of sound which is a genuinely fitting end.

**

The Outlaws are not beyond criticism. They sing with poor diction and their music is full of the echoes of other groups. But they have a sheer brilliance and versatility and energy which leave most groups on this side of the Atlantic looking rather silly.

Dr Feelgood is a currently favoured band in England. Promoted as a bunch of tough throw-backs from Canvey Island, they specialize in primitive rhythm & blues and rock & roll, evoking names from the past like the Coasters, Clyde MacPhatter and Carl Perkins. Their album *Malpractice* (UAS 29880) would do service as a party record, but I suspect that a major part of their appeal is to be found in live performance.

Thursday, 30 October 1975

MUTE MISERY

Paul Simon/*Still Crazy After All These Years*

PAUL SIMON'S LAST album of songs, *There Goes Rhymin' Simon*, was a work of brilliance and depth at first hearing, and has continued to improve with age. For my money it's among the most consummate achievements of contemporary popular music, and is probably the record I would take to a desert island.

Which makes it a hard act to follow. And indeed, the new Simon album *Still Crazy After All These Years* (CBS 86001) seems at first to be plainer, simpler, less rewarding. There's nothing flashy in it, no image or effect or musical idea which draws attention to itself. But closer acquaintance reveals a deliberate obliqueness and a subtlety of approach which grows more and more impressive.

For the album is mainly dealing with a peculiarly modern kind of misery, the mute pain of a relationship which is on the rocks, but can't somehow be ended satisfactorily. Like so much else in our lives, it's repressed and anaesthetised. And this is precisely the effect which Simon achieves—a calm, almost glazed surface of unexceptionable words and pleasantly attractive melodies, with underneath it the bottomless dark depths of fret and worry and hurt.

The title number, which opens the album, doesn't quite perfect the trick. The lyrics, dealing with the thoughts sparked off by a meeting with an old girlfriend, are a shade too depressive, and end very lamely. There's also a slightly soft-centred arrangement of strings and woodwinds. But the second track—'My Little Town'—is something else.

It offers first the pleasure of hearing Simon & Garfunkel again. They sing about a little hometown, with what appears to be the familiar imagery of nostalgia—except that the sound has a hard edge to it, and the printed lyrics have an epigraph from Ted Hughes' 'Crow'. Sure enough, emotional savagery suddenly intrudes with the lines:

Nothing but the dead and dying
Back in my little town.

The song is transformed from a sentimental reminiscence into a vehicle of suppressed bitter rage, well worthy of the great days of the singing partnership.

'I Do It For Your Love' is perhaps the album's centrepiece. It has a suspended, gently cascading tune, and a set of words which seem to recall, in neutral terms, some events of a marriage. But these are pitted against the repeated chorus of the title in a way which suggests, with extraordinary subtlety, the song's true meaning.

This is followed by '50 Ways to Leave Your Lover', which employs straightforward irony to make its point. A flip, catchphrase chorus—'You just slip out the back, Jack/Make a new plan, Stan' etc.—is pitted against painful, realistic verses. Side 1 ends with a short song about the death of á baseball player, an immensely sad and tender piece called 'Night Games'.

***

The opener on Side 2 is designed as the album's hit, and it's a magnificent swinging gospel-style number called 'Gone At Last', with Simon perfectly partnered by Phoebe Snow. 'Some Folks' Lives Roll Easy' is a slow waltz and the only song on the album with a trace of self-pity in it, but 'Have A Good Time' has a vigorous satirical edge. 'You're Kind' is a gentle restrained and finally brutal testimony to the strain of being suffocated by love. The album ends with a very intense but obscure little song called 'Silent Eyes'.

Paul Simon's greatness, as demonstrated yet again in this record, lies in subversion. He revolutionises pop music by revealing its tricks and clichés as the pathetic tatters with which we try to dress our gaping emotional wounds.

Wednesday, 5 November 1975

TOP BANTAM

Leo Sayer/*Another Year*
Horslips/*Drive the Cold Winter Away*

LEO SAYER'S MANY Irish fans should be well pleased with his latest album release, *Another Year* (Chrysalis CHR1087). The bantamweight voice is in good shape, dealing assertively with ten of his own varied, carefully written songs. Manager Adam Faith has again ensured a sensible handling of production, with flexible backing from a good, unobtrusive studio band.

Leo is undoubtedly one highly talented kid, and is only to be found wanting if judged by the highest standards of the singer-songwriter. Which is what he seems most to desire. Which is in turn his biggest single problem—Leo tries too hard, gets sabotaged by his own ambitions, goes over the top. Like the protagonist of the first song on the album, he's too often 'crying to be heard/screaming to be heard.' A man's reach should exceed his grasp, perhaps, but in the words of his last album, this is Just a Boy.

The song I like most on *Another Year* is 'I Will Not Stop Fighting', which closes Side 1. It's sung with a simple directness with just piano backing for most of its length. It's a very attractive, bluesy love song which is clearly not meant to be a standout track, and consequently pushiness and unease are absent from it. On the other hand. 'The Kid's Grown Up' on Side 2 is excellent precisely because it confronts ambition, acknowledges it, turns it into an effective rock & roll growl of defiance.

The songs presumably meant to stand out are 'Moonlighting' and the title track. 'Moonlighting' has been chosen as the single release; it tells the rather implausible story, to a Mexicali beat, of an elopement to Gretna Green. (No kidding). 'Another Year' is a New Year's Eve song, all fashionable disenchantment as emotionally profound as 'Auld Lang Syne'.

Some of the other numbers topple over into melodrama. 'Bedsitter Land', the opener, is quite a strong evocation of bedsitter loneliness and squalor for most of its length, but boils over towards the end. 'Unlucky In Love' fails to arouse compassion for Leo's bad luck in affairs of the heart, partly because of some excruciatingly sustained notes. 'Last Gig of Johnny B. Goode' strains too hard to be a searing revelation of the last days of a disillusioned star.

Scarcely more convincing is 'On the Old Dirt Road', expressing as it does a nostalgia for the blissful days of carefree anonymity. Cynical laughter. 'Streets of Your Town' accuses the listener of similar romanticism by describing vagrants sleeping rough and adding the comment 'I bet you wish you were the same.' Not me, kid.

With any luck, this album may be successful enough to appease Leo Sayer's craving for stardom. Then he might be able to unclench a little and attain to the high quality of which he's so patently capable.

***

Horslips have come out with a Christmas album called *Drive the Cold Winter Away* (Horslips Records M009), complete with a shamrock border in place of the customary holly and a To and From space in which to write your festive particulars.

It's a light and pleasant record, notable for being almost entirely acoustic. Many of the items have a somewhat tenuous connection with Christmas—the hornpipe 'The Piper in the Meadow Straying', for example, gets in on a passing resemblance to 'Deck the Halls'—but the traditional carols 'Rug Muire Mac do Dhia' and 'Ny Kirree fo Naghtey' (a Manx song) are nicely done.

Thursday, 13 November 1975

OLDFIELD'S THIRD

Mike Oldfield/*Ommadawn*
Shusha/*Before the Deluge*

MIKE OLDFIELD'S THIRD album has the title *Ommadawn*, which sounds as if it could have come from *Finnegans Wake*. Along with all those suggestions in it of the holy 'om' and omega and universal dawn, there's the amadán, the fool of Gaelic folk tradition; and probably a lot more besides. But if the music on the album has a comparable depth and richness of connotation, I've entirely missed it. There's more substance than there was in the instantly forgettable *Hergest Ridge*, but nothing to set beside the now classic *Tubular Bells*, which is presumably by this time a millstone round Oldfield's neck.

Ommadawn (Virgin Records V 2043) opens in a dreamy, muffled way with a wash of instrumental and vocal sound—rather a wishy-wash. A guitar and then a mandolin play a vaguely carousel tune over this, and it builds to a head with the crash of a synthesizer. After a bit of tympani and simulated orchestral chords, a jolly version of the tune is played on piano and what sounds like pan pipes. This is reinforced with a lot of extra bits and pieces, and an impressively speedy treatment of the theme takes over on electric guitar.

When that has spent itself there's a slow transition into a passage of steady African drumming, with some female voices far back in the mix singing apparently about 'ommadawn.' As with all of Oldfield's effects, there's a mantra like repetition, hypnotic, and accumulating power from added repetitions chiming in, a harp figure and an organ

311

phrase in this instance. The whole section, which builds to an urgent climax and ends Side 1 is the most effective part of the album.

The second side offers an extension rather than a development of Side 1. There's a similar muddy backdrop of sound, with rather wispy lead playing up front. As the sleeve note proclaims, 'Mike Oldfield plays harp, electric guitars, acoustic bass, electric bass, acoustic guitar, 12-string guitar, classical guitar, mandolin, bodhran, bouzouki, banjo, spinet, grand piano, electric organs, synthesizers, glockenspiel and assorted percussion'... but to what effect? Most of this music is pretty, charming and pointless, like the films of cloud-scapes or wave patterns with which they used to fill programme gaps on television.

***

Another pleasant but bland album is *Before the Deluge* (United Artists UAS 29879), from the Persian chanteuse Shusha. This consists of a number of the lady's own compositions, plus her versions of songs by Jackson Browne and John Prine.

Although celebrated as an interpreter of traditional Persian song, she has opted on this album for a flavourless international style. The backing is as bright and cheery as supermarket strip-lighting, and she sings every word with the same light, expressionless emphasis.

Thursday, 20 November 1975

ROCK FROM JAPAN

Sadistic Mika Band/*Hot Menu*
John Lennon/*Shaved Fish*

SINCE BECOMING WESTERNISED, the Japanese have appeared bent on outclassing all competitors in the various mass markets of capitalism, including the cultural ones. Having contributed the odd pianist or violinist to the top ranks of classical music, and a maverick percussionist who can play in any company, they've now entered the stakes of progressive rock with a group called, rather alarmingly, the Sadistic Mika Band.

Actually, to say they've 'entered the stakes' is to betray a possible prejudice. The Japanese pop music business is twice the size of

Britain's and second only to America's in volume; and the Sadistries are Japan's biggest band, with their third album just released over here. But I doubt that the six members of the group would object to the phrase. Like rock devotees everywhere, they look to Los Angeles and London and intervening points for their standards and influences.

On the basis of their new album, *Hot Menu* (Harvest SHSP4049)— which is the first I've heard—they deserve all the Anglo-American recognition that they desire. From the nimble opening track, 'Time To Noodle', it's clear that this is a group with musical imagination, wit and a quirky individualism. With a line-up of two guitars, keyboards, bass and drums, they go for tight and tricky ensemble playing, strong melodic ideas and atmospheric sound pictures.

The second number, for example—which has another Zappa-like title, 'Mummy Doesn't Go to Parties Since Daddy Died'—is a very attractive dreamy guitar melody which is balanced with the sound of children playing in a genuinely musical and evocative way. As for quirky individualism, how does a Japanese samba grab you? It's right there on Side 1, entitled 'Mada Mada Samba', and I suspect it of containing Japanese puns.

The singing on the album is partly in Japanese and partly in English, and it's the weakest aspect of the group's work. The rhythm guitarist shares it with the girl whose name, Mika, has been adopted by the band, presumably because she's its biggest draw. Neither of them sounds very scrutable, and Mika actually comes over as something of a pain in the final number, 'Tokyo Sunrise', which is a fractured monologue about the mandrax she's swallowed and the drink she wants: more masochistic than sadistic, really.

Nevertheless, this is a group with a style all its own and 'Menu' is a very tasty entrée.

***

Japan, of course, has also given Yoko Ono to the world and to John Lennon, not always to the benefit of either party. Lennon's albums and singles since the break-up of the Beatles have been culled for a new LP release called *Shaved Fish (Collectable Lennon)* on Apple PCS7173; and it reconfirms the belief that the degree of Yoko's influence and collaboration is in inverse proportion to the quality of Lennon's songs.

In other words, songs like 'Woman is the Nigger of the World' and 'Happy Xmas (War is Over)' don't strike me as collectable Lennon, but as forgettable John-and-Yoko. And from the same phase of arid sloganeering comes 'Power to the People', which would surely have been better left to perish along with phrases like 'right on', which completes this song's lyrics.

Still, it's nice, to have the extraordinary, anguished 'Cold Turkey', and for something more uplifting, the soulful 'Instant Karma'. *Plastic Ono Band* is still Lennon's finest album, and the brilliant 'Mother' from it is included here; as are 'Imagine' and 'Mind Games' from the respective albums of the same names.

Thursday, 27 November 1975

PARLOUR SONGS

Michael R. Turner/*The Parlour Song Book*
Michael R. Turner & Anthony Miall/*Just a Song at Twilight*

CHRISTMAS PRESENTS ARE unquestionably a good thing, but it's noticeable how they annually achieve a kind of disappearing trick. At some point early in the New Year they merge imperceptibly into the general clutter of personal or household possessions. I personally find it impossible to remember from one year to the next either what was given or what was received.

Except for special cases. Last year I received *The Parlour Song Book* (Pan paperback, £1.75), a 'casquet of vocal gems' from the Victorian drawingroom, and it has refused to merge. It remains highly visible on the top of the piano, and is constantly drawn upon during parties and sociable evenings for such favourites as 'Come into the Garden, Maud', 'Excelsior!' and 'Father's a Drunkard and Mother is Dead'. The friend who gave the present does a particularly melting rendition of 'Auntie', which begins:

> You're my little true lover,
> You're my little boy blue,
> But I'm your old Auntie, darling,
> And I cannot marry you.

The source of the pleasures—both blithe and excruciating—which these songs afford is well described by the editor, Michael R. Turner, in his introduction: 'A very few of the ballads in this collection are good by any standards; a handful are splendidly, joyously bad, masterpieces in the art of sinking. Most of them, however, are flawed to some extent by hackneyed or at least out-of-date sentiments in the poetry or by clumsy or ingenuous musicianship, or by lack of inspiration or simple wrong-headedness. Because they can all still be enjoyed, despite all their defects, they fall into that category, which is not the same as the mediocre, of good bad art.'

***

TURNER and his co-editor Antony Miall have now produced a second Parlour Song Book entitled *Just A Song At Twilight*: and o dear reader! the manliest lip would tremble at the sight of that dear little treasure nestled close to its mother on the piano. It is in every way the equal of the first book, and in some respects surpasses it. Turner begins his introduction this time, for example, with a word-count of parlour ballads. It transpires that the top five favourite words in the bourgeois lyrics of Victorian society were 'love', 'home', 'old', 'heart' and 'mother'.

The really good songs in this collection include 'In the Gloaming', 'On the Banks of the Wabash', (a gift for the unsophisticated vocal harmoniser), the irresistible 'Sweet Rosie O' Grady' and 'See Me Dance the Polka'; this last comes from a new section devoted to comic songs, at which the Victorians were not very accomplished. But the ones which Turner has chosen survived certainly into my childhood and are presumably still sung by male-voice choirs and by soloists at parish-hall concerts: stately humour about the secret tippler 'Simon the Cellarer' and about the brother-and sister who tittered and laughed because granny had only left to me her old arm-chair—which turns out to be stuffed with money.

Another new section is 'The Emerald Isle'. Thomas Moore is given his due, but I was taken aback at how many of the other perennial sentimental Irish weepies were written by English men and women. The dreaded 'Kathleen Mavourneen' was written by an F.W.N. Crouch; 'The Rose of Tralee' was composed by Londoner Charles Glover; 'Come Back To Erin' was the work of an English lady with the distinctly un-Hibernian pen-name of 'Claribel'. All of which should boost our national self-respect.

If you're thinking of this book as a possible present for somebody this year—and it would make a splendid one—I have to caution you that it is only available at present as a Michael Joseph hardback, costing £8.50. You might as well throw in a piano while you're at it.

Thursday, 4 December 1975

GALLAGHER TOUCH

Rory Gallagher/*Against the Grain*
John Fogerty/*John Fogerty*

AGAINST THE GRAIN (CHR 1098) is Rory Gallagher's first album for Chrysalis Records, though his seventh overall if we include the three put out by his group, Taste. He has long since proved conclusively that a Corkman can play the blues, and indeed is well on the way to becoming an institution. Although his real métier is live performance—and his best albums are live recordings—*Against the Grain* has enough hot licks to keep you listening.

Its first side consists of five Gallagher compositions. 'Let Me In' opens in typical power-driven style, with all four members of the band blasting away on all guns. 'Cross Me Off Your List' gets into more progressive melodic and rhythmic territory. 'Ain't Too Good' is the slow number; 'Souped-Up Ford', a fast rocker, with Rory doing his Chicago ghetto declamatory voice prior to a guitar blitz; and the side ends with a deliberative mid-tempo song called 'Bought and Sold'.

The guitar-playing in all of these numbers is impeccable, but nobody would describe them as great songs. The musical ideas are fluent but hardly original, the lyrics have no great importance attached to them, and Rory's weakest aspect has always been his rather limited vocals. Essentially, these compositions are pleasant vehicles for that trademark guitar work. The other three band members—who play bass, drums and keyboards—are mainly concerned likewise with providing an effective and efficient setting for same.

Side 2 has two further Gallagher numbers, along with three more veteran songs. There's the classic Bo Carter blues, 'All Around Man', full of sexual swagger, and another traditional piece of masculine assertiveness called 'I Take What I Want'. More unusually, there's the splendid Leadbelly cowboy song, 'Out on the Western Plain'. This is beautifully handled by Rory, with sincere and straightforward singing and some attractive acoustic guitar picking.

***

Creedence Clearwater Revival was a major sixties band whose demise was much lamented by fans of otherwise wildly divergent musical tastes. Somehow their music was simple without being infantile, deeply rooted and yet wholly contemporary. The group was created and led by John Fogerty, who hasn't been much in evidence since. But he has now upped and made an album called *John Fogerty* (Fantasy FT526) which recreates a lot of the Creedence sound.

A big component of that sound was the mechanical abrasiveness of early, small-studio rock & roll, which Fogerty has refined to perfection here, as is evident right away in the infectious opener, 'Rockin' All Over the World'. The studio band—there are no musical credits on the sleeve—achieves a rasping, funky backing which is perfectly attuned to Fogerty's voice and guitar.

Most of the songs are his own, but a stand-out track for me was 'Sea Cruise', which was a hit during my schooldays. I guessed it as a Fats Domino number, but the nearest work of reference lists it as a composition of another New Orleans veteran, Huey Smith, with Huey's singer Frankie Ford taking it into the charts in 1959. Fogerty opens it with nautical sound effects, which give way to a boogie piano, croaking saxes and an impassioned rendition of the 'oo-ee, oo-ee baby' chorus. Great.

'You Rascal You', the trad-jazz standard, is also featured as is the Berry Gordy lament, 'Lonely Teardrops'. Musically, though, the most appealing tracks are 'The Wall' and 'Travellin' High'. The latter in particular, which incorporates a horn section has crisp, simple lines tightly played and recorded.

Thursday, 11 December 1975

THE JAZZ CONNECTION

Herbie Hancock/*Man-Child*
Gwendal/*Gwendal 2*
Solution/*Cordon Bleu*

EVER SINCE ITS emergence as a distinct form, jazz has consistently either embodied or allied itself to the biggest aspirations of popular music. Small wonder, then, that in recent years jazz men have made an accommodation with contemporary rock, soul and folk. The seal of approval to this process was first given by Miles Davis, and others of his ilk have followed suit, with some very arresting results.

Pianist Herbie Hancock is in this groove and has just come out with a new album called *Man-Child*, (CBS 69185). It illustrates how much established jazz artists are prepared to learn from contemporary soul and rock musicians about electronic sound and the use of the recording studio as an instrument in itself. *Man-Child* draws on the resources of no fewer than four studios as well as employing on its large roster of musicians three different drummers and three bass guitarists.

The bass is used throughout less as a pulse than as an independent percussive/harmonic instrument, repeating and elaborating on little runs played in and around the drumbeat—very much in the manner developed by the likes of Sly Stone and Stevie Wonder. Also characteristic of these innovations is the way an irresistible dance impulse is always sustained no matter how rich and complex the studio mix becomes. Such is the case with this album—and Wonder himself even appears at one point to help it along, playing a harmonica solo on a track called 'Steppin' In It'.

This is the funkiest of the six numbers: the bass boogies along under some very punchy brass and sax lines. But on the whole I favour the first two titles most. 'Hang Up Your Hang-Ups' opens with bubbling urgency, as guitar and bass repeat simple staccato figures, and then accumulates an almost hypnotic tension as organ, brass, tenor sax and much else interject and decorate these basic ideas. 'Sun Touch' is a slow, sensuous number, with shimmering electronic keyboard work.

Elsewhere the ideas are often spread too thin and the ear wearies of the insistent repetition. But on the whole this is an album which appeals on many different levels of enjoyment.

***

The second album released here by the French group Gwendal (on EMI-Pathe) reveals them as a heavily jazz-oriented bunch of traditional musicians. The material on it ranges from a fairly straightforward treatment of traditional airs like 'Scalloway Lasses' to impressionistic essays like 'Rue Du Petit Music', one of their own compositions.

The most extraordinary music on the album comes in the final number, 'Le Coucou Migrateur', also a composition of their own. Bruno Barre plays an extended solo on electric violin which is like a combination of Jean Luc Ponty and Sean Maguire. The album is worth listening to for this performance alone—it's in every way electrifying.

***

Finally a Dutch group called Solution who play a form of jazz-rock: not the same form as their justly famed Dutch rivals, Focus, but accomplished in its own more conventional way. They've been a top group in Holland for some years, but *Cordon Bleu* (Rocket: Roll1) is their debut album over here.

Its nine tracks display a strong sense of pop melody but also a grasp of jazz dynamics. The line-up is alto-sax, flute, guitars, keyboards and drums, with supplementaries from various studio hands. Bassist Guus Willemse also turns in some pleasant vocals.

Thursday, 18 December 1975

1976

KEEPING UP WITH JONI

Joni Mitchell/*The Hissing of Summer Lawns*

ANY YEAR THAT ended—as 1975 did—with the release of a superb new Joni Mitchell album can't have been all bad. And in fact '75 did very well for itself, with a variety of enduring work from Paul Simon and Carly Simon, the Eagles and the Outlaws, Steely Dan and Procol Harum, and many others besides. Activity was rife on the local scene, and I can't let the occasion pass without mention of the splendid album from the Consort of Saint Sepulchre—here's hoping for a follow-up in '76.

So much for the after-dinner speech. What follows is not so much a review of the Joni Mitchell album—*The Hissing of Summer Lawns* (Asylum 7E-1051)—as an interim report. Miss Mitchell's work long ago exhausted all the critical superlatives. The problem now is not how to assess what she's doing but how to keep up with her. Which is not to say that she's beyond criticism: there are things to dislike in this album, starting with the pompous and even arrogant sleeve note, which begins, 'this record is a total work conceived graphically, musically, lyrically and accidentally—as a whole. The performances were guided by the given compositional structures and the audibly inspired beauty of every player, the whole unfolded like a mystery. It is not my intention to unravel that mystery for anyone.' Spoken like a true prig, Joni.

But all this tends to wither into insignifiance when the music starts, and the extraordinary richness and fecundity of her imagination takes over. As on her last three albums, she employs first-rate jazz musicians here—not Tom Scott and the LA Express, but a mixture of musicians from that group with some from the Jazz Crusaders. The first number, 'In France They Kiss on Main Street', is arranged very similarly to those on *Court and Spark*, and provides a bridge of continuity with that album, evoking as it does the days of her teenage rock & roll revolt. However, that revolt, against 'middle-class circumstances', is the starting-point for a new investigation into the reality of urban bourgeois life and various attempts to combat it or escape from it.

You can take 'The Jungle Line', for example, embracing the vision of the 'primitive'—in painting and music:

Rousseau walks in trumpet paths
Safaris to the heart of all that jazz.

This is sung over an amazing sound, comprising Burundi warrior drums and repeated phrases on a synthesizer. It sounds ridiculous in cold print, but it works—so much so that this is the most exciting track on the album.

***

The other songs seem to follow this pattern, but some of them are still obscure to me, and overall this is undoubtedly the most difficult Mitchell album to date. I'm far from clear as to the scenario of 'Edith and the Kingpin'—it presumably involves the criminal underworld, maybe drugs—and 'Don't Interrupt the Sorrow' is a private trip, though it has some very arresting lines.

'Shades of Scarlett Conquering', however, is in the familiar vein of feminine character-study, dealing with a woman whose style has been formed entirely from old Hollywood movies—another kind of escape. And both 'Harry's House' and 'The Hissing of Summer Lawns' itself are pungent studies of the arid middle-class marriage—the hissing on the lawn being a powerful updating of the imagery of Eden.

Tom Wolfe has given her the title and idea for 'The Boho Dance', which deals with fake bohemianism, including her own. And there's more, much more. As I say, this is an interim report. But what an album!

Friday, 9 January 1976

LIVING DEAD

The Grateful Dead/*Blues for Allah*
Jethro Tull/*Minstrel in the Gallery*

THE LAST GRATEFUL Dead album I heard was *Wake of the Flood*, and much as I enjoyed it, I got the feeling that the band was fading out. Not surprising, when you consider how much a part of the San Francisco 'sixties it was and how much it depended on the precarious spirit of collective spontaneity. And sure though, it's been fourteen months since a Dead album appeared, RIP ... except that in their new LP release, *Blues for Allah*, (United Artists UAS 9895), the Grateful Dead enter their eleventh year of existence with music that achieves new levels of sophistication, vigour, discipline and richness.

If *Blues for Allah* sounds like a title from the Bop era, then that may be an indication of what they've been listening to recently, and of its beneficent influence on them. Opponents of the band have, in the past, been able to point to weaknesses in musicianship which undoubtedly existed but which were deemed unimportant by fans in the context of the overall statement. However, even stern progressive-jazz adherents should be excited and impressed by some sections of this album.

Right away in the first number, 'Help on the Way', there's a strong jazz content in the lightly swinging bass and drum sound and in the loose-limbed and distinctive melody. Jerry Garcia sings the words and embellishes them with beautiful little guitar phrases; the others contribute occasional restrained vocal harmonies. It's a song which has been lodged permanently in my head since first hearing it.

This swings into 'Franklin's Tower', a faster and more pleasing verse-and-chorus number, closer to their familiar vein of old, then come two instrumental pieces end to end—'King Solomon's Marbles' and 'Stronger Than Dirt'—speeding, quicksilver jazz which is most impressive for its balance between anarchy and discipline. Each instrument is fully up front, and yet together they achieve a marvelous, intricate blend. Phil Lesh and Garcia on bass and lead guitars have never sounded better together.

Side 1 ends with a happy, extrovert Bob Weir song celebrating music itself, which contains some very apposite lines about 'a band beyond description':

People join in hand 'n hand
While the music plays the band.

The Dead can actually achieve that sense of the music playing them: they do it in 'Crazy Fingers', which opens Side 2 with a choppy, jaunty kind of sound, Garcia singing inconsequential words over a lolloping organ and guitar, and the occasional ping from finger cymbals. And it's even stronger in 'Sage and Spirit', the following number, in which acoustic guitar, piano and flute create a stream-like piece of free form impressionism.

Its suite of three numbers which ends the album is what I feel least happy about, though mainly because of its excessive length. 'Blues for Allah' itself is a sombre incantation with lines that seem to refer to the war in the Middle East. Thereafter, there's a lot of instrumental meandering over shimmering desert noise which loses me. And I have to add that most of Robert Hunter's lyrics come over as empty poeticisms. But for all that, and for most of the time, there's glorious music here.

***

Which can't, I fear, be said about the Jethro Tull album, *Minstrel in the Gallery* (Chrysalis CHR 10821), released before Christmas. English art school experimentalism has not stood up as well as the Californian varieties. There are arresting moments on this record— 'One White Duck' is an oasis of gentleness in a desert of thudding, unmelodic silliness—but Ian Anderson says it all himself in a line from the song which follows: 'Something must be wrong with me and my brain—if I'm so patently unrewarding.'

Thursday, 15 January 1976

MUSIC BUSINESS

Clive Davis/*Clive: Inside the Record Business*

IF YOU HAPPEN to have a Walter-Mitty trait, try this for size: You're the young president of a huge record company ... you introduce Bob Dylan to Laura Nyro ... you lunch a lot with your personal friends Paul Simon and Art Garfunkel ... to celebrate the signing of her contract, Janis Joplin offers to sleep with you ... a rival company offers you one million dollars of inducements to go over to them, but you turn it down ... It's heady stuff, and furthermore it's all true, folks, and there's a great deal more of the same. It comes from a fascinating and important book called *Clive: Inside the Record Business*—which is the story of Clive Davis's mercurial years with Columbia Records, as told by himself and journalist James Willwerth.

This is a book not just for the armchair fantasist, but also for anybody interested in how music is merchandised in our society or in how large industrial corporations operate. Personally I enjoyed it on all three levels at once. Davis's accounts of inter-office politics and of his 'talent-raiding' attacks on other companies afford the same kind of pleasure to the non-business mind as playing Monopoly. But ultimately he raises bigger questions about the role and position of art in a consumer society than he himself is prepared to entertain.

***

Facts first. Clive Davis started out as a lawyer, a Brooklyn meritocrat driving hard towards the top with no particular interest in music of any kind. In 1960, he was offered a good job in the CBS legal department, which he accepted. Doing legal battle for the artists on the Columbia label—who included Dylan, and Simon & Garfunkel—led him into an involvement with their music and with the artists themselves. It also impressed the corporation heads sufficiently for them to appoint him in 1965, out of the blue, as an administrative vice-president, in charge of the whole domestic records operation. Within a few years he was president of the records division.

CBS is a corporate giant. It operates one of the two biggest American television networks and has diversified into many other fields of entertainment. It's a solid hunk of the bedrock of the American establishment, and in the mid-sixties its records division was devoted to Broadway cast albums, Mitch Mitchell 'sing-along' albums, and crooners like Andy Williams. Profits were dropping steeply. The rock revolution was under way—Clive Davis's first signing was Donovan.

He went on to sign Janis, Santana, Blood Sweat & Tears, Chicago and a host of other cult performers who turned into major stars. Columbia became the dynamic label with the biggest share of the market, on account of Davis's unique combination of gifts: he was a hard-nosed business executive with the ability to spot talent and pick Top Twenty hits. He loved business and he loved music. Ultimately—some would say inevitably—he fell casualty to the contradictions between the two. In 1973 he was fired as suddenly as he had been hired. The company charged him with expense account violations.

The real reasons for his being axed by the corporation are hinted at in Davis's own anguished ruminations: 'The pressure to keep Columbia's profits rising so astronomically took its toll. I had to keep "discovering" new artists or "attracting" major talent almost as if I were feeding an assembly line ... I deluded myself into creating a definite schism of worlds. In my world of music I was happy ... My loyalty, devotion and life were dedicated to the creativity of the artists whom we recorded and to the men around me.'

These are heresies for a corporation man. They smack of the maverick, of the cult of individualism, of a man who puts pleasure alongside business. Davis now has a small new label of his own to run, Arista Records. He's probably better off with that.

The most striking fact to be confirmed by the book is the way in which industrially-organised bureaucratic megastructures in capitalist and Communist countries are each other's mirror image. Davis describes the 'onslaught of revisionism' which followed his dismissal. His name was taboo both in liner notes and at the company convention. He was edited out of a film shown at the convention. In corporate eyes, he had never existed. It's a chilling end to an extraordinary story.

Thursday, 22 January 1976

QUEEN

Queen/*A Night at the Opera*
Natalie Cole/*Inseparable*

SINCE STARTING OUT in the androgynous glam-and-glitter circus of a few years ago, Queen has developed into one of the most interesting rock bands in these islands. One of the most successful too: at the time of writing 'Bohemian Rhapsody' has been at the top of the British singles charts for two months, and *A Night at the Opera* (EMI Records EMTC 103) is the number one album. This week the group opens a two-month tour of America.

'All titles composed, arranged and performed exclusively by

Queen', it says on the album sleeve. 'No synthesizers' is another boast. This pride in their own prowess, although entirely justified, seems to me the key to a latent danger: mere tricksy cleverness, with no substance to it, is always threatening to take over. The danger is intensified by the boys' fondness for melodrama, which is signalled in the above titles. But a surprising proportion of the tracks transcend this and take their place with the best of popular rock music.

The twelve numbers work their way through about half as many distinct genres—nobody's going to accuse this group of lacking versatility. 'Death on Two Legs' is an aggressive heavy rocker, with some fine screeching guitar leading into biting lyrics which are clearly aimed at some particular enemy. It works a treat, but two other cuts in the same vein are less successful. 'I'm in Love with My Car'—an attempt to achieve the ultimate in car imagery—falls down on Brian May's strangulated vocals, and 'Sweet Lady' is melodically shapeless.

There are three jokey attempts at twenties-style pastiche. All of them are quite brilliantly done and are fun to listen to. 'Seaside Rendezvous' in particular is full of vocal wizardry, and 'Good Company' has a catchy tune—except that it sounds too like Paul McCartney for comfort, and since he patented the style, even polished efforts like these ones have a certain second hand air.

The two songs which strike me as outright triumphs, are both couched in the idioms of classic popular song. 'You're My Best Friend' has a bright, catchy melody with a strong hook, perfectly served by a production which is elaborate but not fussy. Very smooth. And 'Love of My Life' is a formal, grave love song, entirely unexpected, sung with real feeling and even restraint by Freddie Mercury. The vocal harmonics are delicate, the baroque like piano and guitar passage in the middle quite lovely, and the whole effect haunting.

Which essentially leaves us with the album's two big extravaganzas, 'The Prophet's Song' and the climactic 'Bohemian Rhapsody'. If you like lavish overdubbing, anguished overblown sentiments, and a general air of apocalypse, then these are for you. Actually, the latter is considerably superior to the former, which has a long bit where they build unaccompanied vocal lines on top of each other; it's excruciatingly overdubbed to the point where the harmonies sound computerised. 'Bohemian Rhapsody', on the other hand, has a humorous side. It may be mostly hokum, but it's a lot more interesting to listen to than your average number one single.

A Night at the Opera ends—appropriately and magnificently— with an electric version of 'God Save the Queen'. Amen.

***

Soul music fans will want to have *Inseparable* (Capitol E-ST 11429), a debut album from Natalie Cole, daughter of the late Nat King Cole. Miss Cole has a fresh voice, full of zest, and a style which is being favourably compared with the young Aretha Franklin's. I can't quite see that, but maybe because the material on the album is not of the first rank.

All ten songs have been composed by its co-producers, Chuck Jackson and Marvin Yancy; they're sound, professional numbers, but none of them quite combines with Miss Cole's voice to produce the required chemistry. Still, an auspicious debut.

Thursday, 29 January 1976

THE BAND AGAIN

The Band/*Northern Lights-Southern Cross*
Gemma Hasson/*Looking for the Morning*

A SWIRLING TIGHTLY integrated sound with organ and accordion prominent. Throaty integrity. The American past in sepia. Homespun sentiments. What else but the Band, back in the record shops almost five years since their last studio album of original songs. We've had their oldies album *Moondog Matinee*, and their live album, *Rock of Ages*, and their backing work on Bob Dylan's records, till it began to look as though they would never put down a new song again. But here they are with eight of them, on *Northern Lights-Southern Cross* (Capitol-ST-11440), and very tasty too.

The Band has always been distinguished by its musical and emotional conservatism; the same five musicians are still playing essentially the same music from Big Pink which made them famous in 1968. Garth Hudson plays around with a synthesizer on most of the numbers here—but its fluid and controlled sounds blend quite naturally into the ensemble pattern. The only other noticeable innovation is a leaning towards Canadian themes in Robbie Robertson's lyrics, reminding us (and maybe himself) of the Band's Canadian origins.

At first glance I assumed that the 'Forbidden Fruit' listed on the sleeve as the opening track was the Oscar Brown Junior classic, but no: it is good old Levon Helm enlarging on the theme of 'people only want what they cannot have', with uxular good humour. He's followed by Richard Manuel, the keyboards man, singing a slow lament; about a dead drifter and his woman called 'Hobo Jungle'— the romanticism here gets too syrupy for me, but 'Ophelia' is a rousing, enjoyable R&B number, with practically a whole band of brass and woodwinds overdubbed by Garth Hudson.

Side 1 ends with the most fascinating and attractive song on the album, 'Acadian Driftwood'. The dictionary says that 'Acadian' comes from the French name for Nova Scotia, and the song is about the French-Canadians who were forced into exile in Louisiana after the fall of Quebec. The lyrics are vividly evocative, with an elegiac chorus sung in very mellow vocal harmonies. The backing is sensitive too, with the wailing fiddle of guest Byron Berline reinforced by Garth Hudson playing a chanter.

Side 2 opens with an uptempo outlaw song, 'Ring Your Bell', which gives the Mounties a mention and has a good driving tune. But the next track, which is called 'It Makes No Difference' (... where I turn, I can't get over you, etc., etc.), strikes me as the album's one dud, musically and lyrically quite dreary. 'Jupiter Hollow', on the other hand, is full of interest; it's about frontiers, which is nothing new for the Band, except that the frontiers here are the contemporary ones of space exploration—inner and outer. The synthesizer is at its busiest on this track, but it isn't overdone.

'Rags and Bones', a song with an untypically urban milieu, ends the album on a strong and affirmative note. Like so many other rock stars, of the late sixties, the Band appear to be back in business with a whole new lease of life.

***

The young Derry singer Gemma Hasson has come out with a fresh-sounding album called *Looking for the Morning* (EMI LEAF 7008). The title comes from an Eric Anderson song, 'Thirsty Boots', and there are other contemporary numbers mixed in with traditional ballads artfully arranged by Paul Barrett. There's Joni Mitchell's 'Urge for Going' for example, and 'Who Will Bury the Children' which was co-written by Gemma Hasson herself. This moving comment on our Northern way of death is sung to an unadorned guitar backing and provides a powerful ending to a creditable album.

Thursday, 5 February 1976

331

BLACK JAMAICA

Bob Marley & The Wailers/*Live!*

REGGAE IS THE most fascinating sub-culture in the whole field of popular music; unless you're a black Jamaican, in which case it is *the* culture.

Jamaican music has been pressing in on the fringes of British and Irish pop for several decades. The West Indian myth of twenty years ago (1957 actually) was 'Island in the Sun' and 'Banana Boat Song' sung by Harry Belafonte who didn't even come from the place. There were also eruptions of real calypso and steel band music into the public consciousness here. But back in Kingston, these indigenous sounds were cross-breeding with American rhythm & blues and rock to produce a style of music which had such an insidious offbeat that you just had to get up and ska or reggae or do the rock steady to it.

The instrumentation was familiar enough: electric guitars, organ, drums. But nobody who didn't grow up with it could reproduce that tantalising, sinuous rhythmic magic. And the lyrics were different too. They weren't asking anybody to tally bananas. They had titles like 'Starvation', 'Judge Dread', 'The Israelites' and images of exile, messiahs, strikes, shanty towns and violence.

Rock stars like the Stones and Paul Simon and Elton John may jet into Kingston now and then to lay down a few album tracks, but reggae has preserved its integrity as a music and has not been assimilated into mainstream pop. Occasional singles get into the charts here—like 'Ooy' by Desmond Dekker & The Aces, or more recently 'No Woman No Cry' by Bob Marley and The Wailers—but the music as a whole remains on the fringes of the big time.

This must have a lot to do with its religious and political content. For most reggae musicians are devout adherents of the Rastafarian Sect, and they express it in their work.

With origins in Marcus Garvey's 'Back to Africa' movement, with a belief in the late Haile Selassie as the king-god of a promised land of Abyssinia, with its 'ganja' smoking and plaited 'dread locks' hairstyle, Rastafarianism is indeed an odd cult: but no odder, if viewed objectively, than any other set of religious beliefs. At any rate it imbues the music with fervent emotional convictions about poverty, inequality, aggression and pride.

***

Recently I've been listening to the *Live!* album by Bob Marley and the Wailers (on Island ILPS 9376), recorded at a concert in London last July. 'This is a real Trenchtown experience', says the MC in his introduction, and with every familiar reference in the music or lyrics the mainly immigrant audience roars assent. Trenchtown, evidently the Liberties of Kingston, is the cradle of reggae, and the opening number is a strutting anthem called 'Trenchtown Rock'.

The titles of the other three songs on Side 1 speak for themselves. 'Burnin and Lootin" is more of a sad warning than an exhortation, with vivid, forceful lines like 'A hungry mouth is an angry mouth'; a theme further developed in 'Them Belly Full (But We Hungry)'. Then it's back to goodtime rock with 'Lively Up Yourself'.

Side 2 opens with 'No Woman No Cry', which is surely one of the all-time great songs of exile. Through the loving repetition of familiar images—logwood fires, oatmeal porridge, the Government Store—Marley's husky, plaintive voice builds up an intense, yearning ache which is unforgettably poignant. The atmosphere lightens with 'I Shot the Sheriff', which is more of a role-playing romance, familiar from Eric Clapton's hit version. And the album ends with the rousing 'Get Up Stand Up' ('Stand up for your rights').

Whether you want to call reggae folk, pop or Jamaican soul music—all of which it is—you certainly ought to give it a listen.

Thursday, 12 February 1976

MINI-RENAISSANCE

Jefferson Starship/*Red Octopus*
Tony Hatch/*So You Want To Be in the Music Business*

FOR THE FAN of American rock music, 1976 is shaping up remarkably like 1967, with interesting and sometimes awesome new albums appearing in the charts from the likes of ... well, the Grateful Dead, Bob Dylan, the Band, Paul Simon, Art Garfunkel, the Jefferson Airplane. There seems to be a miniature renaissance under way, as if the young lions of a decade ago, amazed at having survived into their dreaded thirties without being seriously challenged or compromised, have experienced a new rush of blood to the imagination.

333

Actually, the Jefferson Airplane album is strictly speaking the work of a group called Jefferson Starship: but since it reconstitutes the original Airplane front line of Marty Balin, Grace Slick and Paul Kantner, it can lay a more convincing claim to the clout of the original Airplane than the last few wretched albums produced under that name before the final disbanding in 1973. Missing from the new line-up are guitarist and bassist Jorma Kaukonen and Jack Casady—their places are taken by Craig Chaquico and Pete Sears—but present and correct are veteran violinist Papa John Creach, drummer John Barbata, and David Freiberg, who doubles on bass and keyboards, as does Sears.

It all adds up to the big sound of an eight-piece electric band, with a considerable variety of textures. What's surprising is that most of the numbers are love songs in a distinctly unprogressive vein, sometimes sounding closer to the Mamas and Papas of 1967 than the Airplane's dramatic and defiant 'White Rabbit' and 'Somebody to Love' of that year. Although the album is entitled *Red Octopus* (on Grunt Records FTR 2002), the octopus on the sleeve turns out to be a heart with tentacles: which makes a suitably ambiguous Valentine.

The main source of this imagery is undoubtedly Balin, who is your hardcore pop-music romantic, bruised but still yearning. One of his songs on the album has the wistful and endlessly repeated hook, 'If only you believed in miracles, so would I', which took it to number three in the US singles charts. Another, a big fat mid tempo rhapsody, is called 'There Will Be Love'. Personally, I prefer a cut called 'Tumblin'' to both of these—it still has the pangs, but they're put over with a mellower and more attractively laid-back sophistication.

But even Gracie Slick, the original acid queen with the voice of steel, has signed with Cupid. Her own song 'Al Garimsu (There is Love)' is a pulsating pop ballad with strings and echo and a big beat. And on the more upbeat 'Play On Love', she sings with all the girlish energy of a hungry newcomer making a demo tape. The difference is that she's got the tubes and the experience; which goes for the whole band, a very polished outfit indeed.

The variety extends instrumental tracks—a funk-fiddle interlude from Papa John on 'Git Fiddler', and a clever, adroit, rather staccato dialogue between piano and guitar called 'Sandalphon' by Pete Sears. There are fast and heavy numbers too: 'Sweeter than Honey' and 'I Want to See Another World'.

Another world is not what the album offers, but it presents the old familiar one with professional skill and versatility.

***

VIEWERS of the *New Faces* programme on UTV will be familiar with the well established face of Tony Hatch—he's the panel member you love to hate, the one who hatchets each aspiring star with crisp and brutally candid efficiency. He got there by producing and writing (with his singer wife, Jackie Trent) a bundle of hits, including Petula Clark's 'Downtown'.

Now he's telling you how to get there too, in a book entitled *So You Want To Be in the Music Business* (Everest Books, 95p paperback).

It's as thorough and useful as you would expect, with chapters on forming a group, writing and marketing songs, simple arranging, contracts, recording techniques and a lot else. As always in books of this kind, some of the information is quite arcane, whilst some of the advice is zombie-like ('My advice on what to play is simple. Choose numbers that you can handle.') But overall it should prove invaluable to anybody with any involvement in popular music.

Thursday, 19 February 1976

DIMMING COMET

Various/*Motown Gold*
Eric Carmen/*Eric Carmen*

BERRY GORDY WAS reputedly a car assembly-line worker in Detroit. In 1960 he threw up his job, borrowed six hundred dollars and launched a small local record label, Tammie Records. It started turning out hits almost immediately and continued to do so for over a decade, mushrooming into the multi-million dollar Tamla Motown corporation. It's an American legend in the classical mould, but with one important twist: Gordy and all of his star performers were black.

Motown Gold (Tamla Motown STML12003) is a compilation album, comprising eighteen of the label's numbers which entered the British Top Twenty between 1964 and 1975. As a statement of commercial prowess it's impressive, but like most compilation albums, it's hard to conceive of it catering to any individual taste.

For example, I for one am devoted to Marvin Gaye's recording of

'I Heard It Through the Grapevine'. The tension of the opening guitar figure and the added percussion, the intense isolation of the high voice, the lyrics wringing irony out of betrayal—it's pop artifice at its most subtle and expressive. On the other hand, the hysteria of the Four Tops' 'Reach Out, I'll Be There', leaves me even less moved than it did ten years ago.

Nor am I convinced of any durable quality in the Supremes' records, with or without Diana Ross, though they were certainly a magnetic stage act. Their coy 'Baby Love' is here, as is their group duet with the Temptations, 'I'm Gonna Make You Love Me'; and from 1971 comes Diana Ross's 'I'm Still Waiting' and the Supremes' 'Stoned Love'. Maybe you recall these fondly, but I prefer to lift the stylus over them, to a far better song from the same year, the cool and stylish 'Just My Imagination (Running Away With Me)' from the Temptations.

So it goes, throughout the album; other artistes featured are Stevie Wonder (when he was still little), the Jackson Five, Martha Reeves, Gladys Knight, Smokey Robinson, Jimmy Ruffin, and Syreeta. It does make you realise what a wealth of talent Gordy uncovered, in his famous songwriting/producing teams as much as in his performers. It also makes you wonder whether the Tamla Motown comet, considerably dimmed in recent years, has burnt itself out.

***

It's not often that a group wins acclaim for being imitative, but such was the case with the Raspberries in the U.S. I never did hear them, but the story was that they drew on the styles and sounds of a dozen years ago—early Beatles, Who, Hollies, Beach Boys—to create a music that appealed directly to the teenage audience and obliquely (via pastiche) to the fans with mortgages.

Now their leading light, Eric Carmen—how's that for a pop-music name—has launched out on his own with an album called *Eric Carmen* (Arista Records Arty 120). The déja vu feeling is certainly strong in some of the songs. 'My Girl', for example, has a soaring, extrovert chorus which is pure Beach Boys, and 'Great Expectations' is a straw-boater-and-cane number, complete with imitation tap routine in the middle, very Paul McCartney via Gilbert O'Sullivan.

But this is just one ingredient in what is clearly a big commercial songwriting talent. Carmen has the gift of the hook, the repeated catchy phrase that makes hits. He can also put song lyrics together in a light, witty and reasonably literate way. Already his romantic ballad, 'All By Myself', with its full-blown piano and strings arrangement, has gone to the top across the Atlantic, and you're going to be hearing a lot of it, folks. Cover versions of it and 'Never Gonna Fall in Love Again' and probably 'Last Night' are virtually guaranteed, and every MOR performer in the country will fall upon them with cries of joy.

The rock numbers here—'Sunrise', 'That's Rock 'n Roll' and 'No Hard Feelings'—are too synthesized and mechanical-sounding for me. But the obligatory number from the past, in this case the 1963 Drifters' hit 'On Broadway', is excellent.

Thursday, 26 February 1976

SECOND TIME ROUND

Be Bop Deluxe/*Sunburst Finish*
Jesse Colin Young/*The Soul of a City Boy*

PERSONALLY, I FEEL predisposed to like any group calling itself Be Bop Deluxe. And in fact I did like their album of last year, *Futurama*, very much indeed. I recall at the time praising leader Bill Nelson's grandiose conceptions, and describing the range they covered, from self-indulgent hokum to abundant drama, humour and melodic strength. The best tracks from that album—'Maid in Heaven', 'Sister Seagull' and 'Sound Track'—have stood the test of time.

So what is this reluctance to sing and shout about the new one, *Sunburst Finish* (Harvest SHSP 4053)? Could it be a subconscious reaction against the big promotional push that Be Bop are currently involved in? Bill Nelson has been duly certified as the next Clapton/Hendrix guitarist superstar, the group has just finished a major British tour, and *Sunburst Finish* is 'this year's priority record,' in the words of the record company.

I prefer to think it's a conscious reaction to the music. Nelson's lead guitar is still marvellous, and when it takes over, the music is instantly alive and arresting. But the general effect is messy and over-inflated, the melodies fail to linger on, and Nelson's vocals (which sound throughout as if they're coming from a draughty bathroom) are overall remote and monotonous. Some of this may be due to the fact that Nelson has produced the album himself, in collaboration with the engineer, John Leckie. *Futurama* was produced by Roy Thomas Baker (well-known for his wizardry with Queen).

The copy of *Sunburst Finish* which I have doesn't contain printed lyrics, so I couldn't always be sure what each song was about. The opener, 'Fair Exchange', is an attacking, staccato number which appeared to deal with the general issue of swapping your soul for success. 'Heavenly Homes' is slower, sweeter and indistinct. 'Ships in the Night' is the out-and-out commercial track, a reggae setting of the 'without love I am a desert/without love I cannot win' kind of lyric. 'Crying to the Sky' has a lot of electronic noodling and big effects, and 'Sleep that Burns' is about a night of bad slumber, a dramatic up-tempo piece with a jokey tango bit in the middle to describe a dream.

The songs on the second side are on the whole better than these. 'Beauty Secrets' has a melody which is at least more free-ranging. The ending of 'Life in the Air Age' provides an example of the expressive mimicry of Nelson's guitar work, where he produces a mechanical weeping effect after the line 'grim enough to make a robot cry.' 'Like An Old Blues' is a refreshingly straightforward boogie number. However, 'Crystal Gazing' is puffed out with strings and ethereal trumpets, and 'Blazing Apostles', which seems to be based on the fantasy of a satanic version of the Samaritans, leaves me in absentia.

I haven't mentioned the other three members of the group, all of whom play to a high standard: they're Charles Tumahai, bass, Simon Fox, drums, and Andrew Clark on keyboards.

***

It's almost shocking these days to put on a new record and hear a man singing in his natural, unadorned voice to the accompaniment of an un-electric guitar; it's so human and naked. It makes you wonder how many of our electric superstars would survive such a test.

In fact, there are no new records like that. Jesse Colin Young's *The Soul of a City Boy* (Capitol VMP 1009) is a reissue; the album first came out in 1964, it was Young's first, and it was recorded in one four-hour session. It combines affectionate treatments of old favourites like 'Rye Whiskey', 'Black-Eyed Susan', and 'Drifter's Blues', with half-a-dozen of his own quiet, virile songs, firmly rooted in American tradition. It's a pleasant, lyrical album from what amounts to a whole different era of recording practices.

Thursday, 4 March 1976

A NEW CULT FIGURE

Patti Smith/*Horses*

FROM THE SCENE that brought you Andy Warhol, the Velvet Underground, Yoko Ono and the New York Dolls comes Patti Smith, the latest New York cult figure to be marketed internationally. *Horses* (Arista ARTY 122), her first record album, has been hailed in the States. *Rolling Stone* magazine has designated her 'the queen of rock & roll for the Seventies.' Personally, I don't see it. Let me salt away a few words to be willingly eaten at a future date, should the occasion arise.

The essence of cultism is the private code, the set of references which only initiates understand. *Horses* has its full complement of these. For example, I find from promotional blurb and the *Rolling Stone* article that the singer's younger sister is called Kimberly: hence the song of the same name. Also that 'Birdland', an hysterical nine-and-a-half minute narrative, is all about the UFO experiences of Peter Reich, son of Wilhelm Reich, the orgasm man.

But even when bits of the code are explained like this, comprehension is not greatly increased—for the simple reason that only a fraction of the words can be made out, given Ms Smith's singing, shrieking, stuttering and screaming techniques. It's incredible that no printed lyrics have been issued with the album. Patti Smith is, after all, supposed to be a poet. She has published three volumes of verse, and her cult started with poetry readings. It's only now, approaching the age of 30, that she has decided to be a rock star.

Such words and themes as do emerge are not especially inspiring. Basically, it sounds like your old decadence and sci-fi numbers again. Heroin, violence and alien beings, (the New York avant garde art-mongers have achieved the extraordinary feat of making heroin addiction boring).

Which leaves the music. The band is a regular four-piece setup, nothing out of the ordinary. Mostly they're just asked to repeat a simple harmonic sequence over and over at various speeds and intensities. On 'Redondo Beach' they essay a very lame reggae sound. 'Elegie', on the other hand, achieves a satisfyingly doomy sound, with heavy melancholic piano work from Richard Sohl and effective siren-like guitar playing by guest Allen Lanier (of the group, Blue Oyster Cult).

'Elegie' is one of three tracks on the album which I would voluntarily listen to again. It expresses ennui in a direct and concise way, with the music and voice actually working together. 'Free Money' is also reasonably accessible, concerning the dream of magically acquiring money to buy everything your lover could desire—not a major insight into the human condition, no, but at least recognisably human. And 'Kimberly' actually has a nice tune.

The only non-Patti Smith song on the album is Van Morrison's 'Gloria', but you'd be as well to stick to your original Them recording.

My own taste in rock veers towards the progressive. I liked Zappa, Beefheart, Dylan when they were at their most radical. Steely Dan and the Grateful Dead command my admiration. But *Horses* is not progressive rock in any sense. It's a spurious yoking together of fake punk rock and dimestore Rimbaud. It's like playing 'Roll Over Beethoven' as if it were the Fifth Symphony.

***

Apologies in advance for poaching on a colleague's territory but I just have to say, that *Rock Follies*, on UTV at 9.00 each Tuesday, is the best treatment of the rock music business ever seen on television, or indeed in any dramatic medium. The scripts and lyrics are written by Howard Schuman. They concern the creation and promotion of a rock group called the Little Ladies, comprised of three hard-up actresses.

The real actresses are Julie Covington (who is guaranteed to break through as a successful singer on the strength of her performance), Charlotte Cornwell and Rula Lenska. They are each sublime in carefully differentiated roles, and amazingly, they sing well enough to be a commercial group. Schuman's writing is dead on target: cynical, concise and sardonic.

The series is already half over; catch it, if you can.

Thursday, 11 March 1976

COCKNEY ROCK

Cockney Rebel/*Timeless Flight*
The Eleventh House/*Level One*

'THIRD-GENERATION ROCK' is the phrase of the moment in the popular music journals. The notion is that the first generation was your original rock & roll from the fifties and early sixties; the second generation was your Beatles and their progressive progeny, up to the early seventies; and the third ... well, according to Steve Harley, whose egomania is par for the course, it consists of himself and his group Cockney Rebel.

Actually, there are a few others—like Queen and Be Bop Deluxe— all of them musically articulate, fond of literary and other cultural references, and given to extravagant stage presentation. They don't quite amount to a 'generation' yet, though; the listener is constantly aware of similarities between them and the older crowd.

Steve Harley himself sounds at times like Ray Davies, with a bit of Dylan here and there and lots of Bowie everywhere. In short, he can't hold a note too well but covers with vocal mannerisms. What he can do is put together a strong tune and sell it to an audience: 'Come Up and See Me (Make Me Smile)' was one of last year's most attractive hits. He has also put together a strong band in Cockney Rebel, a five-piece with a fluid, integrated sound which is far from common on this side of the Atlantic.

The new Harley/Rebel album is *Timeless Flight* (EMI EMA 775), and it has a pleasantly mellow, reflective atmosphere on the whole. The lyrics go in for sixth-form versifying, with a lot of obscure colour symbolism, but they are at least personal and specific—objectively wry, in the opening song 'Red is a Mean, Mean Colour', about his personal failings. This number also sets the pace for relaxed, controlled playing by the band, with a fine meandering guitar break by Jim Cregan.

The second track, 'White White Dove', is by contrast aimless and tuneless, but 'Understand' opens with very tasteful piano work from Duncan Mackay and proceeds into interesting words which sound as though they're addressed to his audience ('If only I could put the words together/you'd understand'). Side 1 ends with 'All Men Are Hungry', which has verses about Hemingway and a haunting chorus.

Sub-T.S. Eliot verses kick off the second side, in 'Black or White (And Step On It)', which contains perhaps the most tuneless singing on the album. But 'Everything Changes' is a lively, light boogie number, full of cleverness and deft wit. It's followed by 'Nothing is Sacred', a Dylanesque narrative about a hotel room in Vienna, and the album ends with a terrific song called 'Don't Go, Don't Cry', which both expresses and describes rock mania. A synthesizer plays lightning-fast runs, backing singers chant 'bop-bop ... oo-ee-oo', and Harley sings audacious quatrains, each working on a single rhyme (in the first one, he rhymes safari, Malawi, starry and are we).

Harley is a gifted lad, and he doesn't seem to be entirely carried away by his own abilities and the fans' adulation. He and his band certainly have the potential to do something individual and remarkable.

***

The consensus seems to be growing that jazz-rock, of the chundering, electric kind, has had its day; like any good idea, its combining of jazz expertise with rock hardware has its limits. It can result in a mechanistic anonymous noise which, for all its slickness, its polish and decibels, soon fades into the background. Virtuosity is not enough, with or without electricity.

All of which applies to the album *Level One* (Arista Arty 113) by guitarist Larry Coryell's group the Eleventh House. Coryell has been influenced by playing with John McLaughlin, and he opens with some of the same wailing, aggressive style, but it lacks the genuine fire and conviction of McLaughlin. The numbers are mainly built on simple phrases relentlessly repeated, and the excitement is of the kind you feel when being violently ill whilst drunk.

Thursday, 18 March 1976

WHOLESOME

Maria Muldaur/*Sweet Harmony*
Carole King/*Thoroughbred*

MARIA MULDAUR HAS delivered the goods once again. *Sweet Harmony* (Reprise K54059) is a marvellous album, the most consistent of her three to date. If it has no individual songs quite as strong as 'Midnight At the Oasis' or 'Work Song', it also has none as weak as 'Three Dollar Bill' or 'Tennessee Mountain Home'. In fact, it has no weak tracks at all: it's wholesome and nutritinous all the way through.

One journal has dismissed it as a predictable reworking of a formula, but the only predictions it bears out is that Ms Muldaur would hunt diligently for unusual and fresh material which she could stamp with her own unique brand of sensuous wit and wistfulness. So far as any formula goes, she has discarded the token bawdy song and country song this time and there is no attempt at a follow-up to the 'Oasis' hit. So there.

Instead, there's all the following. First, the title song, Smokey Robinson's soul number 'Sweet Harmony', with the sweet harmonies superbly provided by a six-piece choir which includes Linda Ronstadt and singer-songwriter Wendy Waldman. Next 'Sad Eyes', a Neil Sedaka song unknown to me, invested with all the tenderness and yearning of those distinctive vocal glides and slurs. 'Lying Song' is from the pen of Kate McGarrigle (who wrote 'Work Song'), and is a light-hearted honty-tonk homily on the theme of telling lies, with splendid piano work from James Booker and Howard Johnson on tuba.

Hoagy Carmichael's 'Rockin' Chair' follows, and it's a highlight, an inspired revival of an irresistible song, with a Benny Carter arrangement for a ten-piece band, and Hoagy himself singing along at the very end. Side 1 ends with a complete contrast to this, a driving rocker called 'I Can't Stand It', with a crisp horn arrangement by Howard Johnson and some fiery singing both from Maria herself and from her backing singers.

The second side opens with the wittiest track. It's a delightfully whimsical old number called 'We Just Couldn't Say Goodbye', arranged again by Benny Carter, opening with a straight rendition and then leaping into a hilarious Andrews Sisters pastiche accredited to 'the Bezbo Sisters' (Maria Muldaur, Ellen Kearney, Mary Ann Price). This side also has two Wendy Waldman songs, both reflective and melancholy 'Back By Fall' and 'Wild Bird', the latter arranged with a beautiful simplicity for bass, classical guitar and flute.

'Jon the Generator' is the rock number on Side 2, with a tremendous driving chorus, and the album ends with a genuine gospel song called 'As An Eagle Stirreth In Her Nest'. This is almost entirely carried by the voices, which build up to a terrific climactic intensity, very fitting as conclusion to the best album to appear so far this year.

***

CAROLE KING has a new one out too, called *Thoroughbred* (Ode 77034), and speaking of reworking a formula ... on the other hand, Ms King is a commercial songwriter who knows her craft and is content to work within narrowly defined limits. When you've had an album as big as *Tapestry* and a single off it as big as 'You've Got A Friend', who needs a new formula?

So *Thoroughbred* has all the hallmarks. There's the customary spare, clean production by Lou Adler. There's the seemingly effortless, polished musicianship of pop men like Russ Kuntel on drums, Leland Sklar on bass, Tom Scott on saxes and Waddy Wachtel on guitar (he is also featured on the Maria Muldaur album). There's backing on the vocals from distinguished friends (Crosby, Nash and James Taylor) and above all, there's ten meticulously written and sincerely delivered Carole King songs. It's what you might call the Quiet Good Taste of popular music.

But the song titles indicate how narrow the range is—'So Many Ways', 'Only Love is Real', 'There's a Space Between Us', 'I'd Like To Know You Better', 'Still Here Thinking of You', 'It's Gonna Work Out Fine'—earnest songs about relationships, a little samey and bland.

Thursday, 25 March 1976

KNOCKING ROCK

Various/*Rock Follies*
KGB/*KGB*

ROCK FOLLIES (Island ILPS 9362) is very much the album of the show. If you don't have access to UTV or Harlech, that may not mean a lot; but the show in question, made by Thames Television, has been watched every Tuesday evening for the past six weeks by approximately one-third of the households in Britain. Considering that it presents the most honest, complete and pungently witty accounts of the rock-music business ever seen on television (or film), this represents a conjunction of mass appeal and high-quality entertainment which is rare indeed.

There are probably three prime ingredients in the show's success. The big one, naturally, is Howard Schuman's writing skill, which extends to the song lyrics as well as the script. Then there is the music. In most showbiz dramas this is spurious and unconvincing, but here it's absolutely genuine since it was composed by Roxy Music's sax player and co-writer, Andy Mackay.

Thirdly, there are the brilliant combined acting talents of Julie Covington, Charlotte Cornwell and Rula Lenska, playing the three members of 'The Little Ladies' rock group, struggling to make their way to success in a cartoon society of egomaniacs who are exploiting them from every angle. These friends, lovers, hangers-on, and manipulators are also supremely well acted.

Of these ingredients, the lyrics and music are obviously the only ones that can readily transfer to a record, and the twelve songs on the album can certainly stand on their own feet as shrewd and well-articulated numbers. Schuman's words are blunt and jaundiced about 'Sugar Mountain', the rock stars' haven where 'it's so lush and cool you float on Valium in your swimming pool'; about the housebound wife who plans to take 'some time off/For good behaviour'; about the squalor and adrenalin of the road, about sex exhibited and casual, about instant nostalgia, porn movies, and the whole mass neon fantasy of the rock follies. Mackay's music is match for all this, strongly melodic in 'Good Behaviour', 'The Road' and 'Sugar Mountain', elegantly cool in 'Biba Nova', tender in 'Lamplight', and generally well played by a four-piece group.

The singing is inevitably the weakest feature. Of the three actresses, Julie Covington is the only one with a really good voice, and even it is more of a stage instrument than a studio one. On the screen they have the capacity to convince you of their authenticity, but reduced to voices alone, they can't do full justice to the songs.

Presumably because of this, the production (again by Mackay) has rather muffled them up to keep them warm and mixed them down to keep them inconspicuous, which renders them frequently inaudible. But this is, after all, only the album of the show, aimed at those who have seen it and who want both a memento and something to tide them over till the new *Rock Follies* series begins. As such, it will almost certainly be a big hit, and deservedly so.

***

Old rockers never die, they simply re-group. Hence *KGB* (MCA Records MCF 2749) from the group of the same name. Remember the ace guitarist Mike Bloomfield and keyboards man Barry Goldberg in the Electric Flag? Remember the bassist Ric Grech in Family and Traffic? They've got together with the singer-songwriter Ray Kennedy and drummer Carmine Appice (Vanilla Fudge, etc.) to make KGB.

Unfortunately groups need more than experienced members, they need a chemistry and a dynamic, and such qualities are not in evidence on this debut album. A couple of straightforward macho rockers work pretty well—Kennedy's 'Let Me Love You' and Goldberg's 'It's Gonna Be A Hard Night'—but uneasiness pervades the rest of the proceedings. There are the fashionable gestures of a Beatles revival ('I've Got A Feeling') and a reggae-styled number ('Working for the Children'). There are a couple of Kennedy pop ballads sung with patent insincerity by Bloomfield, there are gospelly passages. But a meaningful name, a decent sleeve, or a sense of group conviction there ain't.

Friday, 2 April 1976

NYMPHETISHISM

Tanya Tucker/*Lovin' and Learnin'*
Alan White/*Ramshackled*
Bob Dylan/*Desire*

TANYA TUCKER IS the current pop Lolita, but by no means the first one. Remember Helen Shapiro, and 'Don't Treat Me Like a Child' and 'Walking Back to Happiness'? And Brenda Lee's 'Sweet Nothin's'? Tanya Tucker doesn't have the voice of either one—she still sounds like a precocious girl rather than a premature woman—but the striking contrast between the two generations of nymphets is the difference in material and backing available to each. Whilst Helen and Brenda had to do what they could with the 'woop-ba-oh-yeah, yeah's', Tanya's album *Lovin' and Learnin'* (MCA MCF 2741) is a set of rather nifty country-rock songs performed by the cream of the Nashville cats.

There is, for example, the splendid Eagles number 'After the Thrill is Gone', ideal material since it's written from a female point of view- a notable aspect of many Eagles songs. There's also Parker McGee's 'Depend On You', an effective statement of bitter betrayal, and the homey and amusing if ethically unsound 'Makin' Love Don't Always Make Love Grow', by the country composer whose name sounds like a kind of ice-cream, Sterling Whipple.

The other numbers, such as 'Don't Believe My Heart Can Stand

Another You' and Dave Loggins' 'You've Got Me to Hold on To' (rather wet) are mainly in the same vein, with a couple of tender interludes ('Leave Him Alone' and 'Here We Are') to leaven the general briskness. Tanya's singing has a youthful bite. The only song on which it sounds downright inadequate is 'Ain't That A Shame', but who could begin to compete with Fats Domino's original? With the help of a Charlie Daniels fiddle solo, she manages to sound at least a little funkier than Pat Boone.

***

The drummer from Yes, Alan White, has come out with a very un-Yes-like solo album called *Ramshackled* (Atlantic K50217). It's also a remarkably self-effacing 'solo' album: White simply played the drums and co-produced, having assembled round him a group of lesser-known but excellent musicians to write, sing and play the nine numbers.

The music is well fleshed-out, in a predominantly jazz-rock vein, but bluesy and without portentousness. The only song that flops is a setting of Blake's 'Spring' from *Songs of Innocence*. Otherwise, 'One Way Rag' gets you moving and listening both, as does 'Giddy'. These have reasonable lyrics and vocals, both of which are a bit thin and anonymous elsewhere on the record.

However, the two instrumental tracks are first-rate. 'Avakak' is particularly fine, with a flashy piano intro by Kenny Craddock and an intricate theme deftly played by Henry Lowther on trumpet and Bud Beadle on sax.

***

You've probably read about Bob Dylan's album *Desire* (CBS86003) and his Rolling Thunder Revue and his new make-up in a hundred other places. So I'll just check in briefly with a late return. So maddening and tantalising and finally boring has Dylan's career long since become to me that I have to make a conscious effort even to listen to his new work.

Hardly a proper critical frame of mind to bring to an album, but in spite of it I was knocked for a loop by 'One More Cup of Coffee'—a magnetically strange, almost Hebraic performance—and held to attention by 'Oh, Sister' and 'Sara', even though the words in both cases often verge on the ludicrous (who else but Dylan would address his wife as 'Scorpio Sphinx in a calico dress ... glamorous nymph with an arrow and bow'?).

But that's just what exasperates about Dylan, a little of the best and a lot of the worst jumbled together. He has assembled round him brilliant performers like Scarlet Rivera and Emmylou Harris to perform radical chic rubbish like 'Hurricane' and 'Joey' and travelogue rubbish like 'Mozambique' and 'Romance in Durango'. And one unforgettable song, as noted. Remember, folks, you read it here last.

Thursday, 8 April 1976

ACID AND HONEY

City Boy/ *City Boy*
The Four Seasons/ *The Four Seasons Story*

CITY BOY IS the name of a new six-man English rock group and also of their outstanding debut album (on Vertigo 6860 126). They come from Birmingham, the source of a number of interesting groups since the Move took the rock scene by storm in the mid-sixties, and they seem to inhabit roughly similar territory to the popular 10CC (whose splendid single 'I'm Mandy Fly Me' is a current hit). Which means often acidly witty lyrics expressed in honeyed vocal harmonies, and an adventurous approach to structuring songs combined with an easy fluency in electric music.

This last is particularly impressive in that no fancy hardware or instrumentation is employed—just the usual range of guitars and keyboards and a lot of percussion—and that, according to the sleeve, the album was recorded in the astonishing time of a week. Bravo, if true.

The most successful song on the album, 'Deadly Delicious', opens with the lines.

> Good God, she's deadly delicious, camper than a holiday,
> Front page in every issue, tighter than a one-act play.

Which gives a neat sense of their own style: most of the songs are little dramas, containing situations, brief character sketches and even dialogue. 'Surgery Hours (Doctor, Doctor)', for example, is the piquant drama of a woman patient willing and indeed anxious to place her male doctor in a compromising position, with the woman's lines chanted in an urgent falsetto. 'Oddball Dance' is the dramatic monologue of a rather deviant person who finds fulfilment at a dance for oddballs of all kinds.

Less originally, 'Sunset Boulevard' presents us with the familiar figure of the washed-up Hollywood star living on fantasies, a subject better understood and handled by American performers (like the Eagles and Dory Previn)—though in this case the song actually incorporates the star addressing her imaginary horde of cheering admirers. 'Deadly Delicious' itself is a biting character portrayal of a contemporary siren, with a section in the middle where one of her victims pleads, 'please ... don't leave the room.'

Humour, as already indicated, is another prominent ingredient of City Boy's work. To quote a further example, 'The Hap-Ki-Do Kid' deals with the celluloid rogue for the martial arts of the Far East ('they say your belt gets blacker by the hour/I know you like your victims sweet and sour'). Perhaps the most attractive element of all is the readiness to go beyond the standard verse-and-chorus formulae of pop songs which are still dominant. All of the numbers on the album extend and multiply their initial ideas in a constant structural variety.

They aren't, of course, uniformly successful. The opening track '(Moonlight) Shake My Head and Leave' has a lovely airborne kind of melody, but the second side opens with a big ballady number called 'Five Thousand Years' which is full of rather empty poetizing; and the album actually ends on a soft, romantic note with a surprisingly hackneyed song called 'Haymaking'.

Nevertheless, *City Boy* is far and away the most exciting debut album to appear so far this year in these islands.

***

Speaking of standard pop songs ... *The Four Seasons Story* (Private Stock DAPS 1001) is a double album containing twenty-eight Four Seasons hits, mainly from the sixties. It doesn't have the recent excellent 'December '63', but it has those favourites of yesteryear. 'Sherry' and 'Big Girls Don't Cry', as well as covers like 'Don't Think Twice', 'Will You Still Love Me Tomorrow', 'Ain't That A Shame' and even 'I've Got You Under My Skin'.

Personally, I find the 'eye-yi-yi's' of Frankie Valli's falsetto acceptable only when cutting through the fug of a crowded room, but for fans and instant nostalgia enthusiasts, this represents an orgy.

Thursday, 15 April 1976

SECOND SNOW

Phoebe Snow/*Second Childhood*
Quicksilver Messenger Service/*Solid Silver*

PHOEBE SNOW MADE her bow with a terrific first album on the A&M label in 1974. She was a bespectacled little white girl from New Jersey with a remarkable smoky, vibrant voice, displaying a natural mastery of inflection and phrasing, and she had written some very effective songs to suit it. There was, for example, the shrewd and anxious love song 'Either or Both' ('Do you like or love Either or both of me? ') and the mordantly funny 'It Must Be Sunday'.

Since that time, her career has been stalled by litigation between rival record companies. It's been a long wait for the second album—*Second Childhood* (CBS 81162)-and apparently rather a detrimental one. For the seven Phoebe Snow compositions on this new release suffer a bit from wordiness and musical sprawl. A typical couplet runs:

> When you feel that your train of thought's been derailed
> Let out your wild wishes from where they've been jailed.
> ('All Over')

She sounds in these songs like an artist who knows that a lot is expected of her, and is consequently striving too hard to be an Artist.

The production (by Phil Ramone) encourages this tendency by being very fancy, with a lot of orchestration and background singing and clever ideas, such as a tuba quintet in a track called 'Sweet Disposition'. All of which is, in my view, mere distracting clutter, for Miss Snow's voice is a choir and an orchestra unto itself. The whole expensive assemblage on this album evokes none of the tremors caused on the last one in 'San Francisco Bay Blues', which Miss Snow sang to a guitar and double bass.

But in despite of all these reservations, this is a Phoebe Snow album, which means that it stands out a mile from the general run of pop music releases. There aren't many contemporary voices which invite comparison with the likes of Ella Fitzgerald and Peggy Lee. Along with a few other singers like Maria Muldaur, Phoebe Snow is in the process of rehabilitating the technically brilliant solo voice as a major instrument in pop.

She shines most brightly here in the non-original songs, and particularly in 'No Regrets', where the restrained but powerfully swinging backing trio allows her vocal exuberance a free rein. The Gershwin song, 'There's a Boat That's Leavin' Soon for New York' evokes from her a beautifully melancholy reading. And soul music gets a look-in, with Holland-Dozier-Holland's 'Goin' Down for the Third Time'.

Of her own songs, 'Pre-Dawn Imagination' is perhaps the most felt, conjuring up a past affair with a wistful directness. 'Inspired Insanity' has the catchiest melody, and might serve as a single, though it's hard to see any one of these tracks making its way in the music-chewing-gum world of singles.

***

First loves are special, but it can be rather daunting to meet them in later life. My own relationship with progressive rock was sparked off by a chance encounter, on the turntable of a record shop, with the music of Quicksilver Messenger Service. That was eight years ago, when the swirling arabesques of San Francisco acid rock were bursting out all over.

The original five members of Quicksilver have now got together again and issued an album called *Solid Silver* (Capitol E St 11462). The sound is flat, the vocals weak and indistinct, and there's an air of competent amateurism about the playing. 'Worryin' Shoes' is a fairly lively blues, 'Witches' Moon' a fairly distinctive instrumental, but most of the songs are without impact. Have they got soft, or have I grown hard? Where are the solos of yesteryear?

Thursday, 22 April 1976

SONG SISTERS

Kate & Anna McGarrigle/*Kate and Anna McGarrigle*

ZEALOUS FANS OF contemporary Amercan songwriting have been looking forward for some time to an album by Kate and Anna McGarrigle. These two sisters from Quebec—they had an Irish father and a French-Canadian mother—have had some outstanding songs recorded by other artists. Linda Ronstadt made a hit out of Anna's poignant 'Heart Like a Wheel', Kate's 'Work Song' was a highlight of

Maria Muldaur's first album, Anna's 'Cool River', appeared on the second, and Kate's 'Lying Song' on the the third Muldaur LP. Kate is also known as the wife of that admirable individual, Loudon Wainwright III.

The long-awaited album, which was recorded exactly a year ago, has at long last been released here (on Warner Bros. BS 2862), to a flood of critical acclaim. Which is about to be swollen further by the following paragraphs. I just hope the record-buying public is as lavish with its sterling as we all are with our radiant adjectives, for it would be refreshing to see a record possessed of integrity and feeling, lacking the affectations of a calculated pose, actually succeed.

Like Joni Mitchell, the McGarrigles have a Canadian quality of clear-voiced innocence, a concern with emotional propriety which, in an American context, seems old-fashioned. Like the Band, they have a Canadian preoccupation with the North American past, which takes in protestant hymns, rural folk songs, jazz, blues, bluegrass and a good deal more. But although their tunes often have the haunting quality of something half-remembered from childhood, there's nothing even faintly quaint or antique about the overall effect. Somehow they contrive to blend a profound sense of genuine rootedness with a high level of sophistication. Which is rare indeed.

The production by Joe Boyd and Greg Prestopino sets all this off to perfection. A small army of musicians is deployed sparingly and with restraint to reinforce and enhance the silvery McGarrigle voices: which are so similar in timbre that they combine to make the purest classical harmonies. Their chasteness is offset by the use of warm-toned instruments—obbligatos and the occasional solo on clarinet, sax, harmonica, fiddle. The arrangements grow out of the sisters' own accompaniments, on piano, guitar, banjo and accordion, and are of a piece with them.

..*

The twelve songs are predominantly gentle and lyrical, but each side kicks off with a rousing up-tempo number to get your attention. Kate's 'Kiss and Say Goodbye' is the infectious song of a woman anticipating the arrival in town of her lover. Anna's 'Complainte Pour Ste-Catherine' is a slightly reggae-styled French-Canadian song, sunny with ringing panache.

Each side also features a song in waltz time by Anna. 'My Town' has a chorus about leaving home, with that strange déja vu musical quality, the whole song coming very close to the anonymity of traditional ballads. 'Jigsaw Puzzle of Life' is a little more syncopated, with a wittily concise use of jigsaw imagery for a love affair.

The two sides are further balanced by each having a song of Kate's performed solo and relatively unadorned. 'Blues in D' is sung in a high voice with an edge of bitterness to it underpinned by clarinet, bass, guitar and her own blues piano. 'Go Leave' uses nothing but a few acoustic guitar chords, and is as direct and affecting a statement as a song can well be:

Go leave, don't come back, no more am I for the taking,
But I can't say that my heart's not aching,
It's breaking in two.

In these two tracks, the album reaches its highest point of emotional intensity.

The remaining two Kate McGarrigle songs, 'Mendocino' and 'Tell My Sister', are gentler and more romantic, with an almost barbershop quality to the back-up singing in the latter. And the album is completed by three non-original songs—two semi-traditional, and Loudon Wainwright's cheerfully inconsequential 'Swimming Song'.

Thursday, 29 April 1976

SONGS FROM THE RUBBISH TIP

Stackridge/*Mr Mick*
Wishbone Ash/*Locked In*

STACKRIDGE IS AN English group which has turned in some very lively and humorous music over the past five years or so. But the current Stackridge album, *Mr Mick* (Rocket Roll 3), is a bit of a dud. It starts very well, with one of the most successful attempts of recent times to reinterpret a Beatles song: the number being 'Hold Me Tight', which they've enhanced with a slower, more sensual rhythm, and a pleasing counter-melody, well up to the original Lennon/McCartney inspiration. And indeed the instrumental which follows, piquantly entitled 'Breakfast with Werner Von Braun', has enough verve to keep you listening.

But the rot sets in immediately thereafter, when Mutter Slater's innocuous West Country voice starts reciting some concerned, warm-hearted lines of verse about a lonely old man called Mick and his stroll towards the local rubbish dump. Yes, listeners, what we've stumbled into here is the concept. From here on, the songs are about the various items on the rubbish tip as they affect old Mick's fantasies, interspersed with narrative links from the versifying mutter.

Like many songs written to a pre-conceived plan, they display their verbal and musical contrivances all too nakedly. The song of a 'busted up steam radio' is followed by that of a discarded cotton reel, and then by the waltz of 'two old ballet shoes/damp and mildewed.' After this strained exhibition of soft-core corn, the concept picks up a little with 'Hey Good Looking', which uses the pretext of Old Mick remembering a holiday romance to give us a little ersatz Caribbean strutting, with at least a vivid tune and some vigour in the singing.

However, the finale, 'Fish in a Glass', carries the concept to its watery grave, billowing along on airily vague poetic references to stardom, revolution and boys in overcoats. Back to the wacky jokes, fellas.

***

It's a bad press all round for English rock bands this week, since the new Wishbone Ash album *Locked In* (MCA MCF 2750) is also pretty lacklustre. At its best, this is a nimble outfit, with sparkling guitar work from the twin leads, Andy Powell and Laurie Wisefield. And the guitar work does stay nifty enough on most of the tracks here. But everything else is fairly ho-hum, from the opening line, 'Last night I had a dream ... ' to the scheduling of two depressive, downbeat numbers in a row at the end, causing the album to drop to a mournful conclusion.

All of which is particularly disappointing given that the album was produced in America by the prestigious Tom Dowd. Either he has had an off-day or I have; the effect, at any rate, is of a routine assignment.

The opening track is called 'Rest in Peace' (once again a rather unfortunate selection to open on), and the guitars fairly bubble on it, even though the basic riffs are too tired to hold your interest for 6 minutes 44 seconds. A slow lament called 'No Water in the Well' follows: it has a decent lyric and tune, but the vocals are too thin to do much with them. 'Moonshine' lifts things a bit, with a quicksilver quality in the tandem vocals and guitar picking, but the first side ends with a terrible song from bassist Martin Turner called 'She Was

My Best Friend'—even the title invites detrimental comparisons with the Queen song, 'You're My Best Friend'.

Side 2 opens with a song asserting that 'It Started In Heaven/but finished with rock & roll'—exactly what, I'm not sure. 'Half Past Lovin" has a nice medium-paced R & B strut-nothing extraordinary, but it's the one track I could live with for a while. Then comes the descent into terminal gloom, with 'Trust in You' and 'Say Goodbye', which outlines a lover's plan to end the affair with a desolate evening of simulated pleasure. Music to swallow pills by.

Thursday, 6 May 1976

NEW YORK CONFORMITY

Barry Manilow/*Trying to Get the Feeling*
Melissa Manchester/*Better Days and Happy Endings*

NEW YORK, HOME of the original Tin Pan Alley, can lay claim to an unrivalled tradition in pop songwriting. For over half a century, great songs and great singers have serviced the Broadway musical industry. The tradition continues—Stephen Sondheim and Barbra Streisand are perhaps its reigning king and queen—but public taste has shifted away from show music.

Nobody is more acutely and astutely aware of this than Clive Davis, the dynamic and much-written-about president of Arista Records. He records in his book about his career at CBS how alarmingly sales of Broadway cast albums plummeted during the 1960s. A different breed of New Yorkers was taking over the limelight: singer-songwriters like Carole King, Paul Simon, Laura Nyro. Davis saw this early on, and moved accordingly.

What's fascinating, though, is the way in which a showbizzy, histrionic strain keeps re-surfacing in New York music. Bette Midler, for example, suddenly came up with a kind of camped-up cabaret version of the Streisand style, highly theatrical. And it seems to me that Clive Davis's current crop of singer-songwriters (Eric Carmen, Barry Manilow, Melissa Manchester) also share a taste for the big dramatic number. All three have an affinity with classical music, and both Carmen and Manilow have 'borrowed' melodic themes from the likes of Chopin and Tchaikovsky upon which to construct throbbing romantic ballads. Which is, of course, a time-honoured practice in pop music.

Manilow has indeed worked in the theatre, but he came to prominence as Bette Midler's Music Director. Since launching a performing and recording career of his own, he has made a massive impact in America, though not so much here as yet. His current album is *Trying to Get the Feeling* (Arista ARTY 123).

Commercially adept as its eleven tracks undoubtedly are, I can't pretend to be pleasurably excited by them. For all the energy poured into them, they sound oddly lifeless—I'd have said 'heartless', but that carries the wrong connotations. Although Manilow has written the music for only six of them, and the lyrics are by various hands, there's considerable uniformity throughout: some are loud and fast, some slow and quiet, but they're all more or less equally shallow.

'Tryin' to Get the Feeling Again', the hit single off the album, represents it well. Manilow's clear, untroubled voice glides through the big strings-and-piano arrangement; the opening verse is feeble, but the chorus works well enough and carries most of the song. It's clean-cut, well-groomed, briefcase kind of music. About as heady as a whiff of Old Spice.

***

There have been portents of stronger stuff in the work of Melissa Manchester. Her first album had a Randy Newman song on it and there were some nice touches of asperity in some of her own lyrics, along with a strong grasp of the Carole King kind of lucid, uncluttered melody. Her new album, however, is a much blander affair, as is indicated by its title, *Better Days and Happy Endings* (Arista ARTY 125).

Apart from a simple little rocker from the cast called 'Rescue Me', the songs here just work their way through a well-worn bundle of romantic formulas. Ms Manchester has a pleasant and even glowing voice, as well as an efficient backing group, but as she moves from 'You Can Make It All Come True' to 'My Sweet Thing' to 'Just You and I' to 'Good News', the appetite doth sicken and so die. Even 'Stand Up Woman', which sounds like an anthem of liberation, turns out to be just the opposite: 'I'll be your Stand Up Woman/Doin' The Best I Can To Lend a Hand'.

All these writers embody to some degree what seems to be a growing conservative and even reactionary trend in pop culture. It's noticeable, for example, how many of their songs are about music itself, as if singing was the ultimate social value. The strings-and-heart-throb style is an unmistakable throwback, except that it's held at arm's length as a piece of machinery. Since New York is broke, perhaps musical conformism and sobriety is to be expected. And perhaps it's unfair to remark that 45 years ago, when things were a lot tougher, Rodgers and Hart had their Manhattan heyday.

Thursday, 13 May 1976

SAN FRANCISCO SOUND

Kingfish/*Kingfish*
Jerry Garcia/*Reflections*

I'VE NEVER BEFORE felt inclined to endorse a publicity blurb, but this one's a plain statement of fact: 'The first Kingfish album, recorded in Bob Weir's new home studio at the end of 1975, demonstrates the group's clean, hard lines and uncanny flexibility, as it moves swiftly and deftly from Mexibilly to direct rock to up-tempo and jazz-related polyrhythmics. Kingfish is a well-seasoned band, a product of the San Francisco cross fertilisation process at its best.'

Ineloquent, but true. The album in question is called *Kingfish* (United Artists UAS 29922), whilst the Bob Weir in question is indeed he of Grateful Dead rhythm guitar and vocals fame. Like the New Riders of the Purple Sage, Kingfish is a group coming to public attention as a kind of Grateful Dead satellite; and indeed Kingfish was formed by bass player Dave Torbert when he split from the New Riders. All of which might seem a mite incestuous and in consequence thin-blooded, but most assuredly is not.

In fact, the immediate impression is that of a band which has been waiting its turn for some time, and has a lot to say. The numbers crowd in on each other's heels, and each of them gets down to business instantly, dispensing with fancy preliminaries. The tightly packed sound of the opener, 'Lazy Lightnin''—the lyrics of which are worthy of its title—is sustained throughout.

Like the man said, there's a variety of styles on show here. 'Supplication', like 'Lazy Lightnin'', works in a sophisticated time signature which gives it a light, buoyant, jazzy feeling. 'Wild Northland' suddenly plunges us into country-rock, with harmony singing well up to Eagles standard. 'Asia Minor', the song of a traveller feeling impelled to push on, has a nervous urgency in the music, with some fine sinewy lead guitar from Robby Hoddinott. The geographical spread—perhaps a symbol of the group's restless energy—widens further still in 'Home to Dixie', a lively updating of a venerable theme. Ironically enough, 'Jump for Joy', in which Weir is not involved either as writer or singer, comes closest to sounding like a Grateful Dead song.

Side 2 has pleasing touches of humour. 'Goodbye Yer Honour' is the upbeat song of a man jumping bail. 'Big Iron' is the splendid old Marty Robbins cowboy ditty, perfect for Weir's deep masculine tones, about Texas Red and the handsome ranger, each with 'a big iron on his hip'. These are followed by a couple of expertly handled love songs, and the album ends with the old spiritual 'Bye and Bye' done as a slow strut, with some very tasty passages from Hoddinott's guitar and the harmonica of Matthew Kelly.

Drummer Chris Herold is the fifth member of the group, which really is a group; there's no sense of Weir as just a guest or as a dominating presence. Kingfish is undoubtedly the brightest new jewel in the San Francisco musical crowd.

***

Meanwhile, back at the commune, Jerry Garcia has sprouted a third solo album, *Reflections* (Round Records UAG 29921). Like most of the indefatigable Garcia's work, it's expansive, mellow, unambitious, and a little ragged round the edges. Four of the tracks come from his pen and that of his longstanding collaborator Robert Hunter, while the other four—rather more enjoyable—are by other hands.

I particularly liked Allen Toussaint's 'I'll Take a Melody', with its sensuous, singalong New Orleans swagger, and Hank Ballard's solid rocker, 'Tore Up Over You'. This latter is propelled along in fine style by guests John Kahn on bass, and Nicky Hopkins and Larry Knechtel on twin pianos. Elsewhere all of the Grateful Dead members take a hand, which can't be bad. But I wish Jerry Garcia's singing voice wasn't so dreadfully flat.

Thursday, 20 May 1976

CHANGING COUNTRY MUSIC

Johnny Cash/*Man In Black*
Jessi Colter/*Jessi*

COUNTRY MUSIC HAS been changing. The Grand Old Opry mainstream flows on, with its familiar mixture of Southern drawl and pedal steel twang, heartfelt banality and lacrymose self-pity, banjo-picking, conservatism and cowboy boots. But all around it, new forces have been at work; the vogue for critical scrutiny, for example, which is exemplified both in the film *Nashville* and in Johnny Cash's autobiography, *Man in Black* (Hodder and Stoughton, £3.75).

Cash is, of course, the most successful country singer of all, and one of the most successful in the whole popular music business. His two albums recorded in prisons (Folsom and San Quentin) have sold over five and six million copies respectively. But almost his entire professional life has been a long and gruesome struggle against addiction to amphetamines and barbiturates. It broke up his first marriage and landed him in prison seven or eight times.

The book gives a graphic and painful account of tormented nights, bouts of violence, suicidal car drives, nightmare concerts where booze, pills and cigarettes had reduced his voice to a whisper. It's a courageous confession, but it won't do any harm to Cash's popularity. For he employs it mainly as a text by which to re-affirm the sanctities of Middle America: God, the flag and mom's apple pie come out on top.

As one of little faith, I find this unconvincing, though Cash has patently won the right to his beliefs. I can't help feeling that the fundamentalist religion in which he was raised, and which he admits caused him terror as a child, had at least some bearing on his later enslavement to drugs. He lays the blame at the feet of show business, and those dreary, empty nights on the road after the emotional high of a big concert. But this is surely an immediate rather than an ultimate cause.

He may be nearer the truth when he writes about the reverence he still feels for his older brother, Jack, a devout, Bible reading paragon, who died in a terrible accident in his early teens. Nobody could be expected to live up to such a peerless model, least of all the insecure and unstable son of an Arkansas cotton farmer.

At any rate, for those interested in the music of the '50s, the account of the sessions at Sam Phillips' Sun Records—which involved Cash with other young hopefuls such as Carl Perkins, Elvis

Presley, Jerry Lee Lewis and Roy Orbison—will be essential reading. And for those interested in the love of a good woman, the picture of Cash's wife June Carter, which emerges is the most attractive aspect of the book. But as for the chapters on their church-going, their trips to the Holy Land, their film *Gospel Road*, their friendship with Billy Graham ... it's all yours.

***

A more important force for change in country music has been the new, young breed of singers and writers currently challenging the Nashville establishment. Waylon Jennings was one of the first, and Jessi Colter is among the most recent of this group: *Jessi* (Capitol E-ST 11477) is an album of the latter's songs, which the former has helped to arrange and produce, and in which his guitar playing features.

It's a fine album, and one which illustrates how far country rock has permeated the soul of Nashville itself. For on its first side at least, this is a driving, spunky country-rock album of songs about the various faces of a woman's love. From the opening lines, when Ms Colter bites into the frustration of awaiting her man in the early hours of the morning ... 'When you're laying spread upon his bed/howling at the moon', it's clear that we're not in Tammy Wynette territory.

The pressure slackens on Side 2, with three rather more conventional slow throbbers in a row, but the playing is immaculate throughout, and Jessi Colter is clearly a refreshing challenge which Nashville will have to reckon with.

Friday, 28 May 1976

FRONTAL

Marvin Gaye/*I Want You*
Dr Hook & The Medicine Show/*A Little Bit More*

MARVIN GAYE HAS always been one of the freer and more original spirits around Motown. Records like 'What's Going On' and 'I Heard It Through the Grapevine' established him as the king of up-market Soul, with an elusive but potent sense of style and purpose. In his new album, *I Want You* (Tamla Motown STML 12025) he has surpassed himself. To say that it weaves a magic spell might be a lame cliché, but it does. Honest.

We'd better establish right away that the spell is an erotic one. If full frontal music about carnal love is not to your taste, this album is not for your ears. Stick with Paul McCartney. But then again, *I Want You* is in no way likely to deprave or corrupt. It's one of the most sophisticated and subtle productions I've heard in an age.

Much of the credit must go to producer Leon Ware, who has written the eleven tracks in collaboration with various hands (Gaye himself in five of them), and taken a major part in the arrangements too. With a large crowd of superb Motown musicians and a mastery of studio techniques, he has created a wide tapestry of sounds, with melodies that shift around chromatically in the most subtle ways, voices drifting in and out, a groundswell of percussion, and those powerful intermittent bass guitar figures holding it all together.

Not forgetting the high, haunting voice of Marvin Gaye. The words he sings are of fairly primitive import, as the titles indicate—'I Want You', 'Come Live with Me Angel', 'After the Dance', 'Feel All My Love Inside' (an unabashed hymn to coition), 'I Wanna Be Where You Are', 'Since I Had You', 'Soon I'll Be Loving You Again.' But he makes a kind of joyful, dreamlike poetry out of them, enhanced by the way the album has been unified into a single statement by the use of fades and reprises.

Exception has been taken to the use of heavy breathing on some of the tracks. Since its introduction on the absurd 'Je t'aime' of some years back, this device has been used by a number of artists, and taken to pornographic lengths by the luscious Donna Summer. But it's used here almost as a percussive effect arising out of the female backing vocals on 'Come Live with Me Angel', where it helps to generate a remarkable erotic intensity. On 'Since I Had You', its use is indeed somewhat extraneous, but that's about the only misjudgment in what is otherwise a quite extraordinary achievement.

***

Dr Hook and the Medicine Show is one of those American groups I've been hearing about for years without actually hearing—till now. They have a new album out called *A Little Bit More* (Capitol E-ST 23795).

The reputation is for a hip, jokey Californian version of country music, and there are indeed a couple of highly amusing numbers here. 'Jungle to the Zoo' is the warning of a caged tiger to his visitors: 'I once was running wild and free as you/But it's one step from the jungle to the zoo.' This is helped along by some terrific guitar effects, bubbling along under the vocal and then breaking out into a wild solo. 'I Need the High' is the ultimate fiddle-and-pedal-steel alcoholic opus—'I need the high but I can't stand the taste.'

In a rock vein, 'Up on the Mountain' tells the story of Al from the alley and Sally, from the valley who played acoustic and electric (and they both took turns playing lead), which has a neat twist at the end. And 'The Radio' has clever lyrics about a melancholic song of broken love which keeps getting played on the radio, to the distress of the lovelorn narrator.

The other half-dozen songs are meant as straight country ditties, which is a little puzzling, drenched as they are in strings and sentiment. It's particularly hard to take 'If Not You', despite Ray Sawyer's pleasantly light, husky voice, with its reminders of Buddy Holly—for the lyrics go, 'Who's gonna water my plants ... who's gonna patch my pants ... who's gonna iron my shirts ... (etc.) ... if not you?' Replies on a postcard, ladies, to Dr Hook.

Thursday, 3 June 1976

SOUTHLAND SOUNDS

Lynyrd Skynyrd/ *Gimme Back My Bullets*
The Outlaws/ *Lady in Waiting*
Donald Byrd/ *Black Byrd*
The Brecker Brothers/ *Back to Back*

CURIOUS HOW BANDS that are commonly bracketed together can make such wildly different impressions on the individual listener. Recently I've been listening to albums by two 'Southland' bands, the well-established Lynyrd Skynyrd, and the rising Outlaws, first and second on the bill of many a live concert south of the Mason-Dixon line. The Lynyrd Skynyrd album (*Gimme Back My Bullets*, MCA MCF 2774) is to me just so much monotonous, loud, heavy riffing, a dreary macho bawl, crashing guitar solos like a series of bad gear changes, the sound perhaps of a band whose potential is all used up.

The Outlaws' album (*Lady in Waiting* on Arista ARTY 126) is by contrast as easy on the ear as birdsong.

They do have a more elegant style, of course, and the extra edge of a band still pushing upwards. But they also have an allround, corporate ability in writing, arranging, playing and singing (in strong and fluent three-part harmony) which makes for a satisfying sense of wholeness. Their first album, which appeared last year, staked a sizeable claim on public attention, and *Lady in Waiting* has itself been awaited with considerable interest.

The wait has been well worth it, for this is a highly-pleasurable, first-rate record which surely establishes them firmly as a major group. They sound like a funkier Crosby Stills Nash and Young, or a younger and more rugged Eagles. As on their debut album, they've calculated their programme to a nicety, opening with an arresting burst of a capella harmony singing on 'Breaker Breaker', offering a considerable variety of tempo and style in the course of the album, and ending with an infectious rouser called 'Stick Around for Rock And Roll' which features an extended guitar work-out by the two leads, Billy Jones and Hughie Thomasson, well-placed and very impressive.

Two songs stand out for me, exhibiting as they do an advance in subtlety and expressiveness. 'Freeborn Man' is the one number not written by an Outlaw. It's a rustic paean to the hobo life:

I'm a freeborn man, my home is on my back,
I know every inch of highway,
every foot of back road,
Every mile of railroad track.

But what they've done with this—apart from delivering it in those clear, ringing harmonies—is to blend it with some passages of jazzy, airborne, instrumental playing, to highly-original effect.

Billy Jones's 'Prisoner' is another high-toned number, with an intriguing and quite complex melody, handled beautifully by Jones's high, sonorous voice and crafty guitar noodling. It demonstrates their sophistication as effectively as 'Lover Boy' and 'Girl from Ohio' show their capacity for potential hit singles, in rock and country modes respectively.

***

The same difference as sketched out above obtains in the jazz-rock field: I've been listening to Donald Byrd's *Black Byrd* (Blue Note BN-LA 047) and *Back to Back* by the Brecker Brothers Band (on Arista

ARTY 128). The former is a graceful, mellifluous treat, while the latter is merely slick, fast, mindless machine music, up-market disco funk, entirely lacking in wit, sensuality or statement. The playing by the whole seven-piece Brecker outfit plus augmentation is as precise as a metronome, but fails to provoke even foot-tapping.

The Byrd recording dates from 1973 and successfully weds his limpid, masterful trumpet style to the fashions of the seventies, an amalgam of soul and rock arrangements, mainly. The man responsible is Larry Mizell, who composed and arranged the tunes and produced the session. The many other musicians involved are not credited, unfortunately; I'd like to know in particular about the flute player, who takes a major part in all seven numbers.

Jazz fans who recall Byrd's work with the likes of Thelonius Monk, Art Blakey and Max Roach may feel a bit stern about the lightweight insouciance of these tracks. But they're restrained, stylish, musicianly, undemanding—which will do to be going on with.

Thursday, 10 June 1976

WORDS WITHOUT SONGS

Bernie Taupin/*The One Who Writes the Words for Elton John*
David Pomeranz/*David Pomeranz*

CURIOUS THINGS, POP song lyrics. Everybody assures you that they're of no importance in contemporary pop, and yet any group who tries to discard them and go for straight instrumentals almost invariably loses its audience. Equally, it's a constantly repeated truism that a good lyric, bereft of its music, can appear to be as grotesque and graceless as a stranded seal. Yet songwriters are forever having them published.

The latest to succumb is Bernie Taupin, *The One Who Writes the Words for Elton John*—this being the title of his collection of lyrics published by Jonathan Cape at £2.95, under the editorship of the well-known illustrators, Alan Aldridge and Mike Dempsey. As you would expect, the book is very handsomely produced on high-quality paper, with lyrics and illustrations on facing pages all the way through, the illustrations including Joni Mitchell, John Lennon,

Charlie Watts, pop artist Peter Blake, and a whole stew of photographers and graphics experts.

However, true to form, the actual lyrics are about as much fun to read as the losing entries in a youth club poetry competition. The 'poetic' ones are verbally and syntactically muddled to the point of gibberish, whilst the simpler, direct ones are mainly American graffiti as perceived by a Lincolnshire farm boy—'Border Song', 'Burn Down the Mission', 'Razor Face', 'Indian Sunset', 'Honky Cat', 'Goodbye Norma Jean', 'Goodbye Yellow Brick Road'.

Why are they so successful? First, because they trigger off Elton John's imagination and he writes catchy tunes for them and sings them with considerable verve, a method of working which makes the John-Taupin partnership almost unique in the music scene. Secondly, I would suggest, because they have the same blunt quality as graffiti or cartoon captions, with a slight aura of mystery or the occasional posh word added to lend them a little class. That's all the mass youth audience wants from a lyricist.

***

David Pomeranz's lyrics also look pretty ropey in cold print. He wrote the song 'Tryin' to Get the Feeling Again', which gave Barry Manilow's career the big boost, but contains some of the worst lines I've ever encountered in a popular song:

> Could you help me rediscover
> the way to re-be her lover
> Once again?

That said, I wish to report that the album *David Pomeranz* (Arista Arty 129) is a highly pleasureable experience, which in my opinion leaves the other Arista stablemates—particularly Manilow and Melissa Manchester—back at the starting gate. For here is a man with a beautifully high, supple voice who can write all varieties of attractive tunes, and who has been blessed with stylish arrangements played by excellent musicians. Even some of his lyrics are pretty fair, if you can believe it.

The people who have worked on the album, from producer Vini Poncia on down, are largely the same as on Melissa Manchester's albums, and indeed Ms Manchester herself supplies the odd backing voice; but there's a whole different level of taste operating here. From the opening verse of the first track—'It's in Everyone of Us'— which is sung by Pomeranz unaccompanied, you know you're in the hands of an unusual talent.

'Tryin' to Get the Feeling Again' is worlds of sensitivity away from the histrionic Manilow rendition. 'Flying' is a magic, falsetto evocation of flight. 'Greyhound Mary' really rocks. 'Home to Alaska' has genuine jazz wit. And so on. Give it a listen.

Thursday, 17 June 1976

MORE COUNTRIFIED ROCK

Fools Gold/*Fools Gold*
Cajun Moon/*Cajun Moon*

ALBUMS FROM TWO new groups this week, which is rare enough. Fools Gold is an American quartet, Cajun Moon (despite the name) an English trio, and they're both involved in country rock, which is becoming rather an overcrowded groove.

The Fools Gold album (on Arista ARTY 131) comes with solid credentials. Some of the tracks were produced by Eagle Glenn Frey, others by rock gitarist Joe Walsh, who's also one of the guest musicians. The group itself is the backing band for Dan Fogelberg, who has contributed two of the ten compositions, and its progenitors and co-writers—Tom Kelly and Denny Henson—have been working together professionally for many's the long year.

Not surprising, then, that this is a smooth and accomplished album, with that apparently effortless flair and clarity which we've come to expect from American recordings of this kind. Fools Gold have no trouble in convincing you of their professionalism and expertise; their only problem is that they sound a little bit like every other band in the field. They're a kind of Flying Eagles/Outlaws of the Poco Purple Sage.

Though, oddly enough, it's the Beatles who are invoked first, with the opening chord sequence of 'Here Comes the Sun' used as the basis of 'Coming Out of Hiding', the first track. There's a solid, chunky sound to this, helped along by the use of four or five guitars, including a slide guitar solo from guest Duncan Cameron. 'Rain, Oh Rain' flows straight down the middle of the country-rock mainstream, whilst 'Choices' picks up the tempo a bit, with a lot of swishing acoustic guitar and good pedal steel from Doug Livingston.

'Rollin' Fields and Meadows' is, as you might expect, a lilting Paean to nature's wonders—'this is the way life was meant to be/I am free'. The first side ends with 'Sailing to Monterey', a song with another venerable theme, the dream about the good life in California, rendered with a little touch of the surfing sound.

Side 2 open strongly with some unaccompanied harmony singing on 'I Will Run', a lively love song. 'Old Tennessee' is a stately waltz and a wistful plea from a young lad in Tennessee to his girl in San Francisco, but 'One by One' is a rather plodding waltz and, in fact, a bit of a bore. 'The Way Love Grows' has been deftly produced by Glyn Johns, with variety in the tempo and sound, and a nice counterpoint between the lead voices and backing tracks. The slow, tender Fogelberg number, 'Love Me Through and Through', brings the album to a lyrical close.

It's a good set, if perhaps a little short on the more rocking kind of number. All it really lacks is a dash of originality.

***

CAJUN MOON (Chrysalis CHR 1116) is an album containing the barest minimum of sleeve information, so I'm only deducing that the three group members play guitar, fiddle and keyboards, and have overdubbed themselves on drums, bass and what have you. The music they produce is a curious medley of British folkrock and Nashville. Both the lyrics and the vocals are often very good, but the whole album is vitiated by a leaden, rhythmic galumphing.

There is one lovely song, called 'Misty on the Water', sung solo over acoustic guitar and a flute-like electronic note. Otherwise, the numbers sound like pantry turns more than anything else, complete with singalong potential. I don't care much for the merrie minstrelsy ones, like 'Calling On' and 'Fiddler John', nor for 'Mistress Music', a lugubrious ditty about the merciless muse, featuring a synthesizer. But 'Close to the Edge' has a beautifully evocative brass-band-like trumpet solo, and 'Losers Can Be Winners' has highly promising lyrics about a lonely pick-up at a drunken party.

Thursday, 24 June 1976

TOP ROCK

Steely Dan/*The Royal Scam*

I'D BETTER JUST say straight away that Steely Dan is my favourite rock group. So I inevitably approach their new album, *The Royal Scam* (Anchor Records, ABCL 5161), with a certain bias, encapsulated in the mad scramble to get it on the turntable. And the fact is, it's as good as anything they've ever done. It's superb.

But then everything about this group is special. To begin with, there is no group. There's just Donald Fagen and Walter Becker. They abandoned the group set-up a couple of years ago in favour of hiring musicians for specific album projects from a pool of ace freelances. Which is only possible because they refuse to perform live on tour. 'We don't mix well,' Becker is quoted as saying in a recent *Rolling Stone*: 'I would go so far as to say it's a direct one-to-one hostile attitude toward fellow members of the race.'

Now, that is not your typical pop star speaking. Nor are the lyrics typical which he writes with his buddy, the aptly-named Mr Fagen. In the past they have inclined towards a largely impenetrable surrealism full of private references. But whereas a lot of rock lyrics are deliberately obscurantist to hide the fact that their authors actually have nothing to say, Steely Dan lyrics always have plenty to say; Becker and Fagen just don't always care whether you get it or not.

On the other hand, they have frequently been very lucid and I've always enjoyed most their songs about the casualties of the urban crack-up: like 'Charlie Freak ' on the *Pretzel Logic* album and 'Daddy Don't Live In That New York City No More' on their last album, *Katy Lied*. It's particularly gratifying, therefore, that they have now composed an entire album of such songs. Nobody needs to complain this time about not understanding.

The tone is set by the sleeve design, which depicts a down-and-out asleep on a ledge, whilst skyscrapers with the heads of roaring tigers and bears tower over him. Thus we come to the opening number, 'Kid Charlemagne', which is addressed to a former purveyor of psychedelic drugs, feted and prosperous in the hippie 'sixties, now washed-up—'And those dayglo freaks/Who used to paint the face/they've joined the human race/Some things will never change.' This is followed by an expression of empathy with those original graffitists and exorcists of sinister implacable forces, the cave painters of Attamira.

'Don't Take Me Alive' has an electrifying lyric, the monologue of a bank robber pinned down by the police and a crowd. 'Green Earrings' is the song of another criminal type, but written in elliptical, gnomic phrases—is he remembering robbing the woman of her jewellery, murdering her or even making love to her? 'Haitian Divorce' tells the baleful story of the marriage between Babs and Clean Willy which goes on the rocks in a rather menacing way in Haiti.

The track which follows this, 'Everything You Did', takes an even more jaundiced view of a marriage: it's the outcry of an enraged and yet prurient husband on the discovery of his wife's adultery. 'Turn up the Eagles/the neighbours are listening,' he yells. Droll fellows, these two. Finally, 'The Royal Scam' itself deals with the experiences of Puerto Rican immigrants into New York city.

Actually, I left out 'Sign in Stranger', which is the one genuinely puzzling song—it has elements of sci-fi fantasy and might just be set in a mental hospital—and also 'The Fez', because 'The Fez' helps to illustrate why Steely Dan's records sell in enormous numbers in the teeth of everything I've said so far. Quite simply, Becker and Fagen write distinctive tunes with powerful choruses, and record them cleanly with excellent, driving rock musicians. You can dance to Steely Dan. They play body music.

Friday, 2 July 1976

THE BEATLE GENERATION

The Beatles/*Rock & Roll Music*
Loudon Wainwright III/*T-Shirt*

THE LATEST ALBUM to arrive on my doorstep has been the Beatles' *Rock 'n Roll Music* (Parlophone PCSP719). Now, this is a new and sobering experience, to see the music of your adolescence revived as though it were something historical and unfamiliar rather than something bred in the bone; and perhaps it's an intimation to the rock critic of maturing years that the time to lay down his stylus is nigh.

At any rate, it's an odd concoction, this album. The re-releasing of all the Beatles' singles was a shrewd commercial gambit on the part of EMI, since there are teenagers buying records today who weren't even born when the Fab Four first went into the studios. But instead of re-releasing the albums—which was presumably impracticable—the company has put together this compilation of twenty-eight tracks on two discs, spanning their whole career from 1963 to 1970. The selection has been based on form rather than content; rock & roll music, any old way you choose it.

This works fine up to half-time, since all the Chuck Berry and R&B songs which they recorded early on can be included—'Twist and Shout', 'Matchbox' (sung by an adenoidal Ringo), 'Roll Over Beethoven', 'Kansas City' and so on. Their own early things like 'Saw Her Standing There' and 'I Wanna Be Your Man' also fit in quite naturally.

However, the concept breaks down once you get past 1965. It means, for example, representing the tremendous 'white' album of '68 with 'Helter Skelter', 'Birthday'—surely its two worst tracks—and 'Back In the USSR'. It also means that a tedious George Harrison number like 'Taxman' is included at the expense of three or four dozen vastly superior songs.

A lot of this comes down to personal taste, of course. I'm still unshakeably convinced that the Beatles' greatest work either collectively or individually is to be found on the *Sergeant Pepper* and *Abbey Road* albums, neither of which is represented here (maybe they're being saved for another day). On the other hand, I'll listen any time of the day or night, to 'Drive My Car', 'Anytime At All', 'Get Back', 'Hey Bulldog' ... ah, great days. You youngsters today have nothing to touch it, I'm telling you.

***

Loudon Wainwright III made his name—if such a name indeed needs to be made—by writing and singing songs which were often riveting in their candour and sense of pain, but also suffused with a hilarious deadpan wit. However, his more recent work has involved diversifying into rock songs and even sentimental mood pieces, using a largish studio band.

The increase in volume has resulted, for me, simply in a loss of intensity, exemplified all the way through his disappointing new album, *T-Shirt* (Arista ARTY 127). Battered targets are selected, and overkill is applied to them: people must be as weary now of hearing the US Bicentennial mocked, for example, as of hearing about it at all. Likewise, 'Hollywood Hopeful', and 'California Prison Blues' fail to ring too many changes out of hackneyed subject matter.

All the same, Loudon being Wainwright, there are things to enjoy here. 'At Both Ends' is a very lively song which takes a rather ambivalent attitude to his own dissipation on tour. Ireland even gets a mention here, with the lines, 'In Dublin town we're going to tip a few/Of that angry land's thick black brew.' Also, 'Prince Hal's Dirge' is an arresting attempt to express the attitudes of a Shakespearean character in contemporary terms. The Prince Hal of the Boar's Head Tavern is a figure with whom Loudon Wainwright can very easily identify. What results is probably the only rock song you'll ever hear which begins 'Gimme a capon,' and includes lines like 'Show me a breach and I'll once more unto it.'

Thursday, 8 July 1976

DISTINCTIVE FLAVOUR

David Batteau/*Happy in Hollywood*
Linda McCartney/*Linda's Pix For '76*
Paul Gambaccini/*Paul McCartney in His Own Words*

DAVID BATTEAU IS a new name to me, but I gather that he's been singing-songwriting for some time; at any rate I'm bewitched by his album *Happy in Hollywood* (A&M AMLH 64576). It's tight, cool, delicate and sophisticated. It has learnt from the best of reggae and soul music a rhythmic flexibility and a spare, muscular use of instrumental resources. It has the deliberation and distinctiveness of a Paul Simon album, and yet it also has a kind of commercial insouciance and impersonality. Definitely a flavour all to itself, in short.

Take the title track—'the sign on the hill/keeps saying/Happy in Hollywood.' Immediately you think of Dory Previn but in place of her mordant anatomising, you get an objective account of a young musician's pilgrimage to the showbiz mecca, his failures and bad times, and his final acceptance of it for sustaining his dream. All of this is sung to a catchy tune which develops a nice clarinet and orchestral counterpoint, and is borne aloft on Jeff Porcaro's fully comprehensive treatment of his drum kit.

Porcaro's drumming is a key element in all ten tracks. Producer Ken Scott has kept it very prominent in the mix, thereby accounting for much of the album's elegant airiness. In 'Festival of Fools', Afro-Cuban percussion adds to the effect, since this is a samba-like evocation of a kind of Mardi Gras festival. In 'Oh, My Little Darling', the upfront drumming combines with bass and guitar to create a marvellous reggae beat, over which a simple melodic idea is very cleverly stretched out.

'My Morning Glory' has pretty ropey lyrics, consisting of a sort of diluted psychedelic fairy story, but its flowing tune, its acoustic guitar and woodwind arangement, and its bridge passage with cello and falsetto voice in unison, combine to make it a thing of surpassing beauty. Finally on Side 1 there is 'Orpheé', a fine version of the Orpheus story employing all the album's effects. Particularly good are the gongs heard in Hades, and the irony of Eurydice's voice coming in on the chorus as she fades away.

It's interesting that Batteau's Orpheus fails because of his musical vanity ('Nobody sings a song like me,' goes the chorus). Music rather than the ego is what Batteau wants to affirm: music, nature and love, rather than his personal hangups. His resonant, resilient voice is remarkably devoid of self-advertisement, and it helps to save the songs when the words get a bit vapid or soft-centered.

They do so more often on Side 2. 'Walk in Love' is ethereal and floating, 'Spaceship Earth' lively and funky, but 'revolution/love is the solution' is a fair sample of their lyrics. 'Dancing on Atoms' fails to emulate John Lennon's 'Across the Universe', with a generally windy string sound terminating in the sound of actual wind.

***

So far as the possibilities of Paul McCartney go, my faith remains lost, in spite of all blandishments of new albums, a special diary called *Linda's Pix For '76* (comprising horrendous Polaroid snaps of the McCartney family) a new book by Paul Gambaccini called *Paul McCartney in His Own Words* (Omnibus Press. £1.95), and the most lavish publicity barrage accompanying all the above.

Wings and McCartney are now being treated with an almost fawning solicitude by the press in general, to atone for the previous scorn and derision. The truth surely lies in the middle: McCartney, half of one of the greatest songwriting teams of the century, has developed into a commercially successful purveyor of forgettable, silly, love songs in expensive packages. If you don't believe me, check out *Wings At the Speed of Sound* (PAS 10010).

Thursday, 15 July 1976

THE BEACH BOYS

The Beach Boys/ *20 Golden Greats*

ME AND MY mates never reckoned the Beach Boys much, back in the early 'sixties. What did we know about drag strips and waxing our boards? What exactly was a T-Bird or a 'little deuce coupé' (pronounced 'coop')? The nearest we could ever get to surf and souped-up jalopies was Easter in Portrush. Besides, they sang a bit funny, all bass and falsetto, but smooth, without the delirious lunacy of the 'fifties groups like Danny & The Juniors or the Diamonds. All in all, they were just a bit too Californian.

Right now, they're riding a whole new wave, the good old nostalgic revival one. *The Beach Boys: 20 Golden Greats* (Capitol EMTV I) is the latest record-company attempt to trade on former glories. It's a 'TV concept album', which means that they're spending a large fortune to promote it via a commercial on the box. Personally, I'd rather see the money invested in discovering new talent, but presumably the shareholders are happy enough.

At any rate, all the 'sixties hits are here in one neat package. The first side opens with 'Surfin' USA', which localised Chuck Berry's 'Sweet Little Sixteen' on those golden Pacific beaches, and closes with 'Sloop John B', which did the same thing for a nice old Caribbean folk song. In between comes eight of those feckless, cheerleading Brian Wilson numbers which were the quintessence of white American highschool pop in their day. It'll be interesting to see whether they do anything for today's teenagers.

***

For us grown-ups, there may be a bittersweet flavour to the experience. At the end of the film *American Graffiti*, which includes some of these numbers in its evocative soundtrack, the subsequent fate of each of the highschool protagonists is flashed up on the screen: one killed in his jalopy, one killed in Vietnam, one an insurance agent in an obscure small town, and one a drop-out writer. This kind of hindsight is unavoidable, and it imbues the innocent inanities of songs like 'Fun, Fun, Fun', 'I Get Around' and 'When I Grow Up (To Be a Man)' with a rather jaded pathos.

This is reinforced by the album's second side, for here we enter into the latter and increasingly melancholy career of Brian Wilson. Having stopped touring with the group in order to concentrate on composition and studio work, he became almost a total recluse, neurotically obsessed with trying to turn a commercial craft into a form of art. One story has it that he worked on 'Heroes and Villains' for nine months, ending up with a work lasting for a couple of hours, out of which the record company took one small snippet which was a medium hit.

For all that—and for all the Maharishi-and-turning-on faddishness which the erstwhile boys from the beach got into—I think these later numbers stand up well. 'Good Vibrations', in particular, is still an exciting recording, with its ethereal opening, its build-up of voices, its effervescent hook, and the surprising way it keeps developing. 'Heroes and Villains', a little comic drama put together with great cleverness, can be seen now as the progenitor of many subsequent works. 'Darlin'' almost anticipates jazzrock, and their treatment of the Phil Spector-Ellie Greenwich song 'I Can Hear Music', is rich and mature.

Who knows ... maybe what we have here is the perfect rock & roll family album: Side 1 for the kids, Side 2 for mum and dad (and Uncle Stew).

Thursday, 5 August 1976

COOL IN THE SUN

The Soft Machine/*Softs*
Kevin Ayers/*Yes We Have No Mañanas (So Get Your Mañanas Today)*

IT'S VETERAN-ENGLISH-progressives' week. The Soft Machine in its fourteenth incarnation—and its first since the departure of the last remaining founder member Mike Rutledge—has come out with an album called *Softs* (Harvest SHSP 4056). Coincidentally, the first departing founder member of the same group, Kevin Ayers, has brought forth his eighth or so solo album. This bears the cleverest title of any record this year—*Yes We Have No Mañanas (So Get Your Mañanas Today)*.

Apart from sustaining Ayers' whimsical banana imagery, this nutritious pun has nothing to do with the album's contents and is markedly superior to them. Not that the ten songs are bad; they're very pleasant on the whole, effervescent and listenable. But since his first emergence, playing bass and singing on the Soft Machine debut LP, Ayers has always seemed to promise more than he has delivered.

The general feeling his work gives out is that composing and singing are sunshine activities, like everything else—scuba diving, for example, which he's pictured doing on the sleeve here. You put together a few polished, ironic lines about love, set them to a simple tune, record it crisply with your musician friends, and peel another grape. What's wrong is the deadpan reserve, the sense almost of disdain for projecting feeling. There's no sense of commitment, even to a deliberate callowness.

Thus, the lyrics of these songs seem to be aiming at autobiographical statements, but they never quite come to grips with their subject. 'Star' opens promisingly:

If you want to be a star, start shining, shine on,
If you're happy where you are, stop whining, it's wrong.

But it peters out in stock lines about 'If you want a love that's true/What you give comes back to you.' 'Mr Cool' is better, with a flip, reggae-style arrangement for lines like 'You want your cake and eat it too, one day the cake turn around and eat you.' Best of all is 'The Owl', which succeeds in making a childlike wit genuinely appealing; it's an extension of the words addressed by the pussycat to the owl in their beautiful peagreen boat.

'Love's Gonna Turn You Round' is as close to rocking as he gets, and has quite thoughtful lyrics. But Side 1 ends with an ill-advised pop version of the Dietrich classic, 'Falling in Love Again'. Nothing could out-camp the original; and this attempt is as bland as semolina.

The story of the second side is much the same, but a word of praise is due to the guitarist Ollie Halsall, rightly singled out for special mention by Ayers. His vivid and fluent work gets free rein at the end of the last track, 'Blue'. And it's nice to see Belfast bass player Charlie McCracken (ex-Taste and ex-Spud) working in such congenial company.

***

With the departure of keyboards mastermind Mike Rutledge, the leading light of the Soft Machine is now undoubtedly Karl Jenkins who joined originally in 1972. Indeed on *Softs*, he has abandoned his oboe and moved over completely to pianos and synthesizers, and most of the compositions are his.

Very accomplished they are too, as is the work of his four team-mates. The new boys are maintaining the Softs' reputation for keeping the popular music world's standards of musicianship up to snuff, and guitarist John Etheridge in particular plays a scorcher.

It's with a certain amount of guilt, then, that I confess to my attention straying often during this album. But only a certain amount; in spite of its many felicities, there's an aura of worthiness about a lot of these numbers with titles like 'Aubade' and 'Nexus' and 'The Tale of Taliesin' and 'Song of Aeolus' (it opens and closes with the sound effect of wind.) Some of it even sounds, frankly, like music for cinema commercials—all scudding clouds and ethereal blondes with slow-motion hair. In these bits, yesterday's progressives have become today's commonplaces.

Thursday, 12 August 1976

READ'S SECOND ALBUM

John Dawson Read/*Read On*
Alexander Robertson/*Shadow of a Thin Man*

ONE OF THE more pleasing debut albums of last year was John Dawson Read's *A Friend of Mine*. It came unaccompanied by hype or hustle; Read had been writing and singing songs for years in his spare time, four-square melodious songs which the album presented in a simple and direct way. It attracted little attention here, but the title song did quite well in America. Quietly launched there as a full-time professional singer-songwriter, Read has come out with a second album called *Read On* (Chrysalis CHR1102).

Listening to it for the first time, I was a little disquieted during the opening tracks. Songs of sentiment can all too easily turn soppy, and the touches of preciosity on *A Friend of Mine* seemed more pronounced here. The first song gives instances of how there's 'one road for angels, another for men'—which might be all right in a book of beauteous gems of wisdom—and the second has lines like, 'but as long as the world's keeping on keeping on, then it's here we belong close together/till forever.'

This Pollyanna strain continues in the next song, which is about

376

the sky at night, and it becomes noticeable how often his tunes follow the same chord progression. But things pick up with 'Me and You', which is a pleasant James Taylorish love song with a light band arrangement; and the album really takes off with 'Old Cold Shoulder'.

This demonstrates, in the nick of time, that Read is not going to stick in the one groove, for it introduces a whole new element of vaudevillian energy and humour, splendidly reinforced by the string playing of the Rodarton Vaudeville Quintet. It's a realistically hilarious account of what greets the man who returns to his woman from the pub much later than he had promised. 'Take Him Down' is a further pleasant surprise, being a rueful treatment of Read's own position as a 30-year-old aspirant to pop stardom, performed in a Dylanesque rock style, with a nicely effective brass section.

The energy level is sustained on Side 2 with 'Some People Are Crazy', which again shows a Dylan influence, with an ironic edge and intensity. This is followed by some more numbers from the romantic job-lot, but 'Thinking (The Things I'm Thinking)' is another success, an infectious and ingenious little song with innocuous-seeming words which carry a strong after-taste.

***

An even newer name, to the public at large, is that of Alexander Robertson. He has come out with a first album which is a real curiosity called *Shadow of a Thin Man* (Arista Sparty 1000). Its cover shows Robertson, holding a ventriloquist's dummy of himself, about to enter on to a burning stage. The music itself is correspondingly theatrical.

It opens with the winding-up of a music-box whose tinkling grows into a full-blooded orchestral overture; the songs which ensue sound as if they ought to come from a show. Robertson's voice has a histrionic projection and enunciation, and he writes accordingly. His orchestral arranger David Whitaker has done him proud, as has his producer Herbie Flowers; a vast number of first-rate musicians are deployed with an imaginative forcefulness, the passages of orchestral linkage are often more exciting than the songs.

Not that the songs are bad; there is, for example, a number called 'Tap! Tap! Tap!' which is a highly enjoyable plea to a girl who's fanatical about tap-dancing and wants to recreate the Astaire-Rogers era. It's just that they're lacking in some vital respect. The lyrics are inventive but too often smart alecky.

Friday, 20 August 1976

SOME NEW NAMES

O/*Within Reach*
Max Merritt & The Meteors/*Out of the Blue*

A BAND CALLED O has upped and made a record album called *Within Reach* (UAG 29942), and United Artists Records are making no secret of the fact. Besides the album itself, they've sent me a tee shirt, a tin badge, a cloth badge and a hideous great poster. The one thing they've omitted is a little information. So I can't tell you anything about the O Band except for what comes off the album.

Which sounds roughly like a credible and polished English version of up-market California rock, covering a spectrum from (say) Jo Jo Gunne to Quicksilver. The instrumental work is a tight and intricate mesh, which can rapidly vary its texture and pace. The sound is virile but not heavy, able to boogie along convincingly on a number like 'Money Talk' and yet be effectively atmospheric on a slow piece like 'Long Long Way'. The lyrics are essentially self-regarding masculine statements about sex and music. And the choruses are sung in smooth harmony.

This last is where the O Band is weakest. Their singing, both solo and harmony, lacks the crisp California attack and precision. It isn't helped either by the producer's attempts to engineer a little colour out of it—this merely blurs the lyrics on a couple of tracks.

On the other hand, the group has a distinctive strength which is invaluable; namely, a strong guitar partnership between 'Pix' Pickford on lead and Craig Anders on electric slide and pedal steel. They produce between them a guitar polyphony which is often richly satisfying, and this set-up also gives them flexibility, the opening number, for example, 'A Smile is Diamond', gets a country-rock feel going with the pedal steel rollicking along at mid-tempo, whilst 'Dontcha Wanna' (which closes Side 1) combines some funky electric slide guitar with piano to produce effective body music.

In between these comes 'Feel All Right', an appeal for female solace from a poor victim of the tough, punishing, relentless life on the road ... or rather poor self-pitying egomaniac bore. Which is followed by 'Lucia Loser', with the first word coming out 'Losh-ya' in best transatlantic fashion.

The most interesting number, for my money, comes on Side 2. It's called 'Still Burning', and it's constructed on a subtle and cunning chord pattern, dancing up and down a series of chromatic steps. 'Paradise Blue' is rather thin by comparison, as is the doleful pedal steel tune, 'Within Reach', which brings to an end this album of the same name. Nevertheless, O is a band with a lot of potential.

***

Max Merritt & The Meteors is another new name to me, but in the case of their *Out of the Blue album* (Arista ARTY 134), the information is copious. Max is 35 and made it big in his native New Zealand before moving to London with his Australian drummer Stu Speer, who is 48. They've been playing in pubs for some years now. You can't fault them for not trying.

This is in fact their second album to be released in these islands. It's a likeable, lively regulation set of ten pop-rock songs, but I can't really see it making a big impression. It just doesn't have a strong enough character of its own. Max sings in a tuneful, lightly husky voice, his songs are soundly put together, and the three pommie Meteors join with him and Stu in a tightly rocking sound.

I can see why it knocks 'em cold in the Windsor Castle in Paddington, and I might even sample the group there sometime. But on cruel vinyl, it just seems to evaporate into the indifferent air.

Thursday, 26 August 1976

LAST WORDS

Karlheinz Stockhausen/*Ceylon/Bird of Passage*
Crystal Gayle/*Somebody Loves You*
Santana/*Amigos*
The Good Old Boys/*Pistol Packin' Mama*

I'M TIDYING UP the in-tray today, since this is my last column. Which is how I come to be confronted with four albums by artists whose names are as follows: Karlheinz Stockhausen, Crystal Gayle, Santana, and the Good Old Boys. In stylistic terms, that reads: avant-garde electronic, mainstream Nashville, Latin-rock progressive, and bluegrass. Not a well-balanced menu, you'll agree—but one that neatly exemplifies the bizarrely disparate kinds of human activity which come together in the enormous supermarket of today's 'popular music'.

For believe it or not, even though these artists are catering to specialised and fragmented audiences, there are things in common between them. Jerry Garcia, for example, is the improbable link between Stockhausen and the Good Old Boys, being Whitmanesque enough to embrace both. He has presided over all the various phases of the Grateful Dead's music, including their ventures into freeform electronic sounds under the influence of Stockhausen's pioneering work with ring modulators and synthesizers. He is also the featured producer of *Pistol Packin' Mama* (UAS 29951), an album which teams the New Riders' guitarist David Nelson with bluegrass luminaries Frank Wakefield, Don Reno and Chubby Wise to form the Good Old Boys.

Not all of us are quite as eclectic as this, though. Stockhausen certainly isn't. He was once asked in a *Newsweek* interview whether he recognised the evidences of his influence on pop music, and replied: 'Naturally, they are so obvious you can't miss them. Basically, it's very superficial. They constantly need new kicks, new colour, a new approach that lasts for a couple of years—and then they look for another influence. They are not basic explorers. They are vulgarisers. And necessarily so—that's why they have sold 500 million records. What this means is that you have to approach people on the lowest level of their consciousness, because this ultimately leads to higher demands, to music which is more developed and far-reaching in its research, creating new soundworlds, giving more far-reaching messages.'

Fair comment, Karlheinz, but that word 'research' gives food for thought. Let us try a medical analogy. Some researchers are probing the genetic basis of life itself; others are still seeking a cure for the common cold (I hope). While the former pursuit is undoubtedly of greater importance and long-term effect, the latter has a more direct bearing on people's everyday lives here and now. Certainly neither is to be despised.

***

Similarly, Stockhausen's own compositions go to the very fundamentals of music and attempt to reorder them radically: as on this current album, *Ceylon/Bird of Passage* (CHR 1110). 'Ceylon' draws on Singhalese music to create a mainly percussive sequence, with restrained electronic colouring. The effect is often hypnotic and arresting. But 'Bird of Passage' has two trumpets and Stockhausen on bird whistle and 'chromatic ring' among other things, and to me—

and most other listeners. I'd suggest—it's the usual kind of serio-comic noodling, squawking and crashing known as 'modern music'. In other words, what he's doing is too abstruse for my ears, but I can see that possibly—probably—it has significance which will grow and clarify over the years.

'On Top Of Old Smokey' is, shall we say, a humbler day's work. Personally, the Good Old Boys' rendition of it and similar works is unlikely to achieve any more plays in this house than 'Bird of Passage', but if you go for top-class bluegrass fiddle, mandolin and banjo, the Good Old Boys are as good as they come. Crystal Gayle's *Somebody Loves You* (UAS 29937) is also good of its kind, which might be expected of Loretta Lynn's kid sister—but another dose of Nashville schmaltz I can live without.

No, the album I actually plan to listen to is Santana's *Amigos* (CBS 86005). Apart from Carlos Santana, the group's line-up is entirely changed from the great days of yore, even featuring a singer now called Greg Walker. It's a more ordinary band, sometimes straying close to routine disco funk. But it has carried over the vital energy, and Carlos' guitar is as incandescent as ever. In short, a guaranteed cure for the common cold.

Thursday, 2 September 1976

Acknowledgements

The editors would like to acknowledge the help and advice given by Lesley Bruce, Lynne Parker, John Fairleigh, Gerry Smyth of the *Irish Times*, Dorothea Melvin, Gerard Fanning, Marilyn Richtarik, Terence Brown, Jonathan Williams and the staff of the Microfilm Room, National Library of Ireland (Dublin), the Linen Hall Library (Belfast), the Fine Arts Department, Central Library (Belfast) and the Library, Trinity College.

INDEX